OXFORD COMPARATIVE CONSTITUTIONALISM

Series Editors

RICHARD ALBERT

William Stamps Farish Professor of Law, The University of Texas at Austin School of Law

ROBERT SCHÜTZE

Professor of European and Global Law, Durham University and College of Europe

Constitutional Change in the Contemporary Socialist World

OXFORD COMPARATIVE CONSTITUTIONALISM

Comparative constitutional law has a long and distinguished history in intellectual thought and in the construction of public law. As political actors and the people who create or modify their constitutional orders, they often wish to learn from the experience and learning of others. This cross-fertilization and mutual interaction has only accelerated with the onset of globalization, which has transformed the world into an interconnected web that facilitates dialogue and linkages across international and regional structures. Oxford Comparative Constitutionalism seeks to publish scholarship of the highest quality in constitutional law that deepens our knowledge of local, national, regional, and global phenomena through the lens of comparative public law.

ALSO PUBLISHED IN THIS SERIES

Poland's Constitutional Breakdown
Wojciech Sadurski

City, State: Constitutionalism and the Megacity
Ran Hirschl

The Global South and Comparative Constitutional Law
Edited by Philipp Dann, Michael Riegner, and Maxim Bönnemann

Constitutional Change in the Contemporary Socialist World

BUI NGOC SON

OXFORD
UNIVERSITY PRESS

OXFORD
UNIVERSITY PRESS

Great Clarendon Street, Oxford, OX2 6DP,
United Kingdom

Oxford University Press is a department of the University of Oxford.
It furthers the University's objective of excellence in research, scholarship,
and education by publishing worldwide. Oxford is a registered trade mark of
Oxford University Press in the UK and in certain other countries

First Edition published in 2020

Impression: 1

Published in the United States of America by Oxford University Press
198 Madison Avenue, New York, NY 10016, United States of America

British Library Cataloguing in Publication Data
Data available

Library of Congress Control Number: 2020936727

ISBN 978–0–19–885134–9

Printed and bound by
CPI Group (UK) Ltd, Croydon, CR0 4YY

Acknowledgments

This book is supported by empirical work. I thank my correspondents, colleagues, and friends in China, Cuba, Laos, South Korea (for the case of North Korea), and Vietnam for kindly sharing their useful knowledge, materials, and assisting the field trips.

This project was started when I was a research fellow of the Centre for Asian Legal Studies (CALS) at the National University of Singapore Faculty of Law. At CALS, I received kindly support, encouragement, feedback, and collaborations. I thank CALS's directors Andrew Harding and Dan W. Puchniak, Gary F. Bell, Weitseng Chen, Jaclyn Neo, Wang Jiangyu, and specially Kevin Y.L. Tan for his encouraging me to study the law of the five current socialist countries. CALS's support of my field trip to Laos is acknowledged.

Major parts of this book have been completed since I joined the Chinese University of Hong Kong Faculty of Law as an Assistant Professor in July 2018. My CUHK colleagues welcomed me and provided support, advice, and suggestions. I particularly thank my deans Christopher Gane and Lutz-Christian Wolff, my mentor Gregory S. Gordon, Rehan Abeyratne, Surabhi Chopra, David Donald, Stuart Hargreaves, Jae Woon Lee, Jyh-An Lee, Mara Malagodi, Benoit Mayer, Bryan Mercurio, Michelle Miao, Ryan Mitchell, Christopher Roberts, Samuli Seppänen, Dicky Tsang, Chao Xi, and James Si Zeng. The CUHK Faculty's Direct Grant for Research made, among others, the field trip to Cuba possible, which I greatly appreciate. I thank Lydia Ching and Michelle Tang for research assistance.

Many colleagues have provided continued support and useful comments on the project as a whole or parts of the project which were presented in various fora. I particularly thank Albert Chen, John Gillespie, Tom Ginsburg, Gary Jacobsohn, David Law, Pip Nicholson, Trang (Mae) Nguyen, Cheryl Saunders, Yoon Jin Shin, Mark Sidel, Mark Tushnet, and Maartje De Visser. I thank Jamie Berezin at Oxford University Press, Richard Albert and Robert Schütze, Series Editors of *Oxford Comparative Constitutionalism,* for supporting the publication of this book.

My biggest thanks go to my families who humanize my meaningful life. I dedicate this book to my virtuous wife Nguyễn Thị Phượng (Jolie) and my lovely daughter Bùi Tố Nguyên (Fifi).

* * *

Some portions of this book have been drawn on my earlier articles: "Constitutional Amendment in Laos" (2019) 17(3) International Journal of Constitutional Law

756; "Constitutional Mobilization" (2018) 17(1) Washington University Global Studies Law Review 113; "Globalization of Constitutional Identity" (2017) 26(3) Washington International Law Journal 463; "Constitutional Mobilization in China" (2017) International Journal of Law in Context 1; "Contextualizing The Global Constitution-Making Process: The Case of Vietnam" (2016) 64(4) American Journal of Comparative Law 931; and "Restoration Constitutionalism and Socialist Asia" (2015) 37(1) Loyola of Los Angeles International and Comparative Law Review 67. These materials have been substantively reworked and improved in this book.

Contents

List of Abbreviations

ANPP	The National Assembly of People's Power
APEC	Asia-Pacific Economic Cooperation Forum
art.	Article
ASEAN	Association of Southeast Asian Nations
CPV	Communist Party of Vietnam
CUP	Cambridge University Press
DPRK	Democratic People's Republic of Korea
ed.	Editor
eds	Editors
KMT	Chinese Nationalist Party
n	note
NA	National Assembly of Vietnam
OCDH	Cuban Observatory of Human Rights
OUP	Oxford University Press
PCC	The Communist Party of Cuba
SPA	Supreme People's Assembly
tr.	Translator
Viet.	Vietnam
Vol	Volume
WTO	World Trade Organisation

Introduction

The Socialist World in Comparative Constitutional Law

I. Paradigm Shift in Comparative Constitutionalism

Research into the role of constitutional change in comparative constitutionalism has become newly energized in recent years. This has been animated by the real waves of formal constitution-making.[1] In addition, in the twenty-first century post-conflict world, from Europe, the Post-Arab Spring Middle East and Africa to the Pacific Islands and Asia, constitution-making and constitutional amendment have ensued, driven by diverse factors such as regionalization, radical revolution, regime change, state-building, and ethnic division.[2] Such experience generates rich data from the comparative study of formal constitutional change. Some scholars have argued that there has been a "paradigm shift" in this field: the change in academic inquiry from a national to a comparative level with new concepts and quantitative research methodologies.[3]

Paradigm shift generally seems to occur in the field of comparative constitutionalism. The last few decades have witnessed the revival of comparative constitutional law.[4] In recent years, the field has experienced significant changes, displaying features of a "scientific revolution," the term put forward by Thomas

[1] Gregory Shaffer, Tom Ginsburg, and Terrance C. Halliday, "Constitution-Making as Transnational Legal Ordering" in *Constitution-Making and Transnational Legal Order* (Gregory Shaffer, Tom Ginsburg, and Terence C. Halliday (eds), Cambridge University Press 2019) 4.

[2] Nimer Sultany, *Law and Revolution: Legitimacy and Constitutionalism after the Arab Spring* (Oxford University Press 2017); Sujit Choudhry (ed),*Constitutional Design for Divided Societies: Integration or Accommodation?* (Oxford University Press 2008); Morris Kiwinda Mbondenyi and Tom Ojienda (eds),*Constitutionalism and Democratic Governance in Africa: Contemporary Perspectives from Sub-Saharan Africa* (Pretoria University Law Press 2013); Joanne Wallis, *Constitution Making during State Building* (Cambridge University Press 2014); Maartje De Visser and Ngoc Son Bui, "Globalised Constitution-Making in the Twenty-First Century: Evidence from Asia" (2019) 8 Global Constitutionalism 297; Special Issue: "Constitution-Making and Political Settlements in Times of Transition" (2017) 6 Global Constitutionalism 12.

[3] Xenophon Contiades and Alkmene Fotiadou, "The Emergence of Comparative Constitutional Amendment as a New Discipline: Towards a Paradigm Shift" in *The Foundations and Traditions of Constitutional Amendment* (Richard Albert, Xenophon Contiades, and Alkmene Fotiadou (eds), Hart Publishing 2017) 369.

[4] Ran Hirschl, *Comparative Matters: The Renaissance of Comparative Constitutional Law* (Oxford University Press 2014). For postwar history of the field, see David Fontana, "The Rise and Fall of Comparative Constitutional Law in the Postwar Era" (2011) 36 Yale Journal of International Law 1.

Constitutional Change in the Contemporary Socialist World. Bui Ngoc Son, Oxford University Press (2020). © Bui Ngoc Son.
DOI: 10.1093/oso/9780198851349.001.0001.

Kuhn.[5] Fundamental change in concepts and experimental practices in comparative constitutional inquiry has been manifested in at least four aspects. The first is the change from "constitutions as judicial review" to what Tom Ginsburg calls "constitutions as products."[6] While judicial constitutional questions have been still prominent, scholars of comparative constitutional law have turned to explore how constitutions are formally produced, amended, and replaced.[7]

The second dimension concerns the shift from the "global north" to the "global south." In his 2014 seminal book *Comparative Matters*, Ran Hirschl lamented that comparative constitutional inquiry has focused on the "constitutional experience of a small set of 'usual suspect' setting-all prosperous, stable constitutional democracies of the global south."[8] While this view is still valid in some ways, the last few years have witnessed the proliferation of comparative work exploring constitutional experience in unusual settings: authoritarianism and illiberal and fragile democracies of both developed and developing countries in different continents.[9] The dynamics of constitutional change in the global south may attract the attention of comparative constitutional academics. In addition, the recent tension and even demise of liberal constitutionalism[10] may animate the inquiry into alternative constitutional experiences.[11]

The third aspect is related to transnational and global concepts of constitutions and constitutional process. A constitution is now conceptualized, not merely a local document made by "we the people" to constitute national identity and national

[5] This term is coined by the philosopher Thomas S. Kuhn. See Thomas S. Kuhn, *The Structure of Scientific Revolutions* (4th edn, University of Chicago Press 2012).

[6] Tom Ginsburg, "Constitutions as Products," https://www.youtube.com/watch?v=XeHZraZJqv8.

[7] Richard Albert, *Constitutional Amendments: Making, Breaking, and Changing Constitutions* (Oxford University Press 2019).

[8] Ran Hirschl, *Comparative Matters: The Renaissance of Comparative Constitutional Law* (Oxford University Press 2014) 192. For similar view, see Sujit Choudhry, "Bridging Comparative Politics and Comparative Constitutional law: Constitutional Design in Divided Societies" in *Constitutional Design For Divided Societies: Integration Or Accommodation?* (Sujit Choudhry (ed.), Oxford University Press 2008) 8; Kent Roach, "Comparative Constitutional Law and the Challenges of Terrorism Law" in *Comparative Constitutional Law* (Tom Ginsburg and Rosalind Dixon (eds), Edward Elgar 2011) 545; Cheryl Saunders, *Towards a Global Constitutional Gene Pool* (2009) 4 National Taiwan University Law Review 3.

[9] Tom Ginsburg and Alberto Simpser (eds),*Constitutions in Authoritarian Regimes* (Cambridge University Press 2013); Mark V. Tushnet, "Authoritarian Constitutionalism" (2015) 100 Cornell Law Review 2, 461; Eric C. Ip, *Hybrid Constitutionalism: The Politics of Constitutional Review in the Chinese Special Administrative Regions* (Cambridge University Press 2019); Helena Alviar García and Günter Frankenberg (eds), *Authoritarian Constitutionalism: Comparative Analysis and Critique* (Edward Elgar 2019); Yap Po Jen, *Courts and Democracies in Asia* (Cambridge University Press 2017); Stephen Gardbaum, "Revolutionary Constitutionalism" (2017) 15(1) International Journal of Constitutional Law 173; Bruce Ackerman, *Revolutionary Constitutions: Charismatic Leadership and the Rule of Law* (Harvard University Press 2019).

[10] Tom Ginsburg and Aziz Z. Huq, *How to Save a Constitutional Democracy* (University of Chicago Press 2018); Mark A. Graber, Sanford Levinson, and Mark Tushnet (eds), *Constitutional Democracy in Crisis?* (Oxford University Press 2018) web.

[11] David S. Law, "Alternatives to Liberal Constitutional Democracy" (2017) 77 Maryland Law Review 223.

governance structures. Scholars have pointed out that the constitution-making and constitutional implementation are influenced by transnational and global ideas, triggers, institutions, and processes.[12] In addition to the theory of transnational constitutional orders, a discourse on the external dimension of constitutions has emerged.[13] Different diffusion mechanisms (coercion, learning, socialization, and competition) identified by social scientists have now migrated into comparative constitutional studies, which are used to explain the ways the constitutions and constitution-making are shaped by external influences.[14]

Finally, there has been a fundamental change in comparative constitutional methodology. Scholars have adopted innovative methods, including quantitative macro-studies.[15] In particular, cutting-edge technological products have been applied to macro-comparative constitutional analysis.[16] Other scholars have conducted field research to support qualitative micro accounts.[17]

To recap, we are in the heyday of comparative constitutional change. Constitution-making and constitutional amendment, animated by both local and global factors and actors which have occurred around the world provide rich empirical data from both the qualitative and quantitative study of comparative constitutionalism.

II. The Gap: Socialist Constitutional Change

The collapse of the Soviet bloc in the late twentieth century, which precipitated a massive transition from communism into constitutional democracy in Europe, is one of the most important catalysts of the revival of comparative constitutional law.[18] Comparative constitutional inquiry has been animated by the reality of constitution-making, constitutional amendments, and the creation of a specialist constitutional court during the post-Soviet era.[19] Scant attention among

[12] T. Ginsburg, T.C. Halliday, and G. Shaffer, *Constitution-Making as Transnational Legal Ordering* (Cambridge University Press 2019) 3–6.

[13] Eyal Benvenisti and Mila Versteeg, "The External Dimensions of Constitutions" (2018) 57 Virginia Journal of International Law 515.

[14] T. Ginsburg, T.C. Halliday, and G. Shaffer, *Constitution-Making as Transnational Legal Ordering* (Cambridge University Press 2019) 3–6; David S. Law and Mila Versteeg, "The Evolution and Ideology of Global Constitutionalism" (2011) 99 California Law Review 1163, 1171–83.

[15] E.g. Versteeg Mila and Zackin Emily, "Constitutions Unentrenched: Toward an Alternative Theory of Constitutional Design" (2016) 110 American Political Science Review 657.

[16] D.S. Law, "Constitutional Dialects: The Language of Transnational Legal Orders" in *Constitution-Making and Transnational Legal Order* (Gregory Shaffer, Tom Ginsburg, and Terence C. Halliday (eds), Cambridge University Press 2019).

[17] E.g. Joanne Wallis, *Constitution Making during State Building* (Cambridge University Press 2014).

[18] On the field's trajectory, see Ran Hirschl, *Comparative Matters: The Renaissance of Comparative Constitutional Law* (Oxford University Press 2014); David Fontana, "The Rise and Fall of Comparative Constitutional Law in the Postwar Era" (2011) 36 Yale Journal of International Law 1, 1–53.

[19] J.H.H. Weiler, "The Transformation of Europe" (1991) 100 Yale Law Journal 8, 2403; Bruce Ackerman, *The Future Of Liberal Revolution* (Yale University Press 1992); Bruce Ackerman, "The

constitutional comparatists, however, has been given to the constitutional system of the five countries that survived the domino fall of communism, namely China, Cuba, Laos, North Korea, and Vietnam.[20]

Although these five countries did not transition into constitutional democracies, constitutional change immediately occurred in these socialist countries in response to the dissolution of the Soviet Union in December 1991. China, North Korea, and Cuba amended their constitutions, Vietnam replaced the Soviet-era Constitution with a new one in 1992, while Laos eventually adopted the first socialist Constitution in 1991. In addition, in response to local and global impetuses, Vietnam, Laos, and Cuba recently adopted new constitutions (in 2013, 2015, and 2019 respectively), while China and North Korea have significantly amended their Soviet-era constitutions in several episodes.

Unfortunately, although national and comparative writings about socialist constitutional law proliferated during the era of the Soviet empire,[21] the fall of the Berlin Wall induced a decline in interest in socialist constitutions. Contemporary socialist constitutions have rarely been incorporated into the mainstream scholarship of comparative constitutional law.[22] Two factors account for this: juris-centrism and western-centrism. First, the field has been methodologically dominated by juris-centrism (or the focus on courts and judicial review),[23] while courts in current socialist countries do not have the power to review the constitutionality of legislation. Second, leading constitutional comparatists, such as Sujit Choudhry, Kent Roach, and Cheryl Sounders, state that comparative constitutional law has jurisdictionally

Rise of World Constitutionalism" (1997) Virginia Law Review 83, 771; Ruti Teitel, "Transitional Jurisprudence: The Role of Law in Political Transformation" (1997) 106 The Yale Law Journal 7, 2009.

[20] For communist resilience generally, Martin K. Dimitrov (ed), *Why Communism Did Not Collapse: Understanding Authoritarian Regime Resilience in Asia and Europe* (Cambridge University Press 2013).

[21] Chin Kim, "Recent Developments in the Constitutions of Asian Marxist-Socialist States" (1981) 13 Case Western Reserve Journal of International Law 483; Chin Kim and Timothy G. Kearley, "The 1972 Constitution of North Korea" (1976) 11(1) Texas International Law Journal, 113; John N. Hazard, "A Soviet Model for Marxian Socialist Constitutions" (1975) 60(6) Cornell Law Review 985; Branko M. Peselj, "Recent Codification Of Human Rights In Socialist Constitutions" (1965) 11(2) Howard Law Journal 342; Nhan Dan, "Constitution of Socialist Republic of Vietnam" (1981) 7(1) Review of Socialist Law 352; Martin Stuart-Fox, "The Constitution of the Lao People's Democratic Republic" (1991) 17(1) Review of Socialist Law 299; William T. D'Zurilla, "Cuba's 1976 Socialist Constitution and the Fidelista Interpretation Of Cuban Constitutional History" (1981) 55(41) Tulane Law Review 1223; L.B. Klein, "The Constitution of Cuba (1976)" (1978) 17 Columbia Journal of Transnational Law 451; Chris Osakwe, "The Common Law of Constitutions of the Communist-Party States" (1997) 3 Review of Socialist Law 155; John N. Hazard, "The Common Core of Marxian Socialist Constitution" (1981–1982) 19 San Diego Law Review 297; Christopher Osakwe, "The Theories and Realities of Modern Soviet Constitutional Law: An Analysis of the 1977 USSR Constitution" (1979) 127 University of Pennsylvania Law Review 1350.

[22] See for example, Vicki C. Jackson and Mark Tushnet, *Comparative Constitutional Law* (Foundation Press 2014); Michel Rosenfeld and András Sajó (eds), *The Oxford Handbook of Comparative Constitutional Law* (Oxford University Press 2012).

[23] For a review of scholarship in this line, see Theunis Roux, "Comparative Constitutional Studies: Two Fields or One" (2017) Annual Review of Law and Social Science 13, 123–39.

focused mainly on a limited set of the established liberal constitutional systems of North America and Europe and a few other states with similar institutional settings.[24] In particular, Ran Hirschl laments that constitutional experience, law, and institutions in a number of non-western nations are "seldom even referred to, let alone thoroughly studied, in mainstream European or North American comparative constitutional scholarship."[25]

More recently, the field has further expanded to incorporate authoritarian constitutions[26], constitutional experience of unusual settings,[27] and non-judicial questions (such as constitution-making, constitutional amendments, popular constitutionalism or political constitutionalism, and economic constitutionalism), but comparative questions in the current five socialist countries have been continuingly ignored or marginalized.[28] The general constraints of time, resources, language, and contextual understanding, as mentioned by Vicki Jackson, are all relevant factors.[29]

This book seeks to fill the academic gap in the existing literature on comparative constitutional law by examining how and why constitutional change (including making new constitutions and formal constitutional amendments) has occurred in five current socialist countries after the fall of the Soviet Union.

III. Comparative Approach and Methodology

This book is a comparative enterprise. This "controlled comparison" follows the "most similar cases" principle in small-N comparative constitutional studies.[30] The five socialist countries share many common features. They all have a communist

[24] Sujit Choudhry, "Bridging Comparative Politics and Comparative Constitutional Law: Constitutional Design in Divided Societies" in *Constitutional Design for Divided Societies* (Sujit Choudhry (ed.), Oxford University Press 2008) 8; Kent Roach, "Comparative Constitutional Law and the Challenges of Terrorism Law" in *Comparative Constitutional Law* (Tom Ginsburg and Rosalind Dixon (eds), Edward Elgar Publishing 2011) 545; Cheryl Saunders, "Towards a Global Constitutional Gene Pool" (2009) 4 National Taiwan University Law Review 3.

[25] Ran Hirschl, *Comparative Matters: The Renaissance of Comparative Constitutional Law* (Oxford University Press 2014) 212.

[26] Tom Ginsburg and Alberto Simpser (eds), *Constitutions in Authoritarian Regimes* (Cambridge University Press 2014); Mark Tushnet, "Authoritarian Constitutionalism" (2015) 100 Cornell Law Review 391–462.

[27] Denis J. Galligan and Mila Versteeg (eds), *Social And Political Foundations of Constitutions* (Cambridge University Press 2015); Mark Tushnet and Madhav Khosla (eds), *Unstable Constitutionalism: Law and Politics in South Asia* (Cambridge University Press 2015); Nimer Sultany, *Law and Revolution: Legitimacy and Constitutionalism After the Arab Spring* (Oxford University Press 2017).

[28] There are some exceptional writings on China from a comparative perspective. See Wen-Chen Chang and David S. Law, "Constitutional Dissonance in China" in *Comparative Constitutional Theory* (Gary Jacobsohn and Miguel Schor (eds), Edward Elgar 2018).

[29] Vicky C. Iackson, "Methodological Challenges in Comparative Constitutional Law" (2010) 28 Penn State International Law Review 323.

[30] Hirschl, *Comparative Matters* (n 4) 244–5.

history, survived the fall of the communist-bloc, have a socialist legal system, and operate a Leninist constitutional system ruled by a communist party, and have an economic system controlled by state-owned enterprises. During the post-Soviet era, the five socialist countries have all adapted their constitutional systems. However, the degree, mechanisms, and influential factors of constitutional change in these countries are not identical but display considerable variations, which warrants further scrutiny in this comparative project.

This book offers inference-oriented qualitative research which aims to advance comparative constitutional knowledge. This mode of research aims to explain why constitutional change happens in the contemporary socialist world and why it happens in certain ways. This explanatory comparative inquiry necessarily makes this enterprise an interdisciplinary project which will engage with comparative constitutional law, political science, sociology, and institutional economics so as to explore and explain the actual operation of the constitution, constitutional process, constitutional actors, and constitutional institutions. Constitutional change in the contemporary socialist countries is an integral part of the broader dynamics of intellectual, political, social, and economic transitions in these countries over the last three decades, and cannot be understood independently from them. Therefore, the understanding of this constitutional change is situated within the broader milieu of intellectual, political, social, and economic changes. To do this, I integrate constitutional theory with social science theories (particularly political theory, sociological theory, and economic theory) to understand the functions, driving forces, and process of constitutional change.

This book relies on primary and secondary sources. The primary sources include materials available in local languages and empirical data gained through fieldwork. The primary resources include constitutions, statutes, regulations, reports, and testimonies available in the local language. This book is supported by fieldwork in socialist countries (except for North Korea) to collect primary materials and to interview local people. I have conducted field trips in Vietnam, Laos, and Cuba, and collected primary resources and interviewed local constitution-makers, legislators, lawyers, legal scholars, and members of civil society. I also traveled to mainland China several times and discussed with local jurists. In the case of North Korea, I traveled to South Korea and, thanks to my colleagues there, was able to collect primary materials related to North Korea. Vietnamese is my native language, and therefore I enjoy direct access to the primary materials available in Vietnamese. My native language also allows me to gain access to materials on the constitutions, and political system in Laos, available in Vietnamese, produced by Laotian scholars, officials, and students who have studied at Vietnamese universities. The primary materials regarding China, Laos, North Korea, and Cuba can be accessed through translation. The book also relies on secondary sources: English national and comparative constitutional writings and interdisciplinary materials.

IV. Argument, Contribution, and Plan

This book integrates conceptual, functional, causal, and institutional accounts to explore and explain how and why the five socialist countries changed their constitutions since the fall of the Soviet era. The book covers the long constitutional trajectory in the five countries, and particularly focuses on constitutional change since the eve of the new century, including: the making of Vietnam's 2013 Constitution, the making of Laos' 2015 Constitution, the making of Cuba's 2019 Constitution, China's serial constitutional amendments through 2018, and North Korea's serial constitutional amendments through 2019. Conceptually, the book adopts a non-binary approach, in order to situate the socialist formal constitution and formal constitutional change within the broader constitutional order and actual social dynamics.

The book argues that socialist constitutional change is progressive. The function of this constitutional change is to facilitate the active role of the party-state (the socialist state under the leadership of a communist party) in improving the material well-being of residents, in terms of their living conditions. This function is epistemologically shaped by progressive convictions in Marxist philosophy. Constitutional reforms have been achieved by institutional improvement of the socialist constitutional system while retaining the dictatorship of the working ruling class presented by the communist party. Therefore, while socialist constitutional identity remains (the instrumental nature of the constitution, the single leadership of the communist party, centralized power, rights and the economy regulated by the state), constitutional change softens and modifies the authoritarian arrangement and introduces new elements which facilitate the improvement of the socialist constitutional system (the dynamic constitution, institutionalization of the party, horizon and vertical distribution of power, universalization of human rights, and marketization of the economy).

This socialist, progressive constitutional change is driven by both top-down and bottom-up dynamics of political economy, including: leadership change; the reformist programs for social and economic development; constitutional and economic globalization, and social demands and domestic social and economic transition.

The legal form for constitutional change is varied, including: implicit replacement through amendment (Vietnam), explicit replacement through amendment (Laos), ordinary replacement (Cuba), and ordinary amendment (China and North Korea). The choice between amendment and replacement is determined by the progressive function of constitutional change: When the socialist elite want to signify the beginning of a new phrase of political, social and economic progress, replacement is the more likely choice. In addition, as the consequence of progressive change within the socialist constitutional order, three legal powers (constituent, amendment, and legislative powers) are blurred (except in the case of Cuba), and socialist constitutional essentials are made unamendable. Although public participation in the socialist constitution-making process is under the party's control, participation in several cases (Vietnam and Cuba) generates popular constitutional dialogue which induces reformative and cultural constitutional change. In addition to domestic participation, transnational influence (international involvement and diffusion) on socialist constitutional change is evident, which creates various responses: convergence, resistance, and engagement.

Based on the prominent appearance of the influential factors that drive and legitimize the substantive and procedural constitutional change, this book identifies five models or variations of socialist constitutional change: universal (Vietnam), integration (Laos), reservation (Cuba), exceptional (China), and personal (North Korea). In the universal model, the global factors and universal norms play a prominent role in shaping and legitimatizing constitutional change. In the integration model, ethnic unity prominently shapes the process and substance of constitutional change. In the reservation model, the reservation of the historical achievement prominently features the process and substance of constitution-making. In the exceptional model, the aspiration and attitude to a distinctive development model prominently shapes constitutional change. In the personal model of socialist constitutional change, a particular leader's power and ideology prominently shape the constitutional change.

This book contributes to a better understanding of dynamic socioeconomic, legal, and constitutional change in socialist countries and comparative constitutional law and theory, generally. In the first instance, the study of constitutional change in the five socialist countries contributes to the understanding of the possibilities and constraints of constitutional development in these countries. This is, in turn, necessary in order to comprehend the dynamics and limits of their legal, political, social, and economic change.

On the second contribution, this book comprehensively examines four aspects of comparative constitutional law and theory: jurisdictional, substantive, theoretical, and methodological.

First, this study contributes to the continued expansion of the jurisdictional sphere of comparative constitutional law into varieties of institutional settings, including socialist ones.

Second, this book enriches the global knowledge of comparative constitutional law by the examination of a variety of the substantive, unique socialist constitutional issues (such as parliamentary constitution-making, constitutional ideology, the constitutional role of the communist party, constitutional mobilization, constitutional regulation of the economy, and legislative constitutional enforcement). This contributes to the development of comparative constitutional law beyond juris-centrism.

Third, this inquiry develops a new theory of progressive constitutional change to understand constitutional dynamics in the socialist, nondemocratic, developing world, which contributes to comparative theorization of constitutional change beyond the empirical base of democratic and developed countries.

Fourth, this book methodologically improves the ways we think about constitutions globally by offering a particular way of thinking about socialist constitutions. This comparative constitutional inquiry goes beyond judicial questions and doctrinal study of constitutional rules and texts, and looks at systematic questions, such as: how the constitutions are produced, how they interact with the socioeconomic context, what ideas and ideology underpin the constitutions, what the political and social forces that drive the constitutional development are, and how the constitutional law is produced and enforced by the complex interplay of different institutional and non-institutional actors.

Besides an introduction and conclusion, the book includes eight chapters divided into two parts. The first part deals with foundational and theoretical issues, while the second part explores the five cases in depth. Part I includes three chapters on theorizing socialist constitutional change, socialist constitutional identity and history. Five chapters in Part II provide in-depth exploration and explanations of constitutional replacement in Vietnam, Laos, Cuba, and the constitutional amendment in China and North Korea, respectively.

PART I
FOUNDATIONS
Theory, Identity, and History

1
Theorizing Socialist Constitutional Change

Introduction

This chapter aims to theorize constitutional change that has taken place in the five socialist countries since the eve of the new century. This chapter focuses on generalization, while ideational and historical backgrounds and five meticulous investigations of constitutional change will be provided in the next two chapters in Part I and five chapters in Part II respectively.

Existing theorizing models of comparative constitutional change feature four approaches, categorized here as conceptualism, functionalism, causalism, and institutionalism. Conceptualist accounts explore foundational concepts, such as constitution and constitutional change. Functionalists are primarily concerned with the actual role of constitutional change in a political landscape: the social, political issues that constitutional change tries to address. Work in this line mainly discusses the role of constitutional change in the creation, transformation, and degeneration of democracies. Causualist accounts try to explain the determinants of constitutional change. While functionalism and causalism tend to be interdisciplinary (integrating comparative constitutional law with social sciences, particularly political science and economics), institutionalism focuses on legal questions. Institutionalists explore legal institutions that govern the way constitutional change occurs, particularly the legal form of constitutional change (amendment and replacement), the legal power to change the constitution (constituent and amendment power), the legal limits on these powers (unamendability), and procedural questions, especially those of public participation and transnational engagement in constitutional change. While conceptual and institutional inquiries mainly deal with legal questions of constitutional change, causalism, and functionalism turn to more interdisciplinary questions.

Constitutional change is multi-dimensional, and therefore cannot be fully understood by using a single viewpoint to conceptualize it. This chapter, therefore, aims to theorize socialist constitutional change, using a holistic approach, which integrates conceptualist, functionalist, causalist, and institutional accounts. Conceptually, I adopt a non-binary approach to constitution and constitutional change, seeking to accentuate and situate the formal constitution and formal constitutional change (including amendment and replacement) within the broader constitutional order. Functionally, socialist constitutional change can be

Constitutional Change in the Contemporary Socialist World. Bui Ngoc Son, Oxford University Press (2020). © Bui Ngoc Son.
DOI: 10.1093/oso/9780198851349.001.0001.

characterized as progressive constitutional change. Epistemologically rooted in Marxist progressivism, the function of constitutional change in socialist countries is to facilitate the active role of the party-state (the socialist state under the leadership of a communist party) in improving the material well-being of local people, through their living conditions. This progressive constitutional change is driven by a range of top-down and bottom-up factors: leadership change; the party's changing policy for social and economic development; constitutional and economic globalization; and social demands and social economic transition. The legal form for constitutional change is varied, including: implicit replacement through amendment, explicit replacement through amendment, ordinary replacement, and ordinary amendment. I conclude by categorizing five variations of the socialist models of progressive constitutional change: universal, integration, reservation, exceptional, and personal.

I. Foundational Concepts

A. Constitution

Zachary Elkins, Tom Ginsburg, and James Melton distinguish between a formal and a functional concept of constitution. The former refers to a written constitutional text, while the latter refers to the broader constitutional order of which the formal constitution is only a single element, albeit the central one.[1] In functional terms, Walter Murphy defines constitution "as the 'constitutional order': the nation's constitutional text, its dominant political theories, the traditions and aspirations that reflect those values, and the principal interpretations of this larger constitution."[2] Ernest A. Young adopts the same functional approach, arguing that the US Constitution includes not only the 1787 Philadelphia charter and subsequent formal amendments but also a wide range of "statutes, executive materials, and practices" which structure the government, empower individuals vis-à-vis the government, and entrench institutional structures and individual rights against change.[3] This functional conceptualization is traceable to the Diceyian definition of English constitutional law as consisting of "rules which directly or indirectly affect the distribution or exercise of the sovereignty in the state."[4]

[1] Zachary Elkins, Tom Ginsburg, and James Melton, *The Endurance of National Constitutions* (Cambridge University Press 2009) 38.

[2] Walter Murphy, *Constitutional Democracy* (The Johns Hopkins University Press 2007) 13.

[3] Ernest A. Young, "The Constitution Outside the Constitution" (2007) 117 Yale Law Journal 408, 412.

[4] A.V. Dicey, *Introduction to the Study of Law of the Constitution* (MacMillan and Co Limited 1920) 23.

The functional concept of constitution is tantamount to the concept of "material constitution" in European public law discourse. The "material constitution" refers to the actual constitutional order. The concept has its root in Marxist historical materialism. "The idea is that in order to explain and understand the constitutional order it is necessary to look into the formation and reformation of societal order. From a Marxist perspective, this means that the organization and regulation of modes and relations of production is critical—as it works as the lynchpin of societal reproduction."[5] The idea of a material constitution has been theorized by other thinkers, such as the Austrian legal philosopher Hans Kelsen, the German philosopher, Hermann Heller, and the Italian constitutional theorist Costantino Mortati.[6] In a recent contribution, Marco Goldoni and Michael A. Wilkinson define four elements of the material constitution: political unity (modern nation-state); a set of governmental (e.g. legislature, executives, and courts) and non-governmental (e.g. family and trade unions) institutions; social relations (class interests and social movements); and political objectives (e.g. democracy, human rights, and social welfare).[7]

In this study, I adopt a non-binary approach to the concept of the constitution, by situating the formal constitution within the broader constitutional order. The formal constitution is integral to the functional or material constitution. The written constitutional texts define the nature of the state, its institutions, its relations with the people, and its political goals, by which they inform actual constitutional relations in some ways. Therefore, the understanding of constitutional order requires taking into account the formal constitutions. The written constitutions, however, were not created and do not operate in a vacuum. Their making and functioning are shaped by the material relations of different social and institutional actors. Therefore, the understanding of the constitutional texts requires situating them within the actual surroundings. This is particularly relevant to understanding socialist constitutions. The socialist states adopt Marxism as the official ideology, and consequently Marxist historical materialism necessarily informs the conceptualization of socialist constitution as the material constitution. With that non-dichotomic approach, in this study, I accentuate and situate the written socialist constitutions within the broader socialist constitutional order. In other words, I locate them with the socialist ideology, the economic system, and political system, and the actual relations of different social and institutional actors (the communist party, the state, and citizens, including social mobilization actors).

[5] Marco Goldoni "Introduction to the Material Study of Global Constitutional Law" (2019) 8 Global Constitutionalism 71.

[6] For a discussion of their theories, see Marco Goldoni and Michael A Wilkinson, "The Material Constitution" (2018) 4 Modern Law Review 81, 567, 569–80.

[7] Ibid. 580–92.

B. Constitutional Change

The conceptualization of constitution is consequential to understanding constitutional change. In current scholarship, constitutional change refers to both *informal* change through judicial interpretation of the constitutional texts and *formal* change through the formal amendment process.[8] In the latter, constitutional change is virtually synonymous with formal constitutional amendment. Consistent with the conceptualization of constitution, I adopt a non-binary approach to constitutional change, situating formal constitutional change within the actual social dynamics.

In fact, Marxist historical materialism is the ideological foundation for the socialist states to justify the constitutional change: the social and economic change (the change in infrastructure) is the base for constitutional change (the change in legal and political superstructure). Therefore, the understanding of formal change to the socialist constitutions must be situated within the framework of broader social, economic, and political change. In addition, the non-binary approach to constitutional change would not exclude the formal making of a new constitution. In the real world, constitutional amendment and constitution-making are indistinguishable in many cases. The process of constitutional amendment may lead to the enactment of a new constitution, as in the case of Hungary. Conversely, formal enactment of new constitutions retains a great deal of constitutional continuity, as in the case of France's fifteen constitutions. In addition, formal constitutional amendment may create significant changes similar to constitution-making, such as in the US Civil War Amendments.[9] In the socialist cases, the distinction between constitution-making and constitutional amendment is very blurred.

Therefore, in this study, I accentuate and situate formal socialist constitutional change (including changes that lead to the enactment of formal new constitutions and formal constitutional amendments) within the real changing ideological, social, economic, and political context.

II. Function: Progressive Constitutional Change

A. The Prevailing Models

Previous scholarship has captured the functions of constitutional change by three prevailing theorizing models: foundational, constructive, and abusive.

[8] Dawn Oliver and Carlo Fusaro, "Changing Constitutions" in *How Constitutions Change: A Comparative Study* (Dawn Oliver and Carlo Fusaro (eds), Hart Publishing 2011) 4.

[9] Michael Rosenfeld, *The Identity of the Constitutional Subject: Selfhood, Citizenship, Culture, and Community* (Routledge 2010) 209. See also, Richard Albert, Malkhaz Nakashidze, and Tarik Olcay, "The Formalist Resistance to Unconstitutional Constitutional Amendments" (2019) 70 Hastings Law Journal 639, 670 (introducing a theory of amendment-as-constitution, the idea that the product of constitution-changing has the same constitution-level status as the product of constitution-making).

Foundationalism holds that formal constitutional change in the extraordinary moment (e.g. an end-result of a liberal revolution) separate from ordinary politics creates the foundation for a new democratic order. This model can be found in Bruce Ackerman's theory of constitutional moment[10] and his normative account of the future of liberal revolution in Eastern Europe.[11] Foundationalism draws on the empirical experience of eighteenth-century constitutional change, mainly in the United States and France. This limits its explanatory power to other cases in other places and at other times. To illustrate, in the late twentieth century, a large number of states in post-communist Central and East Europe successfully transitioned into constitutional democracy accompanied by formal constitutional change without a liberal revolution and an extraordinary constitutional moment.[12]

Foundationalism cannot explain formal constitutional change in the contemporary socialist/communist world. These socialist experiences of formal constitutional change have occurred in a different manner and yielded outcomes different from that which foundationalists expect. The constitutions are not the culmination of a liberal revolution, and there was no "big-bang" constitutional moment that suddenly created a fundamentally new constitutional order. The socialist constitutional order remains but has incremental, not foundational, changes through constitution-making and constitutional amendments.

Constructivism was introduced to respond to the limits of constitutional foundationalism. This conceptual model was first advanced by Ruti Teitel[13] and has since been supported by other scholars.[14] Constructivism is based on the empirical ground of formal constitution-making and constitutional amendment in post-communist Eastern and Central Europe and some Asian jurisdictions such as Taiwan and South Korea in the late twentieth century. Constructivism holds that the adoption of a new constitution or a series of constitutional amendments is constructed of and constructive to gradual shifts from an authoritarian regime to a liberal constitutional regime, replacing violent revolutions with peaceful political transformation.[15] Two positions accompany this constructivist thesis: realism and incrementalism. The realist position is that "constitutional change was so closely associated with political change that it implied a constitutional politics

[10] Bruce Ackerman, *We the People, Volume 1: Foundations* (Belknap Press: An Imprint of Harvard University Press 1993).

[11] Bruce Ackerman, *The Future of Liberal Revolution* (Yale University Press 1992).

[12] Ruti Teitel, "Transitional Jurisprudence: The Role of Law in Political Transformation" (1997) 106(7) Yale Law Journal 2009, 2051–2

[13] Ibid.

[14] Jiunn-Rong Yeh and Wen-Chen Chang, "The Changing Landscape of Modern Constitutionalism: Transitional Perspective" (2009) 4(1) National Taiwan University Law Review 145.

[15] Teitel, "Transitional Jurisprudence" (n 12) 2067.

not readily distinguishable from ordinary politics."[16] In the realist world, "ordinary parliaments became the locus for both ordinary legislation and constitutional making."[17] The incremental position is: "Initial constitutional changes would alter subsequent political situations, where new demands for constitutional reforms would rise and facilitate another round of constitutional changes that would again alter political situations where new changes would be brought about."[18]

Despite being based on post-communist constitutional transformation, constructivism also resonated in the twenty-first century experience of formal constitutional changes in the current communist countries.[19] In a similar way to post-communist countries in Europe, formal constitutional changes in the current communist countries are realist (the ordinary legislature being the locus of formal constitutional change), and incrementalist (constitutional amendments facilitating further constitutional amendment). However, constructivism is intellectually grounded in a liberal understanding of constitutionalism.[20] This limits its explanatory power: constitutional amendments are constructive to constitutional development which may not follow the liberal constitutional paradigm. In addition, constructivism was advanced when globalization (including constitutional globalization) was not yet a prominent global trend. Therefore, it has not yet considered the global and transnational elements of constitutional construction.

A new wave of formal constitutional changes in the twenty-first century has happened in an *abusive* way: constitutional amendments or constitution-making are used to undermine constitutional democracy.[21] This is captured in David Landau's concept of "abusive constitutionalism," grounded on the experience that would-be autocrats in Hungary, Egypt, and Venezuela used constitutional amendments and replacements to undermine democracy.[22] The theorizing model of abusive constitutional change is empirically supported by recent examples of formal constitutional changes in relatively wealthy and democratic countries, which help to validate the model. Constitutional amendment can be used for different purposes in less wealthy and non-democratic countries. When a

[16] Ruti Teitel, *Transitional Justice* (OUP 1999) 207.

[17] William Partlett, "The Dangers of Popular Constitution-Making" (2012) 38 Brooklyn Journal of International Law 193, 205.

[18] Yeh and Chang, "Modern Constitutionalism" (n 14) 161.

[19] Mark Sidel, "Analytical Models for Understanding Constitutions and Constitutional Dialogues in Socialist Transitional States: Re-Interpreting Constitutional Dialogues in Vietnam" (2002) 6 Singapore Journal of International and Comparative Law 42.

[20] Catherine Turner, "Transitional Constitutionalism and the Case of the Arab Spring" (2015) 64 International and Comparative Law Quarterly 267, 280.

[21] Aziz Z. Huq and Tom Ginsburg, "How to Lose a Constitutional Democracy" (2018) 65 UCLA Law Review 78. For further treatment on the regress of liberal constitutionalism, see "*Symposium:* The Limits of Constitutionalism—A Global Perspective" (2018) 85 University of Chicago Law Review 239–608.

[22] David Landau, "Abusive Constitutionalism" (2013) 47 UC Davis Law Review 189, 260, 1686–707.

non-democratic and developing country is struggling for a better constitutional order and socioeconomic development, then amendment may be used as a part of this process. This is the case with socialist countries which cannot be represented by the idea of abusive constitutional change.

B. The Progressive Model

From a functionalist perspective, socialist constitutional change can be characterized as progressive constitutional change. The function of constitutional change in socialist countries is to facilitate the active role of the party-state (the socialist state under the leadership of a communist party) in improving the material well-being of the living conditions of local people. This function is epistemologically shaped by progressivism, a concept articulated by Karl Marx and supported and developed by Friedrich Engels and Vladimir Lenin.

Marxist progressivism, an explanatory and normative theory of human history, is part of the broader history of the grand idea of Progress in Western philosophy.[23] This idea holds "that civilization has moved, is moving, and will move in a desirable direction."[24] Robert A. Nisbet, a prominent scholar of the history of the idea of Progress, writes that at its zenith in Western philosophy in the period 1750–1900 "the concept of progress is distinct and pivotal in that it becomes the developmental *context* for these [equality, social justice, and popular sovereignty] other ideas."[25] Nisbet provides a detailed treatment on how ideas pertaining to two key values, namely individual freedom (the ultimate goal of human progress) and political power (the means to achieve that goal), are intellectually contextualized within the broader idea of Progress.[26] In particular, the idea of Progress provides the philosophical context for the discourse on constitutionalism. According to Ulrich K. Preuss, "at the very beginning of the constitutional epoch in Europe the ideas of revolution, popular sovereignty, political and social progress, and constitutionalism were closely associated with each other in that they mutually support and even explain one another."[27] For example, the French revolutionaries anticipated a constitution created by the constituent power and as the expression of the people's revolutionary spirit, "and clearly this spirit was imbued with the desperate quest for freedom from the misery of their lives."[28]

[23] Henry M. Pachter, "The Idea of Progress in Marxism" (1974) 1 Social Research 41, 136–61.

[24] John Bagnell Bury, *The Idea of Progress: An Inquiry into Its Origin and Growth* (Dover Publications 1932) 2.

[25] Robert Nisbet, *History of the Idea of Progress* (Transaction Publishers 1980) 171.

[26] Nisbet, *History of the Idea of Progress* (n 25) Part II—the Triumph of the Idea of Progress.

[27] Ulrich Klaus Preuss, *Constitutional Revolution: The Link Between Constitutionalism and Progress* (Prometheus Books 1995) 3.

[28] Ibid.

Marx shares with other progressive thinkers the conviction of mankind's unstoppable progress. As Nisbet writes, "it is impossible to think of any major figure of that [nineteenth] century in which the perspective of the inexorable, irreversible, and stage by stage progress toward a golden age on earth is more vividly evident than in Marx's key works."[29] Yet, Marxist progressivism has distinctive directional and substantive features and consequently contextualizes socialist constitutional arrangement in a different way. Directionally, Marxist historical materialism anticipates the human progress from primitive communism, to slave society, to feudalism, to capitalism, to socialism, and ultimately to scientific communism.[30] From this Marxist conviction, the human progress toward socialism is not only necessary but also inevitable. Substantively, Marxist progressivism holds different views about individual freedom as the ultimate goal of human progress, and political power as a means to achieve that goal. As far as individual freedom is concerned, Marxist progressivism is primarily concerned with the emancipation of the working class from capitalist exploitation. The means to this end is a class struggle (socialist revolution) leading to the working class holding political power in a socialist state under the framework of a dictatorship of the proletariat (Marx) or a dictatorship by the communist party representing the proletariat (Lenin).[31] In short, under Marxist progressivism, mankind's progress from capitalism to socialism is led by a party-state or a socialist state under the leadership of a communist party.

Marxist progressivism informs the contents of socialist constitutions generally and the progressive function of socialist constitutional change in particular. Constitutional reforms in the socialist countries aim to facilitate the state-led (and arguably indispensable) progress of these countries toward socialism. To pursue the socialist paradise, the socialist states are compelled to improve the material well-being of the living conditions of the local people (e.g. economic betterment, education, health-care, and social equality). Consequently, socialist constitutional change focuses mainly on social and economic issues. From a socialist, progressive perspective, material improvement is not substantively left to the private sector but essentially depends on the party-state. Therefore, constitutional reforms positively enable or empower (rather than negatively disable or limit) the party-state's actions in economic and social domains to facilitate its active role in improving people's material well-being. These constitutional reforms have been achieved by institutional improvement of the socialist constitutional system while leaving untouched the dictatorship of the working ruling class represented by a communist party. Therefore, while the authoritarian socialist regime remains (the

[29] Nisbet, *History of the Idea of Progress* (n 25) 258.
[30] "Manifesto of the Communist Party" <www.marxists.org/archive/marx/works/download/pdf/Manifesto.pdf>
[31] Nisbet, *History of the Idea of Progress* (n 25) 258, 265.

instrumental nature of the constitution, the single leadership of the communist party, centralized power, rights, and the economy regulated by the state), constitutional change softens and modifies the authoritarian arrangement and introduces new elements which facilitate the improvement of the socialist constitutional system (the dynamic constitution, institutionalization of the party, horizontal and vertical distribution of power, universalization of human rights, and marketization of the economy).

This section has explored the epistemological foundation of the progressive function of socialist constitutional change. However, there must be material factors driving this progressive change. The next part will deal with this issue.

III. Factors: Political Economy of Constitutional Change

Why have the constitutions changed? The explanation of the causal factors of constitutional change has to do with its contextual political, social, and economic surroundings. Understandably, that "why" question is more taken up in interdisciplinary accounts which integrate comparative constitutional with political and economic studies. There are two types of theories of constitutional change: economic and political.

The economic theories of constitutional change are methodologically rooted in institutional economics. To illustrate, drawing on positive constitutional economics, Stefan Voigt proposed the theory of constitutional bargaining. This theory reduces a constitution to a system of rules specifying the procedures for producing collective goods. It also rests on a real as opposed to hypothetical notion of a social contract as explicit agreements between numerous contracting parties. On that basis, Voigt conceptualizes constitutional change as the outcome of a bargaining process between the rulers and various opposition groups.[32]

Echoing institutional economics, in their classical work Zachary Elkins, Tom Ginsburg, and James Melton propose a theory of constitutional renegotiation. The theory is rooted in the quintessential idea that a constitution is the consequence of rational bargaining between relevant parties. Consequently, constitutional change through amendments or replacement is due to the parties' renegotiation as they anticipate that they will be better off under an alternative constitutional arrangement. The renegotiation theory also accounts for the internal and external

[32] Stefan Voigt, *Explaining Constitutional Change: A Positive Economics Approach* (E Elgar 1999) 107–8. For similar economic accounts of constitutional change, see Donald J. Boudreaux and A.C. Pritchard, "Rewriting the Constitution: An Economic Analysis of the Constitutional Amendment Process" (1993) 62 Fordham Law Review 111; Shruti Rajagopalan, *Economic Analysis of Amendments to the Indian Constitution* (Doctoral Dissertation, George Mason University 2013); A.V. Raja, "Democracy and Constitutional Amendments: Economic Reforms in India" in *Internationalisierung Des Rechts Und Seine Öknomische Analyse* (Thomas Eger, Jochen Bigus, Claus Ott, and Georg von Wangenheim (eds), Gabler Verlag, 2008) 747.

pressures that affect the constitutional players' calculus of costs and benefits at the renegotiation table.[33]

The political theories focus on the social, political surroundings of constitutional change. To illustrate, Keith G. Banting and Richard Simeon have theorized the remote and proximate political demands for formal constitutional change in industrial democracies.[34] At the remote level, demands for constitutional change "originate in social and economic forces which shift the relative status of different groups, and which in turn lead the groups to call for alterations in their political relationship."[35] Constitutional change also depends on a more proximate dimension: "the political rules of the game are systematically and unfairly biased against the group, or that they frustrate the group in pursuit of its collective goals."[36]

In the same vein, Gabriel L. Negretto explains the political logic of constitutional replacements and amendments in the context of Latin America. His political theory attributes the causes of constitutional change to political transformations at the state or regime level, a dysfunctional constitutional performance, and balance-of-power shifts. A regime change may lead to the enactment of a new constitution which replaces the existing one. Democratic regimes may also amend existing authoritarian constitutions to facilitate the democratic transitional process. In addition, when a constitution fails to operate as a governance structure that organizes political competition, politicians may replace or amend it. Finally, a constitution can also be replaced or amended when there is a significant change in the balance of political power due to a shift in party competition.[37]

The logic of constitutional political economy in the socialist world may be different. The prevailing economic and political theories tend to draw upon a political competition either as a hypothetical or experimental environment of constitutional change. Socialist constitutional change occurred in different institutional settings dominated by a communist party. Socialist constitutional replacement occurred without regime change. The socialist state replaced or amended the constitution, not to facilitate the transition from socialist regime into a liberal democracy. In contrast, in several cases (e.g. China and Cuba), constitutional change is explicitly aversive to liberal-democratic transition and multiparty politics.

In addition, both economic and political theories explain constitutional change as the political elite's calculus of their material self-interests. This echoes the rational choice theory in modern economics. While the rational choice theory explains a great deal of human behaviors, it has been recently challenged by

[33] Elkins, Ginsburg, and Melton, *The Endurance of National Constitutions* (n 1) 66.

[34] Keith G. Banting and Richard Simeon, "Introduction: The Politics of Constitutional Change" in *The Politics of Constitutional Change in Industrial Nations* (Keith G. Banting and Richard Simeon (eds), Palgrave Macmillan 1985) 10.

[35] Ibid.

[36] Banting and Simeon, "Introduction" (n 34) 12.

[37] Gabriel L. Negretto, "Replacing and Amending Constitutions: The Logic of Constitutional Change in Latin America" (2012) 46(4) Law & Society Review 749, 755–6.

behavior economists and psychologists, such as Daniel Kahneman Amos Tversky who indicates that human behavior is not as rational as we tend to think.[38] Francis Fukuyama has also discussed the weakness of the rational choice accounts, arguing that human behavior is shaped not only by the rational calculation of material self-interests but also by the desire for the recognition of human dignity.[39] In the constitutional field, Mark Tushnet has challenged the instrumental accounts of the role of constitutions and courts in authoritarian regimes, arguing that what shapes the authoritarian leaders' behaviors are not only their calculation of their self-interest but also their "'steady desire', such as a desire for national glory or national economic development."[40]

Socialist constitutional change may be animated by the elites' top-down instrumental consideration of their self-interest, but they might have a progressive desire for the social and economic development to improve the well-being of the local people and ultimately the movement of their societies toward the socialist paradise. The instrumental and progressive motivations may be mixed: to improve the wellbeing of the living conditions of the local people may correspond to the rational concern of rulers' sociological legitimacy and the desire for social and economic progress. Socialist rulers have mixed motivations in changing constitutions, because they are influenced by different dynamics. Due to both top-down and bottom-up dynamics, formal constitutional change occurs in the socialist world to institutionalize the new program for social and economic development which aims to improve the material wellbeing of the living conditions of the local people. The top-down dynamics include: (1) leadership change; (2) reformist programs for social and economic development; and (3) constitutional and economic globalization. Nor should we forget (4) internal bottom-up dynamics, springing from the demands of society for constitutional change to improve the human condition and the domestic social and economic transition.

A. Leadership Change

In the view of the personalization of public power in several socialist states, leadership change often induces constitutional change. Cuba's 2019 constitution-making was triggered by the handover of the presidential position from Fidel Castro Raúl Castro and then to Miguel Díaz-Canel. In China, constitutional amendments responded to Deng Xiaoping's death, Jiang Zemin's succession by Hu Jintao, and the rise of Xi Jinping. In North Korea, the flow of political power from Kim Il-sung

[38] Daniel Kahneman, *Thinking, Fast and Slow* (Farrar, Straus and Giroux 2013)
[39] Francis Fukuyama, *Identity* (Profile Books 2018) 14–24.
[40] Mark Tushnet, "Authoritarian Constitutionalism" (2015) 100 Cornell Law Review 391, 440.

to Kim Jong-il and then to Kim Jong-un was accompanied by corresponding constitutional amendments.

The fact that new leadership brings about constitutional change can be explained by the logic of *socialist constitutional redemption*: the personal commitment to the realization of the socialist constitutional project through formal constitutional change. In Jack M. Balkin's treatment, constitutional redemption (the realization of past constitutional commitments) is a universal phenomenon: "We need a narrative of redemption because all constitutions are agreements with hell, flawed, imperfect compromises with the political constellation of the moment. All constitutions exist in a fallen condition, no matter how good people think they are. They make promises they cannot keep at the time they are enacted, commitments are imperfectly realized, guarantees that often are not guaranteed in practice and that may never be realized at all."[41] Yet, constitutional redemption is contextual because "a different people with a different story and a different set of commitments might have made a different promise; the result, although similar in some respects, might be very different in others."[42]

That universality and contextuality enable possible accounts of comparative constitutional redemption. The phenomenon of redeeming incomplete constitutional promises is universal, but the *substances* of constitutional promises are varied due to a different history. Some people may be committed to liberal constitutional aspirations, while others may adhere to the socialist alternatives. In addition, due to different institutional settings and different constitutional questions to redeem, the *mechanisms* of constitutional redemption are different: they can be informal judicial constitutional interpretation or formal constitutional amendment and replacement.

Socialist constitutional redemption is characterized by faith in progress toward socialism, and is carried out through a formal mechanism. In this narrative of constitutional redemption, socialist constitutional change to respond to leadership change is not necessarily determined by the rational calculation of personal interests. In the five socialist countries, individual communist leaders have played a prominent role in the national history of revolution and reformation: China's Mao Zedong and Deng Xiaoping; Vietnam's Ho Chi Minh; Laos' Kaysone Phomvihane; North Korea's Kim Il-sung and Kim Jong-il; and Cuba's Fidel Castro. They share the belief in the progress of their societies toward socialism, although they articulate different visions to move their societies in that direction. New leadership undertakes formal constitutional change to authoritatively redeem their predecessors' prominent role and hopes.

[41] Jack M. Balkin, *Constitutional Redemption: Political Faith in an Unjust World* (Harvard University Press 2011) 6.

[42] Ibid. 28.

The socialist constitutional redemption takes two forms: glorification and continuation, which both signify the new leaders' faith in the socialist constitutional project. First, as the constitution usually plays a prominent role in the national legal and political systems, it is employed to glorify the predecessors' historical role and dreams. The constitutional preambles are an ideal place to prominently situate and laud the individual leaders in the national history. This constitutional glorification aims to show that the preceding leaders' historical achievements and aspirations are fundamental enough to be respected and recognized not merely by the existing individual leaders but by the whole polity.

Second, socialist constitutional redemption involves continuation. New leaders are committed to continuing the socialist constitutional project set down and implemented by their predecessors. The constitutional injection of personal beliefs and aspirations about historical progress toward socialism (e.g. Cuba's revolutionary Castroism, China's Deng reformism, or Jiang's *Sange Daibiao*, and North Korea's Kim's *Songun jeohgchi*) illustrates the commitment to continuation. In addition, to continue the socialist constitutional project involves more than the insertion of the past leaders' views. Redemption involves articulating the new leaders' new visions on how to take the socialist constitutional project forward. Such new individual visons are generated as the preceding leaders' commitments may be unfulfilled or incomplete. The past progressive constitutional dreams may not be fully realized, and new visions and measures are needed to continue the dream. While the grand commitment to socialism is determined, new social and economic conditions may demonstrate the imperfection of the specific prior commitments (e.g. economic predicament as the consequence of a completely planned economy), and new leaders will create a new vision and measure (e.g. reformist economy and privatization of some economic sectors) to improve the conditions. Consequently, different generations of socialist leaders share the same convictions about the progress of their societies toward socialism, but new social and economic circumstances as the consequence of social incremental evolution render new leaders to articulate different visions and implement different measures to achieve the grand socialist goal. The advent of new leaders involves constitutional change to institutionalize their personal visions.

Glorification and continuation are the base for the legitimacy of the new constitutional visions. As the new visions are associated with individual leaders, their legitimacy is not rooted in the contractual imagination on Rawlsian agreement of reasonable people.[43] Balkin advanced a temporary theory of constitutional legitimacy, which holds that constitutional legitimacy "rests in part on faith in the future and in a story about the past that connects it to the present," and he believes that "this is true [. . .] not only of specifically liberal theories of constitutional legitimacy

[43] John Rawls, *Political Liberalism* (Columbia University Press 1993).

but of many other versions as well."[44] This is true of the socialist versions: the attachment to glorified history and the commitment to continuing and extending the socialist constitutional project make the new constitutional visions sociologically acceptable in the peer-elite's eyes and in the polity at large.

The legitimacy in the attachment to past individual leaders is connected to Frank I. Michelman's *author-based* conception of constitutional legitimacy: "we owe respect to a constitution having such-and-such prescriptive content just because of who that constitution's authors were. Perhaps they were a set of national political ancestors called 'framers.' Or perhaps they were some past popular uprising we personify under the name of 'the People.' In either case, you and I might consider ourselves and the country bound to their word by communal ties of descent, affiliation, and allegiance."[45] In several socialist states, the constitution's authors are personalized, not the amorphous "we the people." They include not only the framers (North Korea's Kim) but also the reformers (e.g. China's Deng). The legitimacy of new constitutional vision depends on its attachment to the constitutionally glorified national political ancestors.

Yet, a non-liberal, socialist theory of constitutional legitimacy is sensitive to two features: formality and paradox. First, the legitimacy of extending the socialist constitutional project rests on the formality of change rather than the interpretative constitutional construction. Without judicial review, the textual form of supreme law renders legitimacy to the personal grand vision. Second, the legitimacy of the new constitutional vision is paradoxical because it is both *underpinned* and *undermined* by its connection to the past leaders. This paradoxical legitimacy is due to both substantive and procedural reasons. Substantively, the new vision presents the elite commitments to socialism, and it may be vulnerable in the increasingly pluralist, social, and political environment in socialist countries, particularly in China and Cuba. Procedurally, the new personal vision to continue the socialist constitutional project presents the elite's hopes and aspirations despite the controlled popular participations in some cases. Consequently, domestic sections of the society who are substantively critical of socialism and/or procedurally marginalized or ignored in the construction of the constitutional project may question its legitimacy.

That said, the impact of leadership renewal on socialist constitutional change is varied. Personal power is the common feature of socialist authoritarianism (and authoritarianism generally), but the significance in the influence of the personal power varies in different socialist countries. Unlike in Cuba, China, and North Korea, the political powers in Laos and Vietnam are less controlled by top individuals, and consequently, it is unlikely that leadership renewal would result in

[44] Balkin, *Constitutional Redemption* (n 41) 44.

[45] Frank I. Michelman, "Is the Constitution a Contract for Legitimacy" (2003) 8 Review of Constitutional Studies 101, 126.

constitutional change. Two factors may explain these variations: the level of institutionalization and the level of constitutional praxis. Political scientists point out that "the relatively institutionalized character of Lao authoritarianism, which has placed the top leadership positions less as powers in themselves, and more under the broad discipline of the LPRP [Lao People's Revolutionary Party]. To express this another way, the LPRP provides a disciplining mechanism for the patron–client relations that continue to function throughout society, which in turn depend on party connections."[46] One consequence is that Laos did not constitutionalize the personal role of individual communist leaders. It is also observed that political power in Vietnam is more institutionalized than in China, particularly through the legislature.[47] Therefore, except for the country's framer Ho Chi Minh, Vietnam did not establish the constitutional status of subsequent communist leaders. Apart from the level of institutionalization, the practice of political power depends more on constitutional praxis than on constitutional theorization. Unlike Deng with the *Kai Fang* theory, Jiang with the Three Represents theory, Kim with the *Songun* theory, or Castro with revolutionary theory, political leaders in Laos and Vietnam normally do not theorize about a grand project which should necessarily be transformed into concrete institutions by the constitution. Constitutional change in Vietnam as well as Laos may be articulated but did not personalize the elite new vision. Consequently, constitutional change depends less on leadership change.

B. Reformist Programs

Another top-down dynamic of socialist constitutional change is change to socio-economic programs. The reformist programs are normally adopted by a communist party. A single communist party monopolizes power in the socialist world. Consequently, once the party changes the program for social and economic development, constitutional change becomes imperative to institutionalize the party's changing plan. Therefore, it is common in the socialist world that constitutional change occurs after a party's national congress in which the party adopts significant changes to its project guiding social and economic progress. To illustrate, the aim of Vietnam's 2013 constitution-making was to institutionalize the party's amended constitution and new social and economic program adopted in the Party's 2011 Eleventh National Congress; Laos' 2015 constitution-making to incorporate the outcomes of the Party's 2011 Ninth Congress; Cuba's 2019 constitution-making to include new ideas and guidance from three political documents adopted in the

46 Simon Creak and Keith Barney, "Conceptualizing Party-State Governance and Rule in Laos" (2018) 48(5) Journal of Contemporary Asia 693, 699.

47 Paul Schuler, "Vietnam as China's Path Not Taken: Explaining Variation in Authoritarian Legislative Institutionalization" (2019) (unpublished paper).

Party's 2011 Sixth Congress and 2017 Seventh Congress; China's 1999, 2004, and 2018 constitutional amendments to respond to the party's Fifteenth, Sixteenth, and Nineteenth Congresses in 1997, 2002, and 2017 respectively; and North Korea's 2016 constitutional amendment to institutionalize the directions adopted in the party's 2016 Seventh Congress.

Why constitutionalize the party's reformist program? This is due to three reasons: vanguardism, separationism, and legitimatization. To begin with, constitutionalization of the party's program is to effectuate the party's vanguardism. In the socialist world, the party is the vanguard force of the both the state and the society, or the polity generally. Consequently, the party's program aims to guild not only the party's work but also to direct the work of the state and more broadly the progress of society. To effectuate the movement of the larger polity, the party's program must be incorporated into the state's fundamental law. Once the party's grand program is constitutionalized, it transforms into the polity's grand program and has a larger effect not only on the party but also on the state and society.

The second reason is separationism in conceptualizing and institutionalizing the party-state relationship. The party-state separation has been the prevailing trend in the socialist world in the global era to prevent the direct interference of the party in the state's activities.[48] This separationism aims to distinguish party leadership from the state's legislature and management. This separationist scheme suggests that the party's program cannot be applied to the state directly. It must be embedded in the state's constitution to authoritatively command the state's work.

The third reason is to *legitimize* the program and the party's rule. To transform the party's program into the polity's constitutional program is not a new phenomenon in the socialist constitutional history, but this is particularly prominent in the global era due to the fact that the external and internal demands of constitutionality as the legitimate condition for governance have become increasingly intense. Externally, in the twenty-first century, the international community has intensified the view of constitutionality as the legitimate condition for the use of political power. Since the fall of the Berlin wall, at least 100 new constitutions have been enacted.[49] "This is not to say that these constitutions are everywhere taken seriously, or that constitutional norms always prevail in cases of conflict with political intentions. But the universal recognition of constitutionalism as a model for the organization and legitimation of political power is shown by the fact that even rulers who are not inclined to submit themselves to legal norms feel compelled

[48] Trần Thành, "Cơ chế Đảng lãnh đạo, Nhà nước quản lý và Nhân dân làm chủ ở Việt Nam" ["The Mechanism of Party Lead, State Manage and People Own in Vietnam"] (2016) Tạp chí Khoa học xã hội Việt Nam [Vietnamese Journal of Social Science] 100.

[49] Cheryl Saunders, "Constitution Making in the 21st Century" (2012) 4 International Review of Law 2.

at least to pretend to be exercising their power within the constitutional framework."[50] The Socialist elites are not necessarily committed to constitutionalism but are compelled to transform the party's grand program for social and economic development into the constitutional framework to signal its constitutionality to the global audiences. In addition, thanks to the globalization of constitutionalism, internal audiences (except perhaps in North Korea) have consolidated their view of constitutionality as the legitimate condition for governance.[51] In response, the socialist elites have constitutionalized their grand program to enhance the legal foundation of the domestic legitimacy of the program and their own ruling status.

C. Globalization

Comparative constitutional scholars have demonstrated that domestic constitution-making has been triggered by external geopolitical events: the 1948 Revolutions throughout Europe, the First World War, the Second World War, the period of French and British decolonization, and the Cold War each animated different "waves" of constitution-making.[52] That constitutional change is triggered by external geopolitical dynamics resonates in the socialist constitutional history. As indicated earlier, the end of the Cold War resulted in constitution-making and constitutional amendments in the remaining socialist constitutions. The legacy of the Cold War has had a lasting effect on constitutional change in some socialist countries. This legacy is manifested in US economic sanctions against Cuba and North Korea, and its democracy program which aims to effect regime change in Cuba. Constitutional change in these countries is indirectly catalyzed by these external sanctions. The sanctions created economic impediments in these countries, which engendered the liberalization of the constitutional economy (e.g. private ownership, and foreign investment) to deal with economic difficulty. The continued impact of the legacy of the Cold War has also triggered aversive constitutional reaction: Cuba enacted a new Constitution to prohibit regime change.

In the twenty first century, external efforts in building global peace have engendered constitution-making in divided societies.[53] Yet, post-conflict

[50] Dieter Grimm, "The Achievement of Constitutionalism and its Prospects in a Changed World" in *The Twilight of Constitutionalism?* (Petra Dobner and Martin Loughlin (eds), Oxford University Press 2010) 3.

[51] Taisu Zhang and Tom Ginsburg, "China's Turn Toward Law" (2019) 59 Virginia Journal of International Law 376 (discussing the "higher social demand for legality" in China); Bui Ngoc Son, "Constitutional Mobilization" (2018) 17 Washington University Global Studies Law Review 113.

[52] Gregory Shaffer, Tom Ginsburg, and Terence C. Halliday, "Constitution-Making as Transnational Legal Ordering" in *Constitution-Making and Transnational Legal Order* (Gregory Shaffer, Tom Ginsburg, and Terence C. Halliday (eds), Cambridge University Press 2019) 4; Jon Elster, "Forces and Mechanisms in the Constitution-Making Process" (1995) 45 Duke Law Journal 364, 368–9.

[53] "Constitution Drafting in Post-Conflict States Symposium" (2008) 49 William & Mary Law Review 1043; Sujit Choudhry (ed), *Constitutional Design for Divided Societies: Integration or Accommodation?* (OUP 2008); Hanna Lerner, *Making Constitutions in Deeply Divided Societies* (CUP 2011); Kirsti

constitution-making as peacebuilding is not the exclusive paradigm of twenty-first century constitution-making. This is in part because peace building is not necessarily associated with constitutional building[54] and in part because several episodes of constitution-building occur without serious conflicts. For example, socialist constitution-making and constitutional amendment have occurred in peaceful societal environments.

Global constitutional change—constitutional change under the pressure of globalization—may be another paradigm of twenty-first century constitutional change. Early on, at the turn of the century, Mark Tushnet had already said that: "No one really knows precisely what globalization is, but nearly everyone thinks that it has some effect on domestic constitutional orders."[55] In fact, this is a growing scholarship exploring the impact of globalization on national constitutional law.[56] Globalization refers to "the ongoing process of economic, political, cultural, and military intertwinement and the mutual interdependence of nations, enterprizes [sic], and people that goes with it."[57] Globalization affects not only constitutional adjudication and the substance of the constitutions, it can also be an external trigger of domestic constitution-making and constitutional amendment process.

Socialist constitutional change is animated by both constitutional and economic globalization. Constitutional globalization refers to the emergence of global constitutionalism, especially in the context of human rights. As Michel Rosenfeld points out, "A large number of nation-states throughout all continents adopted new constitutions that were in the spirit of the ideal of modern constitutionalism—consisting essentially in limitation of the powers of government, adherence to the rule of law, protection of fundamental rights, and guarantees for the maintenance of an adequate level of democracy."[58] In the twenty-first century, the travel of constitutionalism is not limited to the sub-global scales. Tushnet argues that the globalization of constitutional law is inevitable due to top-down pressures (the emergence of global networks of constitutional judges, the involvement of transnational non-governmental organizations (NGOs) in national constitutional matters, the

Samuels, "Post-Conflict Peace-Building and Constitution-Making" (2006) 6 Chicago Journal of International Law 663.

[54] Hallie Ludsin, "Peacemaking and Constitution-Drafting: A Dysfunctional Marriage" (2011) 33 University of Pennsylvania Journal of International Law 239.

[55] Mark Tushnet, *The New Constitutional Order* (Princeton UP 2003) 142.

[56] David S. Law, "Globalization and the Future of Constitutional Rights" (2008) 102 Northwestern University Law Review 1277; Mark Tushnet, "The Inevitable Globalization of Constitutional Law" (2009) 49 Virginia Journal of International Law 985; Anne Peters, "The Globalization of State Constitutions" in *New Perspectives on the Divide Between National and International Law* (Janne E. Nijman and André Nollkaemper (eds), OUP 2007) 251; Jean L. Cohen, *Globalization and Sovereignty: Rethinking Legality, Legitimacy, and Constitutionalism* (Cambridge University Press 2012).

[57] Peters, "The Globalization of State Constitutions" (n 56) 252.

[58] Michel Rosenfeld, "Is Global Constitutionalism Meaningful or Desirable?" (2014) 25(1) European Journal of International Law, 177, 177–8.

incorporation of international human rights treaties into national constitutions, and transnational migration of workers), and bottom-up pressures (competition among nations for investment and human capital).[59] The global spread of constitutionalism as the international standardized norm has been sufficiently intense to oblige even dictators and authoritarians to adopt, at least at the formal level, constitutionalist norms such as human rights.

The socialist states are not immune to the impact of constitutional globalization. In particular, they all changed the constitutions to incorporate or consolidate the norm and institutions of human rights. This has occurred not only in the more globally engaged socialist countries like China, Vietnam, Laos, and Cuba, but also in globally isolated North Korea. Vietnam and Laos depend more on global support, and consequently their constitutions are more vulnerable to alteration to respond to the global spread of constitutionalism. Although China explicitly resists the very notion of constitutionalism, it is not immune to the impact of this idea: eventually China incorporated the constitutionalist idea of human rights into its constitution. Cuba is determined to retain socialism and, like China, is explicitly resistant to western-style constitutional democracy, but its new Constitution is also made to include a statement of human rights as a response to the country's signing of major international human rights treaties. It would be eccentric to conceptualize North Korea in terms of constitutionalism, but this country is not an outlier in terms of the constitutionalization of human rights as the consequence of its ratification of international human rights treaties.

The socialist states incorporate the norm of global constitutionalism on paper to gain international legitimacy and to limit international criticism (e.g. criticism of human rights violations or similar authoritarian practices). Whether the socialist states are committed to implementing constitutionalism in practice is another question. But, the very fact that the socialist states seek to obtain international legitimacy through formal constitutional inclusion of global constitutional norms indicates that their constitutional change is externally triggered by the global spread of constitutionalism, regardless of their intentions and consequences.

In addition to constitutional globalization, economic globalization has engendered constitutional change in socialist countries. "'Economic globalization' refers to the increasing integration of circuits of goods, production, images, information, and money across national borders."[60] In the socialist context, economic globalization requires constitutions to be changed to facilitate the regional and international integration of national economies to deal with local economic difficulties or to consolidate economic development. Accession to the WTO (China, Vietnam, and Laos), East Asian integration (China and North Korea), ASEAN integration

[59] Tushnet (n 56) 987–95.

[60] Fran Tonkiss, "Economic Globalization" in *The Wiley-Blackwell Encyclopedia of Globalization* (George Ritzer (ed.), Wiley-Blackwell 2012) vol. 2, 485.

(Vietnam and Laos), and Latin American integration (Cuba) have engendered constitutional response. The socialist constitutions respond to these external factors in both direct and indirect ways. Directly, the constitutions incorporate economic institutions (e.g. private property rights and foreign investment) to promote further regional and international integration of the national economy. Indirectly, the constitutions facilitate the autonomous role of local governments in promoting cross-border economic relations with neighboring counterparts.

Although there are few remaining socialist constitutions, and each has its own peculiarities, they nevertheless reflect an increasingly interconnected world, and their change cannot be merely understood as the response to local leadership change and the party's changing program. The socialist constitutions, including those of the arguably aberrant North Korea, have been changed to respond to global dynamics. Therefore, the comprehension of the dynamics of socialist constitutional change must be situated within the changing global constitutional and economic plane.

D. Local Dynamics

Constitutions may be changed to respond to global triggers, but they are, after all, local documents and have to respond to local pressures. Tushnet states, "Every society's law is tied to so many aspects of that society—its politics, its particular history, its intellectual life, the institutional forms in which its activities are conducted, and many more."[61] Constitutional law is particularly prominent in this regard. Saunders underlines: "Constitutions are inherently local instruments. They must respond to local needs and they must be 'owned' both by the people of the state concerned and by their political leaders from time to time."[62]

Local pressures for constitutional change are varied. Much has been written about social conflicts as the catalysts of constitutional change.[63] But, constitutional change is also generated by domestic socio-economic development. This catalyst is particularly prominent in the socialist countries where the constitutions represent the codification of ideas in Marxist economic theory and the party's social economic program. In fact, during the last three decades, constitution-making and constitutional amendment in the socialist countries have been driven by the need to have a fundamental institutional framework to both reflect and facilitate social and economic development.

[61] Mark Tushnet, "The Possibilities of Comparative Constitutional Law" (1999) 108 Yale Law Journal 1265.

[62] Saunders, "Constitution Making" (n 49) 9–10.

[63] E.g. Nimer Sultany, *Law and Revolution: Legitimacy and Constitutionalism After the Arab Spring* (OUP 2017); Darin E.W. Johnson, "Conflict Constitution-Making in Libya and Yemen" (2017) 39 University of Pennsylvania Journal of International Law 293.

However, the social and economic catalyst of constitutional change is not limited to the socialist states.[64] Socio-economic development is the common cause of constitutional change. This claim is connected to the contemporary law and development (L&D) scholarship, which shows a strong concern for the relationship between constitutional institutions and social economic development. Kevin E. Davis and Michael Trebilcock call the body of scholarship in this line "new constitutionalism."[65] Legal thought of the contemporary generation of L&D corresponds to the contemporary wave of globalization of legal ideas, as constructed by Duncan Kennedy.[66] The contemporary mode of legal thought is characterized by, among other things, what Kennedy calls "public law neoformalism" which includes international law, constitutional law, and criminal law.[67] In his book *The Law-Growth Nexus: The Rule of Law and Economic Development*, Kenneth Dam energetically examines the relation of different substantive areas of private law to economic development, but eventually claims that public law is more important than private law in the field of economic growth.[68]

Within comparative constitutional law scholarship, theories of constitutional competition introduced in the context of the discourse of global constitutional convergence have also emphasized the relation of constitutions to local economic dynamics. The basic idea is that the constitutional values and institutions can be used as competitive advantages to attract foreign investment. Daniel Farber has proposed the argument of "rights as signals": the government can send a credible message to investors that it will not expropriate investment by constitutional commitments to human rights protected by an independent judiciary, which indirectly affects economic growth.[69] Empirically, Benedikt Goderis and Mila Versteeg have documented that "economic considerations motivated the constitutional entrenchment of property rights and free-market guarantees in South Africa, New Zealand and Egypt."[70] David Law also theorizes about "the impact of global investment and migration patterns on the worldwide development of certain constitutional rights."[71] He has examined "the potential for a constitutional 'race to the top'

[64] See for example, David Brunnstrom, "Philippines Vice President Backs Easing Foreign-Investment Rule" (Reuters, May 2, 2014) <www.reuters.com/article/philippines-binay-constitution-idUSL6N0NN3PJ20140502>

[65] Kevin E. Davis and Michael J. Trebilcock, "The Relationship Between Law and Development: Optimists Versus Skeptics" (2008) 56 American Journal of Comparative Law 895, 905.

[66] Duncan Kennedy, "Three Globalizations of Law and Legal Thought: 1850–2000" in *The New Law and Economic Development: A Critical Appraisal* (David M. Trubek and Alvaro Santos (eds), CUP 2006).

[67] Ibid. 69.

[68] Kenneth Dam, *The Law-Growth Nexus: The Rule of Law and Economic Development* (Brookings Institution Press 2006) 41; Davis and Trebilcock, "The Relationship Between Law and Development" (n 65) 906.

[69] Daniel Farber, "Rights as Signals" (2002) 31 Journal of Legal Studies 83.

[70] Benedikt Goderis and Mila Versteeg, "The Diffusion of Constitutional Rights" (2014) 39 International Review of Law and Economics 1, 3.

[71] David Law, "Globalization and the Future of Constitutional Rights" (2008) 102 Northwestern University Law Review 1277, 1281–2.

driven by competition among countries for capital and skilled migrants: as capital and skilled labor become increasingly mobile, countries will face a growing incentive to compete for both by offering bundles of human and economic rights that are attractive to investors and elite workers."[72] In particular, he emphasizes the idea that countries have competed to attract investors and skilled workers by constitutional commitments to the protection of civil liberties and property rights.[73] Investors will favor investment in the environment where they can make sure that their capital will not be subject to arbitrary confiscation by the state. The state can provide such a guarantee by offering the constitutional protection of property rights.[74] In addition to property rights, capital also will flow to regimes that respect fundamental political and civil rights, such as freedom of expression, rights of political participation, and freedom from political persecution.[75] Law explains that this is because investors favor stability, peace, and transparency, which in turn needs the protection of civil liberty.[76] He also underlines the reason that "respect for human rights attracts investment by improving the quality of a country's workforce."[77]

The global spread of the constitutional court has been also explained as being associated with the incentive to compete in attracting foreign investment.[78] The logic is that countries copy successful constitutional institutions to compete with each other in attracting foreign trading partners and investors. "The more countries successfully attract investment by adopting specific constitutional rules, the more others are likely to follow."[79] The adoption of constitutional review also arguably presents this logic. Tamir Moustafa, for example, argues that the creation of the Egyptian Supreme Constitutional Court stemmed from the need to institutionalize state functions and attract investment.[80] This court was created in 1979 in the context of "elevated concern about the risks of expropriation and the insecurity of property rights that Sadat attempted to attract foreign investment and Egyptian private investment."[81] As Moustafa documented, Sadat established the court with the intention "to keep the foreign investor at ease."[82]

The accounts of the relationship between constitutional law and development has an important implication for causal explanation of the local dynamics of constitutional change: given the integral relationship between constitutional law and

[72] Ibid. 1282.
[73] Ibid.
[74] For details, see ibid 1308–13.
[75] Ibid. 1314.
[76] Ibid. 1316–17.
[77] Ibid. 1319.
[78] Tom Ginsburg and Mila Versteeg, "Why Do Countries Adopt Constitutional Review?" (2014) 30 Journal of Law, Economics, and Organization 587, 596.
[79] Ibid.
[80] See Tamir Moustafa, *The Struggle for Constitutional Power: Law, Politics, and Economic Development in Egypt* (CUP 2007).
[81] Ibid. 76.
[82] Ibid. 77.

socio-economic development, the latter may be the cause of the former's change. However, several claims on the relationship between constitutional law and development must be qualified. Many states that have experienced constitution-making in the last three decades have not yet become constitutional states and do not yet have well-established market economies.[83] What has driven constitutional change in such states is complex, and may include the incentive of reforming the economy and protecting human freedom. Continuing economic development and the growth of rights awareness and practice may in turn exert pressure for continuing constitutional reform.

In constitutional competitions, investors may not rely on formal constitutional commitments to decide whether the investment environment is stable, peaceful, and transparent. In particular, in authoritarian regimes, constitutional commitment and constitutional reality are two different things.[84] Therefore, investors must consider the reality of politics, the workings of the legal system, and even the role of informal institutions and social networks. Also, the idea that civil liberty can ensure stability conducive to investment is also debatable. The practice of some political and civil rights, such as demonstrations, can result in political instability which may slow or block investment flows. Conversely, some authoritarian regimes like those of Vietnam ensure political stability, which is an attractive condition for foreign investment, not by promoting but by controlling civil liberties.[85]

To explain how socio-economic development causes constitutional change, Francis Fukuyama provides a useful intellectual foil. In his book, *Political Order and Political Decay*, Fukuyama explains the changing landscape of political order in the twenty-first century as the interactions between political development and socio-economic development.[86] He situates political development within the more general human socio-economic development which comprises three dimensions: economic development, social mobilization, and ideas of legitimacy.[87] There is no single path of development. Yet, the following general logic is embodied in many cases. Economic development creates new social groups which acquire new ideas of legitimacy and demand for political change.[88] This logic can be extended to the constitutional sphere. Constitutional change is a type of political change at the fundamental level and can be caused by socioeconomic change. Economic development creates new social groups with competing social interests, references, aspirations, and identities. These social groups are imbued with new

[83] IDEA, *Constitution Building after Conflict* 8 (Policy Paper, May 2011).
[84] See generally, Tim Ginsburg and Alberto Simpser (eds), *Constitutions in Authoritarian Regimes* (CUP 2014).
[85] See "Best Countries to Invest In" (*US News*) <http://www.usnews.com/news/best-countries/invest-in-full-list>
[86] Francis Fukuyama, *Political Order and Political Decay: From the Industrial Revolution to the Globalization of Democracy* (Profile Books 2014).
[87] Ibid. 40.
[88] Ibid. 203–4.

ideas about a legitimate constitutional government (e.g. constitutionalism and respecting human rights) and often demand constitutional change. These social demands may compel political leaders to modify the constitutions to incorporate new legitimate constitutional ideas and goals. In addition, social and economic dynamism may prove that the existing constitutions present institutional constraints on continued and sustainable development, and this may place local pressure on constitutional reform.

We now reify the above general logic to explain the correlation of socio-economic and constitutional progress in the socialist states. The reformist progress in the last three decades has been led by the party-state. During the initial stage, the socialist constitutions are changed to deal with economic difficulties to improve the material wellbeing of living conditions of the local people, and to reflect and facilitate the implementation of the party's program to reform the economy: China's 1978 *Gaige kaifang* ("Reform & Opening up"), Vietnam's 1986 *Doi moi* (Renovation), Laos' 1986 *Chintanakan Mai* (New Thinking), Cuba's 2011 Updating the Economic Model, and North Korea's modest post-Soviet efforts toward economic reform. The implementation of the reformist constitutionalized programs has resulted in economic development and social change (the emergence of the new social groups with new interests and new ideas). The socio-economic transition has created local dynamics for further constitutional change. Economic development put pressure on effective legislatures to produce a new legal framework for the economy, an effective administrative system to manage the changing economy, an effective judiciary to handle commercial disputes, and the autonomous local government to boost local economy. Constitutional change is a response to the changing economy's demand for more effective state institutions. In addition, social change as the result of economic development also induces constitutional change. It may be that, except for the case of North Korea, new social groups in the socialist states acquire new ideas about a legitimate constitutional government (the constitutionality in the use of public power; constraints on public power; respecting human rights) and they put pressure (including collective mobilization in China, Vietnam, and Cuba) on the party-state to undertake constitutional reform. In response, the party-states change the constitutions to incorporate new ideas to consolidate the legal foundation of their legitimacy.

IV. Process: The Law of Constitutional Change

How do constitutions change? This question has been the main concern of legal or institutional accounts.[89] The recurring questions in the institutional scholarship of

[89] See for example, Dawn Oliver and Carlo Fusaro, *How Constitutions Change: A Comparative Study* (Hart Publishing 2011); Xenophon Contiades (ed.), *Engineering Constitutional Change. A Comparative Perspective on Europe, Canada and the USA* (Routledge 2012).

constitutional change are regarding the alternative forms of constitutional change (amendment and replacement), the power to change the constitution (the constituent and amendment power), the limits of that power (unamendability), and domestic participation and transnational engagement in constitutional change. This section situates the socialist experience within the comparative models theorizing about the institutional aspects of constitutional change.

A. Form of Change: Amendment and Replacement

What is the difference between constitutional amendment and replacement? What explains the choice between amendment and replacement? What explains the rate of amendment? These questions have been debated by comparative constitutional scholars. This section situates the socialist experience within the contemporary comparative debates on the distinction, choice, and rate of constitutional amendment and replacement.

1. Distinction

Current comparative constitutional scholarship distinguishes between two forms of constitutional change: replacement and amendment. This distinction is not purely theoretical but has practical implications. In the real world of constitutional design, the political elites have to make a choice between amending an existing constitution or replacing it with a new one. To illustrate this point, in the wake of the Arab Spring, Egypt, Tunisia, and Libya made new constitutions "to present the emergence of a new political order," whereas Jordan, Morocco, and Bahrain introduced amendments to their existing constitutions to preserve the overall structure of the constitutional monarchy.[90] In addition to constitutional design, the amendment-replacement dichotomy also informs constitutional adjudication. For example, through a series of judgments starting in 2003, the Colombian Constitutional Court has developed the constitutional replacement doctrine to justify its power to review the substantive aspects of constitutional amendment which is not granted in the Constitution.[91]

The distinction of replacement and amendment is often based on procedural and substantive features. First, amendment follows the procedure articulated by the existing constitution, while replacement may be carried out outside the existing procedural constitutional framework.[92] Second, constitutional replacement involves the making of a new constitution intended "to change the basic structure

[90] Sultany, (n 63) 237.

[91] For more details, see Carlos Bernal, "Unconstitutional Constitutional Amendments in the Case Study of Columbia: An Analysis of the Justification and Meaning of the Constitutional Replacement Doctrine" (2013) 11 International Journal of Constitutional Law 339, 339–40.

[92] Elkins, Ginsburg, and Melton, *The Endurance of National Constitutions* (n 1) 55.

of the state and the political system," while amendment only alters "procedural details and policy issues contained in the constitution."[93] These two procedural and substantive differences between amendment and replacement can be traced back to the German constitutional theorist Carl Schmitt, who contended that constitutional amendment follows the rules and procedures of the existing constitution and can only make additions and deletions and other changes that preserve "the identity and continuity of the constitution as an entirety."[94] As to the substantive point, Walter Murphy holds the same view: "valid amendments can operate only within the existing political system: they cannot deconstitute, reconstitute, or replace the polity."[95]

From a practical point of view, there are several difficulties with the theoretical distinction between replacement and amendment. First, constitutional replacement can be carried out within the amendment procedure of the existing constitution. Hans Kelsen, in fact, disagreed with Schmitt, arguing that a constitution could be entirely replaced by the ordinary amendment procedure.[96] Japan provides a real-life example. Japan's 1946 Constitution (effective in 1947) was adopted as an amendment bill according to the procedure of the Meiji Constitution of 1889, but replaced the latter charter.[97] In terms of substance, amendment could actually transform the existing constitutional order. For instance, a series of constitutional amendments in Indonesia and Taiwan were introduced to transform an authoritarian regime into a constitutional democracy.[98] At the other extreme, new constitutions may differ from the old constitutions in only minor ways, as the cases of Trujillo's Constitutions in the Dominican Republic and Afghanistan's 1990 Constitution.[99]

In response to the difficulties in the procedural and substantive distinction of replacement and amendment, one alternative focuses on the political will and authority of reformers: "Ultimately, the distinction between replacing and amending constitutions is political. It is true that whereas amendments preserve the legal continuity of the existing constitution, constitutional replacements imply its abrogation. This legal effect, however, is not primarily based on the content of the

[93] Negretto, "Replacing and Amending Constitutions" (n 37) 749.

[94] Carl Schmitt, *Constitutional Theory* (Duke University Press 2008) 150.

[95] Walter Murphy, "Merlin's Memory: The Past and Future Imperfect of the Once and Future Polity" in *Responding to Imperfection: The Theory and Practice of Constitutional Amendment* (Stanford Levinson (ed.), Princeton University Press 1995) 177.

[96] Richard Stacey, "Popular Sovereignty and Revolutionary Constitution-Making" in *Philosophical Foundations of Constitutional Law* (David Dyzenhaus and Malcolm Thorburn (eds), OUP 2016) 168. For more details, see L Vinx (ed), *The Guardian of the Constitution: Hans Kelsen and Carl Schmitt on the Limits of Constitutional Law* (Cambridge University Press 2015).

[97] Shigenori Matsui, *The Constitution of Japan: A Contextual Analysis* (Hart 2011) 16.

[98] Jiunn-Rong Yeh, *The Constitution of Taiwan: A Contextual Analysis* (Hart 2016) 38; Denny Indrayana, *Indonesian Constitutional Reform 1999–2002: An Evaluation of Constitution-Making in Transition* (PhD Thesis, Melbourne University 2005).

[99] Elkins, Ginsburg, and Melton, *The Endurance of National Constitutions* (n 1) 55.

reforms or on the procedures by which they are adopted. Rather, it reflects the will and authority of reformers to gain acceptance for their decisions as a new constitutional order at a given historical juncture."[100] In some cases, reformers could deliberately make their decisions on whether the constitutional reform should be a replacement and amendment. Yet, replacement and amendment can be the unanticipated consequence of dynamic interactions of different political and social actors beyond the reformers' political will. Even where replacement and amendment may reflect the reformers' will, the dynamic interactions may result in the change of this will over the course of constitutional change. Imagine, for example, this scenario: the political elite initially had the intention of amending the constitution, but during the amendment process, due to the dynamic interaction among the political elites and also between them and society, they realized that substantive changes were needed, which resulted in the enactment of a new constitution.

I believe that the distinction between replacement and amendment requires taking into account all three features: procedure, substance, and political will. These factors, however, do not explain every case of constitutional change. The distinction between replacement and amendment is contextual rather than universal. There are no clear-cut standards to differentiate amendment from replacement in every case. The distinction depends on the particular case of constitutional change which is in turn shaped by the broader institutional settings, the power of the elite, and social dynamic interactions.

The socialist experiences echo some aspects but present difficulties with other aspects of the theoretical distinction between replacement and amendment. In the main, whether the constitutional change takes the form of amendment or replacement, the substantial continuity of the socialist constitutional order is guaranteed. Core features of the socialist constitutional polity (e.g. communist party leadership, centralized constitutional structure, the economy, and fundamental rights controlled by the state) are preserved, albeit adaptive. This common pattern is defined by the incremental nature in the progressive models of socialist constitutional change which prevents constitutional revolution. Yet, there are variations in the socialist experience of constitutional amendment and replacement, depending on the significance of different features: political will, procedure, and substances.

The first variation is *implicit constitutional replacement through amendment.* This is exemplified by the case of Vietnam: the project of amending the 1992 Constitution led to its replacement by the 2013 Constitution. In this variation, the political elite initiated a project of constitutional change as an amendment project. Constitutional change followed the amendment procedure of the existing

[100] Gabriel L. Negretto, "Constitution-Making in Comparative Perspective" Oxford Research Encyclopedia, Politics (Oxford University Press USA, 2019) <https://oxfordre.com/politics/view/10.1093/acrefore/9780190228637.001.0001/acrefore-9780190228637-e-66#acrefore-9780190228637-e-66-div1-3>.

constitution. But the amendment process is *demanding*,[101] in a similar way to making a new constitution. Consequently, the amendment process included similar phases of constitution-making: agenda setting, design, and approval, and implementation.[102] Agenda setting involves decisions on whether to make a new constitution or to amend the existing one, the nature of the constitution-making body, and the ambit of change. Design involves drafting and deliberating public consultation on draft amended constitution. The final stage is the ratification of the amended constitution. Implementation concerns passing legislations to implement the amended constitution. Despite the amendment project, the scope of substantive changes is extensive, not limited to procedural details and policy issues, but within the existing constitutional order and political system. The project of amendment results in a new constitution effectively replacing the existing constitution. The constitutional replacement is implicit, as the replacement is nowhere formally declared, which differentiates it from the explicit variation below. Despite the replacement, the substantive continuity of the socialist constitutional order and political system is guaranteed.

The second variation is *explicit constitutional replacement through amendment*. This is demonstrated by the case of Laos: the project of amending the 2003 Constitution led to its replacement by the 2015 Constitution. In this variation, the choice of explicit replacement through amendment reflects the elite's political intention. The political elite launched a project of constitutional change as an amendment project, but eventually promulgated a new constitution which explicitly replaced the existing constitution. The constitutional replacement follows the amendment procedures of the existing constitution, which is demanding, in a similar way to the above model. Substantively, the replacement projects allows for a wide range of substantive changes, including the alteration of constitutional identity. In addition, substantive changes animated by explicit replacement through amendment are limited within the existing constitutional order and political system. So, replacement of constitutional text does not result in the replacement of the constitutional and political system. Comparatively, ordinary replacement (as discussed below) and explicit replacement through amendment are different in terms of political intention and procedure but similar in substantive changes. In both cases, substantive changes are extensive but within the existing constitutional and political system. Therefore, in both cases, legal rupture and substantive continuity co-exist.

[101] For demanding amendment, see Xenophon Contiades and Alkmene Fotiadou, "Models of Constitutional Change" in *Engineering Constitutional Change: A Comparative Perspective on Europe, Canada and the USA* (Xenophon Contiades (ed.), 2013) 450; Yaniv Roznai, "Amendment Power, Constituent Power, and Popular Sovereignty: Linking Unamendability and Amendment Procedures" in *The Foundations and Traditions of Constitutional Amendment* (Richard Albert, Xenophon Contiades, and Alkmene Fotiadou (eds) Hart, 2017) 41.

[102] Saunders, "Constitution-Making" (n 49) 4–10.

The third variation is *ordinary constitutional replacement*. The case of Cuba offers a good example: the 2019 Constitution replaced the 1976 Constitution. In this variation, the constitutional change took the form of *replacement* manifested in the following political, procedural, and substantive features. First, the choice of replacement reflected the political will: a project of constitutional change was expressly and deliberately introduced as a project of constitution making aimed at replacing the existing constitution. Second, constitutional change followed the procedures set up by the constitution-makers rather than by the existing constitution. Third, the replacement project opened the door to a wide range of substantive changes, including changes of constitutional identity. But, the constitutional replacement was *ordinary*, not an extra-ordinary constitutional revolution. The reformers intended to replace the constitutional text, not the constitutional order or the political system. Constitutional replacement occurred within the existing constitutional and political structure. This has consequences for the ordinary features of the procedure and substance of constitutional replacement. The procedure for constitutional replacement was not divorced from the existing constitutional framework: the constitutional reform was undertaken by the sitting legislature, not by a constituent assembly, and under the leadership of the existing political elite. Substantive changes are possible, but must take place within the existing political order. Constitutional replacement leads to modification, not replacement of the socialist constitutional identity. The consequence of the ordinary constitutional replacement is co-existence of the legal rupture and substantive continuity.

The fourth variation, presented by the cases of China and North Korea, is *ordinary constitutional amendment*. In this variation, the political elite have the intention of retaining the original constitution and only amending it. Amendment procedures are established by the existing constitution and are similar to the normal legislative procedures. Constitutional amendment can be quotidian, similar to daily politics. The amendments introduce changes to procedural details and policy issues. Several amendments (executive terms, taking oaths, the forms of private ownership, creating economic zones) belong to this variation. But, ordinary amendments could also introduce substantive changes to the constitutional structure, rights, and identity (fundamental principles). In this regard, ordinary amendment has substantive effects similar to constitutional replacement. In fact, although China and North Korea did not engage in constitutional replacement, many of their constitutional amendments have modified or introduced new rights (private ownership), institutional structures (China's supervision commissions, and North Korea's State Affairs Commission), and principles (party leadership, *Juche*, rule of law, protection of human rights, and protection of private economy). In this substantive sense, ordinary amendments in China and North Korea are not very different from replacements in Vietnam, Laos, and Cuba.

2. Replacement Choice

What can explain the elite's choice between amendment and replacement? In their seminal book, Elkins, Ginsburg, and Melton argue that the choice between amendment and replacement is "mostly a function of relative costs and benefits, with intra-constitutional change typically being the preferred choice of actors."[103] Replacement is only employed in certain circumstances (e.g. the party lacking sufficient political strength or the lack of internal flexibility of the constitution) when the means of amendment are not available.[104]

This rational explanation resonates with the socialist experience in some cases. For example, China chose amendment rather than replacement since the former costs less, procedurally. Particularly, since the 2018 circle involved controversial issues (e.g. executive term limit evasion), a replacement process would open the door for criticism and even opposition from some critical sectors of society, and therefore intra-constitutional change through amendment is the first choice. North Korea's choice of amendment is also due to the availability of the means of intra-constitutional change. The cost and benefit explanation may not echo other socialist cases, though. In Vietnam, Laos, and Cuba, amendment could have been feasible given the domination of the communist party in the legislature, and no limits on the scope of amendments. Yet, the socialist elite in these countries chose replacement rather than amendment. Thus, there must be additional determinants.

Negretto explores other determinants of the choice between amendment and replacement, arguing that "constitutions are replaced when they fail to work as governance structures or when their design prevents competing political interests from accommodating the environment. According to this perspective, constitutions are likely to be replaced when constitutional crises are frequent, when political actors lack the capacity to implement change by means of amendments or judicial interpretation, or when the constitutional regime has a power-concentrating design."[105] This thesis may find it germane to explain the determinants of replacement and amendment in competitive environments but not in the socialist context. In Cuba, Vietnam, and Laos, constitutional replacement occurred without constitutional crises. In these countries, as constitutional replacement did not transform the political system, constitutional change could have been undertaken through ordinary or fundamental amendments.

Ultimately, the choice of replacement and amendment in the socialist world is determined by the progressive nature of constitutional change. When the socialist elite want to signify the beginning of a new phase of political, social, and economic progress, replacement is more likely. The new constitution then signals the regime's commitments to far-reaching and comprehensive political, social, and

[103] Elkins, Ginsburg, and Melton, *The Endurance of National Constitutions* (n 1) 76.
[104] Ibid.
[105] Negretto, "Replacing and Amending Constitutions" (n 37) 749–50.

economic reforms to improve the well-being of the living conditions of the local people. The three stories of constitutional replacement can be explained by this logic. Vietnam's constitutional replacement marked the new phase of global integration in the country's development trajectory. The 2013 Constitution signaled the regime's commitments to far-reaching and comprehensive reforms to adapt the country to the global environment. After post-war normalization, and graduation from the class of least-developed countries, Laos' 2015 Constitution signified a new era of development with the view of becoming an upper-middle-income country by 2030. In the same vein, Cuba's 2019 marks a new phase characterized by the "updating" model of political, social, and economic systems.

That progressive logic also explains why constitutional replacement did not occur in China and North Korea. In China, after the new phase of opening policy was codified in the 1982 Constitution, subsequent continuing constitutional reforms have been achieved partially through a series of constitutional amendments. Frequent amendments enable the constitution to adapt to a changing society, and exclude the need of constitutional replacement. In North Korea, partial reforms have been also achieved through frequent amendments, which remove the need for a new constitution. Finally, the constitutionalization of the personal ideology of different generations of political leaders in China and North Korea entails the need for textual constitutional continuity. In this regard, retaining the existing constitution is the way to show continued respect to the previous political leaders.

3. Amendment Rate

Scholars have generalized about the institutional, political, and cultural determinants of constitutional amendment.[106] One classical theory was formulated by Donald S. Lutz. He proposes the concept of amendment rate which "refers to the average number of formal amendments passed per year since the constitution came into effect."[107] He then formulates several general propositions about the amendment rate. According to him, the amendment rate should increase with the length of the constitution, the flexible amendment procedure, and the lack of alternatives to formal amendments.[108] These propositions both resonate with and are debatable in the socialist context.

To begin with, the proposition on the effect of the constitution's length to the amendment rate echoes the socialist experience in some cases. The natural intuition is that since the socialist constitutions are the codification of a social and economic program, they should be long, include provisions on social and economic policy,

[106] Donald S. Lutz, "Toward a Theory of Constitutional Amendment" (1994) 88(2) The American Political Science Review 355; Tom Ginsburg and James Melton, "Does the Constitutional Amendment Rule Matter at All" (2015) 13 International Journal of Constitutional Law 686; Negretto, "Replacing and Amending Constitutions" (n 37) 749.

[107] Ibid. 357.

[108] Ibid. 357–8.

and hence require frequent amendment. The frequent constitutional amendments in China and North Korea seem to bear out this intuition. But, the "length" proposition may not explain the constitutional endurance in China between 2004 and 2018. Particularly, this proposition may not hold in Cuba, Vietnam, and Laos. Cuba's 1976 Constitution lasted for more than four decades with only one amendment, although it was very long, and included many detailed provisions on social and economic policy. This is mainly because Cuba's society and economy remained essentially unchanged for several decades before the country introduced a policy for fundamental but incremental reform in 2011. Vietnam's 1992 Constitution was amended only once in more than twenty years, although its substantive length is almost the same as that of China's Constitution. Similarly, the "length" proposition cannot explain the endurance for more than a decade of Laos' socialist constitutions of 1991 and 2003. The length of the constitutions is an important factor of frequent amendments, but this must be accompanied by the accounts of the significant social and economic changes which require constitutional response.

The amendment rate in the socialist countries may not merely depend on the rigid procedure of amendment. The two-thirds requirement and even referendum requirement (in the case of Cuba) are available but do not present an institutional barrier for constitutional amendment, as such requirements are extremely easy to achieve in socialist institutional settings where a single communist party dominates the legislative platform, political agenda, and mass media.

The proposition for the alternative forms to formal amendments is relevant to the socialist world. There is a persuasive argument that constitutions endure longer when there are alternative forms to formal constitutional change, but these alternative forms are not limited to judicial constitutional interpretation. Constitutional legislation can be a form of constitutional change.[109] In the five socialist countries, judicial constitutional review is absent, but, in several cases, the constitutions are able to enjoy stability, thanks to the legislative interpretation of the constitutional norms and provisions, which limits the number of formal constitutional amendments. For example, Yan Lin and Tom Ginsburg have extensively discussed the legislative constitutional interpretation as the "invisible" mechanism of constitutional change in China.[110] The availability of this informal mechanism explains China's constitutional endurance for more than a decade between 2004 and 2018. In the same vein, in Vietnam, Laos, and Cuba, informal constitutional change can be achieved through the legislature's amendment of the organic constitutional laws on the legislature, the courts, and the government, which prevents frequent resorting to formal amendments.

[109] See generally, Grégoire Webber et al, *Legislated Rights* (CUP 2018).

[110] Yan Lin and Tom Ginsburg, "Constitutional Interpretation in Lawmaking: China's Invisible Constitutional Enforcement Mechanism" (2015) 63 American Journal of Comparative Law 467; Yan Lin, "Constitutional Evolution through Legislation: The Quiet Transformation of China's Constitution" (2015) 13 International Journal of Constitutional Law 61.

B. Constituent and Amendment Powers

Drawing on the work of Emmanuel Joseph Sieyès[111] and Carl Schmitt,[112] comparative constitutional theorists distinguish constituent from amendment power.[113] A related question concerns the limits of the constituent power and amendment power. This section conceptualizes the people's constituent power in Cuba—the only socialist case where this power is practiced, the ambiguity of the three powers in other socialist cases, and unamendability.

1. Ordinary Constituent Power

Constituent power is normally understood as the people's capacity to enact a constitution, which gives rise to a novel legal order.[114] The concept of constituent power "emerges from the secularizing and rationalizing movement of eighteenth-century European thought, known as the Enlightenment and rests on two conditions: recognition that the ultimate source of political authority derives from an entity known as 'the people' and acceptance of the idea of a constitution as something that is created."[115] This concept was theorized by French political writer Emmanuel Joseph Sieyès to justify the French Revolution. Sieyès distinguishes between "constituent power" (*pouvoir constituent*) exercised by the people or "the Nation" in extraordinary moments and "constituted powers" (*pouvoir constitué*) exercised by ordinary institutions—a parliament, an executive, and courts in normal times. In normal times, the people act through ordinary institutions, but in extraordinary times, they repudiate the existing ordinary institutions and execute their original constituent power to directly establish a new constitutional order.[116] German constitutional theorist Carl Schmitt revitalized the interest in constituent power.[117] The concept of constituent power has been vigorously debated in contemporary constitutional theory.[118] Martin Loughlin notes that "since the political domain is a contested space it is not surprising that that concept [of constituent power] is itself contested."[119]

[111] Emmanuel Joseph Sieyès, *What is the Third Estate?* (Frederick A Praeger 1963).

[112] Carl Schmitt, *Constitutional Theory* (Jeffrey Seitzer (tr.)) (Duke University Press Books 2008).

[113] Kim Lane Scheppele, "Unconstitutional Constituent Power" (unpublished paper) <www.sas.upenn.edu/andrea-mitchell-center/sites/www.sas.upenn.edu.dcc/files/uploads/Scheppele_unconstitutional constituent power.pdf>

[114] Hans Lindahl, "Constituent Power and the Constitution" in *Philosophical Foundations of Constitutional Law* (David Dyzenhaus and Malcolm Thorburn (eds), OUP 2016) 147.

[115] Martin Loughlin, "The Concept of Constituent Power" (2014) 13(2) European Journal of Political Theory 218, 219.

[116] Sieyès, *What is the Third Estate?* (n 111) 136–9.

[117] Ibid.; Schmitt, *Constitutional Theory* (n 112).

[118] See Martin Loughlin and Neil Walker (eds), *The Paradox of Constitutionalism: Constituent Power and Constitutional Form* (Oxford University Press 2007); Andrew Arato, *The Adventures of the Constituent Power: Beyond Revolutions?* (CUP 2017); Mark Wenman, *Agonistic Democracy: Constituent Power in the Era of Globalisation* (CUP 2015).

[119] Martin, "The Concept of Constituent Power" (n 115) 218.

The concept of constituent power has informed the study of comparative constitutional law in the context of participatory constitution-making and unconstitutional constitutional amendment. In the first instance, while the idea of constituent power was originally introduced as a conceptual necessity, it generates practical consequences today, in terms of the desire for public participation in the constitution-making process. Discussing features of constitution-making in the twenty-first century, Saunders states that "there is now, effectively, universal acceptance that the authority for a Constitution must derive, in one way or another, from the people of the state concerned. This idea is not, of course, new, but it has been reinforced by the aspirations of people everywhere in the aftermath of the overthrow of authoritarian regimes. Moreover, it now has a practical as well as theoretical dimension. People now expect actually to be involved in the constitution-making process and not just symbolically associated with it."[120] In addition, the concept of constituent power is invocated to defend the doctrine of unconstitutional constitutional amendment: constituent power can change any aspect of the constitution while the amendment power is limited to making changes that do not alter the basic structure made by the constituent power.[121]

The concept of constituent power has usually been discussed in democratic constitutional theory and in the context of democratic institutional settings. How can the socialist, non-democratic experience further the comparative discourse on constituent power? Cuba's real experience with constituent power indicates that, like constitutions, constituent power can be positively conceptualized in a non-democratic constitutional theory and can be practiced in non-democratic institutional setting. Like constitutions, the constituent power in authoritarian regimes may be dismissed as a sham. But, just as authoritarian constitutions have their own functions,[122] authoritarian constituent power may have its own virtues which may complicate comparative constitutional scrutiny.

In non-democratic theory and settings, there may be an ordinary constituent power. The idea of ordinary constituent power seems like an oxymoron from a democratic perspective but may make sense viewed through a non-democratic lens. The ordinary constituent power is constituent in two senses, which are similar to the concept understood in democratic constitutional theory and its practice in democracies. First, the power is practiced by the people, e.g. through a referendum. Second, the power creates a new constitution. Yet, the constituent power is ordinary due to two features. The first is *constituent power without constitutional moment*. This concerns the procedure for exercising the constituent power. The people exercise the constituent power within the existing institutional framework.

[120] Saunders, "Constitution Making" (n 49) 2.

[121] Landau Davide, Dixon Rosalind, and Roznai Yaniv, "From an Unconstitutional Constitutional Amendment to an Unconstitutional Constitution? Lessons from Honduras" (2019) 8 Global Constitutionalism 40, 46.

[122] See generally, Ginsburg and Simpser (eds), *Constitutions in Authoritarian Regimes* (n 84).

At the moment of the exercise of the ordinary constituent power, there may be an unusually high degree of popular engagement, mobilization, and energy, but this is not an extraordinary constitutional moment when people repudiate the existing institutions. When exercising the ordinary constituent power, the people act within the existing institutional framework as the insiders of the existing polity. The second is *constituent power without constitutional revolution*. This concerns the substantive consequence of the constituent power. The practice of the constituent power leads to significant substantive changes but continues the constitutional project. Constituent power modifies rather displaces the cores or identities of the constitutional polity. In other words, ordinary constituent power only results in ordinary constitutional replacement.

Cuba provides a socialist example of ordinary constituent power. The Cuban people exercised their constituent power through a national referendum, which led to the enactment of the 2019 Constitution. The 2019 referendum drew great public engagement and attention, but was not a constitutional moment: the Cuban people acted within the existing institutional framework, and followed the procedure and agenda of the referendum created by the existing socialist government. The constituent power continues the socialist constitutional project but modifies its identities: e.g. distributing the public power, universalizing human rights, and liberalizing the economy. This ordinary feature of the constituent power in Cuba is determined by the incremental nature of progressive constitutional change, which enables constitutional evolution rather than revolution.

2. Blurred Powers

The discourse on constituent and amendment power has been further complicated in the existing comparative constitutional law scholarship. For example, Yaniv Roznai has taken the discourse forward by identifying three powers: the primary constituent power by the people, the secondary primary power (constitutional amendment power) by a separate entrusted body, and the constituted power (e.g. the legislative power).[123]

These three powers may be recognizable in Cuba but are blurred in the four other socialist states: China, Vietnam, Laos, and North Korea. The socialist constitutions of these four states allow the legislature to assume three powers: constitution-making power, amendment power, and law-making power. This ordinary legislature is in fact the locus of both constitutional amendment power and legislative power. Two possible explanations for the ambiguity of the three powers in these socialist states can be offered. The first lies in the socialist authoritarian setting. The distinction of constituent, amendment, and legislative powers rests on democratic foundations. By contrast, the authoritarian constitutional amendment

[123] Roznai, "Amendment Power" (n 101) 23–6.

process in the socialist states is controlled by a centralized power and hence does not have the distinction of powers that it might have in a democratic constitutional amendment process. The second explanation concerns the normative nature of the theoretical differentiation of the three powers. The theorization presents an aspiration on how democratic constitutional powers should be exercised rather than positively describing how they are actually used. In fact, during the process of post-communist democratization in the late twentieth century, there was no clear distinction between constitutional politics and ordinary politics, and the ordinary legislature operated as the locus for both ordinary law-making and constitutional-building.[124] The merging of the amendment power and the legislative power into a single legislature is not a socialist constitutional aberration.

Despite the same authority, the constitutional amendment rules seem to provide that the amendment power should be practiced in a process separate from the ordinary legislative process, e.g. through a requirement for a two-thirds supermajority. In theory, "a two-thirds supermajority requirement, which may seem very demanding in the context of a competitive two-party or multiparty democracy, may not be demanding at all in a dominant party system or even after one party."[125] Despite a single-party rule, several socialist states require a two-thirds super-majority on the constitutional amendment process. In the context of authoritarian constitutional amendment in socialist states, a two-thirds super-majority requirement may have a legitimizing rather than a constraining function: it is used to strengthen the legitimacy of the process and substance of constitutional amendment.

3. Illiberal Unamendability

The distinction between the constituent and constitutional amendment powers constitutes the foundation for the theory of unconstitutional constitutional amendment: the amendment power is constrained by core commitments or basic structures established by the constituent power.[126] The idea of unamendability in the existing constitutional amendment literature is a constitutionalist, liberal, and democratic idea. To begin with, it is an idea of constitutionalism: the entrenchment of core constitutional constraints against the whim of power holders.[127] In other

[124] See Teitel, "Transitional Jurisprudence" (n 12) 2069; Andrew Arato, "Parliamentary Constitution Making in Hungary" (1995) 4 East European Constitutional Review 45.

[125] David Landau and Rosalind Dixon, "Constraining Constitutional Change" (2015) 50 Wake Forest Law Review 859, 872.

[126] Gary J. Jacobsohn, "An Unconstitutional Constitution? A Comparative Perspective" (2006) 4(3) International Journal of Constitutional Law 460; Yaniv Roznai, "Unconstitutional Constitutional Amendments—The Migration and Success of a Constitutional Idea" (2013) 61 American Journal of Comparative Law 657; Mark Tushnet, "Peasants with Pitchforks, and Toilers with Twitter: Constitutional Revolutions and the Constituent Power" (2015) 13(3) International Journal of Constitutional Law 639.

[127] For the relation of the idea of entrenchment to constitutional amendment, see Richard Albert, "Amending Constitutional Amendment Rules" (2015) 13(3) International Journal of Constitutional Law 655, 656. For a critical view on constitutional entrenchment, see Mila Versteeg and Emily Zackin,

words, unamendability is a part of the project of legally limited government. In addition, unamendability is a liberal idea: the entrenched constitutional essentials are associated with the core commitment of enlightenment liberalism to the protection of individuals' fundamental rights. Certainly, unamendable values may include local values (e.g. language or religion) that a polity considers foundational and hence unchangeable.[128] Finally, unamendability is a democratic idea. The constitutional entrenchment aims to protect the core values and institutions of a democracy, such as popular sovereignty and popular elections. Understandably, research on unconstitutional constitutional amendments focuses mainly on constitutionalist, liberal, democratic settings,[129] including the recent accounts of the transitional settings.[130]

The socialist settings have been ignored in the relevant literature on unconstitutional constitutional amendments for understandable reasons. The assumption tends to be that the socialist states are authoritarian, and that consequently their constitutions do not have explicit provisions limiting the amendment power. In theory, the socialist legislature enjoys both constituent and constitutional amendment powers, and thus it is free to amend the constitution. Neither do socialist states have implicit constitutional unamendability since a judicial review of constitutionality is absent as the consequence of authoritarian arrangement. Substantively, as the socialist states are not committed to values of liberal democracy, there seems no basis for entrenching constitutional fundamentals to protect such values.

However, the socialist constitution may entrench unamendable essentials in a different way, and their accounts may enrich the comparative inquiry into unconstitutional constitutional amendments. Of the five socialist states, Cuba is unique in its formal constitutional entrenchment of socialist unamendability. This unique feature is due to the tension involved in Cuba's relations with the United States. In response to the US President's and domestic dissidents' call for fundamental change, the 2002 amendment to the 1976 Constitution excluded from future amendment the irrevocable nature of the political, social, and economic system, and proscription to negotiate under aggression, threat, or coercion by a foreign power.[131] The United States has consistently run democracy promotion programs to promote regime change in Cuba.[132] Understandably, unamendable socialism is again

"Constitutions Un-entrenched: Toward an Alternative Theory of Constitutional Design" (2016) 110(4) American Political Science Review 657.

[128] Silvia Suteu, "Eternity Clauses in Post-Conflict and Post-Authoritarian Constitution-Making: Promise and Limits" (2017) 6 Global Constitutionalism 63.

[129] Yaniv Roznai, *Unconstitutional Constitutional Amendments: The Limits of Amendment Powers* (OUP 2017) 15, 39.

[130] Suteu (n 128) 78–9 (discussing unamendable commitments to official language and Islam in Tunisia's 2014 Constitution).

[131] Constitution of the Republic of Cuba (1967) (Amended 2002) art. 137.

[132] Alessandro Badella, "American Hýbris: US Democracy Promotion in Cuba after the Cold War (Part 1)" (2014) 6 International Journal of Cuban Studies 157.

entrenched in Cuba's 2019 Constitution. Article 229 of this Constitution provides that "The pronouncements concerning the irrevocability of the socialist system established in Article 4, and the prohibition to negotiate under the circumstances specified in paragraph a) of Article 16 in no case may be reformable."[133] This clause makes the regime's commitment to socialism as a political and economic system unamendable. The explicit establishment of irrevocability of socialism necessarily induces explicit unamendability. If irrevocable socialism is unamendable, it naturally follows that the core values of socialism (e.g. party leadership, unity of power, and state-led economy) are unamendable. The unamendability of the prohibition to negotiate under aggression, threat, or coercion by a foreign power also aims to protect the existing socialist regime from external influences. The Constitution cannot be changed to allow the government to enter into international negotiations that would undermine its socialist commitments.

To appreciate the socialist unamendability as embodied in Cuba requires a pluralizing of the idea of unamendability; in other words, to liberate the idea of unamendability from the constitutionalist, liberal, and democratic rationales. With that, it is possible to conceptualize unamendability in socialist settings. Socialist unamendability concerns socialist constitutional essentials that are entrenched against change through amendment. The unamendable constitutional essentials are not values of liberal democracy, but socialist values, such as the leadership of the community party, the unity of power, and the socialist economic system. This socialist constitutional entrenchment performs the expressive function.[134] It expresses the Cuban state's deep commitment to socialist values and their protection from the external influence.

The four other socialist states do not formally include the unamendability clause in their constitutions. But, the cases of Vietnam and Laos suggest that the power to change the constitution is not unlimited in reality. To appreciate this, unamendability can be conceptualized in a functional sense. In fact, amendment scholarship has advanced both formal and functional approaches to unamendability. The former focuses on the formal unamendability clause,[135] while the latter is more concerned with the functional development of unamendability through judicial adjudication.[136] The functional approach may be extended to include non-judicial, political construction of certain constitutional cores as unamendable. What is established by legislators in the constitutional amendment

[133] Constitution of the Republic of Cuba (2019) art. 229.

[134] For the expressive function of constitutional amendment rules generally, see Richard Albert, "The Expressive Function of Constitutional Amendment Rules" (2013) 59(2) McGill Law Journal 225. For the expressive functions of unamendable provisions, see Michel Rosenfeld, *The Identity of the Constitutional Subject: Selfhood, Citizenship, Culture, and Community* (Routledge New York 2010); Gary J. Jacobsohn, *Constitutional Identity* (Harvard University Press 2010).

[135] Suteu (n 128).

[136] E.g., Sudhir Krishnaswamy, *Democracy and Constitutionalism in India: A Study on the Basic Structure Doctrine* (Oxford University Press 2009).

agenda in Vietnam and Laos as "principles" of constitutional amendment can be understood as the functional unamendability: constitutional amendment cannot change the nature of "people's democracy," the leadership of the communist party, and the unity of power. This political construction of unamendability enables incremental constitutional improvement and precludes a constitutional metamorphosis. The communist party is the gatekeeper of the constraints on constitutional amendment. The party closely controls the amendment process to make sure that constitutional evolution is circumscribed within the possible boundaries. The process and the substances of constitutional amendment are closely tied to the party's process of making political decisions, plans, and visions. The party decision was incorporated into the amended constitutions; important changes to the constitutions were approved by the party in advance; and the amended constitutions are the base for implementing the party's long-term plan of socio-economic development.

C. Participation

1. Controlled Participation

Closely related to the global spread of the idea of constituent power is the global trend of involving the public in the constitution-making process. Vivien Hart states: "Participation is now promoted as both a right and a necessity."[137] The logical necessity is that as the people are the authors of the constituent power, the constitution-making process must involve public participation. Yet, beyond this abstract necessity, public participation in constitution-making has now become a right recognized by international law.[138]

The comparative scholarship on participation has focused mainly on democratic constitution-making, especially in the post-conflict contexts.[139] Little attention, however, has been paid to participation in authoritarian constitution-making, such as the socialist one. This may be due to the possible assumption that the socialist constitutional change process is controlled by a single communist party or similar dominant political elite, and hence has little room for public participation. This is true in the cases of China and North Korea's ordinary constitutional amendment process. However, the global spread of the norm of participation in the constitution-making process does affect other socialist states: Vietnam, Laos, and Cuba. This is evident in the public consultation process in the three constitution-making episodes and referendum in the case of Cuba. Participation in socialist

[137] Vivien Hart, "Democratic Constitution-Making" (2003) 107 USIP Special Report 12.

[138] For more detailed discussions, see Maartje De Visser and Bui Ngoc Son, "Globalised Constitution-Making in the Twenty-First Century: Evidence from Asia" (2019) 8 Global Constitutionalism 297, 310–11.

[139] Angela M. Banks, "Expanding Participation in Constitution Making: Challenges and Opportunities" (2008) 49 William & Mary Law Review 1055.

constitution-making may have distinctive aspects which may complicate and enrich a comparative study of participatory constitution-making.

Participation in the socialist constitution-making is a type of *controlled participation,* defined as public engagement in the constitution-making process under the management of the party-state. The rationales of the controlled participation are connected to the progressive function of socialist constitutional change. First, as constitutional change aims to address the material concerns of the local people, the socialist states enable the public to participate in the constitution-making process to identify the populace's material concerns. In this regard, participation, especially through the public consultation process, serves not only to improve or legitimize the constitution but also to help the state to identify problems regarding living conditions and address these accordingly, at the constitutional level. Second, public participation is under the control of the party-state to avoid potential radical constitutional transformation (regime change) and ensure that constitutional change facilitates the movement of these socialist countries toward socialism.

2. Constitutional Mobilization

Participatory constitution-making creates an important opportunity for constitutional mobilization. Yet, constitutional mobilization can also be triggered by other opportunities. This section explores the idea of constitutional mobilization and its manifestations in the socialist countries, particularly Vietnam, Cuba, and China.

I define constitutional mobilization as *the process by which social actors invoke constitutional norms and discourses to advocate for constitutional change*. It is a form of social mobilization which involves social actors, such as human rights activists, intellectuals, constitutional law scholars, lawyers, and civil society groups and organizations. Constitutional mobilization is also a form of legal mobilization as it concerns the law, legal institutions, and legal processes. However, it is a distinctive phenomenon, different from other forms of social and legal mobilization.

To conceptualize its distinctive features, I extend in the constitutional realm three theories on social mobilization and social movements developed by political scientists and sociologists, namely political opportunity, framing, and resource mobilization.[140] *Constitutional opportunities* refers to the general political and constitutional environment in which constitutional mobilization occurs, and particular political and constitutional processes that provoke constitutional mobilization. *Constitutional framing* involves identifying constitutional problems and suggesting constitutional solutions. Constitutional frames are conditioned by people's grievances about the existing constitutional system and their demands

[140] David S. Meyer, "Protest and Political Opportunities" (2004) 30 Annual Review of Sociology 125; David A. Snow et al, "Frame Alignment Processes, Micromobilization, and Movement Participation" (1986) 51 American Sociological Review 464; J. Craig Jenkins, "Resource Mobilization Theory and the Study of Social Movements" (1983) 9 Annual Review of Sociology 527.

for constitutional change. To frame constitutional arguments and demands, social actors refer to distinctive constitutional language, ideas, norms, or symbols. Constitutional mobilization requires distinctively *constitutional resources* in the form of state actors who will play an influential role in constitutional change. Constitutional mobilizers need to garner support from these actors to achieve their constitutional goals. Constitutional resources refer to what Balkin labels as "nodes of power and influence" who "determine which ideas and positions ascend into plausibility and dominance and which are cast into the dustbin of history."[141]

In constitutional mobilization, social actors advocate constitutional change. Constitutional change must be understood as a concept with multiple incarnations, which include both cultural, reformative, and revolutionary change. Cultural change involves changes in the constitutional understanding, behavior, attitude, and consciousness of different social and state actors. Reformative change involves incremental changes within the existing constitutional order. Revolutionary change involves the creation of a new constitutional order.[142] Constitutional mobilization does not always result in constitutional change. Such mobilizations may fail or succeed. Also, the degree to which it may succeed will vary, as an episode of constitutional mobilization may create either minor or major changes.

Under what conditions, how, and why do social actors mobilize for constitutional change in a socialist regime? Given the authoritarian condition of the socialist regime in which the communist party holds a monopoly over public power, the normal intuition is that constitutional mobilization cannot happen there. However, under the socialist regimes in China, Vietnam, and Cuba, constitutional mobilization does occur.

a. *Opportunity*

Constitutional mobilization can occur in the socialist regimes in China, Vietnam, and Cuba thanks to two kinds of opportunity: general and specific. The general opportunity concerns the regime's toleration of civil liberty, to a certain extent. The overall constitutional structure and politics of the socialist regime are not conducive to social mobilization, but, in response to social and political complexity, the regime may soften their suppression of civil liberty by, perhaps, allowing a public discussion of constitutional issues which would permit a constitutional environment to exist wherein social actors may be able to mobilize a constitutional dialogue. In addition to the regime's toleration, the general opportunity includes the development of an active civil society supported by new space of popular debates

[141] Balkin, *Constitutional Redemption* (n 41) 182–3.

[142] Social actors may also seek to defend the existing constitutional values, like the case of Japan in which social actors try to defend the pacifist Constitution against the government. Marie Linton, Guillaume Bression, and Justin McCurry, "Japan's Students at Forefront of Protests to Defend Pacifist Constitution" (*France* 24, September 16, 2015) <www.france24.com/en/20150916-japan-youth-students-abe-reform-security-bills-army-overseas-pacifist-constitution>

(e.g. the cyber space) which enable citizens to engage in constitutional debates and mobilization. Laos and North Korea significantly lack these opportunities, and this is why constitutional mobilization is virtually absent there.

The specific opportunity includes particular legal, political, and constitutional process and events that trigger constitutional mobilization. In China, social actors appropriate different legal and political processes to mobilize for constitutional change, including litigation in the courtroom, petition to the legislative body, and violent protests. In Vietnam and Cuba, the process of constitution-making creates an important opportunity for the operation of constitutional mobilization under socialist regimes. This is because constitution-making is normally a critical moment touching on the fundamentals of a polity. Moreover, the constitution-making process is usually open and inclusive, which attracts the attention and participation of a wide range of social and state actors. However, as this process has multiple steps (including setting an agenda, drafting, state deliberation, public deliberation, ratification) mobilizing actors need to choose the right moment to address their constitutional concerns. For example, it is too early to address constitutional concerns during the initial steps of setting an agenda, when the constitution-makers have just produced a first constitutional draft, or when that draft is discussed within the institutional circle. It is also too late to address constitutional concerns when the constitution-makers are about to approve the new constitution. The most suitable moment to address constitutional concerns is when the regime releases the draft constitution for public deliberation. Social actors ought to seize this moment to mobilize a constitutional dialogue.

b. Frame

Scholars have pointed out that constitutions in authoritarian states operate as *manuals, billboards, blueprints, and window dressing.*[143] Yet, authoritarian constitutions have another function: they operate as the *mobilizing frame*. It functions as the frame for social actors to identity constitutional problems internal to the existing authoritarian regime and mobilize for constitutional change. To develop arguments for constitutional changes, social actors will turn to alternative sources, including transnational sources. International treaties and foreign constitutions operate as the frames for social actors to formulate arguments for constitutional change. However, a sense of nationalism and community identity contextualize global and transnational frames, which results in the dialogical interaction between global and local frames. This dialogical framing also allows social actors to gain public support, to avoid political punishment, and to consolidate the legitimacy of their constitutional arguments.

[143] Tom Ginsburg and Alberto Simpser, "Introduction" in *Constitutions in Authoritarian Regimes* (Tom Ginsburg and Alberto Simpser (eds), CUP 2013) 1–18, 2.

Three dialogical strategies[144] in constitutional framing are also applied. First, social actors *align* transnational constitutional discourse with some unfilled language in the existing constitutional text and in the authoritarian elite's constitutional rhetoric. For example, even authoritarian constitutions and leaders employ language like "democracy," "rule of law," or "human rights" and social actors working for change in such nations use that language to argue that their actions are not in contrast to the existing constitution but, rather, that they are merely seeking to realize the existing constitution's original language.[145] In particular, the framing space is wider when the existing constitution and constitutional rhetoric embrace ambiguous and contradictory language. Second, social actors *amplify* specific constitutional values. As an example of such amplification in an authoritarian context, social actors may focus on specific features of the authoritarian regime like single-party rule or political ideology. Such identity-based mobilization may also underline specific values. For example, as I will discuss later in this paper, Vietnamese gay activists have focused on the constitutional protection of freedom of marriage as a means of advocating for their desired changes.[146] Third, to engage in a national constitutional dialogue, social actors need to *extend* their specific concerns to general, national concerns. For example, social actors may connect their specific grievances against the government to general concerns of the population such as free elections or political competition. Again, an example of this behavior was when Vietnamese gay activists connected their concerns about gay rights to more general human rights in order to gain more popular support and legitimacy for their pursuit of gay rights.[147]

c. *Resources*

The constitutional resources in the socialist regimes are the political elites rather than the judicial elites. They are the forces which have the final say on constitutional issues. Therefore, social actors will approach them as mobilization resources using dialogical strategy.

Law and society scholars have pointed out that activists mobilizing under authoritarian conditions "avoid strategies and tactics common under liberal democratic conditions, such as marches or open and structured association."[148] They try to avoid "direct confrontation with the state, or being seen as a threat to the existing arrangements of power."[149] To survive, social actors mobilizing constitutional change under authoritarian condition also need to adopt a dialogical rather than

144 Douglas NeJaime, "Constitutional Change, Courts, and Social Movements" (2013) 111 Michigan Law Review 893.

145 See chapter on Vietnam for examples of this behavior.

146 Ibid.

147 Ibid.

148 Lynette J. Chua, "Pragmatic Resistance, Law, and Social Movements in Authoritarian States: The Case of Gay Collective Action in Singapore" (2012) 46 Law & Society Review 713, 719.

149 Ibid. 722.

confrontational approach. They also try to avoid confrontational methods such as demonstrating or organizing oppositional bodies. They instead adopt dialogical means to communicate with the public and with political leaders. But, unlike actors mobilizing ordinary legal reform, actors mobilizing constitutional change will inevitably directly challenge the existing constitutional arrangement and those in power. The adherence to the formal constitutional change process initiated by the existing regime and to constitutional rhetoric adopted by those in power is a survival strategy on the part of an applicable authoritarian regime. The government may initiate counter-mobilization against the constitutional mobilization. State actors, however, would not suppress but engage in a dialogue with social actors and the public at large.

3. Constitutional Dialogue

The consequence of participation and mobilization in the socialist states is a constitutional dialogue. This is connected to the fact that the prevailing language of dialogue is in contemporary constitutional theory. Dialogical constitutional theories have been developed on the grounds of constitutional experience in the United States, Commonwealth nations, and common law Asia.[150] The existing dialogical constitutional theories display a narrow focus on constitutional dialogue triggered by the practice of judicial review power. Constitutional dialogue is manifested in three different forms:[151] (1) national institutional dialogues or the dialogues between courts and political institutions about constitutionality;[152] (2) transnational judicial dialogues or dialogues between supreme courts and constitutional courts in different countries about the content and process of constitutional decision-making;[153] and (3) public, national constitutional dialogues. The existing dialogical constitutional theories fail to appreciate the possibility of a broader, public national constitutional dialogue. In particular, when focusing on dialogical judicial review, scholars have largely ignored the possibility of constitutional dialogue without judicial review. I suggest an extension to popular, national constitutional dialogue in which the mobilized public engages in a conversation with political leaders to exchange ideas, opinions, and discuss constitutional questions.

The consequence of controlled participation and constitutional mobilization under the socialist regimes is a constitutional dialogue. The scale of the constitutional dialogue depends on the specific opportunities. The limited opportunities (judicial and legislative process) only create a narrow dialogue among scholars and

[150] Mark Tushnet, "Dialogic Judicial Review" (2008) 61 Arkansas Law Review 205; Alison L. Young, *Democratic Dialogue and the Constitution* (2017); Po Jen Yap, *Constitutional Dialogue in Common Law Asia* (OUP 2015).

[151] I thank Tom Ginsburg for his suggestion of these three manifestations of constitutional dialogue.

[152] On this form, see, for example, Kent Roach, "Constitutional and Common Law Dialogues Between the Supreme Court and Canadian Legislatures" (2001) 80 Canadian Bar Review 481.

[153] On this form, see, for example, David S. Law and Wen-Chen Chang, "The Limits of Transnational Judicial Dialogue" (2011) 86 Washington Law Review 523.

the political elite, as in the case of China. The more generous opportunity of the constitution-making process, however, can generate a broader national constitutional dialogue, as in the case of Vietnam and Cuba. The impact of the constitutional dialogue is determined by the nature of authoritarian institutional settings and the balance of power between communist leaders and social forces. As communist leaders are powerful and social forces are weaker, constitutional dialogue does lead to a *revolutionary* constitutional change or the creation of a new constitutional order. In this context, social actors as rational actors would not be naïve enough to force socialist leaders to give up their power and change the regime in a violent and revolutionary way. Rather, constitutional dialogue can lead to *progressive* constitutional change within the existing socialist constitutional order as in the case of Vietnam and Cuba. The constitutional dialogue itself presents a *cultural* constitutional change, as it indicates the move from a repressive to a more dialogical relationship between the government and the citizens, and facilitates an increased awareness of the public constitutional values.

D. Transnational Influence

Constitutional building, especially in the twenty-first century, is not an exclusively domestic affair but subject to transnational influence. Transnational influence can be a factor triggering constitutional change, as elaborated above. But, it can also be a legal element of the process of constitutional change. Regarding the latter, the transnational influence on domestic constitutional development takes two forms: the involvement of the international/transnational agencies and actors (UNDP, foreign governments, and international experts) in domestic constitutional building,[154] and the diffusion of constitutional ideas and institutions.[155]

Transnational influence is evident in constitutional change in socialist countries. Constitution-making in Vietnam, Laos, and Cuba involves transnational actors and ideas both outside and within the socialist circles. Transnational involvement in constitution-making in Vietnam is mainly outside the socialist circles due to the limit of the pre-existing experience of constitution-making inside the socialist world after the fall of the Soviet Union. Other subsequent experience of constitution-making in Laos and Cuba engages with the pre-existing socialist experience and beyond. In China and North Korea, constitutional amendments

[154] Cheryl Saunders, "International Involvement in Constitution Making" (2019) University of Melbourne Legal Studies Research Paper No. 839 <https://ssrn.com/abstract=3414698> or <http://dx.doi.org/10.2139/ssrn.3414698 >; Tom Ginsburg, "Constitutional Advice and Transnational Legal Order" in *Constitution-Making and Transnational Legal Order* (Gregory Shaffer, Tom Ginsburg, and Terence C. Halliday (eds), Cambridge University Press 2019).

[155] Cheryl Saunders, "Transplants in Public Law" in *The Unity of Public Law? Doctrinal, Theoretical and Comparative Perspectives* (Mark Elliott, Jason N.E. Varuhas, and Shona Wilson Stark (eds), Hart 2018) 257–78; Goderis and Mila Versteeg, "The Diffusion of Constitutional Rights" (n 70) 1.

are either exceptional or isolationist, but are not immune from transnational influences. The idea of human rights, for example, is adopted in the constitutions of these countries through amendments.

To make sense of the transnational influence on domestic constitutional development, Vicki Jackson introduces a useful triad of postures—Convergence, Resistance, and Engagement, which captures the courts' different attitudes in response to the influence of international law and foreign law in domestic adjudication.[156] Like judges, constitution-makers have similar postures in their response to external influences. The transnational influence on socialist constitutional change can be conceptualized within Jackson's extended three models.

1. Convergence

In the Convergence Model, the constitutions operate as an instrument to implement transnational and international norms. In this regard, constitution-makers favor the consistence of some substantive contents of the constitutions with transnational or international standards. A typical example is the attitude to the convergence of the bill of rights with international human rights treaties.[157] This convergence is motivated by both normative force and instrumental consideration. In the first instance, the normative, cosmopolitan value of human rights and human dignity may motivate the posture of convergence.[158] But, the attitude to convergence with universal human rights standards may be driven by instrumental signaling: to gain international legitimacy, constitution-makers incorporate human rights according to international standards to send an authoritative message to the outsider that the regime is a part of the civilized and humane world which respects human rights.[159] Human rights can be used as a signal since the language of human rights is normally vague, and hence it is difficult to gauge the extent to which the human rights commitment is realized. Due to constitutional ambiguity, formal constitutional incorporation of universal human rights does not necessarily compel the governments to realize human rights in practice.

[156] Vicki C. Jackson, "Constitutional Comparisons: Convergence, Resistance, Engagement" (2005) 119 Harvard Law Review 109, 128, 112–15; Vicki C. Jackson, "Transnational Challenges to Constitutional Law: Convergence, Resistance, Engagement" (2007) 35 Federal Law Review 161, 164–77. See also, Jackson *supra* note 14, 8–10. The below sections on convergence, resistance, and engagement are the adaption and the extension from relevant theoretical elaborations in my article, Bui Ngoc Son "You, the People: Cuba's International Constitution" (2020) 52 *NYU Journal of International Law and Politics* (forthcoming).

[157] Jackson, "Transnational Challenges to Constitutional Law" (n 156) 133, 116. See also Tushnet, "The Inevitable Globalization of Constitutional Law" (n 56) 987 (discussing "the convergence among national constitutional systems in their structures and in their protections of fundamental human rights.")

[158] Jackson, "Transnational Challenges to Constitutional Law" (n 156) 133, 167.

[159] Ibid.; Elkins, Ginsburg, and Simmons, *The Endurance* of *National Constitutions* (n 1) 80, 81 ("Signalling refers to the idea that constitutional laws, as the highest legal instrument in a state, send a message about the priority of particular policies").

The possible gap between formal commitment and realization of human rights has given rise to academic discussion on whether human rights treaties and their constitutional incorporation matter. Oona A. Hathaway argues that "ratification of human rights treaties appears to have little favorable impact on individual countries' practices."[160] In contrast, Elkins, Ginsburg, and Simmons find that ratification of human rights treaties results in not only constitutional incorporation of human rights but also better performance of human rights practices because once constitutionalized, rights "become a tool for domestic legal as well as political mobilization."[161] Situating somewhere in the middle, Chilton and Versteeg argue that not all constitutional rights are equally effective, and in particular, find that organizational rights (e.g. the right to form political parties, the right to unionize, the freedom of association, the freedom of religion, the freedom of expression, and the freedom of movement) are surprisingly effective.[162] This is mainly because these rights are less ambiguous and can be claimed by citizens in a more straightforward manner than the personal, social, economic rights.

My contention is that constitutional rights do have a signaling function, but this function is varied. First, countries in which their whole political legitimacy and social and economic development depend on the international recognition of universal standards would have more incentive to use human rights as a signal. Second, regime type matters. As Ginsburg argues, in the international realm, new democracies, which may lack the confidence of the internal public, may constitutionalize human rights as a pre-commitment to "lock- in" democracy domestically.[163] In this regard, rights operate as an internal pre-commitment rather than an external signal. In contrast, authoritarian regimes such as those in the socialist states, which have no commitment to transition into a liberal democracy, may constitutionalize human rights to signal externally. This is mainly because authoritarian regimes are often criticized by international actors for their domestic human rights situation.[164] To counter such criticisms and to legitimize the existing regime in the eyes of international audiences, authoritarian states may constitutionalize rights to send an authoritative message to the outsiders that they even respect human rights at the highest level of the law.

All current constitutions of the five socialist countries incorporate the universal concept of human rights, and this can be understood as Convergence. By

[160] Oona A. Hathaway, "Do Human Rights Treaties Make a Difference" (2002) 111 Yale Law Journal 1935, 1941.

[161] Elkins, Ginsburg, and Simmons, *The Endurance* of *National Constitutions* (n 1) 80, 69.

[162] Adam S. Chilton and Mila Versteeg, "Do Constitutional Rights Make a Difference" (2016) 60 American Journal of Political Science 575, 575–6.

[163] Tom Ginsburg, "Locking in Democracy: Constitutions, Commitment, and International Law" (2006) 38 New York University Journal of International Law and Politics 707, 712.

[164] Jamie J. Gruffydd-Jones, "Citizens and Condemnation: Strategic Uses of International Human Rights Pressure in Authoritarian States" (2019) 52 Comparative Political Studies 579, 582–4 (discussing international criticisms on human rights in authoritarian states).

this incorporation, these socialist countries signal to the outside world that they respect human rights as a normative universal value shared by the civilized world. This signaling is instrumental to the support and acceptance of the international community to the socialist political regime and the socialist models of social and economic development. In addition, the socialist constitutions signal a human rights commitment to gainsay international criticisms of the human rights situation in their countries.

When rights are used as a signaling tool, one may question their meaning in socialist constitutional politics. Without judicial review, constitutional rights can be implemented through legislation or at least inform law-making processes.[165] In addition, due to complex dynamics, once rights are constitutionalized, they may have their own life beyond a centralized control or the regime's anticipation. The socialist states may use rights as a signal, but their citizens and international actors may employ rights as a discursive and mobilizing tool (perhaps except for North Korea). International actors (e.g. US Council on Human Rights, *Human Rights Watch*, and foreign governments, and dissidents abroad) as well as local citizens may invoke the constitutional language of human rights to evaluate the local reality of human rights practice and mobilize for the realization of constitutional rights. The international and domestic discourse and mobilization may exert pressure on the incremental implementation of constitutional commitments to human rights.

2. Resistance

Global constitutional values are not merely adopted but also resisted by local actors. Leading constitutional comparatists, such as Jackson, Tushnet, Scheppele, and Choudhry,[166] are more balanced in their approaches, discussing both positive and negative responses to transnational constitutional influence. Jackson, for example, demonstrates several sources for Resistance to citing transnational or international sources in national constitutional interpretation. These include: the understanding of constitution as self-constituting and self-expressive, the understanding of law as autochthonous identity, several interpretative theories (such as originalism, contractarianism, popular sovereignty, and majoritarianism), and political resistance (nation-building, western dominance, and cultural exceptionalism).[167] However, Jackson focuses on constitutional adjudication.

[165] This is not exceptional to the socialist world. See Webber et al (n 109)

[166] Vicki C. Jackson, *Constitutional Engagement in A Transnational Era* (Oxford University Press 2010); Tushnet, "The Inevitable Globalization of Constitutional Law" (n 56); Kim Lane Scheppele, "Aspirational and Aversive Constitutionalism: The Case for Studying Cross-Constitutional Influence Through Negative Models" (2003) 1 International Journal of Constitutional Law 296; Sujit Choudhry, "The Lochner Era and Comparative Constitutionalism" (2004) 2 International Journal of Constitutional Law 1.

[167] For more details, see Jackson (n 166) 19–30. For Asian cases, see Li-ann Thio, "Reception and Resistance: Globalisation, International Law and the Singapore Constitution" (2009) 4 National Taiwan University Law Review 335; Li-ann Thio, "Beyond the 'Four Walls' in an Age of Transnational Judicial

I submit that the Resistance Model can be extended to constitutional design and discourse. Constitution-makers and the political elite, like constitutional judges, also resist transnational influence. The sources of resistance may also involve the construction of understanding about the nature of the constitution and the law, and political reasons. For example, the understanding of the constitution as expressive of national identity, or as a social contract, or as the embodiment of popular sovereignty will reasonably result in the rejection of foreign influence in constitutional design. Also, the fear of western dominance can engender political resistance to western constitutional influence in constitutional development in the developing countries of the global south. Political interests are also the source of resistance to transnational constitutional influence. Tushnet observes that: "Elite preferences can counter pressures towards the globalization of domestic constitutional law."[168] In theory, for the political incentive of legitimacy or the material incentive of attracting foreign investment by a constitutional commitment for the protection of property rights,[169] several socialist states may also adopt global constitutional norms. However, "political elites willing to forgo the economic benefits of inflows of investment or high-level human capital, so as to ensure that their political power is not diminished by constitutionalizing civil rights and liberties,"[170] and concomitantly, creating judicial institution to enforce these rights and liberties.

The Resistance Model in constitutional design and discourse resonates with Scheppele's idea of "aversive constitutionalism." In her account, "cross-constitutional influence" includes both positive and negative sides.[171] The manifestation of both sides is also varied. Positive responses to cross-constitutional influence include these ideas: "taken entire, reverently accepted, reinvented through bricolage, mistranslated, misunderstood, and mangled."[172] The negative responses also include various ideas, namely "refused, rejected, buried, and maligned."[173] Scheppele, however, focuses more on the negative response, which she believes, is "more crucial to the development of a constitutional sensibility" than positive constitutional adoption.[174] On that basis, she proposes the idea of "aversive constitutionalism," a strong negative model in the constitutional builders' response to cross-constitutional influence. Aversive constitutionalism "is backward-looking, proceeding from a critique of where past (or other) institutions and principles went badly wrong and taking such critiques as the negative building

Conversations: Civil Liberties, Rights Theories and Constitutional Adjudication in Malaysia and Singapore" (2006) 19 Columbia Journal of Asian Law 428.

168 Tushnet, "The Inevitable Globalization of Constitutional Law" (n 56) 996.
169 Law, "Globalization and the Future of Constitutional Rights" (n 56) 1308–13.
170 Tushnet, "The Inevitable Globalization of Constitutional Law" (n 56) 996.
171 Scheppele, "Aspirational and Aversive Constitutionalism" (n 166) 287.
172 Ibid.
173 Ibid.
174 Ibid. 298.

blocks of a new constitutional order. Aversive constitutionalism does not merely refer to those options considered second- or third-best and therefore not chosen, because in fact, there was something better. Aversive constitutionalism identifies a deeper sense of knowing who you are by knowing what you are not; it incorporates a *nation-making sense of rejection of a particular constitutional possibility*."[175] Scheppele's explanation of "aversive constitutionalism" is emphatically temporary. Constitution-builders are more informed by the constitutional past than the constitutional future and hence they have a clearer vision of what not to do than what they are going to do.[176] The negative consequence is a strong sense of constitutional refusal or resistance to past or foreign constitutional influences.[177]

I follow Jackson's idea of constitutional resistance and Scheppele's idea of "aversive constitutionalism" to underline the strong negative sense in these socialist states' reaction to transnational constitutional influence, especially in China. In the model of aversive or resistant constitutionalism, socialist constitution-designers and the political elite decline to adopt a global norm or institution not simply because it is not suitable or because there are better options, but more negatively, because they resist it as a potential threat to the socialist regime and elite power. Constitutional resistance is the consequence of the elite's negative imagination of the past and contemporary constitutional practices.

Vietnam's rejection of a constitutional court, Cuba's anti-capitalism, and in particular, China's forceful anti-constitutionalism campaign provide good examples of resistant constitutionalism. These socialist countries resist western-style constitutional institutions not merely because they are unsuitable or because there are better alternative institutions. There is a more negative sense here: it is resisted as a consequence of the political elite's construction of a negative understanding of the western institutions of liberal constitutionalism as a dangerous device that will threaten both their instrumental interests and the progressive aspiration to achieve socialism.

3. Engagement

The third posture, Engagement, lies somewhere between the other two. It neither rejects nor converges with the external standards. "The engagement model values the insights of foreign and international law, but without necessarily placing a thumb on the scale in any one direction."[178] In the Engagement Model, constitution-makers may consider but are not controlled by the external standards.

Transnational influence within the socialist circles can be explained as the Engagement Model. Laos and Cuba engage with China's constitutional experience,

[175] Ibid. 300 (original italic).
[176] Ibid. 300.
[177] Ibid. 300.
[178] Jackson, "Transnational Challenges to Constitutional Law" (n 156) 171.

and particularly with that of Vietnam. They carefully study and learn from their experience, but do not converge with them. Consequently, new constitutions in Laos and Cuba have adopted several institutions from China and Vietnam (e.g. local government's elected bodies and private ownership), but have not entirely copied these institutions. The adopted institutions are modified and contextualized within the receipt countries.

The transnational constitutional engagement of the socialist countries can be explained as the legacy of the international communist movement. China, Laos, Vietnam, and Cuba all engaged in this transnational political movement, and this historical base consolidates their contemporary diplomatic connection, including constitutional engagement. In addition, common legal origin, geographic proximity, trading relationships, and military alliances are also relevant.[179] Laos and Cuba have practical reasons to consult on constitutional experience from the countries which share their socialist legal system, the socialist political regime, and the socialist constitutional system. Also, geographic proximity (Laos, China, and Vietnam) enables the easy interaction and exchange of constitutional experiences. Moreover, China and Vietnam have become important foreign investors in Laos and Cuba, which may result in the need to adjust the constitutional arrangement along the lines of those of the trade partners, to ease cross-border transactions. Finally, military alliances are also an important factor for intra-socialist constitutional learning.

V. Conclusion: Variations

Constitutional change in the socialist states share the same progressive function: to facilitate the role of the party-state in improving the material wellbeing of living conditions. Yet, this progressive constitutional change is variously driven by a range of top-down and bottom-up dynamics. The legal form and process of change are also varied. Based on the prominent appearance of the influential factors that drive and legitimize the substantive and procedural constitutional change, five models or variations of socialist constitutional change can be identified: universal, integration, reservation, exceptional, and personal.

In the universal model, presented by the case of Vietnam, the global factors and universal norms play a prominent role in shaping and legitimatizing socialist constitutional change. Global integration to boost the national economy is the main factor of constitutional change. The process of constitutional change is influenced by the global return of constituent power, global diffusion of constitutional ideas and institutions, the international norm participation, and international

[179] Goderis and Versteeg, "The Diffusion of Constitutional Rights" (n 70) 3.

involvement. The attachment to the universal norms (e.g. human rights) legitimizes the substantive contents of the new constitution. The universal model of socialist constitutional change in Vietnam is determined by the instrumental approach to global constitutionalism to consolidate the international recognition of the legitimacy of the socialist regime and the reformist model of socio-economic development in the country.

In the integration model, presented by the case of Laos, ethnic unity prominently shapes the process and substance of socialist constitutional change. Improving the economic situation of the different ethnic groups as the material base for ethnic integration is the main function of constitutional change. The process of constitutional change involves consultation with ethnic groups. The attachment to a single one people (the "multi-ethnic Lao people") is the basis for constitutional legitimacy. Ethnic diversity in Laos is the main factor of the integration model of the socialist constitutional change.

In the reservation model, presented by the case of Cuba, the reservation of the historical achievement prominently features the process and substance of constitution-making. To realize the commitments of the Revolution is the main concern of constitutional change. Public participation through consultation and referendum is shaped by the legacy of the people's engagement in and the commitment to direct democracy in the Revolution. The attachment to the revolutionary commitments is the basis for the constitution's legitimacy. The reservation model of socialist constitutional change in Cuba is determined by its unique Revolution and its Caribbean Marxism.

In the exceptional model, presented by the case of China, the aspiration and attitude to a distinctive development model prominently shapes constitutional change. The notion of building socialism with local Chinese characteristics drives constitutional change. The process of constitutional change prominently diverges from the global practice. The attachment to local socialist ideologies is the foundation for the legitimacy of the constitution. China's achievement of national economic development and its prominent role in the global order determine its exceptional constitutional moves.

In the personal model of socialist constitutional change, presented by the case of North Korea, a particular leader's power and ideology prominently shape the constitutional change. Leadership change is normally the main reason for constitutional change. The process of constitutional change is initiated and controlled by a single leader. The substance of constitutional change consolidates the personal power and historical position of particular leaders. The attachment to a particular leader's historical role and achievement is the basis for the constitution's legitimacy.

This classification of various models of socialist constitutional change is emphatic rather than exclusive. It emphasizes the prominent role of a particular element but does not exclude the appearance of other elements which may be less prominent. For example, in the universal model, there may be some exceptional move, but exceptionalism does not dominate the process and substance of constitution-making. Leadership change may be a factor of this exceptional model of constitutional change, but personal power may not dominate this model. Global elements may appear but not in a prominent way in integration, reservation, exceptional, and even personalist models.

2
Socialist Constitutional Identity

Introduction

The Cold War was characterized by the ideological/ideational conflict between Western liberalism and communism. This was embodied in the constitutional sphere as the antagonism between liberal constitutionalism and socialist constitutional theory. Liberal constitutionalism, the conflation of enlightenment liberalism and constitutionalism, is a set of concepts, principles, and practices of a legally limited government in the name of individual liberty.[1] The institutional design to constrain governmental power (separation of power, checks and balances, and the entrenchment of fundamental individual rights) is normally codified in a monist written charter called the constitution.[2] Liberal constitutionalism emerged in the late eighteenth century as the consequence of the American and French Revolutions,[3] was globally diffused after the fall of the Berlin Wall in the late twentieth century,[4] and has arguably regressed in different corners of the globe in recent years.[5]

Socialist constitutional theory, rooted in Marxism-Leninism and Soviet constitutional tradition, is a set of constitutional concepts and principles of a socialist state as the transitional step toward a communist society.[6] In contrast to liberal constitutionalism, socialist constitutional theory anticipates institutional design (the vanguard role of the communist party, democratic centralism as opposed to separation power, state-granted citizens' rights, and state-controlled economy) for "proletarian dictatorship" rather than constrained power and pursues collective social-economic goals rather than

[1] András Sajó and Renáta Uitz, *The Constitution of Freedom: An Introduction to Legal Constitutionalism* (Oxford University Press 2017) 13.

[2] Ibid. English constitutionalism is based on unwritten constitution. See A.V. Dicey, *Comparative Constitutionalism* (J.W.F. Allison (ed.), Oxford University Press 2013) Chapter 1.

[3] Dieter Grimm, *Constitutionalism: Past, Present, and Future* (Oxford University Press 2016) 16.

[4] Bruce Ackerman, "The Rise of World Constitutionalism" (1997) 83 Virginia Law Review 711.

[5] Tom Ginsburg and Aziz Z. Huq, *How to Save a Constitutional Democracy* (Chicago University Press 2018); Mark A Graber, Sanford Levinson, and Mark Tushnet (eds), *Constitutional Democracy in Crisis?* (Oxford University Press 2018); "Symposium: The Limit of Constitutionalism- Global Perspective" (2018) 85 The University of Chicago Law Review.

[6] Chris Osakwe, "The Common Law of Constitutions of the Communist-Party States" (1977) 2 Review of Socialist Law 155.

Constitutional Change in the Contemporary Socialist World. Bui Ngoc Son, Oxford University Press (2020). © Bui Ngoc Son.
DOI: 10.1093/oso/9780198851349.001.0001.

liberal rights. A written constitution is an instrument to formalize this institutional design.

Socialist constitutional theory was embraced by: the first socialist constitution of 1917 of the Russian Soviet Federated Socialist Republic; the constitutions of all Soviet socialist republics which constituted the Union of Soviet Socialist Republics (USSR); and the constitutions of other socialist states, including the People's Republic of Bulgaria, the Hungarian People's Republic, the German Democratic Republic, the Polish People's Republic, the Socialist Republic of Rumania, the Czechoslovak Socialist Republic, the Socialist Federated Republic of Yugoslavia, the People's Republic of Albania, the Democratic Republic of Vietnam, the People's Republic of Korea, the People's Republic of China, and the Republic of Cuba.[7]

After the collapse of the Soviet Union, the former socialist states in Europe transitioned into Western-style democracies, adopting the fundamental values of liberal constitutionalism. China, Vietnam, Laos, North Korea, and Cuba remained socialist states. Laos promulgated the first socialist constitution in 1991, while the four other socialist states updated their constitutions though formal amendment. Their five socialist constitutions are informed by the fundamental values of constitutional socialism.

Before considering the constitutional change in the next part of the book, this chapter introduces fundamental features of the socialist constitutional system and considers how they manifest in socialist constitutions. These core features can be captured by the idea of constitutional identity. Constitutional identity here refers to the identity of the constitution, the sense embraced in Gary Jacobsohn's work,[8] rather than the identity of the constitutional subject as the meaning embodied in Michel Rosenfeld's work.[9] I define constitutional identity as *constitutional ideas and principles essential to a constitutional system*. This chapter demonstrates that the socialist constitutional identity includes five core elements, namely instrumentalism, vanguardism, "democratic centralism," statist rights, and statist economy, which are antithetical to liberal constitutionalism. These are the fundamental, aspirational constitutional principles and ideas characterizing all socialist constitutions, including the five current constitutions in China, Vietnam, Laos, North Korea, and Cuba.

Section I considers theoretical accounts of constitutional identity. Section II examines five socialist constitutional identities. Section III concludes with more general reflections on the implications for comparative constitutional identity.

[7] Ibid.

[8] Gary J. Jacobsohn, *Constitutional Identity* (Harvard University Press 2010).

[9] Michel Rosenfeld, *The Identity of the Constitutional Subject: Selfhood, Citizenship, Culture, and Community* (Routledge 2010).

I. Constitutional Identity

A. Definition

Constitutional identity refers to the shared constitutional principles fundamental to a polity. It is critical to an institutional structure and its workings. It is a part of what Francis Fukuyama calls the "shared mental models," which he conceives as "critical in facilitating large-scale collective action."[10] Douglas North also states that: "Ideas and ideologies matter, and institutions play a major role in determining just how much they matter. Ideas and ideologies shape the subjective mental constructs that individuals use to interpret the world around them and make choices."[11] Constitutional identity shapes the formulation of an institutional model and its workings. Therefore, a study on constitutional identity change is crucial to understanding the possibilities and constraints of institutional and functional changes.

The concept of "constitutional identity," advanced in the work of Gary Jacobsohn, Michel Rosenfeld, and others, is prominent in contemporary comparative constitutional theory.[12] Jacobsohn argues that "the concept of constitutional identity should be at the center of constitutional theory."[13]

A commentator distinguishes between two ideas of constitutional identity: identity of the people and identity of the constitution.[14] Rosenfeld represents the former, while Jacobsohn represents the latter. Professor Rosenfeld conceptualizes constitutional identity as the identity of the constitutional subject or the people which has "emerged in complex and ambiguous relationship with other relevant identities, such as national, ethnic, religious, or cultural identity."[15] Rosenfeld offers a thoughtful and philosophically sophisticated theory of the constitutional subject, which is more relevant to the idea of "constitutional pluralism." However, for the idea of constitutional identity, his theory has to grapple with a number of questions. Who constitutes the people? Are the people really the constitutional subject? In particular, who are the authors of authoritarian constitutions that are

[10] Francis Fukuyama, *The Origins of Political Order* (Farrar, Straus and Giroux 2011) 442.

[11] Douglas C. North, *Institutions, Institutional Change and Economic Performance* (Cambridge University Press 1990) 111.

[12] Jacobsohn, *Constitutional Identity* (n 8); Rosenfeld, *The Identity of the Constitutional Subject* (n 9); Michel Troper, "Behind the Constitution? The Principle of Constitutional Identity in France" in *Constitutional Topography: Values and Constitutions* (András Sajó and Renata (eds), Eleven International Publishing 2010) 187; Michel Rosenfeld (ed.), *Constitutionalism, Identity, Difference, and Legitimacy* (Duke University Press 1994); Mark Tushnet, "How Do Constitutions Constitute Constitutional Identity" (2010) 8 International Journal of Constitutional Law 67.

[13] Jacobsohn, *Constitutional Identity* (n 8) 3.

[14] José L. Martí, "Two Different Ideas of Constitutional Identity: Identity of the Constitution v. Identity of the People" in *National Constitutional Identity and European Integration* (Alejandro Saiz Arnaiz and Carina Alcoberro Llivina (eds), Intersentia 2013) 17.

[15] Michel Rosenfeld, "The Identity of the Constitutional Subject" (1994–1995) 16 Cardozo Law Review 1049.

not ordained by "we the people"? How to distinguish constitutional identity as the identity of people with national, cultural, religious, and moral identities? If constitutional identity collapses into one or more of these identities, is it still a distinctive subject for constitutional inquiry? For these confusing questions, this study does not attempt to pursue the identity of the people as the subject of constitutions.

Instead, I am more concerned with the identity of the constitution as presented in Jacobsohn's work. For Jacobsohn, constitutional identity refers to constitutional goals, aspirations, and commitments that a political community pursues which are normally codified in a national constitutional text.[16] Therefore, "to establish the identity of a constitution, it obviously makes sense to scrutinize carefully the text itself. This provides us with a documentary transcript of how a particular group of framers provided for the governance of their polity, and it often includes their aspirations for its subsequent development."[17] Jacobsohn distinguishes generic and specific constitutional identity. Generic constitutional identity refers to universal attributes of constitutionalism, while specific constitutional identity refers to distinctive features of a particular constitutional system. He insists that: "All constitutional polities represent a blend of characteristics revealing what is particular to the constitutional culture as well as what are widely viewed as common attributes of a universal culture of constitutionalism."[18] Jacobsohn, however, focuses more on specific constitutional identity.[19]

Jacobsohn argues that "the concept of constitutional identity should be at the center of constitutional theory."[20] If so, constitutional identity must be a distinctive concept. First, it must have some features which are different from the concepts of national or cultural identities, although the differentiation is not always easy. For this purpose, I submit that the concept of constitutional identity must be *distinctively constitutional* so that it can be distinguished from the concepts of national or cultural identity. Moreover, the concept of constitutional identity must be *distinctively identitarian* so that it can be distinguished from other constitutional concepts like "unwritten constitution" or "living originalism" which is also concerned with deep constitutional principles.[21]

With that in mind, I define constitutional identity as *constitutional ideas and principles essential to a constitutional system*. It is characterized by the following features. First, constitutional identity is about *philosophical ideas and principles*. It

[16] Ibid. 348.
[17] Ibid. 348.
[18] Ibid. 22.
[19] Ibid. 18.
[20] Jacobsohn, *Constitutional Identity* (n 8) 9.
[21] Akhil R. Amar, *America's Unwritten Constitution: The Precedents and Principles We Live By* (Basic Books 2012). For review of this book and the author's response, see David A. Strauss, "Not Unwritten, After All" (2013) 126 Harvard Law Review 1532; Akhil R. Amar, "American Constitutionalism—Written, Unwritten, and Living" (2013) 126 Harvard Law Review 195. Jack M. Balkin, *Living Originalism* (Harvard University Press 2011).

exists at the fundamental level, resonating with what political scientists variously called "public philosophies," "public sentiments," "deep core," or "worldview" that underpin daily politics "with organizing ideas, values, principles, of knowledge and society."[22] Second, constitutional identity is *constitutional* in the sense that it refers to deep constitutional ideas about the nature of constitution, constitutional structure, constitutional rights, and socio-economic constitutional principles that underpin quotidian constitutional practices, which are normally codified in a nation's constitutional text. Third, constitutional identity is *identitarian* in the sense that the philosophical constitutional ideas present the beliefs about long-term goals, aspirations, and commitments constituting the essence of a constitutional polity.[23]

Although Professor Jacobsohn places constitutional identity at the center of constitutional inquiry, he mainly focuses on the specific constitutional identity of democracies (the United States, India, Israel, and Ireland).[24] This raises the question of whether non-democratic states can acquire constitutional identity. If the answer is negative, then constitutional identity inquiry and, more generally, constitutional inquiry will be centralized around a limited set of American, European, and a few other institutional settings that have met the basic requirements of constitutionalism, and must ignore a number of constitutional experiences in different corners of the globe. My point is that a polity need not be constitutionalist or democratic, or both, to acquire constitutional identity. Every constitutional system has ideas and principles fundamental to its existence, which are not simply ignored by autocrats at will. Authoritarian polities are also committed to fundamental goals and aspirations codified in their constitutions which inform constitutional politics, by which they acquire distinctive constitutional identity. Some concrete constitutional rules may be irrelevant to the real working of authoritarian leaders and the daily lives of citizens, but the operation of the whole authoritarian polity is necessarily directed by fundamental and aspirational constitutional ideas codified in the nation's constitution. Therefore, constitutional identity inquiry should not ignore authoritarian regimes, including socialist regimes.

B. Dynamics

Constitutional identity is not fixed, but changeable. Jacobsohn draws on Alasdair Macintyre's theory of tradition to develop a theory on the dynamic of

22 Vivien A. Schmidt, "Discursive Institutionalism: The Explanatory Power of Ideas and Discourse" (2008) 11 Annual Review of Political Science 303, 306.

23 Jacobsohn particularly underlines the aspirational aspect of constitutional identity. For his extensive treatment on this, see Gary J. Jacobsohn, *The Supreme Court and the Decline of Constitutional Aspiration* (Rowman & Littlefield Publishers 1986). For other discussions on constitutional aspiration, see "Symposium Constitutional Interpretation and Aspirations to a Good Society: The Natural Rights-Based Justification for Judicial Review" (2001) 69 Fordham Law Review 5, 2119.

24 Jacobsohn, *Constitutional Identity* (n 8) 18.

constitutional identity. For Macintyre, "a living tradition is … a historically extended, socially embodied argument, and an argument precisely in part about the goods which constitute that tradition."[25] He considers tradition as the embodiment of "continuities of conflicts."[26] In his understanding, "a tradition becomes mature only insofar as its adherents confront and find a national way through or around these encounters with radical different and incompatible positions."[27] Jacobsohn draws on Macintyre's theory of tradition as a living thing presenting "continuities and conflicts" to support his theory regarding the nature and dynamics of constitutional identity. He argues that constitutional identity "emerges *dialogically* and represents a mix of political aspirations and commitments that are expressive of a nation's past, as well as the determination of those within society who seek in some ways to transcend the past."[28]

To Jacobsohn, the dynamics of constitutional identity are animated by "the universal constitutional condition, which is that in one way or another all constitutions confront or embody the problem of disharmony."[29] He asserts that "the 'disharmonic constitution' does not refer to the incoherence of constitutions (though that may indeed be the condition of some) but to the dissonance within and around the constitution that is key to understanding its identity."[30] So, there are two aspects of the disharmonic constitution: internal and external. The text of a national constitution is itself disharmonic in the sense that it encompasses competing commitments or "contradiction and imbalances."[31] So, the exploration of constitutional identity requires the understanding of alternative visions and aspirations internal to the constitutional text. The external aspect refers to the gap between the aspirational constitutional commitments or ideals and the reality, or in Jacobsohn's parlance, "the lack of agreement evident in the sharp discontinuities that frame the constitution's relationship to the surrounding society."[32] Constitutional disharmony provokes change in constitutional identity. Jacobsohn states that "to apprehend constitutional identity is to see its dynamic quality, which results from the interplay of forces seeking either to introduce greater harmony into the constitutional equation or, contrariwise, to create further disharmony."[33]

Jacobsohn's theory of constitutional disharmony is heuristic to explore constitutional identity change. Other scholars share the common views, although they may use different terms. Hanna Pitkin, for example, contends that: "To understand

[25] Alasdair Macintyre, *After Virtue: A Study in Moral Theory* (University of Notre Dame Press 1981) 207.
[26] Ibid. 6.
[27] Alasdair Macintyre, *Whose Justice? Which Rationality?* (University of Notre Dame Press 1988) 327.
[28] Jacobsohn, *Constitutional Identity* (n 8) 7.
[29] Ibid. 86–7.
[30] Ibid 15.
[31] Ibid. 87. For example, the commitments to both positive and negative rights, ibid 149.
[32] Ibid.
[33] Ibid. 88.

what a constitution is, one must look not to some crystalline core or essence of unambiguous meaning but precisely at the ambiguities, the specific oppositions that this specific concept helps us to hold in tension."[34] Ideology theory in legal sociology also makes similar claims.[35] Alan Hunt argues that: "An ideology is not a unitary entity. It draws its power from its ability to connect and combine diverse mental elements (concepts and ideas) into combinations that influence and structure the perception and cognition of social agents."[36] The idea of disharmony also resonated with the thesis of Marxist dialectic on conflicts as the source of change, which has influenced the political ideology of socialist regimes.

The theory of constitutional disharmony seemingly contradicts the Confucian philosophy of social harmony which has informed political culture in such countries as China and Vietnam. In fact, Confucianism promotes the idea of "harmony but not sameness" (*Analects*, 13:23). Chenyang Li's recent comprehensive treatment of the theme suggests that, in Confucian philosophy, harmony exists with creative tension and does not exclude conflicts and differences.[37] In particular, according to the Book of Change or *I Ching*, one of the Confucian Five Classics,[38] the logics of change essentially lie in the interaction of the two conflicting forces called *Yin* and *Yang*.

However, several points in Jacobsohn's theory must be qualified and refined. To begin with, constitutional identity dynamics are defined by the dialogical interactions between local (specific) and global (generic) constitutional identity. The universal constitutional condition of disharmony, in one way or another, manifests itself in all constitutions, not necessarily liberal constitutions. This is evident if we consider the generic and specific contents of constitutional identity. The legal codification of both generic and specific values and principles in a single charter constitutes conflicting aspirations and commitments. Constitutional identity emerges as the consequence of the dialogical interactions between generic and specific aspirations and commitments. Moreover, within a particular constitutional polity, there are pluralized particularistic values and principles that govern the polity whose dialogical interactions create the dynamics of constitutional identity.

However, although Jacobsohn recognizes that the disharmony between generic and specific aspiration is the condition of change in constitutional identity, he

[34] Hanna F. Pitkin, "The Idea of a Constitution" (1987) 37 Journal of Legal Education 167, 167.

[35] Nicos Poulantzas, *Political Power and Social Classes* (T O'Hagan tr, New Left Books 1973); Alan Hunt, "The Ideology of Law: Advances and Problems in Recent Applications of Ideology to the Analysis of Law" (1985) 19 Law & Society Review 11; Maureen Cain, "Gramsci, The State and the Place of Law" in *Legality, Ideology and the State* (David Sugerman (ed.), Academic Press 1983). I thank John Gillespie for drawing my attention to this literature.

[36] Hunt, *The Ideology of Law* (n 35) 16.

[37] Chenyang Li, *The Confucian Philosophy of Harmony* (Routledge 2014) 12–13.

[38] Surprisingly, this Confucian Classic is extensively explored by a Yale constitutional law professor. Jack Balkin, *The Laws of Change: I Ching and the Philosophy of Life* (Sybil Creek Press 2009).

directs most of his attention to the disharmony of specific constitutional identity. The explanation for this is that his theory is developed on the experience of constitutionalist states (the United States, India, Israel, and Ireland) whose constitutions already incorporate the generic requirements of constitutionalism. If constitutional identity is understood as the identity of the constitution, not the identity of the people as constitutional authors, even non-constitutionalist polities can also acquire constitutional identity. Authoritarian polities are also committed to fundamental aspirations codified in their constitutions, which inform constitutional politics and citizens' activities. Some concrete constitutional rules may be irrelevant to the practice of the authoritarian systems and the daily lives of the citizens. However, the operation of the whole authoritarian polity is inevitably driven by the constitutionally-confided fundamental aspirations, although these aspirations may be imposed by authoritarian leaders. For example, although a Vietnamese citizen may not be aware of a concrete constitutional provision for a certain right, or a Vietnamese political leader may not be aware of a specific constitutional rule on state structure, the whole of the Vietnamese community is inevitably affected by the fundamental commitment to socialist aspirations codified in the nation's constitution.

Fundamental constitutional commitments of authoritarian regimes may not have the intention of limiting the state's power. They may be specific and disharmonic with generic constitutionalist aspirations. Socialist constitutional systems have been constructed on the base of specific kinds of underlying constitutional ideas and principles, and by that, they acquire a distinctive constitutional identity. The disharmony between generic and specific aspirations is an important source of constitutional identity change in socialist polities. The gap between socialist and global constitutional aspirations has engendered efforts to bridge this gap. Therefore, to understand the dynamics of constitutional identity in socialist states, it is important to explore the disharmony between specific socialist constitutional aspirations and generic constitutionalism. I call this *normative constitutional disharmony*. Essentially, constitutional identity change is animated by the universal constitutional condition presented by three elements: internal, external, and normative constitutional disharmonies.

Constitutional disharmony is crucial to the inevitable constitutional globalization. Jacobsohn contends that: "This disharmonic jurisprudential context establishes the incentives, opportunities, and costs inherent in the practice of looking abroad for interpretive inspiration."[39] Consequently, local actors may engage in transnational and global dialogue in defining constitutional meanings and constitutional identity.[40] However, this is not necessarily limited to constitutional interpretation. Domestic constitutional disharmony incentivizes social and institutional actors to

[39] Jacobsohn, *Constitutional Identity* (n 8) 142.
[40] Ibid. 112–17.

look into the pool of global ideas and experiences to seek constitutional consistency by formal constitution-making (the case of South Africa offers a good example).[41] In developing countries in particular (like the socialist countries that are the subject of my enquiry), the gap between national constitutions and global standards of constitutionalism creates the incentives and opportunities for looking abroad for constitution-making or constitutional amendment.

While the global spread of constitutional ideas is inevitable, these ideas are situated within the local context and balanced with local ideas. Jacobsohn argues that global constitutional norms "need to be reconciled with the particularistic commitments of local traditions and practices; the contours of constitutional identity will, to a large extent, reflect how these disharmonies get resolved."[42] The consequence is the interaction and balancing of global and local constitutional identities.

For Jacobsohn, constitutional identity is formulated and evolves through "dialogical enterprises" comprising "interpretive and political activity" occurring in public and private domains.[43] Courts are the principal but not the exclusive shapers and articulators of constitutional identity.[44] A wide range of actors (courts, legislature, executive, and people) engage in constitutional dialogue in the determination and clarification of substantial constitutional meanings and constitutional identities.[45] This argument is supported by the theories of popular constitutionalism developed by such American constitutionalists as Tushnet and Larry Kramer.[46] However, as Heinz Klug rightly comments, "judicial decisions remain at the core of Jacobsohn's empirical analysis."[47] Jacobsohn's theory is informed by the constitutional experience in stable, liberal polities, where judicial review operates as the mechanism of constitutional change. Consequently, he has not yet substantively accounted for the possibility of a non-judicial dialogical mechanism of change in constitutional identity.

In socialist nations where judicial review is absent, constitutional change is normally undertaken through formal constitution-making and constitutional amendment. In particular, the moment of constitution-making creates space for constitutional dialogue among different political actors. The theory of the disharmonic constitution therefore must incorporate constitutional dialogue during the moment of formal constitutional change. Constitutional dialogue at such moments consists not of an elaboration of the meanings of the existing

[41] Ibid. 113. Jacobsohn explains that the South Africa Constitution of 1996 incorporates the international norm of "equal treatment of individuals under law." Ibid.

[42] Jacobsohn, *Constitutional Identity* (n 8) 113.

[43] Ibid. 108.

[44] Ibid.

[45] For a recent account of constitutional dialogue in Asian context, see Po Jen Yap, *Constitutional Dialogue in Common Law* (Oxford University Press 2015).

[46] Mark Tushnet, *Taking the Constitution Away from the Court* (Princeton University Press 1999); Larry Kramer, *The People Themselves: Popular Constitutionalism and Judicial Review* (Oxford University Press 2004).

[47] Heinz Klug, "Constitutional Identity and Change" (2011) 47 Tulsa Law Review 46.

constitution through the dialogical interaction of judges with other political actors, but of dialogical interaction between the public and the government which envisages the meaning of a normative constitution or a desirable constitutional order by taking the existing constitution as a starting point. Constitutional disharmony operates as the condition of the dynamics of constitutional dialogue.

Furthermore, Jacobsohn tends to focus on judicial engagement in transnational dialogue. But there is also transnational engagement in constitution-making and constitutional amendment. Foreign and global sources are important for developing countries, such as socialist countries, which develop their constitutional identity by bridging the disharmonic gap between nation-specific constitutional identity and generic constitutional identity. However, this need not take place by judicial engagement, as judicial review of constitutional questions is absent in contemporary socialist countries. Alternatively, the constitution-making and amendment process allows political actors, constitution-makers, and social actors to engage in a transnational constitutional dialogue in which global and local sources disharmoniously interact and seek balance, provocative to the change in constitutional identity.

II. Socialist Constitutional Identity

A. Instrumentalism

A constitution has multiple functions: it articulates collective ideals and aspirations, creates institutional mechanisms for effectuating future governmental actions, provides the contractual base for divergent interests, co-ordinates political and social actions, and limits governmental power.[48] The last, limiting function defines the nature of generic constitutionalism. C.H. McIlwain famously defined constitutionalism as follows: "Constitutionalism has one essential quality: it is a legal limitation on government."[49] Liberal constitutionalism, a specific type of constitutionalism, associates constitutional limitation with a social contract and natural law theory of the Enlightenment era: a liberal constitution is conceived as a social contract created by the people to establish a legal limitation on the governmental power to protect the natural rights of individuals against government encroachment.[50] In order to ensure that power holders are limited within the existing

[48] Keith E. Wittington, "Constitutionalism" in *The Oxford Handbook of Law and Politics* (Keith E. Whittington, Roger D. Kelemen, and Gregory A. Caldeira (eds), Oxford University Press 2008) 289–92 (summarizing literatures on different functions of constitution).

[49] Charles H. McIlwain, *Constitutionalism: Ancient and Modern* (The Lawbook Exchange 2005) 24.

[50] Richard A. Epstein, *The Classical Liberal Constitution* (Harvard University Press 2014) 18–19.

constitutional framework, a liberal constitution normally creates substantive and procedural entrenchments against constitutional amendment.[51]

The nature and function of socialist constitutions are conceptualized differently. This can be illustrated by the notion of constitutional instrumentalism.[52] The socialist constitutions are an instrument for the working class to: (1) legalize its power; and (2) project a program for social progress toward socialism.[53]

In the first instance, the socialist constitutions are legal documents but are very different from liberal constitutions. They create legalistic rules and principles about governance structure and citizens' rights but do not limit government[54] power. Rather, they legitimize, structuralize, and aggrandize the power of the ruling proletariat class. This instrumentalism is underpinned by the Marxist ideology of revolution. Marxism-Leninism strongly emphasizes the significance of violent revolution and class struggle in the history of the world. Marxists conceive constitutions as an instrument for the proletariat class to organize its power to struggle against the bourgeoisie. When the proletariat class seizes public power, it makes use of the constitution to organize and enhance its power. This instrumentalism is also associated with the Marxist understanding of the nature of state as a coercive organ for the ruling class to repress the ruled class. Socialist states are therefore an instrument for a dictatorship of the working class.[55]

Secondly, socialist constitutions are not purely legal documents. For a socialist polity, the most important aspects of the polity are not only state structure and rights but also a program for social progress toward socialism and ultimately, communism. Consequently, since such a program is so consequential to the polity, it needs to be formally codified in the constitution. The socialist constitutions, therefore, include programmatic, aspirational, ideological statements which lay down a socio-economic program to erect a socialist society and ultimately, to achieve communism. They proclaim the communist ideology (e.g. Marxism-Leninism), the relationships between social classes, the socialist form of the economy, and socialist goals.

Instrumentalism has important consequences for frequent formal constitutional change in the socialist world. For example, the 1918 constitution of the

[51] See for example, John R. Vile, *The Constitutional Amending Process in American Political Thought* (Praeger 1992) 158 (citing Cooley's comment on limits on constitutional amendment in the United States).

[52] On instrumentalist conception of socialist constitutions, see Mark Sidel, "Analytical Models for Understanding Constitutions and Constitutional Dialogues in Socialist Transitional States: Re-Interpreting Constitutional Dialogues in Vietnam" (2002) 6 Singapore Journal of International and Comparative Law 42.

[53] Chris Osakwe, "The Common Law of Constitutions of the Communist-Party States" (1977) 2 Review of Socialist Law 162.

[54] Jan F. Triska, "Introduction" in *Constitution of the Communist-Party States* (Jan F Triska (ed.), Hoover Institution 1968) xi ("Communist party-state constitutions do not limit the respective governments").

[55] Alex Nove, "Some Aspects of Soviet Constitutional Theory" (1949) 12 Modern Law Review 12, 13.

Russian Soviet Federative Socialist Republic was amended in 1919 and 1920, and was formally replaced by the 1924 Constitution of the Union of Soviet Socialist Republics. This, in turn, was formally replaced by the Soviet constitutions of 1936 and 1977. The 1977 Constitution was amended in 1988. The instrumental nature and functions of the socialist constitutions are the determinants of this frequent formal constitutional change. As socialist constitutions organize the power of the ruling class, they "are either amended or scrapped when there is a change in the balance of class forces in society, but not necessarily between antagonistic classes, like the bourgeoisie, on the one hand, and the working class and the peasantry, on the other. The constitution may be changed also as a result of changes in the balance of forces within friendly classes."[56] Furthermore, as the socialist constitutions are not intended to limit the state's power, they normally do not have entrenchment clauses against formal constitutional amendment (except the case of Cuba), and hence the amendment procedure is relatively easy.[57] Furthermore, since the constitutions seek to lay down a socio-economic program, they are often amended or rewritten in response to socio-economic change or a change in the leadership's socio-economic vision and plan.[58] Finally, formal constitutional change is instrumental in legitimizing changes in communist ideology or theory.[59]

B. Party Vanguardism

In liberal constitutionalism, "the will of the people is the source of authority and the basis of legitimate government."[60] This is informed by liberal theories of the social contract, which hold that a legitimate government relies on the consent of the governed. A legitimate government is created through free and equal elections. Therefore, one identity of liberal constitutionalism is "a commitment to periodic democratic elections."[61] This is connected to the notion of political pluralism, which recognizes the multiparty system. Consequently, although political parties may play an important constitutional role in reality,[62] a liberal constitutional polity normally does not entrench the leadership of any political party in its constitution. The liberal democratic constitutions which emerged in Europe after the Second World War include provisions for political parties but do not establish the

56 Cited in Osakwe, "Constitutions of the Communist-Party States" (n 53) 159.
57 Ibid. 61–2.
58 Ibid. 158.
59 Triska, "Introduction" (n 54) xi–xii
60 Louis Henkin, "A New Birth of Constitutionalism: Genetic Influences and Genetic Defects" (1993) 14 Cardozo Law Review 535.
61 Aziz Huq, Tom Ginsburg, and Mila Versteeg, "The Coming Demise of Liberal Constitutionalism?" (2018) 85 University of Chicago Law Review 238.
62 Daryl J. Levinson and Richard H. Pildes, "Separation of Parties, Not Powers" (2006) 119 Harvard Law Review 2311; Stephen Gardbaum, "Political Parties, Voting Systems, and the Separation of Powers" (2017) 65 American Journal of Comparative Law 229.

leadership of any political party, because this would undermine liberal beliefs in political pluralism, participation, and popular sovereignty.[63]

By contrast, the use of public power in the socialist world is constitutionally pre-established as the prerogative of the communist party, conceived as the "vanguard" force of the working class or ruling class of the state and the society. Vanguardism, the identity of socialist constitutions, assumes that the most ideologically and politically advanced sections of the proletariat will play a vanguard role in leading the larger sections of both the working class and other social classes in a struggle against their enemies culminating in the triumph of socialism, and eventually communism.[64] To this end, a communist party is created, and the state and the whole of society are to be placed under the stewardship of the party.[65]

The consequence is that the communist party is not a private entity of civil society, nor an electoral body like political parties in multiparty constitutional democracies, but an integral part of the polity. The constitutional significance of the communist party firstly lies in the formal constitutionalization of its vanguard role. For example, Article 126 of the 1936 Constitution of USSR defines the Communist Party of the Soviet Union (Bolsheviks), as "the vanguard of the working people in their struggle to strengthen and develop the socialist system and is the leading core of all organizations of the working people, both public and state."[66] This provision was incorporated in Article 82 of Mongolia's second constitution of 1940.[67] Article 4 of the Czechoslovak Constitution of 1960 also states that "the guiding force in society and in the state is the vanguard of the working class, the Communist Party of Czechoslovakia."[68]

The state constitution not only establishes the party vanguard role but also incorporates and is subordinate to the communist party program. The party program is conceived as a theoretical document embodying the "vanguard" thinking of the communist party which analyzes, predicts, and directs socio-economic progress toward the ultimate goal of socialism, while the state constitution codifies the party program's most important theoretical statements.[69] Consequently, "the state constitution is hierarchically inferior to the communist party program," because "the communist party is looked upon as 'the mind, the honor, and the conscience' of the people" and "the communist party is universally regarded as the motive force of society."[70] The constitutional provisions derive their source, legitimacy, value,

[63] Ingrid Van Biezen, "Constitutionalizing Party Democracy: The Constitutive Codification of Political Parties in Post-war Europe" (2011) 42 British Journal of Political Science 187.

[64] Erwin Marquit, "Dictatorship of the Proletariat and Vanguard Party in Historical Context" (2005) 18 Nature, Society, and Thought 549, 554.

[65] A. James McAdams, *Vanguard of the Revolution: The Global Idea of the Communist Party* (Princeton University Press 2017) 3.

[66] 1936 USSR Constitution, art. 126.

[67] Cited in John N. Hazard, "The Common Core of Marxian Socialist Constitution" (1981–1982) 19 San Diego Law Review 304.

[68] Cited in Ibid. 306.

[69] Osakwe, "Constitutions of the Communist-Party States" (n 53) 160–1.

[70] Ibid. 161.

and effect from the party program. In this regard, the state constitution is the supreme law of the state, but the party program is the supreme law of the whole polity.

Party vanguardism results in party-controlled constitution-making in the socialist world. Osakwe states: "In theory the constitution is a manifestation of popular will. It is an act of the people adopted through a referendum. But the practical reality of a socialist constitution is that it is a document entirely conceived by the communist party, then channelled to the government for its blessing, after which the masses are put on notice as to their right to acquiesce in the document in a national referendum."[71]

Another consequence of party vanguardism is the constitutional convention that the party is placed above the state constitution. Osakwe explains: "It is an unarticulated principle of socialist law that the provisions of the constitution are not intended to be binding upon the communist party. The constitution is the supreme law of the land only with regard to the various state agencies, social organizations other than the communist party, private individuals, and groups ... It is this special role of the Party as the only 'thinking organ' within the Soviet body politic that places it above the law which, by inference, is designed to guide the non-thinking segments of society-the state organs, the various social organizations, and the ordinary citizenry."[72]

C. Democratic Centralism

Liberal constitutionalism emerged from radical revolutions aimed at dethroning absolute monarchs. The experience of the past autocratic monarchs reminded the people not to give their power to a single hand. Through exercising their constituent power, the people created a government in which the constituted legislative, executive, and judicial powers were separated and practiced by three different institutions. Montesquieu's model of separation of the legislative, executive, and judicial powers is considered to be the necessary institutional guarantee of limited government to protect the individual's liberty in a liberal constitutional state.[73] Nowadays, the separation of power takes different forms in different liberal democratic states.[74] Despite classical and contemporary criticism of both its practical and conceptual limits,[75]

[71] Ibid.

[72] Ibid.

[73] Aileen Kavanagh, "The Constitutional Separation of Powers" in *The Philosophical Foundations of Constitutional Law* (David Dyzenhaus and Malcolm Thorburn (eds), Oxford University Press 2016) 222.

[74] Bruce Ackerman, "The New Separation of Powers" (2000) 3 Harvard Law Review 633.

[75] Christoph Moellers believes that "The contemporary academic discussion of the idea of separated powers is defined by a simple, powerful, and mistaken narrative: once upon a time, there was a 'classical' system of separated powers, in particular within the constitutional nation-states of Europe." Christoph

"the separation of powers in some form is arguably the essence of [liberal] constitutionalism."[76]

Marxist constitutional theory rejects the principle of separation of powers. First, this is due to the Marxist conception of the separation of powers as a capitalist evil. "Marxism-Leninism sees any such separation of powers as bourgeois formalism, designed to mask the exploitative character of the bourgeois state as a whole."[77] Second, the principle of the separation of power is at odds with the Marxist conception of the nature and mission of the socialist state. In Marxist theory, the socialist state is conceptualized as "a transitional arrangement whose only reason for existence is to prepare society for the full communist society, and in the meantime, its principal functions include the organization of the national economy and national defense, the creation of the 'new man', the protection of society from destruction by internal enemies—in short, the general orchestration of the national movement towards the stateless and lawless society known as communism. In order to do this, all the functional subdivisions of the state must necessarily work together."[78] Furthermore, they must work together under the orchestration of the vanguard communist party. "All the three departments of government are subordinate to the communist party from which they take their general orders and individual directives."[79]

That does not mean that there is no distribution of the three powers into different departments in the socialist world. Yet, the powers are structurally, institutionally, and personally distributed according to a distinctive socialist principle called "democratic centralism," an antithesis of Montesquieu's tripartite government. Although "both democratic and centralist ideas can be traced back to Marx and Engels,"[80] it was V.I. Lenin who integrated the two ideas to formulate democratic centralism as the principle of the communist party's organization and activity.[81] Put simply, this principle aims to combine "democratic" discussions and centralized actions. After "democratic discussion," superiors will issue a "conclusion" or order which must be obeyed without question by their inferiors.[82] Democratic centralism was then applied to constitutional design and state activity. In the constitutional realm, this principle means that state powers are centralized

Möllers, *The Three Branches: A Comparative Model of Separation of Powers* (Oxford University Press 2013) 8. See also, Laurence Claus, "Montesquieu's Mistakes and the True Meaning of Separation" (2005) 25 Oxford Journal of Legal Studies 419.

[76] Eric Barendt, "Is there a United Kingdom Constitution?" (1997) 1 Oxford Journal of Legal Studies 141. See also M.J.C. Vile, *Constitutionalism and the Separation of Powers* (Oxford University Press 1998); Eoin Carolan, *The New Separation of Powers: A Theory for the Modern State* (Oxford University Press 2009).

[77] Osakwe, "Constitutions of the Communist-Party States" (n 53) 173.

[78] Ibid.

[79] Ibid.

[80] Stephen C. Angle, "Decent Democratic Centralism" (2005) 33 Political Theory 525.

[81] Ibid.

[82] Nove, "Some Aspects of Soviet Constitutional Theory" (n 55) 19.

in the popularly elected representative body. Within this formal scheme of united power, all other state bodies are subordinate to the supreme legislature. The centralization of power in the socialist legislature is formalist rather than realistic. The communist party remains the *coryphaeus* of the unitary scheme of the powers. The legislature is the formalist forum to institutionalize and legitimatize the party's vanguard orchestration of the centralized powers. Labor divisions among the three state organs are possible, but they must work together. This socialist constitutional arrangement aims to strengthen and co-ordinate rather than constrain power.

D. Statist Rights

The ultimate goal of liberal constitutionalism is the protection of fundamental rights of individuals. Backed by natural law theories and the liberal political theories of the Enlightenment, fundamental rights are understood in the liberal sense as the universal rights inherent in an individual as a human being.[83] For a liberal constitutionalist, the constitutional protection of these universal rights is important as they protect both the *individual* from state interference so that she can "make up her own mind about what she wants to do with her life" and *society* from degeneration into authoritarianism.[84] These functions stem from the need to ward off the dangers identified by a liberal constitutionalist: "the natural tendency of unchecked government to slip toward despotism and of majorities to impose their references on all."[85] A liberal constitution materializes the commitment to individual liberty by providing for a bill of rights and institutional devices that would prevent government encroachment on these rights.[86] Once rights are constitutionally entrenched, they have a legal binding effect on government actions and are justicably enforced: government encroachment of constitutional rights is subject to constitutional review by the courts (ordinary courts or specialist constitutional courts).[87]

Socialist constitutions include a lengthy list of fundamental rights "to demonstrate the superiority of socialist democracy over bourgeois democracy" and "to prove to the world that socialism holds personal freedom and individual liberty in high esteem."[88] Differing from liberal constitutional rights, socialist constitutional rights are statist rights, that is to say rights posited by the state.[89] According

[83] András and Uitz, *The Constitution of Freedom* (n 1) 374.
[84] Ibid. 373.
[85] Ibid.
[86] Mark A. Graber, *A New Introduction to American Constitutionalism* (Oxford University Press 2013) 36.
[87] András and Uitz, *The Constitution of Freedom* (n 1) 374.
[88] Osakwe, "Constitutions of the Communist-Party States" (n 53) 190.
[89] For comparative discussion the difference between American liberal constitutional rights and fundamental rights in the Soviet Union, see Thomas E. Towe, "Fundamental Rights in the Soviet Union: A Comparative Approach" (1967) 115 University of Pennsylvania Law Review 1251.

to Osakwe, socialist constitutional rights are not inalienable natural rights but rights granted, modified, or eliminated by the state; have "social content and meaning determined by the social, economic, and political structure of a given society in which the rights in question exist and function"; are inseparable from citizens' duties and obligations to the state and the society; and are reconciled and subordinated to "the overriding interests of society at large."[90] These features of socialist constitutional rights are underpinned by Marxist legal positivism, constitutional instrumentalism, and historical materialism. Marxist legal positivism holds that rights are positively granted and withdrawn by the state. Constitutional instrumentalism suggests that rights serve as a means of realizing state policy. Inga Markovits indicates that socialist constitutional rights are not an entitlement conferred upon autonomous individuals but a proclamation of state policy.[91] A constitutional right to work, for example, "does not entitle a citizen to sue the state for employment," but is the constitutional pronouncement of the state labor policy which is not judicially enforceable, although it may "find reflection in court decisions that protect employment and people who work."[92] One consequence of the instrumentalist nature of socialist constitutional rights is that they do not function as limits upon a government, but are rather themselves limited by the government. The realization of the socialist constitutional rights as state policy and the concomitant duties to the state empowers the state to interfere in individual lives, and to justify such interference.[93] Historical materialism, which emphasizes the material determination of the historical evolution of society, justifies specific meanings and applications of constitutional rights in particular circumstances.

E. Statist Economy

Limited government goes in tandem with a free market in a liberal constitutional polity. Liberal constitutionalism prioritizes constitutional capitalism: the constitutional protection of the fundamental values of a capitalist market system, e.g. the limits of state intervention, co-operation, competition, freedom of contract, and private property rights.[94] Richard A. Epstein writes in the American context that "the classical liberal tradition of the founding generation prized the protection of

[90] Christopher Osakwe, "The Theories and Realities of Modern Soviet Constitutional Law: An Analysis of the 1977 USSR Constitution" (1979) 127 University of Pennsylvania Law Review 1390–5.
[91] Inga Markovits, "Socialist vs. Bourgeois Rights—An East-West German Comparison" (1978) 45 University of Chicago Law Review 615.
[92] Ibid. 616.
[93] Ibid. 617.
[94] Richard A. Epstein, "The Wrong Rights, or: The Inescapable Weaknesses of Modern Liberal Constitutionalism" (2018) 85 University of Chicago Law Review 407–8.

liberty and private property under a system of limited government."[95] The liberal logic is that "the best way to maximize human welfare writ large is to first limit the use of force and fraud and then to encourage and foster cooperation and competition in the markets for goods, services, and ideas."[96] These objectives can be achieved by creating constitutional rules that both limit the use of public power and recognize each individual as "both an autonomous agent who is responsible for his or her own actions and one who is entitled to reap the gains that come from the acquisition of property and the creation of successful contractual and social relations."[97]

Marxist economic theory denounces private ownership and the free market system as an evil instrument deployed by the capitalists to exploit the workers. Alternatively, to ensure the movement of the society toward socialism and ultimately communism, Marxist economic theory proposes the socialist form of the economy, which is embodied in the socialist constitutions. The socialist constitutions confirm these statist features of the socialist economy: socialist ownership and the planned economy. Socialist ownership means that the state or collective-co-operative organizations (e.g. collective farms and trade unions) are the owners of the means of production and distribution.[98] In particular, some socialist constitutions nationalize all lands, while others allow the private and collective ownership of land.[99] A related issue is that the socialist form of property ownership recognizes the ownership of personal property (property satisfying personal needs) but not private property (property generating capital).[100] A planned economy is one in which different economic units are centrally planned and managed by the state.[101] Consequently, the socialist, statist constitutional economic provisions strongly empower rather than limit the state's intervention in the economy.

III. Conclusion

Constitutional identity is a distinctive concept and a distinctive object for comparative constitutional inquiry. The prevailing trend in comparative constitutional studies is the focus on rules and institutions. However, underlying these rules and institutions are deeply constitutional ideas. A constitution implicitly or explicitly includes fundamental ideas which provide not only concrete guidance for the concrete political conduct of concrete constitutional actors, but also general directive

95 Richard A. Epstein, *The Classical Liberal Constitution* (Harvard University Press 2014) 17.
96 Epstein, "Modern Liberal Constitutionalism" (n 94) 406.
97 Ibid. 407.
98 Osakwe, "Constitutions of the Communist-Party States" (n 53) 166.
99 Ibid.
100 Ibid.
101 Ibid.

beliefs, aspirations and commitments that propel the workings of the whole constitutional system. So, a study about constitutional identity is distinctive in that it focuses not on rules and institutions but rather on deeply constitutional ideas, values, and principles. It may refer to rules and institutions as the embodiment of constitutional ideas. Constitutional identity inquiry is also different from studies on unwritten or living constitutionalism in that it takes the written constitutions seriously as the embodiments of constitutional principles. Given that constitutional identity inquiry is concerned with philosophical constitutional ideas, it may overlap to an extent with inquiry into the philosophical foundation of constitutional law.[102] However, unlike abstract constitutional philosophical inquiry, constitutional identity inquiry is more concrete, as it identifies the philosophical constitutional ideas codified in a nation's constitution and defining the essence of a given constitutional order.

Socialist constitutions have their own identities, although they are not committed to constitutionalism. Socialist constitutions have codified goals, aspirations, and commitments that the polity will pursue. In particular, the expression of constitutional identity in socialist constitutions is much stronger than in classical liberal constitutions. Classical liberal constitutions are predominantly legalistic documents and tend to include mainly judicially enforced legal norms. Liberal constitutional identities are mainly implicit in their constitutional provisions about rights and structural institutions. Liberal constitutional identities tend to be explicitly articulated in constitutional preambles. By contrast, the socialist constitutions are both legalistic documents and the codifications of a program for social progress toward socialism. It is the latter's progressive nature and function that defines the strong expression of constitutional identity in both the preambles and the body of the socialist constitutional texts. As the socialist constitutions project a socio-economic program to achieve socialism, they necessarily define the distinctively socialist principles, ideas, hopes, and aspirations that stimulate the progress of society toward the anticipated socialist paradise.

Socialist constitutions are often dismissed as merely descriptive documents. Louis Henkin, for example, states that the socialist constitutions of Eastern Europe after the Second World War "describe the kind of government and the institutions of government that have already been established and indicate plans and make promises for the future ... Ordinarily, such constitutions have not been enforceable as law and had little normative character."[103] The establishment of constitutional identities in the socialist constitutions suggests that this popular view should be revisited. The socialist constitutional identities do have normative implications for

[102] E.g. David Dyzenhaus and Malcolm Thorburn (eds), *Philosophical Foundations of Constitutional Law* (Oxford University Press 2016).

[103] Louis Henkin, "Elements of Constitutionalism" (1998) 60 International Commission of Jurists Review 11, 11.

the legitimacy of a socialist state. A socialist state cannot simply ignore the grand socialist commitments explicitly codified in the supreme law of the land without undermining its legitimacy. Law, policy, and state actions departing from the socialist constitutional commitments would generate social mistrust in the regime and undermine the sociological foundation of the regime's legitimacy. For example, China's Anti-Rightist Campaign (1957–58) significantly departed from the statist rights commitment established by the 1954 Constitution, and this is one of the reasons for the difficulty with "popular acceptance of regime ideals of justice."[104] The socialist constitutional identities logically inform state actions and provide the fundamental blueprint for judging the constitutional legitimacy of the regime.

The next chapter will explore how socialist constitutional identity informs the constitutional history of the five countries that are the subject of my inquiry (China, Vietnam, Laos, North Korea, and Cuba) during the Soviet and transitional era, while the second part of the book will deal with socialist constitutional change (including identity change) in the global era.

[104] Pitman B. Potter, "Riding the Tiger: Legitimacy and Legal Culture in Post-Mao China" (1994) 138 China Quarterly 325, 329, 333.

3
Socialist Constitutional History

Introduction

This chapter examines constitutional history in the following five socialist countries: China, Vietnam, Laos, North Korea, and Cuba. Their constitutional history can be analytically divided into three periods: pre-socialist, Soviet-era, and transitional. During the pre-socialist period, when socialist states had not yet been created and socialist policies had not yet been enacted, the five countries had their own constitutional history, which was predominantly informed by traditional values (e.g. Confucianism in China, Vietnam, and Korea, and Buddhism in Laos) and liberal modern values, although some socialist ideas were also partially adopted in some cases, such as the 1946 Constitution of Vietnam. In the Soviet era, except for the belated constitution-making in Laos, the four other countries made, replaced, or amended the socialist constitutions which were predominantly informed by five elements of socialist constitutional identity. Immediately after the collapse of the Soviet bloc, the five countries adapted their socialist constitutional system in the early 1990s in a transition with three separate elements: independent states, economic reforms, and institutional adjustment. The examination of socialist constitutional history has implications for comparative constitutional history: the global polarization between the liberal and socialist constitutional models, intra-socialist constitutional convergence and divergence, and constitutional transition without constitutionalism.

This chapter is structured as follows. Section I examines the pre-socialist constitutional experience. Section II deals with constitutional history during the Soviet era. Section III turns to the constitutional transition after the fall of the Soviet bloc. Section IV concludes with reflections on the implications for comparative constitutional history.

I. Pre-Socialist Period

The examination of pre-socialist constitutional history in the five countries under consideration is important in three senses. First, it serves as the background for understanding their socialist constitutional history: socialist constitutions did not emerge in a vacuum, as the countries had some pre-existing constitutional experience. Second, some elements of their pre-socialist constitutional history were

Constitutional Change in the Contemporary Socialist World. Bui Ngoc Son, Oxford University Press (2020). © Bui Ngoc Son.
DOI: 10.1093/oso/9780198851349.001.0001.

incorporated into their socialist constitutions, which helps to explain the constitutional divergence within the socialist world during the Soviet era. Finally, in countries like China, Vietnam, and Cuba, pre-socialist constitutional values inform nationalist aspirations and are cited in the current debates on socialist constitutional change.

A. China

The idea of ancient constitution[1] resonates in China as indicated by the discourse on the Confucian form of constitution and constitutionalism.[2] However, modern constitutional history began here at the turn of the twentieth century, not as the evolution of autochthonous institutions but as the consequence of the impact of Western constitutionalism.[3] Two important factors affected constitution-making in China in the late nineteenth century and early twentieth century: the pressure of constitution-making applied by revolutionaries and the world-wide expansion of Western modern constitutionalism.[4] The revolutionary demand for constitution-making sprang from the weakness of the Qing dynasty, the last imperial dynasty in China: it "suffered corruption and inefficiency in its administration of domestic affairs, and defeat and humiliation in its dealings with foreign Powers."[5] Regarding the second factor, since the middle of the nineteenth century, ideas of modern constitutionalism spread through China via various channels, such as missionaries, foreigners in China, and Chinese students returning from Western countries and Japan.[6] This created the impression among the Chinese reformists and revolutionaries that powerful countries were powerful because they had a constitutional government,[7] and that China too could become powerful if it constitutionalized its government.[8]

To mollify the public and to save the regime, the Imperial Court reluctantly adopted an *imperial constitution-making* approach, by setting up a constitutional monarchy.[9] These attempts, however, failed to save the regime. The 1911

[1] Adriaan Lanni and Adrian Vermeule, "Constitutional Design in the Ancient World" (2011) 64 Stanford Law Review 907.

[2] For recent account, see Su Li, *The Constitution of Ancient China* (Zhang Yongle and Daniel A. Bell (eds), Edmund Ryden (tr.), Princeton University Press 2018). For early accounts, see Hawkling Lugine Yen, *A Survey of Constitutional Development in China* (AMS Press 1968); Wm Theodore de Bary, "The 'Constitutional Tradition' in China" (1995) 9(7) Journal of Chinese Law 7.

[3] Jianfu Chen, *Chinese Law: Context and Transformation* (Brill 2016) 90–1.

[4] William L. Tung, *The Political Institutions of Modern China* (Martinus Nijhoff 1964) 2.

[5] Ibid. 3.

[6] Ibid. 5.

[7] Pan Wei-Tung, *The Chinese Constitution: A Study of Forty Years of Constitution-making in China* (1945) 3.

[8] Tung, *The Political Institutions* (n 4) 5.

[9] See generally Jiang-Guohua, "A Hundred Year's Celebration of The Constitutional Practice in The Late Qing Dynasty" (2008) 9 Historia Constitucional 341.

Xinhai Revolution overturned the dynastic regime and created a republic. The revolutionaries then engaged in *republican constitution-making*. The imperial and the republican efforts of constitution-making altogether led to the enactment of several constitutional documents, including: the Principles of Constitution of 1908, the Nineteen Articles of 1911, the Provisional Constitution of the Republic of China of 1912, the Constitutional Pact of 1914, the Constitution of the Republic of China of 1923, the Provisional Constitution of the Republic of China for the Period of Political Tutelage of 1931, and the Constitution of the Republic of China of 1946.[10]

1. Principles of Constitution of 1908

The victory of Japan in the Russo-Japanese War (1904–1905) raised the Qing court's awareness of the power of modern constitutionalism over autocracy. "Demand louder that China should adopt [modern] constitutionalism in order to become strong and wealthy."[11] In the summer of 1905, the Qing government issued edicts appointing five special commissioners to study the modern system of constitutional government in Japan, England, the United States, Germany, and France, and to consider its possible creation in China.[12] After their return in July 1906, all commissioners recommended constitution-making to create a constitutional monarchy, "which, in their opinion, was the only way to avert a revolution."[13] The court explained the significance of constitution-making in an edict issued by Empress Dowager on September 1, 1906:

> We sent our High Ministers to various countries to study and investigate their governmental systems and administrative methods. Now, these Ministers have returned, and in their report all submitted their opinion, as the result of their study and investigation, that the weakness and inefficiency of our country is due to the lack of close touch between the government and the people and the entire separation of those who are in office and those who are not. The officials do not know how to protect the people, and the people how to defend the country. That other countries are wealthy and strong is primarily due to the adoption of a constitution, by which all the people are united in one body and in constant communication, sane and sound opinions are extensively sought after and adopted, powers are well divided and defined, and financial matters and legislation are discussed and decided upon by the people. Moreover, other countries look to one

[10] The English version of these documents are available at Tung, *The Political Institutions* (n 4) 318–66.

[11] Chozo Ichiko, "Political and Institutional Reform 1901–11" in *The Cambridge History of China*, vol. 11 (John F. Fairbank and Kwang-Ching Liu (eds), Cambridge University Press 1978) 388–9.

[12] E-Tu Zen Sun, "The Chinese Constitutional Missions of 1905–1906" (1952) 24 The Journal of Modern History 251.

[13] Tung, *The Political Institutions* (n 4) 7.

another for improvement, and amend their constitutions and change their laws to their highest efficiency. So it is not a mere accident that their governments are in such a good working order and their peoples enjoy so great happiness.[14]

Yet, the court considered immediate constitution-making unrealistic: "*At present no definite plan has been decided upon and the people are not educated enough for a constitution; if we adopt one hastily and regardless of the circumstances, it will be nothing more than a paper constitution. Then how can we stand before the people and ask them to repose confidence in us*?"[15] So, preparatory steps for constitution-making were necessary. The Qing government issued the *Principles of the Constitution* on September 22, 1908, a preparatory document which laid down the principles for constitution-making to create a constitutional monarch. The *Principles* included fourteen principles concerning "the powers of the sovereign" and nine principles on "the rights and duties of the subjects." The *Principles* copied seventeen articles from the Meiji Constitution but did not borrow the provisions limiting the royal power from its Japanese counterpart.[16] In fact, this document aimed to institutionalize the absolute monarch, defining the emperor as the supreme ruler to be "honored forever," concentrating all legislative, executive, and judicial powers and placing them in the hands of the emperor, and giving the people (conceived as the 'subjects') only parsimonious rights, such as freedom of speech, press, and assembly.[17] Understandably, constitutionalists and intellectuals criticized the Principles and "ardently demanded an immediate inauguration of constitutional government."[18]

2. Nineteen Articles of 1911

Faces with serious domestic pressures, especially revolutionary uprisings in different provinces, the National Legislative Council, the body of 200 elective and appointed members, hastily drafted, presented to the throne, and then adopted the *Nineteen Articles* on November 3, 1911. The document aimed to limit the royal power, providing that "the Power of the Emperor shall be limited by the Constitution."[19] It vested the constitution-making and constitutional amendment power in a bicameral legislature. It stipulated a parliament-based cabinet government. The legislature would select the Premier, who would then recommend other cabinet members.[20] The throne only had the formalist power to appoint the selected and recommended cabinet members.[21]

14 Payson J Treat, "Constitution Making in China" (1911) 2 The Journal of Race Development 151.
15 Ibid.
16 Tung, *The Political Institutions* (n 4) 9.
17 Principles of Constitution 1908.
18 Ichiko (n 11) 397.
19 Nineteen Articles 1911, art. 3.
20 Ibid. art. 8.
21 Ibid.

3. Provisional Constitution of 1912

The lack of sincere interest in constitution-making to truly transform the regime into a constitutional polity led to the failure of these reluctant attempts at imperial constitution-making, to save the imperial regime. The result was the 1911 Xinhai Revolution. Led by Sun Yat-sen, the Revolution overthrew the monarchical government of the Qing, to create a constitutional republic. The revolutionaries selected Sun Yat-sen as the Provisional President of the new republican government on December 19, 1911. The Provisional President promulgated the Provisional Constitution on March 11, 1912, drafted by the Legislative Council. The document included fifty-five articles divided into seven chapters. The Constitution provided for popular sovereignty, a republic, a list of fundamental rights of citizens, and a presidential system with separation of powers between the legislature (Legislative Assembly), the executive (Provisional President, Vice President, and the Cabinet), and the Judiciary.[22]

4. Constitutional Pact of 1914

To protect the infant republic and to head off a war between Northern and Southern China, a modus vivendi was reached between the court and the revolutionaries. Accordingly, Sun soon resigned from the presidency in favor of Yuan Shikai, a powerful warlord in Beijing, in return for Yuan's support of the republic.[23] Yuan, who was neither a revolutionary nor a constitutionalist but rather an opportunist military politician, behaved as president almost as though he was an emperor, thanks to "his own military power, foreign support, and deft political manipulation."[24] Yuan tried to achieve his goal through abusive constitution-making: he promulgated the Constitutional Pact on May 1, 1914, to replace the Provisional Constitution. The document, consisting of sixty-eight articles, elevated the president to the status of a dictator by concentrating and placing all the major powers in the hands of the president, and reduced the legislature to "a subsidiary organ."[25] Sun led a movement to defend the Constitution which Yuan was emasculating. Sun failed, but Yuan could not realize his dream of a "life presidency" and died when there was a further uprising against him. [26] China then became embroiled in the Warlord Era.

[22] Provisional Constitution of the Republic of China 1912.

[23] See generally, Ernest P. Young, *Yuan Shih-kai's Rise to the Presidency* (Center for Chinese Studies, University of Michigan 1968).

[24] Michael Gasster, "The Republic Revolution Movement" in *The Cambridge History of China*, vol. 11 (John F. Fairbank and Kwang-Ching Liu (eds), Cambridge University Press 1978) 530–1.

[25] Tung, *The Political Institutions* (n 4) 53.

[26] X. Xiao-Planes, "Of Constitutions and Constitutionalism: Trying to Build a New Political Order in China, 1908–1949" in *Building Constitutionalism in China* (Stephanie Blame and Michael W. Dowdle (eds), Palgrave Macmillan 2009) 43.

5. Constitution of the Republic of China of 1923

The warlords used the constitution not as a tool to limit brutal forces but to legitimize their claims.[27] Their influence was reflected in the enactment of the Constitution of the Republic of China on October 10, 1923, by a new Parliament. While the Constitution defined China as a unitary republic, it clearly divided the central and local powers, making it a type of federal constitution.[28] It also created a cabinet system and a bicameral legislature. The Constitution was, however, unenforceable due to the turmoil created by the warlords.[29]

6. The Constitution of the Republic of China in the Period of Political Tutelage of 1931

The warlords were defeated by Chiang Kai-Shek in 1928, a leader of the Chinese Nationalist Party (Kuomintang or KMT) previously created by Sun Yat-sen, and consequently, the national government of the Republic of China was established in Nanking.[30] However, the KMT engaged in a civil war with the Chinese Communist Party (created in 1921) until 1936, when the two parties entered into an alliance to confront the Japanese invasion.[31] The KMT sought to materialize Dr. Sun Yat-sen's three-stage program of Chinese political transformation. The three stages included a military government for ending the rule of the warlords and unifying the nation, a constitutional democracy under the KMT's political tutelage, and finally a full liberal constitutional democracy.[32] To implement the second stage, the Constitution of the Republic of China in the Period of Political Tutelage was enacted in 1931.[33] This Constitution included eight chapters, namely: general principles; rights and duties of the people; essentials of political tutelage; the people's livelihood; education of the citizens; division of power between the Central and local governments; organization of the governments; and an annex.[34] William L. Tung remarks that: "The provision on the rights and duties of the people was similar to that in most of the Western democratic constitutions. People's livelihood was much emphasized here and the State would afford every encouragement and protection to the private enterprises."[35]

[27] A.J. Nathan, "A Constitutional Republic: the Peking Government, 1916–28" in *The Cambridge History of China*, vol. 12 (Cambridge University Press 1983) 279.
[28] Qianfan Zhang, *The Constitution of China: A Contextual Analysis* (Hart 2012) 24.
[29] Tung, *The Political Institutions* (n 4) 72.
[30] Suisheng Zhao, *Power by Design: Constitution-making in Nationalist China* (University of Hawaii Press 1996).
[31] Albert H. Chen, "Pathways of Western Liberal Constitutional Development in Asia: A Comparative Study of Five Major Nations" (2010) 8 International Journal of Constitutional Law 874.
[32] Ibid.
[33] Ibid. 118–48.
[34] Tung, *The Political Institutions* (n 4) 126.
[35] Ibid.

7. Constitution of the Republic of China of 1946

To realize the third stage, a new Constitution of the Republic of China was promulgated in December 1946.[36] The Constitution consisted of fourteen chapters: general provisions; rights and duties of the people; the National Assembly; the President; Administration; Legislation; Judiciary; Examination; Supervision; powers of Central and local governments; system of local government; election, recall, initiative, and referendum; fundamental national policies; and enforcement and amendment of the Constitution.[37] Most notably, the Constitution established five Yuan or branches, including the Executive, the Legislative, the Judiciary, the Examining, and the Supervisory, modeling Sun's doctrine of the separation of five powers. The KMT government was defeated by the Chinese Communist Party on the mainland and retreated to Taiwan in 1949. The Constitution of the Republic of China of 1946 remains in effect in Taiwan today, albeit with subsequent amendments.[38]

B. Vietnam

Like China, Vietnam also had an ancient constitution influenced by Confucian thinking.[39] But efforts of modern constitution-making in the country can only be traced back to the first half of the twentieth century when Vietnam was under French colonial rule and the Nguyen dynasty was titular at Huế.[40] During this period, Vietnamese nationalists adopted the fundamental values of Western liberal constitutionalism so as to counter the colonial power.[41]

In the early twentieth century, Western ideas of liberal constitutionalism were introduced in Vietnam by Confucian nationalist intellectuals (most notably, Phan Bội Châu, Phan Chu Trinh, and Huỳnh Thúc Kháng) through their revolutionary movements and organizations (such as the Eastern Exodus Movement, and Vietnam Restoration League, Restoration Movement, and the Tonkin Free School).[42] They were particularly inspired by the Meiji Constitution, Chinese institutional reform (the Hundred Days Reform), the 1911 Revolution by Sun Yat-sen, and the writings of Chinese reformists, such as Kang Youwei and Liang Qichao.[43]

[36] Ibid. 202.

[37] Ibid. 203.

[38] For Taiwan's liberal constitutional transition, see Wen-Chen Chang, *Transition to Democracy, Constitutionalism and Judicial Activism: Taiwan in Comparative Constitutional Perspective* (JSD Diss, Yale Law School 2001); Jiunn-Rong Yeh and Wen-chen Chang "The Emergence of Asian Constitutionalism: Features in Comparison" (2011) 59(3) American Journal of Comparative Law 805.

[39] Bui Ngoc Son, "Confucian Constitutionalism in Imperial Vietnam" (2014) 8(2) National Taiwan University Law Review 373.

[40] Bui Ngoc Son, "The Introduction of Modern Constitutionalism in East Asian Confucian Context: The Case of Vietnam in the Early Twentieth Century" (2011) 7(2) National Taiwan University Law Review 423, 425.

[41] Ibid. 430.

[42] Ibid. 441.

[43] Ibid. 426–37.

Consequently, constitutionalism under the Western form became an inextricable part of their anti-colonialism, as they believed that constitutionalist institutions and values were instrumental to the modernization of the nation, enabling them eventually to reclaim sovereignty from their invaders.[44] On the grounds of Western liberal constitutional framework, the Confucian patriots criticized the arbitrary power of colonialists and the despotic power of the imperial government.[45] The Confucian patriots then called for national independence and creation of a constitutional government mirroring Western standards such as a written constitution, popular sovereignty, a popularly elected parliament, a multi-party system, separation of powers, liberal rights, and judicial independence.[46]

During World War I, new Western-style intellectuals emerged in Vietnam who resembled the traditional intellectuals in their advocacy of Western liberal constitutionalism. They included Nguyễn An Ninh; Phan Văn Trường; the La cloche fêlée [1923–1926] and L'Annam [1926–1928] newspapers; Phan Anh and the Thanh Nghi group; and Nguyễn Tường Tam and the Self-Reliance Literary Group (*Tự lực Văn đoàn*). The Francophiles, such as Nguyễn Văn Vĩnh and the Đông Dương Magazine [1913–1919] group, Phạm Quỳnh and the Nam Phong Magazine [1917–1933] group, Bùi Quang Chiêu, and the Constitutionalist Party, also supported the creation of a Western-style constitution in Vietnam under the tutelage of the French.[47] Despite forceful calls for constitution-making by different actors, no constitutional documents were enacted in Vietnam before the August Revolution of 1945. But the social importance of these diverse constitutional movements was by no means insignificant. These movements familiarized and inspired the Vietnamese people with novel notions of Western constitutionalism and helped the public gain full access to the ideas and institutions of Western modern constitutionalism.

Hồ Chí Minh is best known as a Vietnamese hero and the founder of the Communist Party of Vietnam and the State of Vietnam. He gained a status in Vietnam comparable to Mao Zedong in China, but he differed from Mao Zedong in substantial ways. While he adopted several ideas of communism such as violent revolution, a revolutionary party, and international connection of the communist community as a means to gain the independence for the nation, in order to envisage a government in an independent Vietnam, he adopted several political schools of thought other than communism, including Western modern constitutionalism.[48]

[44] Ibid. 428–30.
[45] Ibid. 430.
[46] Ibid. 446–50.
[47] Phan Đăng Thanh, *Tư tưởng Lập hiến Việt Nam nửa đầu Thế kỷ 20 [Vietnamese Constitutional Thoughts in the First Half of the Twentieth Century]* (Jud Publ'g House 2006)
[48] For more illustrations, see Bui Ngoc Son, "Confucianism and Constitutionalism in Vietnam" (2013) (unpublished Ph.D. dissertation, University of Hong Kong) 264–77 <http://hub.hku.hk/bitsbitst/10722/197124/2/FullText.pdf> [hereinafter Confucianism and Constitutionalism].

During the prerevolutionary period and early years after the August Revolution of 1945, Hồ Chí Minh adopted fundamental ideas of Western liberal constitutionalism in his vision of government for an independent Vietnam.[49] In this regard, he more resembled Sun Yat-sen than Mao Zedong. Consequently, his first 1946 Constitution shared some values with Sun Yat-sen's 1946 Constitution and was different from Mao Zedong's 1954 Constitution. It is discernible through the works of Hồ Chí Minh during the given time, such as The Ballad on the Demands of Vietnam (1922), Screams to the League of Nations (1926), and Declaration of Independence (September, 1945), that he advocated the Western ideas of the rule of law and liberal rights.[50] In addition, he insisted on the enactment of a written constitution as an instrument not for class struggle in a communist sense, but for the realization of the rule of law and liberal rights in the Western sense.[51] Hồ Chí Minh also rejected a Soviet-style government—the "workers', peasants', and soldiers' government"—in favor of a popular government.[52] He accepted the Western idea of a free and equal election, and in fact organized such an election after the revolution, which was different from the elections in the Soviet Union.[53]

Several intellectual and practical factors led Hồ Chí Minh to adopt Western liberal constitutional concepts. Two factors should be noted. Firstly, his early study of political works by Enlightenment thinkers such as Rousseau and Montesquieu, and his thirty-year overseas experience, particularly in Western nations such as the United States, the United Kingdom, and France where constitutionalism had been developed, may have shaped his liberal constitutional thinking.[54] Secondly, the failure of the Nghệ-Tĩnh Soviets was a practical factor that may have generated Hồ Chí Minh's conviction that a Soviet government was unsuitable for Vietnam.[55] Although the practice of the Soviet government was merely at the village level, its failure brought about a more general implication. Thus, the radical proposal of the Soviet government might not be appropriate to the revolutionary context in Vietnam, in that it might exclude the involvement of many strata other than the

[49] Thiem H. Bui, "Liberal Constitutionalism and the Socialist State in an Era of Globalization: An Inquiry into Vietnam's Constitutional Discourse and Power Structures" (2013) 5 The Global Studies Journal 47.

[50] See generally Ibid.

[51] See generally Ibid.

[52] Bui (n 48) 287.

[53] Ibid. 272.

[54] Ibid. 262–5.

[55] Two months after its founding, the Communist Party led a peasant insurrection whose paroxysm brought about the abolition of the local machinery of government and the replacement by the Soviet regime in two provinces, Nghệ An and Hà Tĩnh, best known as *Xô viết Nghệ- Tĩnh* (Nghệ-Tĩnh Soviets) (1930–1931). The Nghệ-Tĩnh Soviet revolt lasted many months and then was fiercely suppressed by the colonial authorities. The problem of the regime of Nghệ-Tĩnh Soviets was that, while the members of the Soviets were narrowly limited to the workers and the poor peasants, their enemies were broadly defined to include not only the foreign colonialists but also a number of strata in the Vietnamese society; the intelligentsia, the rich farmers, and the other "haves." This isolated the Soviets from other forces of the society, which enable the colonialists to quell the movement quickly. See Martin Bernal, "The Nghe-Tinh Soviet Movement 1930–1931" (1981) 92 Past & Present 148.

workers, peasants, and soldiers in the revolution. That is why after that abortive experience, Hồ Chí Minh and the League for Independence of Vietnam, or the Việt Minh front, introduced a commitment to create a democratic republic with a popular government in order to rally all forces in society to revolution.[56]

1. The 1946 Constitution

Immediately following the Declaration of National Independence, in the first meeting of the provisional government on September 3, 1945, Hồ Chí Minh proposed creating a constitution, stating: "Previously, because we were ruled by a despotic monarchy and then by an equally despotic colonial regime, our country did not have a constitution. Our people did not enjoy democratic liberal rights. We must have a democratic constitution."[57] In order to enact a constitution, he then suggested "organizing as soon as possible a general election in concordance with the principle of universal suffrage."[58]

On September 8, 1946, Hồ Chí Minh, the President of the Provisional Government, issued a decree for general suffrage in Vietnam and for the convocation of the first National Assembly following a general election.[59] The decree stated, "[t]he Vietnamese people represented by the National Assembly are the supreme power to ordain for Vietnam a democratic republic constitution" acknowledging that the people were the possessors of the constitutive power and a representative body established by popular election was to make the constitution.[60] The decree also provided that in order to draft and propose a constitution to the constituent National Assembly, a constitution drafting committee comprising seven members would be established.[61] The Constitution Drafting Committee was founded on September 20, 1945, and was presided over by Hồ Chí Minh and six other members.[62] The first constitutional draft was presented at the session of the Provisional Government on October 24, 1945, and then released to the public in the newspaper *Cứu Quốc* (National Salvation) on November 10, 1945 for public deliberation.[63]

The National Assembly was created on January 6, 1946, after the general election.[64] It was a pluralist constituent assembly, consisting of 120 delegates of Vietminh (communists), forty-six delegates of the Democratic Party of Vietnam, twenty-four delegates of the Social Party of Vietnam, 143 non-party delegates,

[56] Bui (n 48) 269–70.
[57] Chí Minh Hồ, *Complete Works*, vol. IV (Nat'l Politics Publ'g House 2000) 8.
[58] Ibid.
[59] Bernard B. Fall, *The Viet-Minh Regime: Government and Administration in the Democratic Republic of Vietnam* (Inst of Pac Relations 1956).
[60] Decree No. 14/SL (September 8, 1945) (Viet.).
[61] Ibid.
[62] They included including Vĩnh Thụy (formerly monarch Bảo Đại), Vũ Trọng Khánh, Lê Văn Hiến, Đặng Thai Mai, Nguyễn Lương Bằng, and Trường Trinh. Decree 34/SL (September 20, 1945) (Viet.).
[63] Phan (n 47).
[64] Bui (n 48) 272.

and seventy non-elected delegates of the League of Vietnam Revolution (or Việt Cách), and the Nationalist Party of Vietnam (or Việt Quốc).[65] Two months after its founding, the National Assembly, in its first session on March 2, 1946, decided to establish its own constitution drafting body, the Select Committee for the Constitution, which consisted of eleven members from various political parties and a completely different entity from the Provisional Government's Constitution Drafting Committee.[66] At the same time, the government's National Construction Committee introduced another constitutional draft. The Select Committee for the Constitution, after examining the two drafts by the government, referencing foreign constitutions, and taking into account public opinion, produced its own draft and presented it at the second session of the National Assembly on October 29, 1946.[67] This constitutional draft was deliberated in the National Assembly for more than one week and was eventually approved on November 9, 1946, by a majority of 140 to 2 votes.[68]

The 1946 Constitution was not a Soviet-style constitution. Rather, it adopted several values of Western liberal constitutionalism. Its preamble recognized the idea of constituent power held by the people.

Article 1 defines the polity as a "Democratic Republic" and declares the principle of popular sovereignty: "All powers in the nation belong to all Vietnamese people, irrespective of race, gender, prosperity, class, and religion."[69]

Next, Chapter II is dedicated to fundamental rights. The Constitution guaranteed: equal rights in all fields; equality before the law; the right to participate in government; gender equality in all domains; right of freedom of speech, of the press, of association and meeting, of belief, and of movement; and the right to own property.[70] In addition, the Constitution provided a separate section on political rights concerning popular participation ("election, recall and referendum").[71] The Constitution was committed to universal suffrage; free, direct, and secret voting; the right to recall their representatives; and the right to a referendum on the Constitution and on important issues concerning the destiny of the country.[72]

[65] See generally ibid. The election was held in hard conditions when internal struggles happened between communist force and anti-communist forces like Việt Quốc and Việt Cách, and the French were returning to Indochina. The Communist Party self-dissolved and transformed to the Association of Marxist-Leninist Studies. The communists participated in the election as members of Vietminh. Việt Quốc and Việt Cách, anti-communist parties, boycotted the election. To appease the internal tension and unify internal force against the returning French, before the election, a compromise between Vietminh and Việt Quốc-Việt Cách forces had been reached which allowed the later to participate in the National Assembly without election.

[66] Bui (n 48) 276.

[67] Ibid. at 277.

[68] Ibid.

[69] Constitution of the Democratic Republic of Vietnam (1946), art. I (Author's Translation of 1946 Vietnamese Constitution and hereafter).

[70] Hiến pháp Việt Nam Dân chủ Cộng hòa [Constitution] (1946), arts 6–14 (Viet.).

[71] Ibid. arts 17–21.

[72] Ibid.

Chapters III through VI of the Constitution deal with the structure of the state. The Constitution established a tripartite political system: the People's Parliament, the unicameral legislature elected every three years; the Government created by Parliament, including the President of State, the Vice-President, and the Cabinet with the latter consisting of the Prime Minister, the Ministers, and the Vice-Ministers; and the judiciary comprising the supreme court, the courts of appeal, and the courts of second and first instance.[73] The local governments included the People's Councils and the Administrative Committees.

In structuring the central government, the principle of concentration rather than separation of power was accepted due to wartime conditions.[74] It is understood that a concentrated power is more suitable for rallying an entire national force to fight against invaders, and to deliver a political decision quickly in the war context. This leads to the connection between the People's Parliament and the government.

However, the form of government established by the Constitution was more likely a semi-presidential system with the adoption of several features of American presidentialism and European parliamentarism, which made it distinctive from the Soviet-style concentrated government. The President of State, albeit selected by the Parliament rather than by popular election, had a dual role similar to the President of the United States, namely as the head of both the state and the executive branch.[75] In addition, important powers were vested in the president: to represent the country; to assume the function of Commander-in-chief of the National Army, nominate or dismiss generals and high-ranking officers of the Infantry, the Navy, and the Air Force; to sign decrees to nominate the Prime Minister, the members of the Cabinet, and the high-ranking officials of governmental agencies; to preside over the Government Council; to promulgate the laws voted by the People's Parliament; award medals and diplomas of honor; to promulgate special amnesties; to sign treaties with other countries; to accredit Vietnamese diplomatic representatives abroad and receive diplomatic representatives from other countries; and to declare war and the end of war. The President also had the relative veto power—a distinctive element among the various checks and balances in the United States presidential system.[76] Besides the presidential features, the 1946 Constitution also adopted several features of European parliamentarism. A clear

[73] Ibid. arts 22–70.

[74] Nat'l Assembly Office, *Lich Sû Quóc Höi Vidt Nam, 1946–1960 [History of Vietnam's National Assembly, 1946–1960]* (Nat'l Politics Publ'g House 1994) 104.

[75] Compare "Hiến pháp Việt Nam Dân chủ Cộng hòa [Constitution]" (1946), art. 31 (Viet.) (Laws approved by the People's Parliament must be promulgated by the President of the Democratic Republic of Vietnam no later than ten days after he receives notification. But within that term the President shall be entitled to request the People's Parliament to proceed to a new discussion. If the laws are maintained by the People's Parliament after further discussion, the President shall be compelled to promulgate them.), *with* U.S. Constitution, art. 1, § 7.

[76] Ibid.

example was the parliament-based process of government formation. Another parliamentary indicator was the institution of a vote of no confidence. The distinctive feature of the 1946 Constitution was that it adopted two separate forms of a vote of no confidence: a vote on individual ministers and a vote on the collective Cabinet. This mechanism allowed Parliament to remove both individual ministers and the Cabinet as a whole.[77]

The judiciary is relatively closed to the idea of a separation of powers which underlines the importance of its independence. The Court system includes the Supreme Court, the Courts of Appeal, and the Courts of Second and First Instance, organized separately from the central government and local government. Judicial independence was guaranteed by the provision that: "The judges must always carry out their judicial duties in conformity with the law. No other authority is allowed to interfere with the functions of the Judiciary."[78]

Apart from civil liberties and the semi-presidential government, the Constitution also adopts the Western mechanism of the popular constitutional amendment. The final chapter (VII) prescribes the constitutional amendment process as follows: 2/3 majority of the Parliament could propose the amendments; a special constitutional amendment committee would be established; and the constitutional amendments, after being approved by the Parliament, would be ratified by the people in a popular referendum.[79]

Given these characteristics, some Western experts in Vietnamese modern history and particularly Vietnamese constitutional history have concluded that the Western democratic features of the 1946 Constitution differ from the Soviet constitution. According to David G. Marr, "there were a few borrowings from the Soviet constitutional model in the [Democratic Republic of Vietnam] text, notably people's councils and administrative committees meant both to serve their constituency and to obey directives from above."[80] Instead, the Constitution adopts several liberal and democratic values common in Western constitutional government. In Mark Sidel's assessment, "many of the rights enumerated were intended to indicate the democratic nature of the new government and to reach out to other forces in Vietnamese society"[81] and the provisions on "election, recall and referendum" are "the best evidence of the more democratic and participatory nature of the 1946 Constitution."[82] Bernard B. Fall, an American journalist and analyst, remarks that: "The Constitution gives a generally 'Western democratic' impression to the readers in that it does not deal in economic theories and does not make use

[77] Ibid. art. 54.
[78] Ibid. art. 69.
[79] Ibid. art. 70.
[80] David G. Marr, *Vietnam: State, War, and Revolution (1945–1946)* (University of California Press 2013) 106.
[81] Mark Sidel, *The Constitution of Vietnam* (Hart Pub 2009) 29.
[82] Ibid. 29–30.

of stereotyped communist phases, such as the 'working people' or the 'victory of the dictatorship of the proletariat.' As a matter of fact, neither does it resemble the new French Constitution of 1946, with its detailed social provisions (right to strike, collective bargaining, and creation of an Economic Council). Like the Democratic Republic's Declaration of Independence, it appears designed to provide 'reader appeal' in the Anglo-Saxon countries, and particularly the United States."[83] Inside Vietnam, it is popular to view the 1946 Constitution as "a constitution not less democratic and progressive than any constitution in the world. It is a paradigmatic constitution in many aspects."[84]

From my point of view, the 1946 Constitution reflects fundamental ideas and institutions of Western constitutionalism: political pluralism, popular sovereignty, constitutional referendum, civil liberties, governmental accountability, some forms of checks and balances, and judicial independence.

The 1946 Constitution's liberal features may have some connections with Ho Chi Minh's liberal constitutional thinking. Inside Vietnam, Ho Chi Minh is normally regarded as the author of the 1946 Constitution. The famous military commander Võ Nguyên Giáp, who served in Hồ Chí Minh's Government, asserts that: "History verifies that Hồ Chí Minh is the founder of our Party, our Nation, and our National Assembly, and the author of the immortal Declaration of Independence and the first Constitution of Vietnam's Democratic Republic."[85]

Hồ Chí Minh in fact played an important role in the birth of the 1946 Constitution. He suggested constitution-making immediately after the national liberation, proposed electing the National Assembly to make the constitution, and established the Constitutional Drafting Committee under his leadership, which, in fact, produced a draft constitution. It is very hard to gauge exactly to what extent Hồ Chí Minh's constitutional ideology actually influenced the drafting of the 1946 Constitution. However, at least, it can be postulated that Hồ Chí Minh might have inserted his constitutional ideas into the constitution-making process, particularly during the time he served as leader of the Constitution Drafting Committee of the Provisional Government. As the leader of the Committee, he might have sketched the basic framework for the future constitution of Vietnam. Later, the draft constitution by Hồ Chí Minh's Constitution Drafting Committee became the basis for the work of the Collective Committee for Constitution under the National Assembly.

As a result, the fundamental contents of the 1946 Constitution were basically in accordance with Hồ Chí Minh's constitutional vision. The 1946 Constitution was genuinely, to use Hồ Chí Minh's terminology, a "democratic constitution" created

[83] Fall (n 59) 159.

[84] *Giáo trình Luật Hiến pháp Việt Nam [Textbook on Vietnamese Constitutional Law]* (People's Polices Publ'g House 1998) 82.

[85] Vietnam's National Assembly Office, *Hiến pháp năm 1946 và sự kế thừa, phát triển trong các hiến pháp Việt Nam [The 1946 Constitution and its Endowment and Development in the Vietnam's Constitutions]* (National Politics Publishing House 1998).

in the line with "popular rights ideals."[86] The document was the basis for pursuing democracy and liberal rights rather than an instrument for class struggles. Furthermore, the rights provisions in the Constitution were basically in accordance with the rights petitions and statements in the 1919 Demands of the Annamite People, the 1926 The Screams to the League of Nations, and the September 2, 1945, Declaration of Independence. Finally, the political system established by the Constitution meshes well with Hồ Chí Minh's project of a democratic republic with a popular government. That government, instead of a "workers', peasants', and soldiers' government," was the government of the entire people, constituted and removable by the people through their representatives. Therefore, it can be concluded that the 1946 Constitution reflects a certain degree of Hồ Chí Minh's liberal constitutional thinking.

However, the liberal features of the 1946 Constitution are also closely related to the domestic context in which constitution-making had taken place. Although the 1946 Constitution was adopted after a communist revolution, it was drafted, deliberated and adopted by a pluralist national assembly—a constituent assembly. In the words of David G. Marr, "the second session of the National Assembly has proved to be the most wide-ranging, substantive public deliberation by an official body ever to take place in Vietnam to date."[87] The public deliberation reflected the views and the choices of political forces other than communism, which advocated more Western-style liberal and democratic values.[88] The communists constituted only 36 percent of the members of the National Assembly. Even for the communists, with the experience of the Nghệ-Tĩnh Soviets, it is unlikely that the Soviet government model was a choice congenial to Vietnam at that time. Before and after the 1945 revolution, the central concern of Vietnam was national liberation. Therefore, Vietnam needed to rally the resultant force of people for the complete liberation of the nation. A communist constitution as an instrument for class struggle might have resulted in social division and hence was not likely to be appropriate to the mission of national liberation. A democratic constitution which affirmed the power of the entire people, established a government of the entire people, and guaranteed basic rights for an entire people was more likely to serve as a talisman for rallying an entire people for national liberation.

In addition to internal factors, the fact that Vietnamese constitution-makers in 1946 adopted a Western-style constitution is due to external factors. At the closing meeting of the second session of the National Assembly after the Constitution was adopted, Hồ Chí Minh avowed:

86 Hội Luật Gia [Bar Association], *Pháp lý Phục vụ Cách Mạng [Legislations Severving Revolution]* (Bar Association 1975) 278.

87 Marr (n 80) 106–7.

88 Ibid. 107.

> The National Assembly has made an achievement which glorifies the nation, which is to adopt the Constitution. 14 months after the nation was liberated, it has made the first constitution in the history of our nation. At the same time, that Constitution is the first constitutional hallmark in (South) East Asian history. That Constitution may not be perfect, but it has been created in accordance with the real situation. The Constitution declares to the world that Vietnam has been independent. The Constitution declares to the world that in Vietnam there has been every liberal right. The Constitution declares to the world that in Vietnam women have been equal to men to enjoy every liberal right of a citizen. The Constitution demonstrates the spirit of union among the Vietnamese nationalities and the spirit of integrity and justice among the classes.[89]

This speech illustrates that the Constitution is both expressive of nationalism and instrumental to international recognition. The recurrent reference to "declare to the world" indicates that political leadership used the Constitution to communicate with the world and to advertise national independence and the nation's commitment to shared liberal values to gain international recognition by which to socialize or acculturate the nation into the world's "civilized" community for the ultimate end of complete national independence. In particular, the liberal rights in the Constitution are used to attract support from Western powers. The historical context helps explain this. At the given time, the preoccupation of Ho Chi Minh's newly established government was for complete national independence to be recognized and supported by the world community rather than the ties to Moscow or Beijing. However, the Democratic Republic of Vietnam failed to receive significant recognition from the international community,[90] especially Western powers such as France or the United States. France returned to Vietnam immediately after Ho Chi Minh's declaration of national independence. "Ho Chi Minh tried to negotiate with France and also to seek recognition from the United States of America, but both countries rejected his pleas."[91] In this brittle context of international relations, the constitutional commitments to liberal rights shared by Western powers were instrumental in seeking their support and recognition of the legitimacy of the new established government.

That, however, does not mean that there is no *socialist influence* on the 1946 Constitution. Marr argues that the 1946 Constitution was influenced by the French Third Republic[92] but carefully noted that: "There were a few borrowings from the Soviet constitutional model in the DRV text, notably people's councils

[89] Chí Minh Hồ, *Complete Works*, vol. IV (Nat'l Politics Publ'g House 2000) 440.

[90] Thaveeporn Vasavakul, "Vietnam: Doi moi Difficulties" in *Government and Politics in Southeast Asia* (John Funston ed 2001) 372.

[91] Nhu Dung Hopt-Nguyen, "Vietnam" in *Oxford Public International Law* (2009) <http://opil.ouplaw.com/view/10.1093/law:epil/9780199231690/law-9780199231690-e1873>.

[92] Marr (n 80) 106.

and administrative committees meant both to serve their constituency and to obey directives from above."[93] The influence of Western liberal constitutionalism in the 1946 Constitution is dominant, although there are some vestiges of soviet socialist constitutional theory in that document.

C. Laos

The history of the Laotian state can be traced back to the Kingdom of Lan Xang (literally Million Elephants), a united kingdom existing from 1354 to 1707, one of the largest kingdoms in Southeast Asia.[94] The political structure of this kingdom is marked by Buddhism, which spread to Laos in the seventh–eighth centuries CE, via the kingdom of Dvaravati.[95] Buddhism was reinforced in the Kingdom of Lan Xang, identified by Stuart-Fox as a "Buddhist kingdom."[96] Together with heredity, Buddhism constituted one of primary sources of the legitimacy of ruler.[97] Particularly, the Buddhist concept of *karma* suggests that "a king must have accumulated considerable religious merit in previous existences" and therefore "he owned his exalted position primarily to the workings of the immutable law of *karma*."[98] The king possessed absolute power in theory, but in reality he was constrained both by the expectation that as a Buddhist monarch he would abide by the ten Buddhist precepts of just rule, and by his need of the support of the powerful members of the aristocracy and regional *chao meuang* who sat on the King's Council.[99] The kingdom of Lan Xang therefore can be considered as an example of Buddhist constitutionalism.[100] The imperial government was limited ideationally by the Buddhist principles of just rule and institutionally by local autonomous actors. This is comparable to Confucian constitutionalism in China and Vietnam in which imperial power was constrained by the Confucian principles of just rule and by scholars sitting in different imperial institutions.[101]

The unity of the kingdom of Lan Xang was underlined by dynastic disputes, which led to the division of the kingdom into three kingdoms in the eighth

[93] Ibid.

[94] For an extensive study of this kingdom, see Martin Stuart-Fox, *The Lao Kingdom of Lan-Xang: Rise and Decline* (White Lotus Press 1998).

[95] Martin Stuart-Fox, *Laos: Politics, Economics, and Society* (F Pinter and Lynne Rienner Publishers 1986) 3.

[96] Martin Stuart-Fox, *Buddhist Kingdom, Marxist State: The Making of Modern Laos* (White Lotus 1996).

[97] Martin Stuart-Fox, "Politics and Reforms in the Lao People's Democratic Republic" (2005) 126 Murdoch University's Asia Research Centre 5.

[98] Stuart-Fox, *Laos* (n 95) 5.

[99] Stuart-Fox (n 97) 5.

[100] For Buddhist constitutionalism in general, see Benjamin Schonthal, "Formations of Buddhist constitutionalism in South and Southeast Asia" (2017) 15(3) International Journal of Constitutional Law 705.

[101] See Bui Ngoc Son, *Confucian Constitutionalism in East Asia* (Routledge 2016) ch 2.

century, Luang Prabang in the north, Champasak in the south, and Vientiane in the center.[102] During the first half of the twentieth century, Laos was colonized by France.[103] In 1893, French Indochina was added with Laos together with Cambodia, and three Vietnamese regions of Tonkin (north), Annam (center), and Cochinchina (south).[104] Under the French rule, Laos was far from an integrated political unity, as "a small group of elite Lao families was allowed to consolidate its power; thus, the Lao emerged from colonial rule (after World War II) more divided, isolated, and backward than ever."[105]

1. The Issara Constitution of 1945

On March 9, 1945, Japanese forces seized France's colonial power in Indochina.[106] In Laos, Crown Prince Savang Vatthana called "in the name of the king" for popular opposition to the Japanese.[107] On April 8, 1945, under Japanese pressure, however, he was forced to declare the independence of Laos.[108] The Japanese were defeated, Prince Phesarath as viceroy and prime minister declared the independence of the unitary kingdom of Laos.[109] At the same time, the French had returned to Luang Prabang, and the king welcomed the return while he dismissed his prime minister, whereupon a provisional People's Assembly met in Vientiane to vote to depose the king, and enacted a provisional constitution, and appointed a provisional government called Lao Issara (Free Laos).[110]

The Lao Issara government's provisional Constitution stipulated a constitutional monarchy with three basic state branches: the National Assembly as the legislature, the Government, and the judiciary.[111] The king's actions would be approved by the legislature.[112] The Constitution also provided for basic rights, such as equality before the law, the right to free speech, freedom of expression, freedom of assembly, freedom of association, the right to privacy, property, employment, and education.[113] The king declared all of the National Assembly's activities illegal.[114] The provisional government negotiated with the court: the king would legitimize it and

[102] Stuart-Fox, *Laos* (n 95) 8.
[103] For this period, see Martin Stuart-Fox, *A History of Laos* (Cambridge University Press 1997) ch 2.
[104] For the making of Indochina, see Pierre Brocheux and Daniel Hémery, *Indochina: An Ambiguous Colonization, 1858–1954* (Ly Lan Dill-Klein, Eric Jennings, Nora Taylor, and Noémi Tousignant (trs), University of California Press 2009).
[105] Robert Dayley, *Southeast Asia in the New International Era* (Westview Press 2017) 163.
[106] Stuart-Fox, *Laos* (n 95) 17.
[107] Ibid.
[108] Ibid.
[109] Ibid.
[110] Ibid. 17–18.
[111] Gerald Leather, "Laos: A Constitution in Search of Constitutionalism" in *Constitutionalism in Southeast Asia,* vol. 2 Reports on National Constitutions (Clauspeter Hill and Jőrg Menzel (eds), Konrad-Adenauer-Stiftung 2008), 129.
[112] Ibid.
[113] Ibid.
[114] Stuart-Fox, *A History* (n 103) 62.

its Constitution in return for the position of constitutional monarch.[115] On April 24, 1945, French troops reoccupied Vientiane, and the Lao Issara government fled to Thailand.[116]

2. The Royal Constitution of 1947

The French also realized that constitution-making was necessary for Laos to be within the French Union.[117] Therefore, the Constituent Assembly, elected on the base of universal male suffrage in December 1946, approved a constitution of the Kingdom of Laos in March 1947.[118] The Constitution declared unity of the kingdom and recognized French as the official language.[119] It then provided for basic institutions of a constitutional monarchical polity, namely the King, the National Assembly, the Government, and the Royal Council.

The limited monarchical powers included the power to issue orders and regulations and to promulgate laws and treaties approved by the National Assembly.[120] The King was also able to act as the Supreme Head of the Armed Forces and declare war, subject to the National Assembly's approval.[121] The Government consisted of the Prime Minister appointed by the King, and other members, separate from the legislature selected by the Prime Minister and approved by the National Assembly.[122] The Government could be dismissed by a legislature vote of no confidence.[123] On the base of universal male suffrage, the National Assembly was elected for a four-year term, increasing to five years by a constitutional amendment in 1956.[124] This body could be dismissed by the King.[125] The Royal Council consisted of nine members, later increasing to twelve members, appointed by both the King and the National Assembly on an equal basis.[126] The Royal Council operated as a supreme court, having the power to review legislations passed by the National Assembly.[127]

Some criticized the Constitution for lacking fundamental rights and the confirmation of the national independence, as the 1945 Constitution had.[128] The 1947 Constitution of the Kingdom of Laos had remained in force during the civil war and the second Indochina War, with several subsequent amendments, until it was

115 Ibid. 65.
116 Ibid.
117 Ibid.
118 Ibid.
119 Ibid. 129.
120 Ibid.
121 Ibid.
122 Ibid. 130.
123 Ibid.
124 Ibid.
125 Ibid.
126 Ibid.
127 Ibid.
128 Ibid.

abolished by the forced abdication of the king and the proclamation of the creation of the communist government in December 1975.[129]

D. North Korea

Before the division into the North and the South in 1948, the Korean peninsula was ruled by an independent Confucian government and was then annexed to Japan in 1910. The Confucian government in pre-modern Korea did not have a written constitution in the modern sense, but practiced a form of Confucian constitutionalism: Confucian *li* (rituals) operated as the constitutional norms which constrained the imperial power.[130] The legacy of Confucian culture is currently still evident in North Korea. Some Confucian norms also resonate in North Korea's socialist constitution.

E. Cuba

The first socialist constitution of Cuba was promulgated in 1976, but the socialists (the *fidelistas* or the followers of Fidel Castro) attributed its historical origins to the early experience of constitution-making in the early years of the nineteenth century Cuban independence movement, when Cuba was under Spanish colonialism.[131] During this period, "independence fighters" enacted several constitutional documents, including: the 1869 Constitution of Guaimaro, the 1878 Constitution of Baragua, the 895 Constitutions of Jimaguayu, and the 1897 Constitution of La Yaya.[132]

Some of these documents were informed by several ideas from Western liberal constitutionalism. For example, the wealthy *mambisas*, who drafted the Guaimaro Constitution, "studied Montesquieu, Locke and the other philosophers from the American and French revolutions," and consequently the constitution incorporated "the doctrine of separation of powers and the natural law theory of inalienable rights."[133] At the same time, the contextual factors determined the function of

[129] Ibid. 133.

[130] Chaihark Hahm, "Confucian Constitutionalism" (SJD diss, Harvard Law School 2000); Chaihark Hahm, "Constitutionalism, Confucian Civic Virtue, and Ritual Propriety" in *Confucianism for the Modern World* (Daniel A. Bell and Hahm Chaibong (eds), Cambridge University Press 2003) 31–53; Chaihark Hahm, "Conceptualizing Korean Constitutionalism: Foreign Transplant or Indigenous Tradition?" (2001) 1(2) Journal of Korean Law 15; Chaihark Hahm, "Ritual and Constitutionalism: Disputing the Ruler's Legitimacy in a Confucian Polity" (2009) 57 American Journal of Comparative Law 135.

[131] William T. D'Zurilla, "Cuba's 1976 Socialist Constitution and the Fidelista Interpretation of Cuban Constitutional History" (1980–1981) 55 Tulsa Law Review 1223, 1224.

[132] For more details on these documents, see D'zurlla, "Cuba's 1976 Socialist" (n 131) 1226–32. See also R. Alomar, "Cuba's Constitutional Moment" (2017) 23 Texas Hispanic Journal of Law and Policy 1.

[133] D'zurlla, "Cuba's 1976 Socialist" (n 131) 1226–7.

colonial constitution-making. Given the war situation and the setting of a colony, the main function of constitution-making is not to create a framework for governance but to struggle for complete independence. Through constitution-making, independence movement figures declared their aspiration to create a constitutional government, which would raise the people's awareness of constitutional values and inspire them to struggle for full independence, the condition for the realization of these constitutional values. In addition, through constitution-making, they can explicitly call for complete independence through the power of constitutional language. For example, the Jimaguayu and La Yaya Constitutions in their respective preambles and provisions on peace treaty uncompromisingly demanded "absolute and immediate independence."[134]

Cuba regained independence from Spain in 1898 and then enacted *six constitutional texts* before the advent of the socialist Constitution in 1976. During the sixty years following independence, only two occasions (in 1901 and 1940) of constitution-making involved the people to varying extents[135] while the rest were imposed by the political elite's "fiat" as the consequence of political turmoil.[136] The Constitution of 1901 was adopted by an elected assembly when Cuba was under American occupation after the Spanish–American War. Consequently, it was strongly influenced by American constitutionalism: it stipulated a government structure "almost identical to those of the United States" and included a similar bill of rights.[137] Later, several provisional regimes enacted their Constitutional Laws in 1934 and 1935 respectively.[138]

In 1940, a constitutional convention adopted a "popularly acclaimed" constitution which endured for twelve years.[139] This Constitution aimed to limit the executive power and deal with economic matters, and was inspired by the 1917 Mexican constitution, the 1918 German (Weimar) constitution, and the 1931 Spanish Constitution.[140] Notably, the Constitution provided for judicial review of constitutionality of the legislation, the power exercised by the Supreme Court section of Constitutional and Social Guarantees, an "unusual practice" for a country adhering to the Roman civil law tradition.[141] The government of Fulgencio Batista

[134] Ibid. 1231.

[135] International Commission of Jurists, *Cuba and the Rule of Law* (International Commission of Jurists 1962) 78.

[136] Klein L.B., "The Socialist Constitution of Cuba (1976)" (1978) 17(3) Columbia Journal of Transnational Law 451, 453.

[137] D'zurlla, "Cuba's 1976 Socialist" (n 131) 1233. See also, Albert P. Blaustein, "The Influence of the United States Constitution Abroad" (1987) 12(3) Oklahoma City University Law Review 435, 464; Charles E. Chapman, "The Cuban Constitution and Congress" (1925) 14(1) California Law Review 22.

[138] Klein, "The Socialist Constitution" (n 136) 453–4.

[139] Ibid. 455. For acclamation of the constitution, see also Jonathan Wachs, "Reviving the 1940 Cuban Constitution: Arguments for Social and Economic Rights in a Post-Castro Government" (1994) 10(1) American University Journal of International Law and Policy 525.

[140] D'zurlla, "Cuba's 1976 Socialist" (n 131) 1237–8.

[141] Ibid.

who led a coup d'etat in 1952, suspended the 1940 Constitution and passed the Constitutional Law in April that year.[142]

II. The Soviet Era

During the Soviet era, except for the case of delayed constitution-making in Laos, the four other socialist constitutions adopted socialist constitutions, modeled on the Soviet constitutional model. These socialist constitutions have been revised or replaced several times to reflect and promote social progress as anticipated by the communist party. Despite this replacement and amendment, the socialist constitutions strictly adhered to the socialist constitutional identity.

A. China

After defeating the KMT, the Chinese Communist Party founded the People's Republic of China (PRC) in October 1949. In the early stages, the new communist regime in mainland China relied on the Common Program of the Chinese People's Political Consultative Conference as a provisional constitution. *Socialist constitution-making* then triumphed in mainland China, with the enactment of four constitutions in 1954, 1975, 1978, and 1982. While imperial and republican constitution-making was influenced by different ideas and experiences of western liberal constitutionalism (a written constitution to constrain power, popular sovereignty, fundamental rights, and the separation of powers),[143] socialist-constitution-making was shaped by Marxist constitutional ideas and the Soviet experience of constitution-making.

1. 1954 Constitution

While the 1946 republican Constitution and the socialist 1954 Constitution are substantively different and promulgated by competing regimes, they share a similar feature: both were the "foreign product."[144] The difference is the former was influenced by the Western liberal constitutional model, while the latter was influenced by the Soviet constitutional model, particularly the 1936 Soviet Constitution or the "Stalin

[142] Klein, "The Socialist Constitution" (n 136) 455–6.

[143] Albert H. Chen, "Pathways of Western Liberal Constitutional Development in Asia: A Comparative Study of Five Major Nations" (2010) 8 International Journal of Constitutional Law 874; Xiaohong Xiao-Plannes, "Of Constitution and Constitutionalism: Trying to Build a New Political Order in China, 1908–1949" in *Building Constitutionalism in China* (Stéphanie Balme and Michael W Dowdle (eds), Palgrave Macmillan 2010) 56.

[144] Jerome A. Cohen, "China's Changing Constitution" (1979) 1 Northwestern Journal of International Law and Business 62.

constitution."[145] That is in part due to the influence of Soviet leader Joseph Stalin on Chinese constitution-making.[146] Archival resources reported that Stalin urged and suggested to the PRC's founding father Mao Zedong and other communist leaders that they replace the provisional constitution (the Common Program) with a formal one to consolidate the legitimacy of the new regime.[147] When Mao visited the Soviet Union in the early 1950s, Stalin again suggested the adoption of a formal constitution, among others.[148] "Although Mao outwardly expressed support for China's new constitution, he did not share Stalin's enthusiasm for a constitution and a representative body during the initial stage of China's socialist development. Mao nevertheless did what Stalin wanted."[149] Mao's "selective and strategic" approach in dealing with Stalin and the Soviet Union is due to "practical concerns" (e.g. technological, financial, and military assistance from the Soviet Union) and "ideological commitment" (e.g. building socialism in China).[150]

In addition to the "constitutional Stalinization," the influence of socialist constitutional documents is also notable. To illustrate, in preparing for constitution-making, Mao urged every member of the Politburo and of the Central Committee of the Communist Party to read the Stalin Constitution, the 1918 Russian Soviet Federated Socialist Republic Constitution, and several constitutions of other socialist states (Romania, Poland, East Germany, and Czechoslovakia), among others.[151] The report on the draft constitution stated: "It is obvious that the experience of the advanced socialist states, headed by the Soviet Union, has been of great help to us. Our Draft Constitution embodies the experience of our own country and that of other countries. It is not only the product of the people's revolutionary movement in China but also a product of the international socialist movement."[152]

The constitution-making process includes these activities: Mao proposed a constitution-making plan; the Constitution Drafting Small Group (including Mao himself and three of his secretaries) wrote the draft constitution close to his plan; the draft was presented to the Politburo for discussion; the draft was sent to the thirty three-member Constitution Drafting Committee (twenty communist party members included) for deliberation; the Committee of the Central People's

[145] For an extensive study on the soviet influence on this document, see Fan Jizeng, "Constitutional Transplant in the People's Republic of China: The Influence of the Soviet Model and Challenges in the Globalization Era" (2015) 2 Brics Law Journal 50.

[146] Hua-yu Li, "The Political Stalinization of China: The Establishment of One-Party Constitutionalism, 1948–1954" (2001) 3 Journal of Cold War Studies 28.

[147] Xiuyuan Hu, *A Nuanced History: China's Constitutional Making in the 1950s* (Undergraduate Honors Thesis in Legal Studies: University of California, Berkeley 2014) 13.

[148] Ibid.

[149] Li (n 146) 29.

[150] Li (n 146) 31.

[151] Glenn D. Tiffert, "Epistrophy: Chinese Constitutionalism and the 1950s" in *Building Constitutionalism in China* (Stéphanie Balme and Michael W. Dowdle (eds), Palgrave Macmillan 2010) 66–7.

[152] Shaoqi Liu, *Report on the Draft Constitution of the People's Republic of China*, delivered at the First Session of the First National People's Congress of the People's Republic of China on September 15, 1954 (1954) 18.

Government adopted the draft; the draft was released for public consultation in three months; and finally the National People's Congress adopted the official Constitution on September 20, 1954.[153] Although the process included the deliberation of a constitution drafting body of diverse members and public discussions, the process was initiated and closely overseen by the party.[154] The party's control of the constitution-making process was to make sure that the document would embody the party policy. Public discussion was also instrumental to legitimizing the new constitutional framework for the new regime.

Unsurprisingly, the 1954 Constitution largely emulates the Stalin Constitution (forty-four articles in the former wholly or partially borrowing from the latter),[155] and shares common features of socialist constitutional identity.

The 1954 Constitution is an *instrument* to legitimize the new communist regime and to pursue socialism. In addition to the process, the substance of Constitution is also instrumental in structuring and legitimizing the communist power and in the incremental achievement of the goal of socialism. In the first instance, the Constitution "is the contemporary form of the mandate by which the CCP has organized the public power of the Chinese state."[156] Prominent Chinese law expert Jerome Alan Cohen articulates the instrumental nature of the Constitution, stating that the document "was perceived to be a useful creature of Party convenience. It established the basis for a strong, unifying national government and allocated responsibilities among different agencies, bringing greater clarity and order to a people who have always dreaded, and frequently experienced, political confusion. It also confirmed, both at home and abroad, the legitimacy of a regime that felt understandably insecure about its prestige."[157] The document also serves as a transitional framework for the new regime to gradually reach the paradise of socialism. The instrumental nature defines the transitional function of the document. The Constitution was not designed to be permanent but a transitional document for the incremental transformation of China into a true socialist country.[158] Constitution-makers aimed to create a transitional framework "to bring about the socialist industrialization of the country and, step by step, to accomplish the socialist transformation of agriculture, handicrafts and capitalist industry and commerce."[159] Speaking at the meeting of the Constitutional Drafting Committee, Mao said that it would take around fifteen years for China "to transform into a true socialist country," implying that the Constitution's life is around fifteen years.[160]

[153] For more details, see Hu, "A Nuanced History" (n 147) 14–22.
[154] Tiffert, "Epistrophy" (n 151) 67.
[155] Fan (n 145) 57.
[156] H. Arthur Steiner, "Constitutionalism in Communist China" (1955) 49 American Political Science Review 5.
[157] Cohen (n 144) 63.
[158] Hu, "A Nuanced History" (n 147) 12.
[159] Constitution of the People's Republic of China (1954) preamble.
[160] Hu, "A Nuanced History" (n 147) 12

The Constitution is also an embodiment of *party vangardism*. This is presented not only in the communist party led-constitution making process but also in the constitutional document. The constitutional preamble attributes the "great victory" to the leadership of the Communist Party.[161] It also makes it clear that "the people's democratic united front" led by the Communist Party "will continue to play its part" in the transition to socialism.[162]

A constitutional structure under the principle of *democratic centralism* was based on the Soviet model. This principle is clearly stated in Article 2: "The National People's Congress, the local people's congresses and other organs of state practice democratic centralism."[163] To practice this principle, the National People's Congress, like the Supreme Soviet, albeit unicameral, is "the highest organ of state authority,"[164] while other state institutions are subordinate to it. The Standing Committee, like the Presidium of the Supreme Soviet, acts as a permanent body of the Congress.[165] The State Council, like the Soviet Council of Ministers, is "the executive organ of the highest state authority" [the Congress] and "the highest administrative organ of state."[166] At the local level, the local people's congresses and local people's councils "were modelled on the local soviets and their executive committees in the soviet republics" although China is not federal like the Soviet Union.[167] The court system and the distinctive Leninist institution called procuracy[168] (practicing the procuratorial power over government agencies and citizens "to ensure observance of the law"[169]) also followed the Soviet model.[170] The functional independence of the courts is stipulated in the constitution,[171] but its meaning and practice (e.g. courts' relation with the Party; the absence of judicial review) is very different from the Western liberal constitutional polity.[172]

Statist rights are also evident in the Constitution. The document included a lengthy list of citizens' fundamental rights. In particular, it incorporated "a bundle of social rights aimed at demonstrating is socialist identity."[173] Constitution-makers seem to consider rights less important than state structure: rights are only

[161] Constitution (n 159) preamble.
[162] Ibid.
[163] Ibid. art. 2.
[164] Ibid. art. 21.
[165] Ibid. art. 30.
[166] Ibid. art. 47.
[167] Cohen (n 144) 63.
[168] On the introduction of this institution in China, see George Ginsburgs and Arthur Stahnke, "The Genesis of the People's Procuratorate in Communist China 1949–1951" (1964) 20 The China Quarterly 1.
[169] China 1954 Constitution (n 159), art. 81.
[170] Cohen (n 144) 63.
[171] China 1954 Constitution (n 159) art. 78 ("In administering justice the people's courts are independent, subject only to the law.")
[172] For detailed discussion, see Jerome Alan Cohen, "The Chinese Communist Party and 'Judicial Independence': 1949–1959" (1969) 82 Harvard Law Review 967.
[173] Fan (n 145) 59.

articulated in the Constitution before the last chapter on national symbols and after all chapters on state institutions. These rights provisions are the declaration of state policy rather than a citizen's entitlement. For example, Article 91 provides that: "Citizens of the People's Republic of China have the right to work. To guarantee enjoyment of this right, the state, by planned development of the national economy, gradually creates more employment and better working conditions and wages."[174] This provision is more like the declaration of the state labor policy. Some social rights (e.g. rights to rest and leisure, social insurance, and education) are specially provided for the "working people,"[175] which entails a corresponding state policy.

Finally, the Constitution protects a *statist economy*. Following the Soviet model of ownership,[176] the Constitution protects state, co-operative, collective ownerships of means of production, the state sector as the leading force in the national economy,[177] the state ownership of "all mineral resources and waters, as well as forests, undeveloped land and other resources,"[178] and "the rights of citizens to own lawfully-earned incomes, savings, houses and other means of life."[179] Yet, as a transitional constitution, capitalist ownership was tolerated.[180] But, it makes it clear that capitalists would be under the control of the state, providing that: "The policy of the state towards capitalist industry and commerce is to use, restrict and transform them."[181]

The enforcement of the 1954 Constitution is limited. The document "was generally well received in China" but "was not implemented with serious effort."[182] The Anti-Rightist Campaign, a communist campaign to castigate critics of the government, introduced by Mao and lasting roughly from 1957 to 1959, is at odds with the constitutional commitment to fundamental rights.[183] In addition, the Congress was not convened annually throughout the decade 1965–1975, despite the constitutional requirement.[184] The limitations of constitutional enforcement are due in part to the instrumental nature and function of the constitution. When the Constitution was made to legitimize the regime and to send a signal to the outside world about alternative and allegedly "superior" commitments,[185] how it was implemented domestically became less important.

[174] China 1954 Constitution (n 159) art. 91.
[175] Ibid. arts 92, 93, 94.
[176] Fan (n 145) 58.
[177] China 1954 Constitution (n 159) art. 5.
[178] Ibid. art. 6.
[179] Ibid. art. 11.
[180] Ibid. art. 5.
[181] Ibid. art. 10.
[182] Zhang, *The Constitution of China* (n 28) 45.
[183] Cohen (n 144) 66.
[184] Cohen (n 144) 66.
[185] Mao said "Our constitution is of a new, socialist type, different from any of the bourgeois type. It is far more progressive than the constitutions of the bourgeoisie even in its revolutionary period. We are superior to the bourgeoisie." Tse-tung Mao, "On the Draft Constitution of The People's Republic of

2. The 1975 Constitution

Since the 1954 Constitution was considered a transitional document, formal constitutional amendment or replacement became necessary when socialist transformation took place. The socialist transformation in agriculture occurred shortly after the constitution's enactment, and in industry and commerce at the end of the 1950s,[186] and consequently, the need for formal constitutional change was discussed by the Party in 1956.[187] Yet, it was not until 1975 that the second socialist Constitution of the PRC was enacted as the consequence of the Cultural Revolution.[188] Compared to its predecessor of 106 articles and 15,000 words, the new Constitution is extremely short: it only has thirty articles and 2,000 words.[189]

The 1975 Constitution is an *instrument* for dictatorship of the proletariat with an extreme socialist ideology. It is said "to present the final triumph of Mao over the Russian School of ideologues in that it embodied his revolutionary ideas in place of those of the Soviets."[190] Consequently, although it was criticized for presenting the "extreme Left ideology," it is more reflective of Chinese reality than the previous constitution.[191] The constitutional preamble restates the "great victories both in socialist revolution and socialist construction and in the Great Proletarian Cultural Revolution" and then is committed to "continued revolution under the dictatorship of the proletariat" guided by "Marxism-Leninism-Mao Tsetung Thought."[192] Notably, the commitment to this mixed socialist ideology is not only expressed in the preamble but also declared in Article 2 of the Constitution: "Marxism-Leninism-Mao Tsetung Thought is the theoretical basis guiding the thinking of our nation."[193]

Party *vanguardism* was now constitutionally confirmed in the same Article: "The Communist Party of China is the core of leadership of the whole Chinese people. The working class exercises leadership over the state through its vanguard, the Communist Party of China."[194] The Constitution retained the provision on *democratic centralism*,[195] but explicitly placed the state power under the Party's control. The document explicitly provides that the National People's Congress is under the Party's leadership;[196] the Premier of the State Council is appointed and removed

China" in *Selected Works of Mao Tse-tung* (1954) <https://www.marxists.org/reference/archive/mao/selected-works/volume-5/mswv5_37.htm>.

186 Cohen (n 144) 65.
187 Chen, *Chinese Law* (n 3) 100.
188 On the 1975 constitution, see Chin Kim, "The 1975 Constitution of the People's Republic of China" (1977) 1 Hastings International and Comparative Law Review 1; John Gardner, "The Chinese Constitution of 1975" (1976) 11 Government and Opposition 212.
189 Cohen (n 144) 66.
190 Chen, *Chinese Law* (n 3) 101.
191 Ibid.
192 The 1975 Constitution of the People's Republic of China preamble.
193 Ibid. art. 2.
194 Ibid. art. 2.
195 Ibid. art. 3.
196 Ibid. art. 16.

by the Congress by the proposal of the Party's Central Committee;[197] and the armed forces are led by the Party with the Central Committee's Chairman commanding the country's armed forces.[198] The Constitution abolished the office of state presidency.[199] Fundamental *rights* are condensed into four articles as opposed to fourteen articles in the preceding constitution, and are more statist as a consequence of the Anti-Rightist Campaign. These rights are not supposed to be the entitlements for citizens to make claims and challenge the state but are to support the leadership of the Communist Party of China, support the socialist system and abide by the Constitution and the laws of the People's Republic of China.[200] The constitutional *economy* is more statist without the toleration of capitalist elements. The Constitution only recognizes two forms of ownership: the socialist (or state) ownership and the collective ownership of the working people.[201] This "reflects the complexion of socialist transformation of the means of production."[202] It confirms that the state "promotes the planned and proportionate development of the socialist economy."[203]

The 1975 Constitution institutionally departed from the Soviet constitutional model in substantive aspects but ideologically adhered to fundamental Marxist-Leninist constitutional concepts and principles. This document, is, in fact, a mixture of Mao socialist ideology informed by Chinese reality with a Marxist-Leninist constitutional identity.

3. The 1978 Constitution

Mao's death in 1976 and the castigation of the so-call Gang of Four (four communist officials prominent during the Cultural Revolution) led to the enactment of a new Constitution in 1978.[204] The document is an instrument to express the change in communist leadership and new communist policy, especially the Four Modernizations (four goals to modernize agriculture, industry, national defense, and science and technology).[205] The 1978 Constitution abolished radical features of the preceding charter (e.g. the legislature as the body of the communist party) and restored the Soviet style of centralized institutional structure (including the procuracy) provided by the 1954 Constitution.[206] Yet, reminiscent of the Cultural Revolution, the Constitution retained the radical commitments to "class struggle"

[197] Ibid. art. 17.
[198] Ibid. art. 15.
[199] Albert Chen, *Introduction to the Legal System of the Peoples Republic of China* (5th edn, LexisNexis 2019) 49.
[200] China 1975 Constitution (n 192), art. 26.
[201] Ibid. art. 5.
[202] Kim, "The 1975 Constitution of the People's Republic of China" (n 188) 14.
[203] China 1975 Constitution (n 192), art. 10.
[204] On this constitution, see Chin Kim and Timothy G Kearley, "The 1978 Constitution of the People's Republic of China" (1979) 2 Hastings International and Comparative Law Review 251.
[205] Zhang, *The Constitution of China* (n 28) 47.
[206] Chen, *Chinese Law* (n 3) 101.

and "dictatorship of the proletariat"[207] and the explicit confirmation of the vanguard role of the communist party[208] and explicit provisions for the party's control of the armed forces and state institutions.[209] The Constitution restored statist provisions of fundamental rights and included new rights, especially "the freedoms of thought and expression."[210] The statist arrangement of the constitutional economy basically remained, including the two forms of ownership[211] and the state economic sector as the "leading force of the national economy."[212]

Two sets of amendment to the 1978 Constitution were introduced in 1979 and 1980. The first set dealt with, among other issues, the restructuring of local governments, while the second deleted a provision on the right to "speak out freely, air their views fully, hold great debates and write big-character posters,"[213] which was designated to depress the "Democracy Movement" initiated in late August 1978.[214] These constitutional amendments exemplify the feature of constant amendments of socialist constitutions in response to the instrumental needs of the communist elite.

4. The 1982 Constitution

In the 1980s, two new instrumental needs motivated the Chinese communist elite to engage in a new project of constitution-making. The first was to create a new constitutional framework to facilitate the "Open Door" economic reform, the landmark economic policy initiated by Deng Xiaoping in 1978.[215] The second was to repudiate the negative legacies of the Cultural Revolution.[216] A party official document stated that "the kind of chaotic situation that was obtained in the 'cultural revolution' must never be allowed to happen again in any sphere."[217] The constitution-making process was under the strict control of the Party.[218] The constitution-making initiative was formally decided by the Central Committee of the Party, followed by the National People Congress's approval in September 1980.[219] A constitution-making body called the "Constitution Revision Committee" was comprised of 103 members, including all members of the politburo and the Central Committee's Secretariat.[220] The Party assigned communist

[207] China 1978 Constitution (n 192), preamble.
[208] Ibid. art. 2.
[209] Ibid. arts 19 and 22.
[210] Kim and Kearley, "The 1978 Constitution" (n 204) 253.
[211] China 1978 Constitution (n 192), art. 5.
[212] Ibid. art. 6.
[213] Ibid. art. 45.
[214] Chen, *Introduction* (n 199) 50.
[215] Zhang, *The Constitution of China* (n 28) 48.
[216] William C. Jones, "The Constitution of the People's Republic *of* China" (1985) 63 Washington University Law Quarterly 707, 712.
[217] Fan (n 145) 65.
[218] Chen, *Chinese Law* (n 3) 103.
[219] Ibid.
[220] Ibid. 104.

leader Peng Zhen to articulate guidelines for constitution-making, who proposed that the new constitution should include, among its principles, Deng's Four Fundamental Principles[221] (the adherence to socialism, people's democratic dictatorship, leadership of the Communist Party of China, and Mao Zedong Thought and Marxism-Leninism). The constitution was drafted according to these ultimate guidelines, released for public discussion in four months, and finally adopted by the National People's Congress on December 4, 1982.[222] Ye Jianying, the chairman of the constitution drafting committee, stated that: '[We] might draw some experience of constitution-making from the other advanced states, particularly borrowing some from new socialist constitutions."[223] One of the important socialist constitutions that inspired the Chinese 1984 constitution-makers is the 1977 Soviet Constitution.[224] This Constitution is the current constitution in China, and in 2014 the Party declared its day of adoption to be the nation's Constitution Day.[225]

The Constitution is an instrument to express the Party's new ideology and policy in constitutional terms.[226] Its preamble now incorporates "Deng Xiaoping Theory," in addition to Marxism-Leninism and Mao Zedong Thought, as the guiding ideology of the Communist Party.[227] In addition, inspired by a provision in the Soviet charter,[228] the Chinese counterpart provided for the principle of constitutional supremacy in Article 5: "The state upholds the uniformity and dignity of the socialist legal system. No law or administrative or local rules and regulations shall contravene the constitution."[229] This provision, however, is not a commitment to constitutionalism. Rather, it indicates the dual nature of the socialist constitution as the political document and the supreme law in the socialist legal system. Constitutional supremacy is meant to ensure "the uniformity and dignity of the socialist legal system" rather than to constrain the state actions.

Party vanguardism also witnessed a new development. The 1982 Constitution refers to the leadership of the CPC in its preamble, rather than expressly mandating this in a constitutional provision as in the 1975 and 1978 documents. Jianfu Chen explains this change as being due to the fact that "major efforts have been made for such [party] control to be exercised through state mechanisms."[230] Yet, the nature of the Party vanguardism does not substantively change but is now pursued under the framework called "The system of multi-party cooperation and

221 Ibid.
222 Zhang, *The Constitution of China* (n 28) 50.
223 Fan (n 145) 65.
224 Ibid.
225 Jerome A. Cohen, "China's New National Constitution Day: Is It Worth Celebrating?" (2014) 24 ChinaBrief 3.
226 Jones (n 216) 713.
227 China 1982 Constitution preamble.
228 Fan (n 145).
229 China 1982 Constitution (n 227), art. 5.
230 Chen, *Chinese Law* (n 3) 121.

political consultation led by the Communist Party of China."[231] This unique system establishes that "The CPC is the only party in power in the People's Republic of China while under the precondition of accepting the leadership of the CPC, the eight other political parties participate in the discussion and management of state affairs, in cooperation with the CPC."[232]

Democratic centralism has been continuingly established as a constitutional principle,[233] but the detailed provisions on institutional structure contain important changes, such as the expansion of power of the National People's Congress, the restoration of the position of President, and two-term limits on the Presidency and membership of the National People's Congress's Standing Committee.[234]

The statist rights also have new developments.[235] The Constitution restored and expanded the rights provisions in the 1954 Constitution.[236] The bill of rights is now placed before the structural provisions to signal the regime's commitment to depart from the Cultural Revolution's legacy and respect individual rights.[237] Borrowing from a provision in the Soviet Constitution, a new right to dignity is included[238] "for comforting people with painful memories from the decade of the Cultural Revolution when innocent individuals were oppressed or tortured by cruel and inhumane punishment beyond what was established by law."[239] Yet, following the Soviet model, the practice of rights "may not infringe upon the interests of the state, of society and of the collective, or upon the lawful freedoms and rights of other citizens."[240] This provision defines the nature of statist rights.

The statist constitutional economy continues to feature the "socialist public ownership" of the means of production (ownership by the whole people or the state, and collective ownership by the working people),[241] and the state economy as "the leading force in the national economy."[242] Private property rights are protected, including the right to inherit private property.[243] The constitutional economy was affected by an amendment in 1988, providing the constitutional base for private economy and the commercial transfer of land use rights, which in fact legitimized the existing economic practices.[244]

231 China 1982 Constitution (n 227), preamble.

232 "The System of Multi-Party Cooperation and Political Consultation" (Ching.org.cn) <http://www.china.org.cn/english/Political/29034.htm>

233 China 1982 Constitution (n 227), art. 3.

234 Jones (n 216) 730.

235 Fan (n 145) 66.

236 Hungdah Chiu, "The 1982 Chinese Constitution and Rule of Law" (1985) 4 Series in Contemporary Asian Studies 6.

237 Fan (n 145) 66.

238 China 1982 Constitution (n 227), art. 38.

239 Fan (n 145) 66–7.

240 China 1982 Constitution (n 227), art. 51.

241 Ibid. art. 6.

242 Ibid. art. 7.

243 Ibid. art. 13.

244 Chen, *Chinese Law* (n 3) 105.

B. Vietnam

1. The 1959 Constitution

After the Điện Biên Phủ victory, the Geneva Conference divided Vietnam into two separate zones, North and South, with the Democratic Republic of Vietnam ruling in the North from Hanoi, and the Republic of Vietnam, under the support of the United States, ruling in the South from Sài Gòn (presently, Hồ Chí Minh City).[245] The Democratic Republic of Vietnam enacted the second constitution, a charter for implementing socialism in the North, modeled after the Soviet constitutional system, in December 1959;[246] whereas the Republic of Vietnam in the South enacted its own two constitutions in 1956 and 1963 respectively.[247] Hồ Chí Minh was formally the president of the drafting committee of the 1959 Constitution, but the document was drafted with the predominant direction by the socialists of the Party of Labor (the renamed communist party), particularly under the influence of the Secretary-General of the Party Trường Chinh.[248] This explains the radical differences between the 1946 Constitution and the 1959 Constitution.

Bernard B. Fall provides a useful description of the socialist features of this constitution.[249] According to him, this document "deals in extreme detail with economic theories and makes abundant use of stereotyped communist phrases and ideas."[250] To illustrate, its preamble "contains all the communist cliches of the past decade, from the 'planned development of agriculture' to the 'wholehearted solidarity' with the other nations of the Soviet orbit."[251] On institutional structure, the National Assembly was introduced to replace the former People's Parliament, now defined as " 'the highest organ of state authority,' a turn of phrase that can be found in all constitutions of the Soviet bloc.' "[252] Its standing committee's new powers "are strictly parallel to those of the USSR's Presidium of the Supreme Soviet."[253] Socialist influences can be also found in the constitutional provisions on the "state control

245 Ibid. 330–1, 335.

246 On the 1959 Constitution, see Bernard B. Fall, "North Vietnam's Constitution and Government" (1960) 34 Pacific Affairs 284.

247 For more details, see Robert Devereux, "South Vietnam's New Constitutional Structure" (1968) 8 Asian Survey 627, 628–45; J.A.C. Grant, "The Vietnam Constitution of 1956" (1958) 52(2) American Political Science Review 437, 444–62; Milton Sacks, "Restructuring Government in South Vietnam" (1967) 7 Asian Survey 515.

248 Trường Chinh was the Secretary-General of the prewar Indochina Communist Party and became the Secretary-General of the Party of Labor when it was formed in 1951. After the Geneva Conference, Trường Chinh resolved to follow Stalin's example and build socialism in the North Vietnam. See William Warbey, *Ho Chi Minh and the Struggle for an Independent Vietnam* (Merlin Press 1972) 117–18.

249 Bernard B. Fall, "Constitution-Writing in a Communist State: The New Constitution of North Vietnam" (1960) 6 Howard Law Journal 157.

250 Ibid. 159.

251 Ibid.

252 Ibid. 163.

253 Ibid.

organs," people's courts, the Leninist people's procuracies, local government, and statist rights and duties of citizens, and the "new economic policy."[254]

2. The 1980 Constitution

After the Vietnam War, the new Constitution of the Socialist Republic of Vietnam (SRV) was promulgated in December 1980, the charter for enforcing socialism throughout Vietnam.[255] Like China's 1982 Constitution, the SRV's 1980 Constitution strictly adhered to the *1977* Soviet *Constitution*. It defines the Socialist Republic of Vietnam as "a state of proletarian dictatorship whose goals are to build socialism successfully and advance to communism," among others.[256] Party vanguardism and socialist ideology are established in Article 4: "The Communist Party of Vietnam, the vanguard and general staff of the Vietnamese working class, armed with Marxism-Leninism, is the only force leading the state and society, and is the main factor determining all successes of the Vietnamese revolution."[257] Ho Chi Minh's ideology is not explicitly established in the body of the constitution, but the commitment to his ideology is expressed in the preamble, which stated that: "Let our entire people strengthen unity and act upon the sacred testament of our great President Ho Chi Minh."[258]

Article 6 stipulates that all state organs "are organized and function according to the principle of democratic centralism."[259] The Leninist constitutional structure consists of the supreme National Assembly, the collective presidency (the Council of State), the other institutions (Council of Ministers, the procucracies, and the courts) are subordinate to the National assembly. Statist rights are prominent. Constitutional rights and duties are based on these principles: "Each for all, all for each." The rights of citizens are inseparable from their obligations. The state guarantees the rights of citizens, and citizens must fulfill their obligations towards the state and society.[260] The statist features of the constitutional economy include: "the centrally-run economy";[261] socialist ownership of the means of production (state ownership and collective ownership of the working people);[262] the leading role of the state sector in the national economy,[263] and the state's protection of the citizens' right to private ownership.[264]

[254] Ibid. 164–7.
[255] On the 1980 Constitution, see William J. Duiker, "The Constitutional System of the Socialist Republic of Vietnam" in *Constitutional Systems in Late Twentieth Century Asia* (Lawrence Beer (ed.), University of Washington Press 1992).
[256] 1980 Constitution of Vietnam, art. 2.
[257] Ibid. art. 4.
[258] Ibid. preamble.
[259] Ibid. art. 6.
[260] Ibid. art. 54.
[261] Ibid. art. 16.
[262] Ibid. art. 18.
[263] Ibid. art. 18.
[264] Ibid. art. 27.

During the period when the 1959 and 1980 Constitutions were implemented, Vietnamese constitutional thinking was predominated by Marxist-Leninist political and legal ideology. This is understandable in political circumstances where political leaders were gravitating toward the Soviet model and in an intellectual environment where most constitutional scholars were educated in the Soviet Union. The 1959 and 1980 Constitutions were established with the hegemony of communist ideology, and this stymied the dynamics of constitutional discourse. As Professor Mark Sidel points out, from 1959 to 1980, in Vietnam, "there were only occasionally alternative voices heard in the north on issues of constitutionalism."[265] Statements of political elite and "scientific work" on the 1956 and 1980 Constitutions were dominated by the dogma emulated from "historical materialism," "scientific communism," and soviet constitutional tradition, including: the class nature of state and law, the dichotomy of capitalism and socialism, dictatorship of the proletariat, the leadership of the communist party, democratic centralism, concentration of power, and socialist legality.[266] "Constitutional law" was eventually conceived as the "bourgeois" product and was not taught at law schools. The alternative course called the "Law on the State of Vietnam" was taught in a highly ideological manner. Limits were placed on alternative voices to constitutional discourse.

C. Laos

The Issara government is the forerunner of the communist government, or the Lao People's Democratic Republic. For the Issara leaders in Thailand, the French tutelage of Laos was unacceptable.[267] However, "the government-in-exile was unable to obtain international recognition or assistance from any state other than Thailand."[268] In this context, the more effective way "was Vietminh directed activities along the Lao-Vietnamese boarder."[269] On August 13, 1950, with the consultation of Vietnamese communist leaders (Ho Chi Minh and Vo Nguyen Giap), the Lao communist movement called Pathet Lao (the Land of the Lao) was created in north-western Vietnam, with Souphanouvong as prime minister and minister of foreign affairs, and Kaysone Phomvihane as minister of defense.[270] On March 22,

[265] Sidel, *The Constitution of Vietnam* (n 81) 62.

[266] See for example, Institute of Legal Studies (ed.), *Hiến pháp nước Cộng Hòa Xã Hội Chủ Nghĩa Việt Nam [The Constitution of the Socialist Republic of Vietnam]* (Legal Publishing House 1980); Vietnam Lawyers Association (ed.), *Nhà nước và pháp luật [State and Law], Volume 1- Những vấn đề cơ bản về hiến pháp Việt-Nam (31-12-1959)* [*Fundamental Issues on the Vietnam Constitution (31 December 1959)*] (Labor Publishing House 1971).

[267] Stuart-Fox (n 95) 18.

[268] Ibid.

[269] Ibid.

[270] Ibid. 19.

1955, the communist party of Laos, which has its roots in the Communist Party of Indochina, was officially created as the Lao People's Party (Phak Passon Lao), and has had its current name, Lao People's Revolutionary Party (Phak Pasason Pativat Lao), since 1975. By the end of the second Indochina War, the communist-backed Pathet Lao prevailed over the US-backed Royal faction in the coalition government called the Provisional Government of National Unity.[271] In December 1975, the Pathet Lao dissolved the coalition government, forced the king to abdicate, and declared the creation of the Lao People's Democratic Republic.[272]

For the next sixteen years, the communist government ruled Laos without a constitution. Stuart-Fox provided two possible explanations for this delay of constitution-making.[273] The first concerns the possible disagreement "between the Lao leadership and their Vietnamese counterparts and advisers" on a suitable constitutional form in Laos.[274] The second difficult question is how the constitution should provide for the protection of the rights of minority groups occupying a half of the national population.[275]

D. North Korea

1. The 1948 People's Democratic Constitution

In 1910, the Korean peninsula was annexed to Japan. Japan's surrender to the Allies on August 14, 1945, led to a new phase of modern constitution-making in Korea.[276] By 1948, the Korean peninsula was divided into the North, occupied by the Soviet Union and the South, occupied by the United States. Governments on both sides enacted their own constitutions in 1948.[277] The Constitution of the Republic of Korea (or South Korea) embraced many features of American liberal constitutionalism,[278] while the People's Democratic Constitution of the Democratic People's Republic of Korea (or North Korea) enacted by the Supreme People's Assembly (SPA) imitated the Stalin 1936 Constitution of the Soviet Union.[279]

[271] Robert Dayley, *Southeast Asia in the New International Era* (Westview Press 2017) 165.

[272] Ibid. For more details on the triumph of communism in Laos, see Macalister Brown, "The Communist Seizure of Power in Laos" in *Contemporary Laos: Studies in the Politics and Society of the Lao People's Democratic Republic* (Martin Stuart-Fox (ed.), University of Queensland Press 1982) 17–38.

[273] Stuart-Fox (n 95) 69.

[274] Ibid.

[275] Ibid.

[276] Wen-Chen Chang, "East Asian Foundations for Constitutionalism: Three Models Reconstructed" (2009) 3 National Taiwan University Law Review 111, 119.

[277] Yeh Jiunn-Rong and Wen-Chen Chang, "The Emergence of East Asian Constitutionalism: Features in Comparison" (2011) 59 American Journal of Comparative Law 805, 818.

[278] Kyong Whan Ahn, "The Influence of American Constitutionalism on South Korea" (1997) 22 Southern Illinois University Law Journal 71, 73.

[279] T. Kim, "Comparison of the Constitution of South and North Korea—Prospects for a Constitution for a Unified Korea" (1982) 10 Korean Journal of Comparative Law 1, 3.

Like the Soviet model, the North Korea Constitution designs a centralized constitutional structure: the SPA as the highest organ of state power, the Presidium as its standing committee and the collective head of state; and the Cabinet practicing the executive power authorized by the SPA. A lengthy list of fundamental rights accompanied by duties is provided. Interestingly, copying a provision in the Soviet Constitution, the North Korea Constitution provides for the protection of "national minorities," while a study in 1964 indicates that there is only the Korean nation in the Korean peninsula.[280] However, the statist constitutional economy reflects the reality of North Korea in the early stages of socialism, which led to the compromise of socialist identities and non-socialist legacies.[281] This is evident in the constitutional provisions which stipulate multiple ownership of the means of production (state, co-operative, and private); confiscation of land owned by the Japanese state and Japanese nationals, and the Korean landlords; protection of private property; the nationally planned economy with the participation of privately owned economy.[282] The Constitution was amended four times in 1954, 1955, 1956, and 1962 to deal with some minor institutional issues.[283]

2. The Socialist Constitution of 1972

The completion of collectivizing lands and socializing all means of production together with the consolidation of Kim Il-sung induced the SPA's enactment of the second Constitution of North Korea in 1972.[284] The new charter aims to eliminate the non-socialist legacies and consolidate the socialist identities. It is, therefore, called the "Socialist Constitution."[285] It defines North Korea as "an independent socialist state"[286] under "the dictatorship of the proletariat."[287] The Constitution explicitly establishes that the regime will be guided by the Democratic People's Republic of Korea's ideology called *Juche*, "a creative application of Marxism-Leninism to the realities"[288] of North Korea. *Juche* (literally self-reliance), considered "the Korean way to socialism," was introduced by Kim II Sung in 1955 in his critical response to the "dogmatic and formalistic tendencies" to copy the "Marxist-Leninist practice" in other socialist countries.[289]

[280] Youn-Soo Kim, "The 1972 Socialist Constitution of the Korean Democratic People's Republic" (1977) 3 Review of Socialist Law 281, 283.

[281] D. Yoon, "The Constitution of North Korea: Its Changes and Implications" (2004) 27(4) Fordham International Law Journal 1289

[282] Constitution of the Democratic People's Republic of Korea 1948, arts 5, 6, 8, and 10.

[283] Kim, "The 1972 Socialist Constitution" (n 280) 284.

[284] Ibid.; Yoon (n 281) 1295. On this constitution, see also John N. Hazard "A Comparativist's View of the 1972 Constitution of the Democratic People's Republic of Korea" (1974) 7(1) Studies in Comparative Communism 73; C. Kim and T.G. Kearley, "The 1972 Socialist Constitution of North Korea" (1976) 11(1) Texas International Law Journal 113.

[285] Yoon (n 281) 1295.

[286] Socialist Constitution of the Democratic People's Republic of Korea (1972) art. 1.

[287] Ibid. art. 10.

[288] Ibid. art. 4.

[289] Geir Helgesen, "Political Revolution in A Cultural Continuum: Preliminary Observations on the North Korean 'Juche' Ideology With Its Intrinsic Cult Of Personality" (1991) 15 Asian Perspective 187,

The ideology of *Juche* therefore underlines the importance of "underlying historical and cultural conditions of Korea—including the people's manners and customs" in the course of "socialist revolution."[290] In the party's official teaching, "the Juche idea defined man as the master who dominates the world, not merely as part of it, and thus established a new world outlook which, unlike preceeding [sic] ones, regards the world and its changes and progress with man, its master, at the centre."[291]

Democratic centralism is confirmed as the constitutional principle of all state organs' formation and actions.[292] Chapter VI details the centralized constitutional structure, including sections on the supreme people's assembly, the national defense commission, the presidium of the supreme people's assembly, the cabinet, the local people's assembly and committee, the public prosecutor's office, and courts. One distinctive feature of the centralized constitutional system is the presidency. As the reflection of the consolidated power of Kim II-Sung, the Constitution stipulated an individual Presidency created by the Supreme People's Assembly with a four-year term without a term limit. In formal constitutional terms, the President guides the Central People's Committee, convenes and guides the State Administration Council when necessary, and "is the supreme commander of the entire armed forces of the Democratic People's Republic of Korea and the Chairman of the National Defense Commission, and commands the entire armed forces of the state."[293] In reality, Kim was selected as the first President and held this position until his death in 1994.[294] While the Constitution defines the SPA as "the highest organ of state power,"[295] the real power lay with the President.[296] The powerful presidency is considered a distinctive feature of North Korea's 1972 Constitution: it is different from the collective Presidium or symbolic individual presidency in other socialist countries at the same time.[297]

Chapter V provides for the citizens' fundamental rights and duties. Rights are shaped by the statist constitutional principles. "One for all and all for one" is established as the "collectivist principle" of the rights and duties of citizens.[298] This means that the practice of rights would be situated within collective duties to the

190, 194. See also, Christopher Hale, "Multifunctional Juche: A Study of the Changing Dynamic between Juche and the State Constitution in North Korea" (2002) 42(3) Korea Law 283.

[290] Helgesen, "Political Revolution" (n 289) 190.
[291] Ibid. 188.
[292] Socialist Constitution of Korea (n 286) art. 9.
[293] Ibid. arts 91, 92, and 93.
[294] Yoon (n 281) 1296.
[295] Socialist Constitution of Korea (n 286) art. 73.
[296] Yoon (n 281) 1296.
[297] Youn-Soo Kim, "The 1972 Socialist Constitution of the Korean Democratic People's Republic" (1977) 3 Review of Socialist Law 281, 287.
[298] Socialist Constitution of Korea (n 286) art. 49.

state, the community, and other citizens. In addition, the implementation of rights is accompanied by the state's empowerment: "The State shall effectively guarantee genuine democratic rights and liberties as well as the material and cultural well-being of all its citizens."[299] To reflect the social reality, the provision for the protection of national minorities was removed.

Chapter II is devoted to the statist principles of the socialist constitutional economy. It establishes that the regime "relies on the socialist production relations and on the foundation of an independent national economy."[300] The State, social, and co-operative organizations' ownership of the means of production are recognized.[301] The non-socialist elements of the constitutional economy were deleted, including the taxation system, private ownership of means of production, and the right to run private businesses.[302] Private property was limited to property for private use only.[303]

E. Cuba

Fidel Castro led a revolution against the Fulgencio government, and a Fundamental Law was enacted by the Council of Ministers in 1959, which "changed the government of Cuba into a virtual constitutional dictatorship."[304] The period between 1959 and 1976 is "a period of constitutional irregularity."[305] The Fundamental Law was amended 16 times to reflect changes in policy before its repudiation in 1961.[306] Then, in preparing for a new constitution, legal scholars as well as government and communist party officials "studied the Marxist theory and socialist institutions."[307] In 1965, a constitutional commission was created but failed to draft a new constitution.[308] Explaining the delayed constitution-making, John N. Hazard wrote that "for years the Soviet communist party's leaders tolerated the presence within the commonwealth of a state without a modern socialist constitution, either because the principles applied in practice conformed to those of 1957 or because they knew that an acceptable draft was in preparation."[309]

299 Ibid. art. 64.
300 Ibid. art. 19.
301 Ibid. art. 20.
302 Yoon (n 281) 1297.
303 Socialist Constitution of Korea (n 286) art. 22.
304 D'zurlla, "Cuba's 1976 Socialist" (n 131) 1239.
305 Klein, "The Socialist Constitution" (n 136) 460.
306 Ibid. 460. For details of the amendments, see the International Commission of Jurists, Cuba, and the rule of law (Geneva, 1962) 98–112.
307 Klein, "The Socialist Constitution" (n 136) 458.
308 D'zurlla (n 131) 1242.
309 J.N. Hazard, "Soviet Model for Marxian Socialist Constitutions" (1974–1975) 60(6) Cornell Law Review 985, 989.

1. The Socialist Constitution of 1976

After preparatory work and as the culmination of the official policy called "institutionalization"[310] restored in 1970, the new *socialist Constitution* was adopted in 1976.[311] The two-year (1974–1976) constitution-making process involved these activities: the Council of the Ministers and the Political Bureau of the Cuban Communist Party provided the "guidelines" for constitution-making; "a small group of comrades" prepared the preliminary constitutional draft (the *Anteproyecto*); the *Anteproyecto* was studied by the Council of the Ministers and the Political Bureau; it was then sent to public discussions which involved some 6,200,000 people; the First Party Congress approved the preliminary constitutional draft after minor changes; and the final draft (the *Proyecto*) was ratified by a national referendum.[312]

As one commentator stated, "Like the constitutions of all communist party states, the Cuban constitution is an instrument of social engineering."[313] It is a charter for "the construction of socialism and, under the direction of the Communist Party" and ultimately building "a communist society,"[314] as declared in its preamble. Article 1 defines Cuba as "an independent and sovereign socialist state of workers, and peasants and all other manual and intellectual workers."[315] The constitutional articulation of this socialist and communist program is situated within the nation's distinctive history of independent movement against Spanish colonialism, the "proletarian internationalism," and "the fraternal friendship, help cooperation of the Soviet Union and other socialist countries" and the "solidarity of the workers and people of Latin America and of the world."[316]

Party vanguardism is expressed in the preamble and Article 5: "The Communist Party of Cuba, the organized Marxist-Leninist vanguard of the working class, is the highest leading force of the society and the State, which organizes and guides the common effort toward the goals of the construction of socialism and the progress toward a communist society."[317] Yet, the distinctive feature is the additional establishment of the non-communist ideology of José Martí as the guiding ideology of the regime. The preamble declared that the Constitution of the Republic shall be guided by José Martí's desire: "I want the fundamental law of our republic to be the

310 H.J. Berman and V. Whiting, "Impressions of Cuban Law" (1980) 28(3) American Journal of Comparative Law 475, 477 (reporting that "the policy of institutionalization has restored the prestige not only of law but also of the legal profession.") for comparative experience, see W.R. Baerg, "Judicial Institutionalization of the Revolution: The Legal Systems of the People's Republic of China and the Republic of Cuba" (1992) 15(1) Loyola of Los Angeles International and Comparative Law Review 233.
311 Klein, "The Socialist Constitution" (n 136) 451, 459.
312 Ibid. 451, 461–5.
313 D'zurlla (n 131) 1242.
314 Constitution of the Republic of Cuba 1976 preamble.
315 Ibid. art. 1.
316 Ibid. preamble.
317 Ibid. art. 5.

tribute of Cubans to the full dignity of man."[318] This is attributed to the need to incorporate nationalist values into the Constitution.[319]

Democratic centralism is also confirmed: "State organs are set up, function and carry out their activity based on the principles of socialist democracy, unity of power and democratic centralism."[320] These principles reject the doctrine of separation of powers, aim at concentrating power on the "working people" presented by the National Assembly, but allow for distribution of government functions.[321] This reflects Fidel Castro's view: "There is a division of functions, but there is no division of power. Power is one, the power of the working people exercised through the National Assembly and the state bodies dependent on it."[322] Within the centralized constitutional structure, the National Assembly (like the Supreme Soviet) is defined as the "supreme organ of State power"[323] and other state institutions (the Council of State equivalent to the Presidium of the Supreme Soviet, Council of Ministers constituting the Government, People's Supreme Tribunal, and Office of the Attorney General equivalent to the Soviet procuracy) subordinate to it. Yet, compared to the socialist community, one distinctive feature[324] of the constitutional arrangement in Cuba is that the President of the Council of State is concurrently the Head of Government with the power to "assume the leadership of any ministry and central agency of the administration."[325] This may reflect the influential role of Castro in the nation's communist revolutionary history, who became the President of the Council of State after the adoption of the constitution.

Statist rights are also prominent. Rights are balanced with duties. Article 40 provides that: "All citizens have equal rights and are subject to equal duties."[326] Work is both "a right and duty and a source of pride for every citizen."[327] The exercise of the freedom of speech and of the press must be "in keeping with the objectives of socialist society."[328] Yet, other provisions on citizenship reflect the local distinctive conditions. For example, Article 30 and Article 32 stipulate the conditions relating to the acquisition and loss of citizenship, which reflect the "legacy of national tradition."[329]

The socialist constitutional economy shares some core statist features. The Constitution establishes a socialist economic system "based on the people's socialist ownership of the means of production and on the abolition of the exploitation of

[318] Ibid. preamble.
[319] Klein, "The Socialist Constitution" (n 136) 474.
[320] Cuba 1976 Constitution (n 314) art. 66.
[321] Klein, "The Socialist Constitution" (n 136) 499.
[322] Ibid.
[323] Cuba 1976 Constitution (n 314) art. 69.
[324] Klein, "The Socialist Constitution" (n 136) 505.
[325] Cuba 1976 Constitution (n 314) art. 91.
[326] Ibid. art. 40.
[327] Ibid. art. 44.
[328] Ibid. art. 52.
[329] Klein, "The Socialist Constitution" (n 136) 479.

man by man."[330] Article 16 provides that: "The state organizes, directs and controls the economic life of the nation in accordance with the central plan of socioeconomic development."[331] The constitutional economy is also reflective of the social reality. For example, in addition to "the socialist state property," private ownership of "small farmers or to cooperatives formed by the same"[332] is recognized due to "the survival on the island of private ownership of small plots of agricultural land."[333]

III. The Post-Soviet Transition

The constitutions of the five remaining socialist states immediately reacted to the fall of communism in Eastern Europe in 1989 and the dissolution of the Soviet Union in December 1991. In the following years (1992 and 1993), the four socialist states amended their constitutions (China, North Korea, and Cuba) or replaced the current one (Vietnam), while Laos eventually adopted the first socialist constitution in 1991. This experience of constitution-making, amendment, and replacement took place during the transition era. The socialist transition is not the triple transition of the post-communist states in Europe,[334] but has relevant features. In response to the external fall of communism and internal dynamics, the triple socialist transition included independent states, economic reforms, and institutional adjustment, which were addressed in the transition constitutions. As liberalism now triumphed over communism, Marxist-Leninism was removed or supplemented by the local socialist ideology, which in some cases mixed socialist and capitalist ideas. Economic reforms, perhaps, are the key feature of the transition constitutions of the remaining socialist states. The socialist constitutional economy now adopted more capitalist values although the socialist features have remained dominant. Full democratization of the socialist constitutional structure was not the case, but institutional adjustment was introduced.

A. Factors

The fall of communism in Eastern and Central Europe in 1989 and the dissolution of the Soviet Union in December 1991 were major external factors of the transitional constitutional change in the five remaining socialist countries: China,

[330] Cuba 1976 Constitution (n 314) art. 14.
[331] Ibid. art. 16.
[332] Ibid. art. 15.
[333] Klein, "The Socialist Constitution" (n 136) 484.
[334] Claus Offe, *Varieties of Transition: The East European and East German Experience* (Polity Press 1996) 29–49.

Vietnam, Laos, North Korea, and Cuba.[335] This external event effected three aspects of constitutional response. First, the post-cold war radical changes of world geopolitics required the adjustment of fundamental commitments in international and diplomatic relationship of the socialist countries, and this was necessarily addressed at the constitutional level. Second, the fact that western liberalism prevailed over communism required changes in constitutional commitment to the communist ideology. Third, as the five socialist countries depended on aid from the Soviet Union and trade partners from Eastern and Central Europe, the post-communist traumas engendered economic difficulties, and this needed to be addressed in the constitution.

In addition to the external collapse of communism, the internal institutional dynamics was an equally important factor. While communism was collapsing in Europe, internal institutional adaption had already occurred in the five countries, which is the key reason for their resilience, despite the domino effect of the communist fall in Europe. Rather than strictly adhering to the constitutional provisions of the statist market of the traditional socialist constitutions, extra-constitutional economic institutions and practices were at play to facilitate socio-economic changes. China, Vietnam, and Laos undertook relatively similar market reforms: China launched the *Gǎigé kāifàng* ("Reform & Opening up") policy in 1979; Vietnam started reform policy in 1979 culminating in the introduction of the comprehensive economic reform program called *Đổi Mới* (Renovation) in 1986; and Laos initiated the *Chintanakan Mai* (new economic thinking) in the same year.[336]

In North Korea, although such comprehensive program of market reform was not adopted, institutional adaption was at play to address economic difficulties: the Joint Venture Act was adopted in 1984 to attract foreign investment, and the Jajin-Sonbong Free Economic Trade Zone was created in 1991.[337] Like North Korea, Cuba lacked a comprehensive program of market reform, but local economic dynamics were evident: e.g. the rise of the private economic sector and foreign trade through joint ventures, despite the lack of a constitutional base.[338]

The external decline of communism and the internal rise of market economic institutions triggered constitutional responses. Laos eventually adopted the first socialist constitution in August 1991, shortly before the Soviet Union's dissolution,

[335] Steven Saxonberg, *Transitions and Non-Transitions from Communism: Regime Survival in China, Cuba, North Korea, and Vietnam* (Cambridge University Press 2013).

[336] Norihiko Yamada, "Legitimation of the Lao People's Revolutionary Party: Socialism, Chintanakan Mai (New Thinking) and Reform" (2018) 48 Journal of Contemporary Asia 717, 722.

[337] Dae-Kyu Yoon, "Constitutional Change in North Korea" in *Constitutionalism in Asia in the Early Twenty-First Century* (Albert H. Chen (ed.), Cambridge University Press 2014) 101, 109.

[338] Matias F. Travieso-Diaz and Steven R. Escobar, "Cuba's Transition to a Free-Market Democracy: A Survey of Required Changes to Laws and Legal Institutions" (1995) 5 Duke Journal of Comparative & International Law 379, 387; Shari-Ellen Bourque, "The Illegality of the Cuban Embargo in the Current International System" (1995) 13 Boston University International Law Journal 191, 205.

which is significantly different from a standard socialist constitution. In the following year, 1992, Vietnam adopted a new constitution to replace the 1980 Soviet era Constitution, while North Korea and Cuba introduced important amendments to their constitutions. China also adopted "far-reaching" amendments to its Constitution in 1993.[339]

B. Triple Transitions

1. Independent States

The transitional constitutions of the socialist countries has addressed two aspects of the independent states: independence in international relations; and independence in constitutional ideology.

Consider first the independence in international relations. As the soviet empire collapsed, the five constitutions abandoned their commitments to the exclusive relationships with the socialist world and opened up to the larger international community. To illustrate, the amended preamble of China's Constitution is committed to "persevere in reform and opening to the outside world."[340] Vietnam's 1992 Constitution stipulates in Article 14 that the country "pursues a policy of peace, friendship and expanded international relations and cooperation with all countries in the world, irrespective of their political and social systems."[341] In the same vein, Laos' 1991 Constitution provided in Article 12 that the state "promotes the relations and cooperation with all countries."[342] In North Korea, the amended constitution underwent a commitment that "the state shall establish diplomatic as well as political, economic, and cultural relations with all friendly countries."[343] Specifically, the attitude to the capitalist South Korea is "more receptive to co-existence."[344] The Constitution states that the communist government is committed to "complete victory of socialism in the North half of Korea" but supports "peaceful reunification and great national unity (article 9). Finally, Cuba's Constitution provides in Article 12 that the state "maintains relations of friendship with the countries having a different political, social and economic regime."[345]

The second aspect is the independence of constitutional ideology. While the communist regimes remained, their ideology did not exclusively depend on Marxism-Leninism but incorporated local ideology. To illustrate, in its preamble, China's Constitution was continuingly committed to "the guidance of Marxism-Leninism

339 Chen, *Introduction* (n 199) 51.
340 China constitution preamble.
341 Constitution of the Socialist Republic of Vietnam 1992, art. 14.
342 Constitution of Lao People's Democratic Republic 1991, art. 12.
343 Socialist Constitution of the Democratic People's Republic of Korea (amended through 1992) art. 17.
344 Yoon, "Constitutional Change in North Korea" (n 337) 108–9.
345 Constitution of the Republic of Cuba (amended though 1992) art. 12.

and Mao Zedong Thought," but anticipated "theory of building socialism with Chinese characteristics."[346] This signals the message that China has its own way to achieve socialism. The preamble and Article 4 of Vietnam's new 1992 Constitution now added "Ho Chi Minh's Thought" to the communist party's ideology along with Marxism and Leninism.[347] Cuba's Constitution further underlined local ideology, providing in Article 5 that the Communist Party of Cuba was "a follower of Martí's ideas and of Marxism-Leninism."[348] North Korea's Constitution deleted the reference to Marxism and Leninism and only retained the *juche* ideology.[349] The Lao Constitution of 1991 did not have any explicit reference to Marxist-Leninist ideology although it mandated in Article 3 that the Lao People's Revolutionary Party (the communist party) is "the leading nucleus" of the political system.[350] The country's "long-standing aspirations" are not explicitly to erect socialism but to build "Laos a country of peace, independence, democracy, unity and prosperity."[351]

These ideological constitutional changes were driven by both the external collapses of communism and the internal institutional dynamics. Externally, the fall of the Berlin Wall and the Soviet Union indicated that Marxism-Leninism was not the prevailing ideology of the world. The exclusive and rigid commitment to this ideology would prevent the socialist countries from communicating with the majority of the world in which liberalism triumphed. This explains the ideological flexibility, which induces the de-emphasis or even deletion of the reference to Marxism-Leninism and the greater emphasis on local ideology. Ideological flexibility and the articulation of local ideology also allow the socialist countries to address local issues generated by internal institutional dynamics.

2. Marketization

The focus of the transition constitutions of the five social constitutions is to change the constitutional economy by incorporating market values. One of the main concerns of the opening international policy is to integrate the national economy into the international economy to ameliorate domestic economic hardship when external aids and trade partners from the socialist world have collapsed. Domestic institutional dynamics requires a new constitutional economy which both reflects and consolidates economic reforms. The transition constitutions of the five socialist states were committed to socialism but altered the program of social progress to achieve socialist goals, leading to the adoption of opening and reforming principles of the constitutional economy. The difference, however, is between the

346 Ibid. preamble.
347 Ibid. preamble, art. 4.
348 Ibid. art. 5.
349 North Korea Constitution (n 343), art. 3.
350 Lao 1991 Constitution art. 3.
351 Ibid. preamble.

comprehensive change of constitutional economy in China, Vietnam, and Laos, and the *partial* change in North Korea and Cuba. This reflects the reality that the formers states introduced comprehensive programs for market reforms while the latter states only have partial reformist policies.

Consider first the comprehensive one. The constitutions in China and Vietnam, respectively, replaced the planned economy with the "socialist market economy" (Article 15) or "socialist-oriented market economy" (Article 15), while the Lao Constitution introduced the "market economy with the adjustment of the state" (Article 16). This constitutional economy includes two competing components: socialist and market. While the socialist components remain statist and dominant features (state ownership, the leading role of state economic sectors, and the state's management of the economy), market principles and institutions were substantively incorporated into the constitutions. The transition constitutions explicitly adopt market principles such as competition, co-operation, and legal equality of economic sectors (Laos' Constitution, Article 14; Vietnam's 1992 Constitution, Article 16). They also adopt major market institutions, such as multi-sector economy including private economy (Lao Constitution, Article 13); multi-ownership including private ownership (Lao Constitution, Article 14; Vietnam Constitution, Article 15).

In particular, given the economic hardship without Soviet aid and the limited socialist trade partners, attracting foreign investments worldwide became the chief constitutional concern. Vietnam's new 1992 Constitution signaled the commitment that: "The State encourages foreign organizations and individuals to invest capital and technology in Vietnam in accordance with Vietnamese law and with international law and practice; ensures the legal ownership of capital and assets as well as other interests of foreign organizations and individuals. Enterprises with foreign invested capital shall not be nationalized. The State encourages and creates favorable conditions for the Vietnamese who live abroad to invest in the homeland" (Article 25). Lao's Constitution provides that "The state promotes and give advice on the development of economic relations, under many forms, with foreign countries" (Article 18). There was also a commitment that the state shall protect private ownership of foreign investors (Article 14). China had already addressed the concern of foreign investment in its original 1982 Constitution "The People's Republic of China permits foreign enterprises, other foreign economic organizations or foreign individuals to invest in China or to undertake various forms of economic co-operation with Chinese enterprises or other Chinese economic organizations" (Article 12).

The constitutions of North Korea and Cuba did not project a comprehensive plan for a socialist market economy, but partially introduced market elements to the constitutional economy. The North Korea Constitution underlined the independent national economy and technological and scientific development as the base for economic development (Articles 26 and 27). Local institutions, enterprises and organizations were encouraged to enter joint ventures and co-operation of enterprise with foreign corporations and individuals (Article 37). Several investment laws (such as the Foreign Investment Act in 1992, the Foreign Enterprise Act in 1992, the Contractual Joint Venture Act in 1992, and the Foreign Economic Trade Zone Act in 1993) were adopted to implement this constitutional commitment.[352] In Cuba, the Constitution allowed for limited private ownership of the means of production (not "fundamental means of production" which belongs to "social ownership") and private property (Articles 14 and 15).[353] In addition, the Constitution removed the state's monopoly on foreign trade[354] and, like North Korea, encouraged foreign investments through joint ventures (Article 18). The Constitution also allowed "quasi-private companies"[355] by recognizing "the property of mixed enterprises, economic partnerships and associations" (Article 23).

3. Institutional Adjustments

While constitutional changes occurred largely in economic areas, the centralized constitutional structure under the communist party's vanguard leadership was largely unaffected by constitutional amendments in China, North Korea, and Cuba. China introduced some changes to the local government,[356] Cuba modified the election mechanism,[357] and North Korea created a separate constitutional institution called the National Defense Commission.[358] The new constitutions in Laos and Vietnam confirmed the principle of democratic centralism (Articles 5 and 6, respectively). The constitutional system remained largely centralist, in the style of the soviet model, but the distribution of power was relatively clearer. For example, unlike the Soviet model, the Laos Constitution separated the Standing Committee of National Assembly from the President of state. In the case of Vietnam, the presidium was abolished, and the single presidency and the Standing Committee of the National Assembly were created as two separate institutions.

The bills of rights in China, North Korea, and Cuba remained largely the same after constitutional amendments. One notable change in Cuba, however, concerned the right to religious freedom. In 1991, the Communist Party of Cuba removed the requirement that party members must be atheist.[359] This was reflected in a new constitutional commitment that "recognizes, respects, and guarantees freedom of conscience and religion" (Article 55).

[352] Yoon, "Constitutional Change in North Korea" (n 337) 109.
[353] For further details see, Bourque, "The Illegality of the Cuban Embargo" (n 338) 203–4.
[354] Ibid. 204.
[355] Ibid. 205.
[356] See Chen, *Introduction* (n 199) 51.
[357] M.B. Wise, "Cuban Constitutionalism: Will There Be Changes" (2013) 51(2) Duquesne Law Review 467, 51.
[358] Yoon, "Constitutional Change in North Korea" (n 337) 109.
[359] Jill I. Goldenziel "Sanctioning Faith: Religion, State, and US-Cuban Relations" (2009) 25 Journal of Law and Politics 179, 180.

The new bills of rights in Laos and Vietnam are largely statist but less so compared to a traditional socialist bill of rights. Most notably, the term "human rights" appeared in the 1992 Constitution for the first time in Vietnamese constitutional history and as an exception to the five transition constitutions of the socialist states. However, human rights are analogized to citizens' rights: "In the Socialist Republic of Vietnam, human rights in all respects, political, civic, economic, cultural and social are respected, find their expression in the rights of citizens and are provided for by the Constitution and the law" (Article 50). This is a constitutional response to the country's accession to two major international human rights treaties (the International Covenant on Economic, Social, and Cultural Rights; and the International Covenant on Civil and Political Rights) in 1982. In the Constitution of Lao, the "Lao citizens" were often placed before the state in the constitutional rights provisions, which aimed to signal to the world the state's recognition of the importance of fundamental rights vis-à-vis the state. The Constitution even established the principle that rights "cannot be violated by anyone" and that prohibited state actions are "physically harmful to the people and detrimental to their honor, lives, consciences and property" (Article 6).

IV. Conclusion

The examination of socialist constitutional history has three implications for comparative constitutional history. The first implication is the global polarization between the liberal and socialist constitutional models. A theory of "world society" in sociology suggests that a hundred nation-states around the world shared "standardized forms," including "constitutional forms emphasizing both state power and individual rights."[360] Such neo-institutional accounts are echoed in the theory of global constitutional convergence in recent studies of comparative constitutional law.[361] The thesis holds that national constitutions share similar rights provisions, although limited variables (liberitarian vs statist) are recognized.[362] Macro-accounts of global constitutionalism are extensive, covering all national constitutions over the last six decades. The convergence thesis, therefore, aims to capture the global patterns of modern constitutional history, not merely the recent constitutional globalization.

While the accounts of global neo-institutionalism and global constitutionalism have their own merits, they seem to underestimate the differences generated by

[360] John W. Meyer et al., "World Society and the Nation-State" (1997) 103(1) American Journal of Sociology 144, 152.

[361] David S. Law and Mila Versteeg, "The Evolution and Ideology of Global Constitutionalism" (2011) 99 California Law Review 1163. For critical discussions, see R. Dixon and E.A. Posner, "The Limits of Constitutional Convergence" (2011) 11(2) Chicago Journal of International Law 399.

[362] Ibid. 1170.

local conditions and factors. During the Cold War era, there was no single dominant form of constitutional construction. Indeed, ideas of liberal constitutionalism informed the constitutional discourses and constitution-making in the five aforementioned countries to various degrees, but liberal constitutionalism did not become the dominant constitutional model, especially when communism and concomitantly the socialist constitutional theory and the Soviet constitutional model triumphed.

The early socialist experiences may challenge the global claim of the existence of the standardized constitutional form of modern states. The socialist state of China was created in 1949, but its first constitution was only enacted in 1954. In Laos, the socialist state was established in 1975 and operated for sixteen years without a constitution until 1991. After the Revolution, Cuba's socialist state was created in 1958, but its first socialist constitution was only enacted in 1976. The case of Cuba is explained as being due to the fact that "The revolutionary government saw the locus of democracy not in institutions of the Party or the State, but in the unmediated and direct relationship between the people and its revolutionary core."[363] More generally, the absence of a constitution as the form of modern socialist states in their early experience may indicate that constitutional enactment has not yet become the global standard for a modern state, at least in the socialist world, because there may be alternative forms of legitimizing the modern states. The legitimacy of the socialist states may sociologically depend more on the actual political communications between the government and its people than on the formal institutionalization of government power.

During the Cold War, the landscape of modern constitutional configuration was polarized between the liberal and socialist constitutional models. Countries in the two camps have written constitutions but the mere existence of the written *form* of the constitutions does not suggest a global constitutional convergence. The *functions* of these constitutions are not merely different but conflictive. Unlike liberal constitutions, the socialist counterparts did not establish legal constraints on the government: rather, they are the instruments to project a program of social progress, which necessarily entails strong empowerment of the government. In addition, the substances of the constitutions are also radically antagonist. Certainly, like the liberal constitutions, the socialist constitutions have provisions on government structure and the bill of rights. However, this alone does not suggest the existence of a form of a world constitutionalism, at least during the Cold War. A close examination of these structural and rights provisions may reveal great polarization. The separation of powers, mechanisms of checks and balances, and constitutional review were rejected within the socialist centralized constitutional system.

[363] Larry Catá Backer, Flora Sapio, and James Korman, "Popular Participation in the Constitution of the Illiberal State—An Empirical Study of Popular Engagement and Constitutional Reform in Cuba and the Contours of Cuban Socialist Democracy 2.0" (2019) 34 Emory International Law Review 4.

Socialist rights are not natural rights to limit the state power but the declarations of policy accompanied by state's duties and empowerments. Finally, the socialist constitutions include substantive contents that cannot be found or are less prominent in liberal constitutions, such as the provisions of the party leadership, regime's ideology, and principles of the national economy.

In addition to the confrontational context of world politics, the conflict of constitutional identities is the key explanation for the global constitutional polarization. The liberal and socialist constitutional models are underpinned by contradictory constitutional ideas, principles, aspirations, and hopes. These constitutional contradictions were translated into the formal constitutions and created the global constitutional polarization.

One study of the written constitutions of ninety-one postcolonial nations during the latter part of the twentieth century reveals the "subglobal," not purely global scales of constitutional influences.[364] The postcolonial society is not a single world society but "a world of empires, a series of societies fractured along imperial and transnational lines."[365] Constitutional norms were diffused within these imperial and transnational lines. For example, the constitutions of the ex-British countries adopted the Westminster parliamentary model, while the constitutions of the ex-French countries were modeled after the presidential system of the French Fifth Republic.[366]

Another implication for comparative constitutional history is intra-socialist constitutional convergence and divergence. The idea of subglobal constitutional convergence is useful in understanding the transnational constitutional influence within the socialist world. The aforementioned socialist constitutions were influenced by the socialist constitutional theory and the soviet constitutional model, culminating in intra-socialist convergence during the utopia of the Soviet Union. Except for the delay of socialist constitution-making in Laos, the socialist constitutions of China, Vietnam, North Korea, and Cuba (particularly, the ones enacted in 1982, 1980, 1972, and 1976 respectively) were all instrumental in projecting the working class's program of social progress toward socialism under the leadership of the communist party. They created a centralized constitutional system, granted statist rights to the citizens, and established the socialist economy dominated by the state.

Global constitutionalists identify several mechanisms of global constitutional influences, such as learning, competition, conformity, and networks.[367] These overlap and complicate the coercive (political influence and the problem of legitimacy), mimetic (standard responses to uncertainty), and normative

[364] Julian Go, "A Globalizing Constitutionalism?: Views from the Postcolony, 1945–2000" (2003) 18(1) International Sociology 71, 74.

[365] Ibid. 73.

[366] Ibid.

[367] Law and Versteeg (n 361) 1173.

(professionalization) mechanisms of institutional isomorphic change proposed by neoinstitutionalists.[368] While the mechanisms of global constitutional influences aim to capture the fully global scale, they resonate in subglobal scales. The intra-socialist constitutional convergence can be explained by the logic of conformity.[369] The five socialist countries are allies of the Soviet Union and depended on the latter's economic and military support. To conform to socialist and Soviet constitutional norms became necessary to ease and facilitate political, diplomatic, economic, and military activities. This intra-socialist constitutional isomorphism is also instrumental to guaranteeing the continued support and alliance with the Soviet Union.

The constitutional convergence within the socialist lines should not blind us to the reality that intra-socialist constitutional divergence occurred at the same time. While the socialist constitutions lay down the programs for building socialism, these programs are not identical to one another and to that of the Soviet Union. At least four factors influence the intra-socialist constitutional divergence: the pre-socialist legacy; local ideology; local politics; and transitional justice.

To begin with, the interaction of the socialist constitutional elements with the preceding legacies creates an intra-socialist constitutional divergence. In this regard, the constitutional preambles provide a good foil with which to understand the divergence. The preambles of the aforementioned socialist constitutions (except for North Korea's, which lacks a preamble) refer to the non-socialist legacies of the national history: China's Sun Yat Sen's republic revolution; Vietnam's thousand-years of struggle for independence; and Cuba's independence movement against Spanish colonialism. In some cases, national legacies are explicitly incorporated in the constitutional body. For example, Article 2 of Cuba's Constitution of 1976 provides that the national symbols (namely, the flag of the solitary star; the anthem of Bayamo; the emblem of the royal palm) are "those which have presided for over one hundred years in the Cuban struggles for independence, for the rights of the people and for social progress."[370] Vietnam's 1980 Constitution provides in Article 38 that the state shall "protect and develop cultural and spiritual values of the nation."[371] The socialist constitutions also deal with non-socialist institutional legacies. North Korea's 1948 Constitution had to resolve the legacies of Japanese colonialism, evident in its distinctive provisions on lands owned by the Japanese state and Japanese nationals. Cuba's Constitution has distinctive provisions on citizenship as a reflection of institutional legacies.

Local ideology is the second factor of the intra-socialist constitutional convergence. In addition to Marxism-Leninism, the socialist constitutions incorporate

[368] Paul J. DiMaggio and Walter W. Powell, "The Iron Cage Revisited: Institutional Isomorphism and Collective Rationality in Organizational Fields" (1983) 48(2) American Sociological Review 147, 150.
[369] Law and Versteeg (n 361) 1177.
[370] Cuba 1976 Constitution art. 2.
[371] Constitution of the Socialist Republic of Vietnam 1980 art. 38.

local socialist ideology (China's Mao Zedong's Thought and Deng Xiaoping's Theory, Vietnam's Ho Chi Minh's testament, and North Korea's *Juche*) and even non-socialist ideology (Cuba's José Martí's ideology). The articulation of the local socialist ideology indicates that while the constitutions lay down the program to progress toward socialism, countries have their own visons of how to reach the socialist goals. In the case of Cuba, the goals include Martí's non-socialist aspiration to the "full dignity of man."

The third influential factor of the divergence is local politics. The divergence of this institutional design is determined by the local political reality. The reality of multi-parties in China results in a unique arrangement for party-vanguardism: the system of multi-party co-operation and political consultation led by the Communist Party. Due to its distinctive political historical role, the Vietnamese Fatherland Front, the umbrella of mass movements associated with the Communist Party, is constitutionally recognized as "a firm prop of State."[372] The Constitution of North Korea stipulated a powerful individual presidency due to the influential role of Kim Il-sung. The socialist Constitution of Cuba created a dual presidency as a reflection of the influential role of Castro.

The last factor of divergence concerns transitional justice. Several socialist constitutions have various ways to tolerate non-socialist economic arrangements (multi-ownership of the means of production, private economic sectors, and private property) in the early stages of transition from a non-socialist into a socialist regime. In the case of Vietnam, as the 1980 Constitution was adopted after the Vietnam War, it inevitably deals with local transitional issues. One example is the distinctive commitment in Article 74 that the state will grant "privileges to disabled soldiers and families of fallen combatants" and reward "persons or families who have rendered meritorious services to the revolution."[373]

The general logic of adaption explains the intra-socialist constitutional divergence. The adoption of an external constitutional norm normally entails the adaption to suit the local intellectual, political, social, and economic milieu. Apart from this general logic, nationalism is an important determinant of the intra-socialist constitutional convergence. The constitutional narrative and provisions of national legacies indicate the constitutional pride of the respective countries in their own history. Consequently, the socialist constitutions include both socialist and non-socialist elements, although the former is hegemonic. Nationalism also explains the fact that the socialist constitutions envisage the visions of local political leaders as the means of achieving socialism. The incorporation of non-socialist aspirations and values is also an indicator of the nationalist sentiment.

[372] Ibid. art. 9.
[373] Ibid. art. 74.

Constitutional change in the five socialist countries, as the immediate response to the fall of the Soviet bloc, has implications for the possible conceptualization of constitutional transition without constitutionalism.[374] The changes to socialist constitutions in the five remaining socialist countries immediately after the collapse of the Soviet bloc can be conceptualized in transitional terms. They, of course, are different from transitional stories from the post-soviet Central and Eastern Europe, but the differences should not be exaggerated due to the shared factor, concern, and mechanism of the constitutional change. Constitutional change in the five socialist states and the post-socialist states in Central and Eastern Europe was affected by the same global factor: the fall of communism worldwide. Consequently, constitutional change in these states had to deal with the same concern: how to reconstruct the polity in a world where the Soviet empire no longer existed. While democratic reconstruction can be seen as the great divergence, economic reconstruction is the convergence. Both socialist states and the post-socialist states were confronted with economic difficulties due to the lack of Soviet aid and a limited market, and hence constitutional change has to do something to facilitate economic reform.

The five socialist constitutions deal with this *directly*: introducing market reforms to the constitutional economy while keeping minimum changes to the existing constitutional political structure. The form is consequential to the latter: directly dealing with economic reforms would confer a sociological legitimacy to the existing socialist political structure. The post-socialist states in Central and Eastern Europe dealt with the same economic question, but did so *indirectly*: they were committed to institutions of constitutionalism (separation of powers and human rights enforced by constitutional courts) to facilitate economic reforms. The base for this commitment is the liberal idea in constitutional economics that economic development requires preventing the "state's threat to expropriate the gains from reform" and "the most effective constitution will be one that maximizes constraints on the state's discretionary powers to intervene in the economy."[375] The fact that the post-socialist constitutions adopted institutions of constitutionalism stemmed not merely from a political concern of democratization but also from economic concern. How the post-socialist constitutions affected economic reform, in reality is another question.[376]

[374] The theory of transitional constitutionalism is pioneered by Ruti Teitel. See Ruti Teitel, "Transitional Jurisprudence: The Role of Law in Political Transformation" (1997) 106(7) The Yale Law Journal 2009; Ruti Teitel, *Transitional Justice* (Oxford University Press 2000). For other accounts of transitional constitutionalism, see Jiunn-Rong Yeh and Wen-Chen Chang, "The Changing Landscape of Modern Constitutionalism: Transitional Perspective" (2009) 4(1) National Taiwan University Law Review 145; Tania Groppi, Valeria Piergigli, and Angelo Rinella (eds), *Asian Constitutionalism in Transition: A Comparative Perspective* (Giuffrè 2008).

[375] J. Hellman, "Constitutions and Economic Reform in the Postcommunist Transitions" (1996) 5(1) East European Constitutional Review 46, 47.

[376] On this question, see Katarzyna Metelska-Szaniawska, "Constitutions and Economic Reforms in Transition: An Empirical Study" (2009) 20(1) Constitutional Political Economy 1.

Finally, the mechanism for constitutional change was relatively similar. In both socialist and post-socialist states, with a few exceptions, changes were introduced to the existing socialist constitutions. In both cases, there was no distinction between constitutional and ordinary politics: extra-ordinary participatory constitution-making was absent, and the legislatures were the ordinary political platform for addressing transitional constitutional issues.

PART II
VARIATIONS
Five Models of Socialist Constitutional Change

4
The Universal Model
Vietnam

Introduction

On November 28, 2013, the National Assembly of Vietnam (NA) adopted a new constitution, the fifth enacted under the leadership of the Communist Party of Vietnam (CPV) and the culmination of a three-year constitution-making process. This chapter focuses on this constitutional change, but the background of the preceding change is useful. The 2013 constitution-making circle addressed several issues raised but not solved in the preceding circle of constitutional amendment a decade before that. In December 2001, the NA adopted, for the first time, important amendments for the 1992 Constitution. In the earlier years of 1998, 1999, and especially, 2000, party officials and academics called for amending the charter to reflect the changes in Vietnamese society after ten years of *Doi moi* (renovation). The dynamics of economic transformation as the result of the *Doi moi* policies, especially the speedy diversification of sectoral structures of the economy, in particular the remarkable rise of the private sectors, induced the need for amending the 1992 Constitution to reform the state machinery to better manage the changing society. Apart from the state institutions, some provisions of the 1992 Constitution regarding the economy, educational, scientific, and technological policies looked out of date in the new transitional context. Ten years of national transition coupled up with globalization resulted in the emergence of novel sectors of the economy focused on education, science and technology. Therefore, although in 2001 Vietnam reformed the state institutions, the country also wished to reflect economic, educational, scientific, and technological advancements into the Constitution. Consequently, the NA adopted the constitutional amendments in December 25, 2001, at its plenum session after long deliberation.[1] The amendments were then promulgated by the President of State in January 7, 2002 and effective the next day.

Initially, some legislators and legal scholars called for a fundamental amendment or new constitution because they believed that the 1992 Constitution was

[1] For an excellent elaboration of contentious debates in the process of amending the 1992 Constitution in 2001, see Mark Sidel, "Analytical Models for Understanding Constitutions and Constitutional Dialogues in Socialist Transitional States: Re-Interpreting Constitutional Dialogues in Vietnam" (2002) 6 Singapore Journal of International and Comparative Law 42–89.

Constitutional Change in the Contemporary Socialist World. Bui Ngoc Son, Oxford University Press (2020). © Bui Ngoc Son.
DOI: 10.1093/oso/9780198851349.001.0001.

adopted in the early stage of the *Doi moi* when Vietnam did not have the necessary conditions to introduce a comprehensively new constitution.[2] However, the Party refuted both a fundamental amendment and replacement and instead channeled the amendments to individual institutional issues. For the party, foundational amendment is delicate because this change would open a range of issues, such as party leadership (Article 4 of the Constitution) and other political and economic policies pronounced in the Constitution, which the party and the state were not willing to relinquish.[3] Consequently, even though some Assembly delegates and scholars repeatedly exhorted to broaden the scope of amendment, the Party has successfully limited the amendment to the following key issues: introducing the concept of "socialist rule of law state," the principle of the distribution of powers, a new mechanism which allowed the NA to hold a vote of confidence on individual officials elected or approved by it; and limiting the procuracy's jurisdiction.[4]

Apart from the main preoccupation of the state machinery, there are several amendments reflecting the rising demands of economic and social renovation. Several articles of Chapter 2 Economic System were revised in response to the dramatic private sector growth of the economy. The amended articles have strengthened the state's commitments to "actively integrate into the international economy" and "carry out the national industrialization and modernization"[5] as well as have introduced a new "foreign invested economic sector in various forms" to galvanize more growth.[6] Nevertheless, the new constitutional framework of the economy also softens the dogma of "socialist orientation."[7] The amendments acknowledge that "all economic sectors are important constituents of the socialist-oriented market economy."[8] In Chapter 3 Culture, Education, Scientific and Technology, the amendments further strengthened the state and party commitments to the relevant policies. The development of education was prioritized as "a primary national policy."[9] Similarly, the amended Constitution also accentuates the "development of science and technology [as] a primary national policy."[10]

A decade later, Vietnam planned to amend the 1992 Constitution for a second time, but the result was instead its implicit replacement by the new Constitution adopted by the NA on November 28, 2013. This chapter investigates this 2013 constitutional change. Compared with previous experience in Vietnam and with

[2] Pham Quoc Anh (ed.), *Nhung Van de Co ban cua Hien phap 1992 Sua doi [Fundamental Issues of the Revised 1992 Constitution]* (People's Police Publishing House 2006) 42–3.
[3] Mark Sidel, *The Constitution of Vietnam: A Contextual Analysis* (Hart 2009) 114.
[4] For more detail, see Sidel, "Analytical Models for Understanding Constitutions" (n 1) 42.
[5] The 1992 Constitution (revised art. 15).
[6] Ibid. art. 27.
[7] Mark Sidel, *The Constitution of Vietnam* (n 3) 122.
[8] The 1992 Constitution (revised) art. 16.
[9] Ibid. art. 35.
[10] Ibid. art. 37.

the experience in the other four socialist countries, the 2013 experience features the local adherence to universal norms in the process and substance of socialist constitutional change. This model of socialist constitutional change is, therefore, characterized here as the universal model.

Consider first the universal features of the constitution-making process. Drawing from the work of Saunders, Mark Tushnet, Vivien Hart, and others, the following universal features of constitution-making process in the twenty-first century can be identified: global pressures on constitution-making, the global return of constituent power, public participation as an international norm, the international involvement, and the impact of global diffusion of constitutional ideas and institutions.[11] However, as Tushnet argues, constitutional design "results far more from on-the-ground political circumstances than from reason and choice."[12] A constitution is eventually a local document, expressing the will of a given people, meeting local needs, and handling local issues. Therefore, universal norms and forces of constitution making are inevitably contextualized by their interaction with local socioeconomic factors, political culture, the domestic institutional and political environment, and the elites' political ideology. The Vietnamese experience in 2013 echoes the universal norms of constitution-making process. This 2013 constitution-making features the prominent appearance of the aforementioned global elements. The adherence to these universal norms informs and legitimitizes the process of the constitution-making. But, the global norms are contextualized by their intricate interaction with socialist, local elements: the party's reformist program, legislature's constituent power, party's control of participation, and the party's control of international involvement. Procedurally, the interplay of global and socialist factors results in a more open national constitutional dialogue and a less authoritarian paradigm of constitutional imposition.

Let us now turn to the universal features of the substances of constitutional change. The substances of socialist constitutional change in Vietnam are animated by the universal condition of constitutional disharmony as theorized by Gary Jacobsohn.[13] The three aspects of dissonance (internal to the socialist constitution of Vietnam, between the socialist constitutional ideals and external Vietnamese reality, and between the socialist and global constitutional norms) result in the pragmatic incorporation of universal ideas, principles, and institutions into the socialist Constitution of Vietnam, e.g. people's constituent power, limited power, and human

[11] Cheryl Saunders, "Constitution-Making in the 21st Century" (2012) 1 International Review of Law 2; Vivien Hart, "Democratic Constitution Making" (*US. Inst. Peace Special Report No. 107*, July 2003) <www.usip.org/sites/default/files/sr107.pdf>; Mark Tushnet, "Constitution-Making: An Introduction" (2013) 91 Texas Law Review 2983, 1987; Laurel E. Miller and Louis Acuoin (eds), *Framing the State in Terms of Transition: Csae Studies in Constitution Making* (United States Institute of Peace 2010); Sujiy Choudhry and Tom Ginsberg (eds), *Constitution-Making* (Edward Elgar Pub 2016)

[12] Mark Tushnet, "Some Skepticism about Normative Constitutional Advice" (2008) 49 William & Mary Law Review 1473, 1495.

[13] Gary J. Jacobsohn, *Constitutional Identity* (Harvard University Press 2010) 86–7.

rights. The consequence is the progressive change of the socialist constitutional order: the dynamic constitution, constitutionalization of the party, distribution of powers, universalization of human rights, and the marketization of the economy.

This chapter is based on original, empirical work: my interviews with constitutional scholars, constitution-makers, members of the Constitutional Amendment Committee, constitutional advisors for top political leaders, Assembly deputies, and National Assembly officers, constitutional scholars, and social actors engaging in constitutional mobilization.[14] In addition, the chapter is drawn on my actual engagement in the Vietnamese constitutional debate process. This primary work is combined with the analysis of Vietnamese materials available in online popular media, the NA's webpage, live television broadcasts of the NA's debates on the draft constitution, national law journals, Vietnamese books, and proceedings of workshops and conferences held in Vietnam.[15]

The remainder of this chapter unfolds in four parts. Section I introduces the background of Vietnamese 2013 Constitution making. Section II describes the process leading up to the birth of the 2013 constitution. Section III analyses the global and local factors affecting this process and its consequences. Section IV analyses the substantive changes. Section V concludes.

I. Factors

The Vietnamese constitution-making process in 2013 was driven by both global and local dynamics. Consider first the global dynamics. Constitution-makers mentioned to me several global factors that resulted in constitution-making in Vietnam, including international economic integration, Vietnam's ratification of international human rights treaties, and the globalization of Vietnamese legal scholarship.[16] They said that Vietnam needs to reform the constitutional system to better integrate into the global community.[17] The Party even instructed constitution-makers to reference foreign constitutional experience.[18] Vietnamese constitution making was animated by the fact that Vietnam has become deeply integrated into the global community. The *Đổi mới* program provided for the implementation of opening (*mở cửa*) policies in Vietnam. Accordingly, the state has been opening up not only to its people but also to the outside world broadly conceived, and not exclusively to socialist nations as was the case in the previous

[14] Due to sensitive nature of the issue, most interviewees remained anonymous, but their other details are specified. When the footnotes are addressed as "interviews," this indicates that the statements or evidence are drawn on several interviews which will not be specified.

[15] The English translations of Vietnamese documents are my own.

[16] Interviews.

[17] Ibid.

[18] Ibid.

pro-Soviet period. This was explicitly stated in the 1992 constitution.[19] Under this constitutional commitment, Vietnam has been integrating into the international community to a considerable extent.

Vietnam has also joined most major international human rights treaties, including the International Covenant on Civil and Political Rights; the International Covenant on Economic, Social, and Cultural Rights; the Convention on the Elimination of All Forms of Discrimination Against Women; the International Convention on the Elimination of All Forms of Racial Discrimination; the Convention on the Rights of the Child and its two Optional Protocols on the Involvement of Children in Armed Conflict and on the Sale of Children, Child Prostitution, and Child Pornography; and the Convention on the Rights of Persons with Disabilities.[20] Vietnam has also ratified twenty-four conventions of the International Labour Organization.[21]

As to the reporting obligations under international treaties, the country submitted and presented a report on the implementation of the International Convention on the Elimination of All Forms of Racial Discrimination from 2000 to 2009 and a report on the Convention on the Rights of the Child from 2008 to 2011 in 2012. It also presented a report (for the 1993–2010 period) to the Committee of the Convention on the Economic, Social, and Cultural Rights in 2011, and submitted a report to the Committee on the Elimination of All Forms of Discrimination Against Women in 2012.[22] Vietnam has submitted and defended reports at the United Nations Human Rights Council in accordance with the guidelines of Resolution 5/1 (June 18, 2007) of the Council to review the implementation of human rights in Vietnam. A report was submitted and defended in February, 2014,[23] shortly after Vietnam was selected, together with thirteen other countries, on November 12, 2013, to serve on the Human Rights Council for a period of three years beginning on January 1, 2014.[24]

In addition, Vietnam has integrated considerably into the global market by joining international and transnational organizations, including the World Bank, the International Monetary Fund, and the Asian Development Bank. Notably, it

19 1992 Constitution art. 14.

20 "Ratification Status for Viet Nam" (*United Nations Human Rights: Office of the High Commissioner*) <http://tbinternet.ohchr.org/_layouts/TreatyBodyExternal/Treaty.aspx?CountryID=192&Lang=E> accessed February 6, 2017.

21 "International Labour Standards in Viet Nam" (*International Labour Organisation*) <www.ilo.org/hanoi/Areasofwork/international-labour-standards/lang--en/index.htm> accessed May 8, 2020.

22 See Working Group on the Universal Periodic Review [of Vietnam], "National Report Submitted in Accordance with Paragraph 5 of the Annex to Human Rights Council Resolution 16/21: Vietnam, Report Submitted to the UN Human Rights Council (18th Session)" 17, (November 8, 2013) UN Doc A/HRC/WG6/18/VNM/1 [hereinafter Universal Periodic Review National Report].

23 Ibid.

24 "General Assembly Elects 14 Members to UN Human Rights Council" (*UN News Centre*, November 12, 2013) <www.un.org/apps/news/story.asp?NewsID=46476#.VCPP1qO_hI0>.

has been a member of the World Trade Organization since January 11, 2007.[25] The nation also joined the Asia-Pacific Economic Cooperation Forum (APEC) in November 1998. Within the Asian region, Vietnam is a member of the Association of Southeast Asian Nations (ASEAN) and of the ASEAN Intergovernmental Commission on Human Rights,[26] and it signed the ASEAN Human Rights Declaration on November 18, 2012.[27]

The fact that Vietnam has deeply integrated into the global community in the early twenty-first century has resulted in the need for a new constitutional framework which reflects, to a certain extent, the general rules and principles familiar to the global community. The maintaining of the 1992 constitution, which was ideologically, institutionally, and technically influenced by the constitutional system of the Soviet Union, may constrict Vietnam's communication with the world. Alternatively, to make a new constitution that presents (at least formally) some level of global constitutional convergence by adopting general constitutional concepts, principles, and institutions may help Vietnam further integrate economically and politically into the global community. By doing this, Vietnamese political leadership can also gain more international legitimacy. This explains in part the fact that the Vietnamese government referred to the enactment of the new Constitution as a national achievement in the report it prepared and presented under the Universal Periodic Review process to the UN Human Rights Council on February 2014.[28]

These global factors co-exist with local concerns and dynamics. The first is to incorporate the Party's reformist program. Constitutional change is necessary to incorporate new policies for social, political, and economic development reflected in the revised Political Creed adopted by Party's Eleventh National Congress in 2011. In addition to the Party's reformist program, socio-economic development after nearly three decades of *Đổi mới* is the driving force of constitution-making. Vietnamese constitution makers believed that "it is necessary to amend the 1992 Constitution to guarantee the synchrony of both economic and political renovation, to build the socialist rule of law state of the people, by the people, and for the people, to perfect the socialist-oriented economic institutions, to better ensure human rights, and citizens' rights and duties, to construct and defend the nation, and to be active and subjective in international integration."[29] The 1992

[25] See "Member Information: Viet Nam and the WTO" (*World Trade Organisation*) accessed February 6, 2017 <http://www.wto.org/english/thewto_e/countries_e/vietnam_e.htm>.

[26] On this institution, see Hsien-Li Tan, *The ASEAN Intergovernmental Commission on Human Rights: Institutionalising Human Rights in Southeast Asia* (CUP 2011).

[27] ASEAN Intergovernmental Commission on Human Rights, "The Adoption of the ASEAN Human Rights Declaration (AHRD) at the 21st ASEAN Summit and the Special Meeting of the ASEAN Intergovernmental Commission on Human Rights (AICHR)" (*AICHR*, November 26, 2012) <http://aichr.org/press-release/the-adoption-of-the-asean-human-rights-declaration-ahrd-at-the-21st-asean-summit-and-the-special-meeting-of-the-asean-intergovernmental-commission-on-human-rights-aichr/>.

[28] Universal Periodic Review National Report 3.

[29] Nguyễn Sinh Hùng, Tờ Trình Về Dự thảo sửa đổi Hiến pháp năm 1992 [Proposal on Amendments to the 1992 Constitution], Statement No 194/TTr-UBDTSĐHP (submitted by the Drafting Committee

Constitution was basically a charter for economic renovation. It set down in constitutional terms the Renovation program, which focused mainly on economic reform. Consequently, it included new provisions facilitating economic liberalization, but basically retained the overall political structure established by the previous 1980 constitution. Therefore, Vietnamese constitution makers in the 2010s attempted to introduce more political changes to promote the "socialist rule-of-law state" and human rights. At the same time, they committed to furthering economic reform and international integration. All together in consideration, nearly three decades of social and economic transition generates the need for a new charter for a comprehensive "renovation" of the nation.

Local social and economic transition also creates new challenges to the legitimacy of the communist rule and constitutional change is a response to these challenges. The success in defending the nation from foreign invasions conferred considerable legitimacy on Vietnam's communist political leadership. Additionally, the *Đổi mới* achievements were the base for social acceptance of the communist leadership during peaceful periods. However, by the early 2010s, serious problems had emerged and challenged the legitimacy of Vietnamese political leadership. Most importantly, after nearly three decades of development as the result of the Renovation program, the economy had stagnated considerably due to ideological and institutional constraints,[30] which resulted in social and cultural problems. Furthermore, corruption had become serious enough to challenge domestic legitimacy of the party-state. Notable examples of this were the tremendous losses and revelations of grave corruption at the Vietnam Shipbuilding Industry Group (Vinashin) and Vietnam National Shipping Lines (Vinalines) in 2012.[31] Political leaders did acknowledge the gravity of the situation.[32] In particular, in an interview with official media, President Trương Tấn Sang conceded that the situation was so serious that the people's trust in the Party and the regime had been challenged and

for Amendment of the 1992 Constitution to the National Assembly of the Socialist Republic of Vietnam, November 28, 2013) (translated by author).

[30] For an explanation of the reasons, see Khuong M Vu, "The Institutional Root Causes of the Challenges to Vietnam's Long-Term Economic Growth" (2014) 13 Asian Economic Papers 159.

[31] The *Vinashin* case is one of the most serious economic criminal cases in Vietnam, with losses of around 950 billion VND (around USD 43 million) according to the indictment of the procuracy at the trial on March 27, 2012. "Xử vụ án tại Vinashin: Thiệt hại kinh tế gần 950 tỷ đồng" ["The Trial of the Vinashin Case: The Economic Losses Are Around 950 Billion VND"] (*VOV*, March 27, 2012) <http://vov.vn/Phap-luat/Xu-vu-an-tai-Vinashin-Thiet-hai-kinh-te-gan-950-ty-dong/204387.vov>. The *Vinalines* case involved losses of 1686 billion VND (around USD 80 million) according to the government's inspector. "Vinalines Thua Lỗ Hàng Nghìn Tỷ Đồng 'Vì Suy Thoái'" ["Vinalines Lost Billions of VND 'Because of Recession'"] (*VnExpress*, May 12, 2012) <http://kinhdoanh.vnexpress.net/tin-tuc/vi-mo/vinalines-thua-lo-hang-nghin-ty-dong-vi-suy-thoai-2719874.html>.

[32] Đảng Cộng sản Việt Nam [Communist Party of Vietnam], *Văn kiện đại hội đại biểu toàn quốc lần thứ XI* [*Documents of the XIth National Congress*] (2011) 185.

had declined.[33] The past glorious triumphs are thus no longer sufficient to confer legitimacy on the socialist leadership.

Constitutional change has become one of the solutions to the problem of political legitimacy. Revising the Constitution comprehensively so as to provide a platform for the Party, the state, and the people to engage in an open dialogue on substantial issues of state building could help secure and enhance the legitimacy of the Constitution itself, of the Party's leadership, of political institutions, and of the socialist regime. In this regard, it is the dialogic process of constitution making that is instrumental to political legitimacy. Substantively, constitutional reform to incorporate new global legitimate ideas and to relax institutional constraints on economic development is also instrumental to the legitimacy of the Party's leadership.

II. The Making of the 2013 Constitution

A. Agenda Setting

A few years after the 2001 constitutional amendment, the need to further revise the 1992 Constitution emerged. In mid-2005, the Politburo of the CPV issued two important documents pertaining to legal and judicial reforms that stipulated further constitutional reform. To begin with, Resolution No. 48-NQ/TW on lawmaking strategy, dated May 24, 2005, mobilized, among other things, the possible creation of a constitutional review system.[34] The other document by the Politburo, Resolution No. 49-NQ/TW on judicial reform strategy, dated June 2, 2005, is also suggestive of constitutional reform.[35] The second Resolution suggested reorganizing local courts so as to make them independent from the local government, and encouraged studying the potential transformation of Vietnam's Soviet-style procuracy system into a Western-style prosecution system. The implementation of these reforms would necessarily entail revising the constitution.

Inspired by the Party's initiatives, alternative proposals concerning constitutional review, the court system, and the procuracy system were actively discussed among legal scholars, legislators, government members, judges, procurators, and others, which put further pressure on constitutional reform. Notably, in April

[33] Niềm tin với Đảng đang bị Thách thức [Trust in the Party Has Been Challenged] (*Vn Express*, Janurary 21, 2013) <http://vnexpress.net/tin-tuc/xa-hoi/niem-tin-voi-dang-dang-bi-thach-thuc-2416524.html>.

[34] Nghị quyết *số* 48-NQ/TW về việc chiến lược xây dựng và hoàn thiện hệ thống pháp luật Việt Nam đến năm 2010, định hướng đến năm 2020 [Resolution on the Strategy for the Development and Improvement of the Vietnam Legal System to 2010 and Direction for the Period Up to 2020] No. 48-NQ/TW (promulgated by the Politburo of the Communist Party of Vietnam, May 24, 2005).

[35] Nghị quyết *số* 49-NQ/TW về Chiến lược cải cách tư pháp đến năm 2020 [Resolution on the Judicial Reform Strategy to 2020], Resolution No. 49-NQ/TW (promulgated by the Politburo of the Communist Party of Vietnam, June 2, 2005).

2008, at the meeting of the NA's Standing Committee, the Chairperson of the Legal Committee proposed that constitutional revision was imperative to reform the constitutional supervision system, the court system, the procuracy system, and local government.[36] The Chairperson of the Judicial Committee further supported amending the Constitution to allow for the implementation of a judicial reform program.[37] In response, NA President Nguyễn Phú Trọng, later the General Secretary of the CPV, announced that the Politburo was supportive of constitutional revision, but noted that the revision of the state's Constitution must take place after the revision of the Party's constitution or political creed (*cương lĩnh*), which was to be carried out at the Eleventh National Congress of the Party in early 2011, and also observed that a comprehensive revision was not ready at this time.[38] Hence, as of 2008, discussions on constitutional reform tended to focus on individual amendments to resolve some institutional questions that had been raised but not ultimately handled by the 2001 constitutional amendment.

In mid-2010, constitutional amendment was included in the NA's work plan for 2011.[39] Constitutional amendment was then subject to extensive discussions in a number of workshops, seminars, national law journals, and mass media. Importantly, more substantial constitutional questions emerged in these fora.[40] The focus of constitutional discussions moved from individual to comprehensive amendments. Many legal scholars, legislators, lawyers, activists, dissidents, and some senior politicians supported a fundamental rather than fragmentary revision.[41]

[36] Nghĩa Nhân, "Sửa đổi Hiến pháp 1992- Yêu cầu Cấp bách" [Amending the 1992 Constitution: The Urgent Requirement] (*Pháp luật Việt Nam*, April 18, 2009) <http://phapluattp.vn/250285p0c1013/sua-doi-hien-phap-1992-yeu-cau-cap-bach.htm.>.

[37] Ibid.

[38] Ibid.

[39] Nghị quyết Chương trình xây dựng luật, pháp lệnh năm 2011, điều chỉnh Chương trình xây dựng luật, pháp lệnh năm 2010 và bổ sung Chương trình xây dựng luật, pháp lệnh của Quốc hội nhiệm kỳ khóa XII [Resolution Adopting the 2011 Law- and Ordinance-Making Program, Adjusting the 2010 Law- and Ordinance-Making Program, and Supplementing the Law- and Ordinance-Making Program of the Twelfth National Assembly] No. 48/2010/QH12 (promulgated by the National Assembly of the Socialist Republic of Vietnam June 19, 2010).

[40] In particular, the Institute of Legislative Studies under the NA's Standing Committee held a series of workshops on constitutional issues as a preparatory step in the constitutional amendment process. Although the themes of these workshops were merely about the methodology to assess the effectiveness of the 1992 Constitution and foreign experiences of constitution making, the attendees—including legislators, legal scholars, and officials—took the opportunity to critically discuss the substantial limits of the Constitution and propose possible amendments. Notably, the discussions were not limited to academic fora but reached the public as well, thanks to reporting by the mass media. I attended some of these workshops.

[41] See, e.g., Thu Hà, "Cựu chủ tịch Quốc hội bàn chuyện sửa Hiến pháp" [Ex-President of the National Assembly Commenting on Constitutional Amendment] (*Tuần Việt Nam*, June 16, 2010) <http://tuanvietnam.net/2010-06-24-cuu-chu-tich-quoc-hoi-ban-viec-sua-hien-phap>; "Đã đến lúc không thể tránh né những vấn đề cốt tử" [It is Now Impossible to Avoid Essential Issues] (*Tuần Việt Nam*, September 2, 2010) <http://tuanvietnam.net/2010-09-02-da-den-luc-khong-the-tranh-ne-nhung-van-de-cot-tu->; "Việc nước mà dân không biết thì không thể dân chủ được" [If the People Are Not Aware of National Affairs, It Will Be Undemocratic] (*Tuần Việt Nam*, September 3, 2010) <http://tuanvietnam.net/2010-09-02-trang-page>.

From January 12 to 19, 2011, the CPV's Eleventh National Congress took place at Hanoi. At this Congress, the Party amended its 1991 Constitution (*cương lĩnh*). For our purposes, the most notable changes were the greater emphasis on direct democracy, human rights protection, the construction of a rule-of-law state, controlling state power, and responsible government.[42] In the context of Vietnam, the revision of the Party's Constitution necessarily leads to a corresponding revision of the state's constitution. Hence, constitutional revision came under discussion at the Party's Eleventh Congress. The Party urged "immediate study of revision and supplementation of the 1992 Constitution in conformity with the new situation."[43]

Following the Party's initiative, in the session on August 4, 2011, the NA enacted a resolution[44] approving the Proposal for Amending and Supplementing the 1992 Constitution (hereinafter Constitutional Proposal) submitted by its Standing Committee and establishing the Drafting Committee for Amendment to the 1992 Constitution (hereinafter Constitutional Amendment Committee.)[45] The Constitutional Proposal insisted that the revision guarantee the socialist rule-of-law state, the leadership of the Communist Party, and the socialist-oriented market economy. Within this socialist ambit, the Proposal suggested revisions to nearly all of the content rather than some individual articles of the 1992 constitution, ranging from the preamble to the last chapter. Some suggestions were more related to economic, social, cultural, and educational policies. The Constitutional Proposal, however, suggested considering other substantial political questions, namely direct and indirect democracy, the distribution of power, the control of power, the protection of human rights, the relationships among the major state institutions, constitutional review, and decentralization of the central–local relationship. These questions had been actively discussed by scholars, legislators, and officials in the early stages and were then fiercely debated during the later stages of the constitution-making process.

In addition to approving the Constitutional Proposal, the NA also established a Constitutional Amendment Committee, responsible for "organizing the review

[42] Đảng Cộng sản Việt Nam [Communist Party of Vietnam], Đại hội [Documents] (n 32) 63–90.

[43] Ibid. 247 (translated by author).

[44] Nghị quyết số 06/2011/QH13 ngày 6 tháng 8 năm 2011 của Quốc hội về việc sửa đổi, bổ sung Hiến pháp năm 1992 và thành lập Ủy ban dự thảo sửa đổi Hiến pháp năm 1992 [Resolution Amending and Supplementing the 1992 Constitution and Setting Up the Drafting Committee for Amendment of the 1992 Constitution] No. 06/2011/QH13 (promulgated by the National Assembly of the Socialist Republic of Vietnam, August 6, 2011).

[45] For the report, see Ủy ban thường vụ Quốc hội [Standing Comm. of the Socialist Republic of Vietnam], Tờ trình số 11/TTr-UBTVQH13 ngày 02/08/2011 của Ủy ban thường vụ Quốc hội về việc triển khai thực hiện chủ trương nghiên cứu, sửa đổi, bổ sung Hiến pháp năm 1992 [Report No. 11/TTr-UBTVQH13 on Implementation of the Policy on Study, Amendment, and Supplementation of the 1992 Constitution], Report (August 2, 2011) [hereinafter Standing Comm. of the Socialist Republic of Vietnam, Report No. 11/TTr-UBTVQH13].

of the implementation of the 1992 constitution, preparing the draft of constitutional amendments, and submitting it to the National Assembly for consideration and approval."[46] The Committee was composed of thirty members, headed by Nguyễn Sinh Hung, the NA's President.[47] They were influential members of the Party, including eight members of the Politburo and nineteen members of the Party's Central Committee. They concurrently held key positions in the state: the President and Vice-President of the NA, the Vice-President of the State, chairpersons of the NA's committees, the Deputy Prime Minister, the Presidents of the Supreme People's Court and the Supreme People's Procuracy, and the Ministers of National Defense, Public Security, Internal Affairs, Justice, and Planning and Investment. Other members were the heads of Vietnamese political and social organizations under the Party's control, such as the Fatherland Front, the General Confederation of Labor, the Women's Association, the Communist Youth Association, the Peasants' Association, and the Lawyers' Association. The Committee also included two heads of the Academy of Social Sciences and the Academy of Science and Technology, who were concurrently members of the Party's Central Committee. It should be noted that only five of the thirty members were trained in law.[48]

The NA's resolution provided that the Committee could create an editorial board which would assist it with drafting the amendments.[49] The Committee issued Resolution 03/NQ-UBDTSDHP (dated August 6, 2011) and Resolution 33/QD-UBDTSDHP (dated September 12, 2011) to create the Editorial Board of Draft Amendment to the 1992 Constitution (hereinafter, Editorial Board of Draft Constitutional Amendment).[50] Headed by Phan Trung Lý, Chairperson of the NA's Legal Committee, the Board consisted of forty-three members who were state officials and scholars from different backgrounds, including legal scholars. It was divided into six teams charged with studying and providing assistance on six groups of constitutional issues: (1) the political regime and state apparatus; (2) the society and economy; (3) national defense and international relations; (4) constitutional rights and duties; (5) the judicial bodies; and (6) review of constitutional implementation.[51]

[46] Resolution No 06/2011/QH13 art. 2 (translated by author).

[47] Ibid. art. 1.

[48] They were Uông Chu Lưu (Vice-President of the National Assembly), Lê Minh Tâm (President of the Lawyers' Association), Phan Trung Lý (Chairperson of the National Assembly's Legal Committee), Hà Hùng Cường (Minister of Justice), and Trương Hòa Bình (President of the Supreme People's Court).

[49] Resolution No. 06/2011/QH13 art. 3.

[50] Ủy Ban Dự Thảo Sửa Đổi Hiến Pháp Năm 1992 [Drafting Committee for Amendment to the 1992 Constitution] Báo Cáo Kết quả hoạt động của Ủy ban dự thảo sửa đổi Hiến pháp năm 1992 từ khi được thành lập đến nay và dự kiến hoạt động trong thời gian tới [Report No 74/BC-UBDTSĐHP on the Results of the Activities of the Drafting Committee for Amendment to the 1992 Constitution from its Establishment to Now and the Plan For Future Activities].

[51] Ibid.

B. Design

1. First Draft and First Legislative Debate

From August 2011 to March 2012, the Constitutional Amendment Committee was busy with reviewing the implementation of the 1992 Constitution to further diagnose its limitations and determine the scope of constitutional revision. At the same time, public intellectuals further published critical comments on the 1992 Constitution and constitutional amendment proposals.

As a special step in the Vietnamese constitutional amendment process, the report on the review of the implementation of the 1992 Constitution and the scope of constitutional amendment was examined by the Politburo in April 2012 and then by the Central Committee in May 2012. The Central Committee issued a "conclusion" (*kết luận*) on this review and on some fundamental aspects of constitutional amendments.[52] Some conclusions pertaining to the enhancement of democracy, human rights protection, a rule-of-law state, and constitutional review were relatively conducive to further debate. However, other conclusions called for the retention of the existing constitutional principles, such as the prominent leadership of the Party, the leading role of the state economic sector, and the state's prerogative powers over land, which tended to limit the debates.

On the grounds of the Party's conclusions, from June to October 2012, the Editorial Board worked on drafting the constitutional amendments under the direction of the Constitutional Amendment Committee. Meanwhile, public intellectuals continued to debate the constitutional issues in mass media, law journals, and workshops.

In plenary sessions on November 15 and 16, 2012, the NA discussed the first draft of the revised constitution submitted by the Constitutional Amendment Committee. The draft was published on the NA's webpage, and the discussion was televised live. The draft restructured the body of the constitution, revised 100 existing articles, and introduced around ten totally new articles.[53] Hence, it had the appearance of a new constitution rather than a constitutional amendment. Yet, the draft retained substantial constitutional principles enshrined in the 1992 constitution, and reconfirmed the Central Committee's "conclusion." Building on the confirmed socialist constitutional background, the draft introduced considerable revisions, viz., the new principle of controlling state power; the requirement of the Party's responsibility to the people; a clear definition of the NA as the holder of

[52] The announcement of the result of the Central Committee's meeting is available on the webpage of the government: "Thông báo Hội nghị lần thứ 5 BCHTW Đảng khoá XI" ["Announcement on the 5th Conference of the Party's Central Committee Term XI"] (*Báo Điện Tử Của Chính Phủ Nước Cộng Hòa Xã Hội Chủ Nghĩa Việt Nam* [*Online Newspaper of the Government of the Socialist Republic of Vietnam*], May 15, 2012) <http://baodientu.chinhphu.vn/Home/Thong-bao-Hoi-nghi-lan-thu-5-BCHTW-Dang-khoa-XI/20125/138101.vgp>.

[53] The 1992 Constitution has 147 articles.

legislative power, the government as the holder of executive power, and the courts as the holder of judicial power; an adjustment of the NA's authority; strengthening the power of the President of State vis-à-vis the Prime Minister and the government; some new human rights provisions; and two independent institutions, namely the Council of National Elections and the Council of State Audit.

Throughout the duration of the parliamentary debates over the constitutional draft, contentious constitutional questions emerged.[54] To begin with, many deputies were concerned with the nature of the draft. They argued that as the draft introduced comprehensive revisions to the 1992 constitution, it should be considered the draft of a new constitution. On the content of the draft, the issue of controlling state power drew particular attention among the deputies. Many supported the introduction of this new principle but commented that the draft revised constitution did not yet articulate the concrete institutional mechanisms needed to realize this principle. In particular, some deputies criticized the lack of an institution to control the legislature. This criticism was closely related to the issue of constitutional review. The Constitutional Amendment Committee reported to the NA that there were two options concerning constitutional review which had been controversially debated among its members—namely, either to strengthen the current system of constitutional supervision or to create a special body of constitutional review named the Constitutional Council, following the French experience. The Constitutional Amendment Committee decided to favor the first option without serious justification. This caused strong resistance among the deputies. Virtually all commentators in the parliamentary session favored the creation of a special institution of constitutional review. Some agreed with the proposal for a Constitutional Council, while others moved further to call for a constitutional court. Among the supporters of a special institution of constitutional review, the most notable were two deputies, Hà Hùng Cường, the Minister of Justice, and Trần Văn Độ, the Vice Chief Judge of the Central Military Court, who are also famous legal scholars in Vietnam. Their support was weighty because they occupy relatively high positions in the state and enjoy renown within the legal community.[55]

The next question of contention was the issue of a constitutional referendum. The draft revised constitution introduced a lengthy new article articulating the procedure of constitutional amendment. The draft stipulated that the NA would have the power to decide whether a constitutional amendment would be voted on in a national referendum. This caused differing views among the NA deputies. Another controversial issue was the role of the state economic sector. Some deputies disagreed with the continued constitutional confirmation of the leading role

[54] I watched the live television broadcasts of these debates. The transcripts of the debates are available at Dự Thảo Online [Online Drafts], <http://duthaoonline.quochoi.vn/DuThao/Lists/DT_DUTHAO_NGHIQUYET/View_Detail.aspx?ItemID=32&TabIndex=4>.

[55] For more detail, see Bui Ngoc Son, "The Discourse of Constitutional Review in Vietnam" (2014) 9 Journal of Comparative Law 205–7.

of the state economic sector and argued for the removal of its constitutional entrenchment. Other issues pertaining to land ownership, the structure and role of the judiciary, the powers of the procuracies, and the model of the local government were also actively discussed in the NA forum.[56]

2. Second Draft, Consultation, and Mobilization

At the close of the November 2012 meeting, the NA passed the Resolution on Organizing the Collection of People's Opinions on the Draft Amendment to the 1992 Constitution.[57] The Resolution required the Constitutional Amendment Commission to revise the draft Constitution according to deputies' comments and then release it to the public for comment. It recognized that public consultation on constitutional amendment is essential to forming a social consensus, enabling popular will to be reflected in the constitution, and strengthening public awareness of constitutional amendments and their implementation. The Resolution requested that the people comment on all constitutional issues ranging from the preamble, fundamental principles of the political system, state policies, state institutions, and fundamental rights to the constitutional amendment procedure, constitutional enforcement, and techniques of constitution drafting. Those to be consulted included individuals of different backgrounds, governmental institutions of all levels, political-social organizations, civil society institutions, academic institutions, and journalist institutions. The forms of collecting public constitutional comments varied, and included the postal system; the NA's webpage; conferences, workshops, and seminars of different types and scales; and other channels.

On the eve of launching the public constitutional consultation, the Politburo issued an *Instruction on Organizing the Collection of People's Opinions on the Draft Amendment to the 1992 Constitution*.[58] The *Instruction* required that the public constitutional consultation be in accordance with the Central Committee's "conclusion" and other political documents of the Party. It also commanded the Central Military Commission and the Central Party Committee on Public Security to "strictly lead the activities of ensuring national defense, social security and order; co-operate with the concerned agencies and organizations to timely counter and prevent acts of abusing democracy and appropriating the people's opinion collection process to spread misleading propaganda against our Party and the State."[59]

[56] See the detailed debates at Dự Thảo Online <http://duthaoonline.quochoi.vn/DuThao/Lists/DT_DUTHAO_NGHIQUYET/View_Detail.aspx?ItemID=32&TabIndex=4>.

[57] Nghị quyết tổ chức lấy ý kiến nhân dân về Dự thảo sửa đổi Hiến pháp năm 1992 [Resolution on Organizing the Collection of People's Opinions on the Draft Amendment to the 1992 Constitution], No 38/2012/QH13 (promulgated by the National Assembly of the Socialist Republic of Vietnam, November 23, 2012).

[58] Chỉ thị của Bộ Chính trị về việc tổ chức lấy ý kiên nhân dân về dự thảo sửa đổi Hiên pháp [Instruction on Organizing the Collection of People's Opinions on the Draft Amendment to the 1992 Constitution], Instruction No. 22-CT/TW (promulgated by the Politburo of the Communist Party of Vietnam, December 28, 2012).

[59] Ibid. (translated by author).

Yet, in a press conference on December 29, 2012, Phan Trung Lý, the Head of the Editorial Board of Draft Constitutional Amendment, confirmed that there were no limits on public comment on the draft revised constitution. In particular, in response to a query regarding Article 4 of the 1992 constitution, which confirmed the leadership of the Communist Party, Lý said: "The people can comment on Article 4 as well as all other issues in the draft, without any taboo."[60] This meant that, in theory, the Central Committee's "conclusion" would not limit constitutional discussions among the population.

From January 2 to March 31, 2013, the public constitutional consultation process took place throughout Vietnam. Virtually all state-owned online media displayed the draft revised constitution and installed special entries for popular comment on the constitutional amendment. Notably, a set of materials that included the draft revised constitution, its comparison with the 1992 constitution, the rationale for the amendments, and question sheets[61] was distributed to all households. The NA, the government, the Supreme People's Court, the Supreme People's Procuracy, and the Fatherland Front collected their members' comments on the draft constitution, and their reports on this collection process were published on the NA's website. All local governments collected their officials' constitutional comments, and their reports were also reflected in mass media. National law schools and legal institutes held numerous conferences, workshops, and seminars on constitutional amendment, attended and reported by mass media. Individual scholars, group scholars, and legal institutions published a number of books on the theme, and distributed copies to constitution makers and legislators.[62] In addition, writings on the constitutional issues abounded in popular online media and newspapers[63] and in academic law journals.[64]

[60] Chung Hồng, "Không có Cấm kỵ trong Góp ý Sửa Hiến pháp" ["There Is No Taboo in Commenting on the Constitutional Amendment"] (*Vietnamnet*, December 29, 2012) <http://vietnamnet.vn/vn/chinh-tri/103205/khong-co-cam-ky-khi-gop-y-sua-hien-phap.html> (translated by author).

[61] The question sheets asked people to provide general comments on the draft revised constitution as a whole and to express their agreement or disagreement with particular constitutional revision proposals.

[62] These volumes had been prepared slightly earlier but were distributed to Assembly delegates and constitution makers at the time of the public constitutional consultation. They contain important material for understanding Vietnamese constitutional development and discourse and are worth noting here: Phạn Văn Hùng (ed.), *Bàn về sửa đổi và bổ sung Hiến pháp 1992* [*Discussions on Amendment and Supplementation of the 1992 Constitution*] (2012); Phạm Hồng Thái (ed.), *Sửa đổi bổ sung hiến pháp 1992: Những vấn đề lý luận và thực tiễn* [*Amending the 1992 Constitution: Practical and Theoretical Issues*] (2012); Nguyễn Đăng Dung (ed.), *Những vấn đề về hiến pháp và sửa đổi hiến pháp* [*Issues Concerning the Constitution and Constitutional Amendment*] (Dân trí Publishing House 2012).

[63] These included Vietnamnet, Vnexpress, Tuổi trẻ, Thanh niên, Lao Động, Pháp Luật Thành phố Hồ Chí Minh, Nhân dân, Đại đoàn Kết, Công an Nhân dân, etc.

[64] Namely, the Legislative Studies Journal (Tạp chí Nghiên cứu Lập pháp), the State and Law Review (Tạp chí Nhà nước và Pháp luật), the Journal of Law and Democracy (Tạp chí Dân chủ và Pháp Luật), the Journal of Legal Science (Tạp chí Khoa học Pháp lý), and the Journal of Jurisprudence (Tạp chí Luật học).

Commentators actually touched on all constitutional questions. More specifically, questions pertaining to the Party's leadership, popular sovereignty, a constitutional referendum, the control and distribution of state power, judicial independence, land ownership, and the model of local government were extensively debated. In particular, the call for popular ratification of the future constitution became more vehement.

During the process of public constitutional consultation, new constitutional questions emerged as well. Most notable was the call for a possible change of the nation's name, the Socialist Republic of Vietnam, by removing the word "Socialist." Alternative names proposed included the Democratic Republic of Vietnam, the Republic of Vietnam, and the People's Democratic Republic of Vietnam.[65] Next were the issues concerning the power of the President of State. Some commentators were dissatisfied with the symbolic position of the President of State and called for a more powerful presidency to be created through popular election and the granting of more executive powers to the position, such as the power to invalidate legal regulations of the government or Prime Minister deemed inconsistent with presidential decrees, the power to preside over the government's meetings in necessary cases, and the power to require that the Prime Minister report to the President on consequential economic and social problems.[66]

Other emerging questions concerned new provisions in the second draft of the revised constitution. Firstly, the draft required in Article 70 that "the armed forces must be absolutely loyal to the Communist Party of Vietnam, the Fatherland, and the people." The emphasis on the military's foremost loyalty to the CPV triggered serious resistance from public intellectuals, domestic and overseas dissidents, and others.[67] Secondly, the draft introduced a new provision (Article 15) concerning the restriction of human rights for reasons of "national defense, national security, social security and order, community morality, and health." This stipulation resulted in contentious debate among members of the public. Many criticized the provision on the grounds that it would legitimize the violation of human rights in Vietnam.[68] A related issue pertaining to the limitation of gay

[65] Ban Biên tập dự thảo sửa đổi Hiến pháp năm [Editorial Board of Draft Amendment to the 1992 Constitution], Báo cáo Tổng hợp ý kiến nhân dân về Dự thảo sửa đổi Hiến pháp năm 1992 (từ ngày 02 tháng 01 2013 đến ngày 30 tháng 4 2013) [Synthesized Report on the People's Opinion on the Draft Amendment to the 1992 Constitution (Janurary 2, 2013–April 30, 2013)] <http://duthaoonline.quochoi.vn/DuThao/Lists/DT_DUTHAO_NGHIQUYET/View_Detail.aspx?ItemID=32&TabIndex=2&TaiLieuID=1066>.

[66] P. Thảo, "Bàn luận sôi nổi về tăng quyền hạn của Chủ tịch nước" [Hot Debates on the President's Powers] (*Báo Dân trí*, January 12, 2013) <http://dantri.com.vn/xa-hoi/ban-luan-soi-noi-ve-tang-quyen-han-cua-chu-tich-nuoc-1358381356.htm>.

[67] See, e.g. Bảo Cầm, "Tổ quốc và nhân dân phải được đặt lên hàng đầu" [The Fatherland and the People Must Be Put at the Forefront] (*Thanh Niên*, February 20, 2013) <www.thanhnien.com.vn/chinh-tri-xa-hoi/to-quoc-va-nhan-dan-phai-duoc-dat-len-hang-dau-476838.html>.

[68] See, e.g. Hoàng Xuân Phú, "Teo dần quyền con người trong Hiến pháp" [Human Rights Are Gradually Shrinking in the Constitution] (*Cùng viết Hiến pháp [Let's Draw Up the Constitution]*, February 1, 2013) <https://cungviethienphap.wordpress.com/2013/02/01/teo-dan-quyen-con-nguoi-trong-hien-phap/>.

and lesbian rights was also hotly discussed,[69] as draft Article 39 stipulated that "men and women have the right to marry or divorce." Thirdly, in response to the NA delegates' support of the new mechanism for constitutional review, the second draft introduced a new Article 120, which provided for the creation of a Constitutional Council with an advisory power. In most constitutional consultation fora, commentators disagreed with the latter provision, criticizing the proposed Constitutional Council as being just a dependent institution of the NA with no definitive power, and hence as being incapable of effective constitutional enforcement. Instead, they called for a more powerful and independent constitutional council or a constitutional court to be created.[70] Last but not least, the second draft removed the provision confirming the leading role of the state economic sector, which was strongly supported by economists, legal scholars, and business people.[71]

During Vietnam's public constitutional consultation, the rise of constitutional mobilization was striking. The most notable phenomenon was *Petition 72*,[72] an initiative comparable to China's *Charter 08*.[73] *Petition 72* was signed by a group of seventy-two senior Vietnamese scholars (known as the "72 Group"), and by April 2013 had garnered the support of around 14,000 Vietnamese people inside and outside Vietnam.[74] The Petition included seven points: (1) multiparty elections; (2) protection of human rights in accordance with international standards, removing restrictions on human rights for public goals, and creating an independent Human Rights Committee; (3) multiple forms of ownership of land, including private ownership; (4) the separation of powers and other forms of checks and balances; (5) removal of the new provision requiring the loyalty of the armed forces to the Communist Party; (6) a constitutional referendum; and (7) extension of the time for public constitutional consultation until the end of 2013.[75]

[69] See, e.g. Ngọc Quang, "GS Nguyễn Minh Thuyết nói về điều 71 và sự tồn tại của người đồng tính" [Professor Nguyễn Minh Thuyết Talks About Article 71 and the Existence of Homosexual Persons], (*Báo điện tử Giáo dục Việt Nam*, February 4, 2013) <http://giaoduc.net.vn/Xa-hoi/GS-Nguyen-Minh-Thuyet-noi-ve-dieu-71-va-su-ton-tai-cua-nguoi-dong-tinh-post109105.gd>.

[70] Bui (n 55) 191, 208–9.

[71] "Sửa đổi Hiến pháp: Phải bình đẳng giữa DN nhà nước và tư nhân" [Amending the Constitution: State-Owned and Private Enterprises Are Equal] (*VOV Online*, February 4, 2013) <http://vov.vn/kinh-te/sua-doi-hien-phapphai-binh-dang-giua-dn-nha-nuoc-va-tu-nhan-246155.vov>.

[72] For more detail, see Bui Ngoc Son and Pip Nicholson, "Activism and Popular Constitutionalism in Vietnam" (2017) 42 Law and Social Inquiry 677.

[73] For China's *Charter 08*, see Liu Xiaobo, *Charter 08 and the Challenges of Poitical Reform in China* (Jean-Philippe Béja et al. eds, 2012).

[74] Bauxite Việt Nam, "Danh Sách Người Ký Kiến Nghị Sửa Đổi Hiến Pháp 1992 (Từ Đợt 1 Đến Đợt 34)" ["The List of Signatures to the Petition to Amending the 1992 Constitution (From 1st Course to 34th Course)"] (*Bauxite Việt Nam*, August 16, 2013) <www.boxitvn.net/bai/16449>.

[75] Ibid. The petition is available on the blog of the group:

Nhóm 72 [72 Group], "Kiến Nghị Về Sửa Đổi Hiến Pháp 1992" ["Petition to Amending the 1992 Constitution"] (*Bauxite Việt Nam*, April 14, 2013) <http://boxitvn.blogspot.com/2013/01/kien-nghi-ve-sua-oi-hien-phap-1992.html>.

Another movement called "Declaration of Free Citizens" first appeared on Facebook and then spread widely on the Internet, receiving 10,000 signatures. It called for a constitutional convention to be assembled, the removal of Article 4 and the establishment of a multiparty system, the separation of state powers vertically and horizontally, and a civilian military. The *Cùng viết Hiến pháp* ("Let's Draw Up the Constitution") group should also be mentioned. This group, which included Vietnamese scholars in the United States (specializing in non-legal disciplines), created its website on February 1, 2012, in an attempt to provide a forum for "democratic dialogues" on constitutional revision issues.[76] This group garnered particular attention from the public due in significant part to the reputation of the founding members.[77] Through its website, the group published and republished discussions, conducted surveys of popular opinion on the constitutional amendment, and offered constitutional proposals. Other collective activists included Vietnamese bishops, seven NGOs, and vulnerable groups, which shared the commonality of supporting more liberal constitutional ideas and institutions.[78]

Eventually, the process of public consultation on the draft Constitution concluded at the end of April 2013, as set out in the approved agenda. In response to calls for an extension, the Constitutional Amendment Committee issued a document stating that although the official time for collecting people's opinions on the draft Constitution had passed, the people could continue to comment on it until September 30, 2013, that being when the NA was scheduled to approve the new constitution.[79] The Constitutional Amendment Committee produced an extensive synthesized report on the public consultation on the draft constitution. According to this report, in the span of three months, there were 26,091,276 popular constitutional submissions, and 28,149 conferences, workshops, and seminars were held to discuss the draft constitution.[80]

[76] Cùng viết Hiến pháp ["Let's Draw Up the Constitution"] <https://cungviethienphap.wordpress.com/>.

[77] "Nhóm Cùng Viết Hiến Pháp gửi đề xuất" ["The Group Let's Draw Up the Constitution Submits Their Proposal"] (*BBC Tiếng Việt [BBC Vietnamese]*, April 6, 2013) <www.bbc.com/vietnamese/vietnam/2013/04/130406_cvhp_proposal l>.

[78] For a discussion of these collective constitutional suggestions, see Lã Khánh Tùng, "Các tổ chức Phi Chính phủ ở Việt Nam với Tiến trình Sửa đổi Hiến pháp trong năm 2013" ["The NGOs in Vietnam and the Constitutional Revision Process in 2013"], in *Sự tham gia của nhân dân vào Quy trình Lập hiến lý luận, thực tiễn trên thế giới và ở việt na* [*People's Participatino in the Constition-making Process: Theory and Practice Around the World and in Vietnam*] (Đào Trí Úc et al. (eds), VNU Press 2013) 252 .

[79] Ủy Ban Dự Thảo Sửa Đổi Hiến Pháp Năm 1992 [Drafting Committee for Amendment to the 1992 Constitution], V/v Tiếp tục triển khai Nghị quyết của Quốc hội lấy ý kiến nhân dân về Dự thảo sửa đổi Hiến pháp [On Continuing Implementation of The National Assembly's Resolution on Organizing the Collection of People's Opinions on the Draft Amendment to the 1992 Constitution] No. 250/UBDTSĐHP (March 6, 2013).

[80] Ban Biên tập dự thảo sửa đổi Hiến pháp năm 1992 [Editorial Board of Draft Amendment to the 1992 Constitution], Báo cáo Tổng hợp ý kiến nhân dân về Dự thảo sửa đổi Hiến pháp năm (TỪ NGÀY 02 Tháng 01 2013 ĐẾN NGÀY 30 Tháng 4 2013) [Synthesized Report on the People's Opinion on the Draft Amendment to the 1992 Constitution (January 2, 2013–April 30, 2013)] 1.

3. Third Draft and Second Legislative Debate

In May 2013, the Constitutional Amendment Commission worked quickly to digest the comments received through the public consultation and to prepare the third draft of the revised constitution, which would be submitted to the NA for its second debate in its meeting from May 20 to June 21, 2013. As the process of constitutional amendment came closer to the final stage, Party and Assembly leadership began to decide on substantial issues and direct the legislative debate to a narrow scope.

The third draft of the revised constitution reconfirmed the primacy of the CPV, the unity of power, the class foundation of the people, the military's loyalty to the CPV (which, however, was deemed second to its loyalty to the Fatherland), the state's exclusive ownership of land, the restrictions on human rights, and the constituent power of the NA. These issues had been controversially debated among the public and had met with serious criticisms from constitutional activists, but nonetheless they were not the subject of any considerable movement in the third draft. This caused some skepticism among legislators about the meaningfulness of the public constitutional consultation when they met as a group on May 27, 2013, to review the public consultation process and discuss the third draft of the revised constitution. To illustrate, Hà Hùng Cường, the Minister of Justice, criticized the collection of people's opinions on the constitutional amendment as cursory and perfunctory, and continued to call for a constitution that would be a "production of the people," implying that the third draft had failed to fully express the people's will.[81] In a similar vein, Dương Trung Quốc—an active legislator—agreed that never had the constitution been as fervently discussed in Vietnam as it was in 2013, but he doubted whether this necessarily meant that the people's opinions had been fully collected, and insisted on the necessity of the people's ratification of the revised constitution.[82]

Apart from reconfirming the constitutional dogmas, the Party and Assembly leadership provided alternatives to some limited constitutional issues to be debated in the NA. Among other things, the third draft of the revised constitution offered open answers to the following constitutional questions: first, whether to confirm the leading role of the state economic sector or to acknowledge the equal importance of, and competition among, different economic sectors; second, whether to create a Constitutional Council or not, and if so, with or without an advisory power; third, whether to retain the 1992 constitution's provisions on local government, which articulated the same structure of local government in all geographical

[81] L Thư, L Nhung, T Chung, and C Quyên, "Bộ Trưởng Bộ Tư pháp: Lấy ý kiến Nhân dân về Hiến pháp Gấp gáp" ["Minister of Justice: The Collection of People's Opinions on the Constitution Is Hasty"] (translated by author) (*Vietnamnet*, May 27, 2013), <http://vietnamnet.vn/vn/chinh-tri/122929/bo-truong-tu-phap--lay-y-kien-dan-ve-hp-gap-gap.html>.

[82] Lê Nhung, "Hiến pháp 'Treo' đến Bao giờ" ["When Will the Postponement of the Constitution End?"] (*Vietnamnet*, May 27, 2013) <http://vietnamnet.vn/vn/chinh-tri/122866/hien-phap--treo--den-bao-gio-.html>.

areas, or whether to instead allow statutes to establish different models of local government suitable to different areas. Notably, in response to the call for alteration of the nation's name during the period of public constitutional consultation, the Constitutional Amendment Commission had planned to submit to the NA two options—either to retain the current name, the Socialist Republic of Vietnam, or to return to the former name, the Democratic Republic of Vietnam[83]—but this plan was quickly retracted.[84]

Over two days, June 3 and 4, 2013, the NA debated the third draft of the revised constitution in a plenary session, which was televised live.[85] Party and Assembly leadership were successful in achieving Assembly consensus on substantial constitutional dogmas. There was broad agreement among the delegates on the constitutional confirmation of the Party's leadership, retention of the nation's current name, the unity of power, the military's loyalty to the Party, and the state's exclusive ownership of land. Moreover, many delegates, in speeches that had perhaps been prearranged, provided verbose justifications for these constitutional dogmas in an attempt to propagandize them to the public and to obtain social consensus.[86]

However, delegates' positions on the open-answer constitutional questions were considerably divided. To illustrate, many insisted on retaining the current constitutional review system without any change, while many others vehemently supported the introduction of a Constitutional Council and even called for its adjudicative power. Many defended the leading role of the state economic sector, while many others advocated for an equal and competitive economy. Also, many advocated retaining the current system of the People's Council and the People's Committee, while many others argued for a diversification of the models of local government.[87]

On the following day, June 5, 2013, when delegates discussed the legislative work plan for 2014, an important proposal emerged not to enact the revised constitution in October 2013 as scheduled. Many delegates submitted that because there was much dissension on important constitutional issues at the NA meeting, the enactment of the revised constitution should be postponed to early 2014 after having more serious deliberation among the people and their representatives. A delegate stated:

> There is a lot of content and many points which have not achieved a high level of agreement (among the Assembly delegates), while 500 Assembly delegates do not

[83] Lê Nhung, "Sẽ Trình Quốc hội Phương án Đổi Tên Nước" ["The Plan to Change the Nation's Name Will Be Submitted to the National Assembly"], (*Vietnamnet*, May 17, 2013) <http://vietnamnet.vn/vn/chinh-tri/121655/se-trinh-qh-phuong-an-ten-nuoc.html>.

[84] P Thảo, "Không Trình Quốc hội Phương án Đổi Tên Nước" ["The Plan to Change the Nation's Name Will Not Be Submitted to the National Assembly"] (*báo điện tử Dân trí*, May 20, 2013) <http://dantri.com.vn/xa-hoi/khong-trinh-quoc-hoi-phuong-an-doi-ten-nuoc-1369484129.htm>

[85] I watched the live television broadcasts of these debates. For the transcripts of the debates, see Dự Thảo Online.

[86] Ibid.

[87] Ibid.

merely work within this meeting hall but represent 85 million people. Therefore, this [the enactment of the revised constitution] needs the consensus of different strata among the people.... I suggest extending the necessary physical time for the birth of the new constitution.[88]

While some delegates were more concerned with the postponement of the constitutional enactment, public intellectuals continued to call for a constitutional referendum. To illustrate, at the meeting of the Fatherland Front on July 4, 2013, Mr. Lù Văn Que persisted in calling for a popular vote on the new constitution, stating: "If the Party releases the Constitution for the people's ratification, this will enhance the trust between the two, and evil actors cannot sabotage it."[89] Also, on July 3, 2013, the 72 Group submitted to the NA and top political leaders a second petition, which continued to advocate in favor of a constitutional referendum and multi-form land ownership.[90]

C. Approval

Despite the calls for postponement and the holding of a referendum, the new Constitution was scheduled to be approved by the NA at the sixth session of its XIIIth term, which ran from October 21 to November 29, 2013. According to the initial plan, the NA would discuss the constitutional draft in two plenary meetings. The NA did discuss the draft in its plenary meeting on October 5, 2013, which was televised live.[91] The Constitutional Amendment Committee pronounced the "conclusion" of the controversial questions, which meant that these issues would not be discussed; they included confirmation of the current nation's name, the leadership of the CPV, the loyalty of the military to the Party, the leading role of the state economic sector, and withdrawal of the right to use land for developmental projects and other public purposes.[92] The conclusion of these issues was justified on the ground of the continued implementation of socialism in Vietnam.

[88] Linh Thư, "Kiến nghị Chưa thông qua Hiến pháp sửa đổi" ["Suggestion Not to Enact the Revised Constitution"] (translated by author) (*Vietnamnet*, June 6, 2013) <http://vietnamnet.vn/vn/chinh-tri/124237/kien-nghi-chua-thong-qua-hien-phap-sua-doi.html>

[89] Cẩm Quyên, "Tiếp tục đề xuất Dân phúc quyết Hiến pháp" ["Continuing to Propose a People's Referendum on the Constitution"] (translated by author) (*Vietnamnet*, July 4, 2013 <http://vietnamnet.vn/vn/chinh-tri/129820/tiep-tuc-de-xuat-dan-phuc-quyet-hien-phap.html> (quoting Speaker's Name)

[90] Nhóm 72 [72 Group], "Góp ý tiếp về Hiến pháp và Luật đất đai" ["Continuing Comments on the Constitution and the Land Law"] (*Cùng Viết Hiến Pháp*, 3 July 2013), <https://hienphap.wordpress.com/2013/07/06/gop-y-tiep-ve-hien-phap-va-luat-dat-dai-boxit-viet-nam/>.

[91] I watched the live television broadcasts of these debates. For the transcripts, see Dự Thảo Online (n 47).

[92] P Thảo, "Chốt phương án không đổi tên nước" ["Conclusion on Not Changing the Nation's Name"] (*Báo Dân trí*, October 22, 2013) <http://dantri.com.vn/xa-hoi/chot-phuong-an-khong-doi-ten-nuoc-1382889308.htm>.

Notably, the proposal for a Constitutional Council was eventually rejected on the ground that this was "a new issue and there are different opinions."[93] As substantial issues had been concluded, enlivened discussions among the NA delegates almost disappeared. Instead, they provided more justifications for the options that had been selected. There were, however, some active voices on the question of the structure of local government.[94]

An unusual controversial voice was that of Trương Trọng Nghĩa, a delegate and lawyer from Ho Chi Minh City, who was well-known to the public. He stated that the public was very much hopeful in this round of constitution making, as they believed that the Constitution was "the solution for every problem."[95] Mr. Nghĩa then said: "I believe that constitutional revision is the consequential affair whose influence may impulse or impede the steps of history. Posterity will adjudge whether the National Assembly's XIIIth term has done something to impel, not to impede, the development of the nation."[96] The implication of his statement seems to have been that it was not clear that the new Constitution would be useful for Vietnam in moving forward and that the National Assembly's XIIIth term must bear responsibility for any consequences it might cause.

Mr. Nghĩa's comment might have been beyond the political leadership's anticipation. Perhaps in an attempt to avoid a similar voice of dissent, after the first meeting, the second plenary meeting was canceled; instead, on November 18, 2013, the NA delegates met in groups and individually submitted a document on "issues that have different opinions."[97]

During the NA's consideration of the final draft of the constitution, as substantial issues had been decided, active public discussion on constitutional issues virtually disappeared. The mass media just spread information about the NA's activities without publishing controversial discussions as it had done the previous time. The most notable event was that the seventy-two Group submitted to the NA a petition calling for the postponement of constitutional ratification as they believed that the final draft failed to include substantial

[93] "Đề xuất bỏ Hội đồng Hiến pháp" ["Suggestion on Abolishing the Constitutional Council"] (translated by author) (*Vietnamnet*, October 22, 2013) <http://vietnamnet.vn/vn/chinh-tri/145857/de-xuat-bo-hoi-dong-hien-phap.html>.–

[94] For the transcripts of the debates, see Dự Thảo Online.

[95] Lê Kiên, "Hậu thế sẽ đánh giá Quốc hội khóa XIII" ["Posterity Will Adjudge the National Assembly's XIIIth Term"] (translated by author) (*Tuổi trẻ*, November 5, 2013) <http://tuoitre.vn/tin/chinh-tri-xa-hoi/20131105/hau-the-se-danh-gia-quoc-hoi-khoa-xiii/578379.html>.

[96] Ibid.

[97] "QH bỏ thảo luận hội trường về Hiến pháp" ["The National Assembly Dropped the Plenary Meeting on the Constitution"] (translated by author) (*BBC Tiếng Việt*, November 17, 2013) <www.bbc.com/vietnamese/vietnam/2013/11/131117_constitution_debate>.

changes, which meant the continuation of "an out-of-date legal framework of a totalitarian regime."[98]

The final version of the Constitution was eventually adopted by 97.59 percent of NA members on November 28, 2013.[99] Two delegates carried blank votes on the constitution. One of them was Dương Trung Quốc,[100] an active delegate and famous historian. In an interview with the *Tuổi trẻ Newspaper*, he explained that the nation needed "more substantial steps."[101] The 72 Group released a "declaration" against the new Constitution and called for civil disobedience.[102] The *Cùng viết Hiến pháp* group issued a farewell statement, saying: "We need to say the most important thing that the constitution, adopted by the National Assembly on November 28, 2013, is different from our suggestions and from the opinions of the majority of our audience."[103] Meanwhile, the constitution-makers and political leaders claimed that the new Constitution truly presented the will of the people and would serve as "the legal political foundation for comprehensive renovation of the nation in the new era."[104]

D. Implementation

After its adoption, the government undertook legal reform at both central and local level to implement the new Constitution. the National Assembly has revised or enacted new organic laws and laws related to human rights (e.g. the Penal Code,

98 Nhóm 72 (72 Group), "Lời Kêu gọi Dừng việc thông qua Dự thảo Hiến Pháp nước CHXHCN Việt Nam" ["Call for Suspending Adoption of the Draft of the Constitution of the Socialist Republic of Vietnam"] (translated by author) (*Bauxite Việt Nam*, November 16, 2013) <http://boxitvn.blogspot.com/2013/11/loi-keu-goi-dung-viec-thong-qua-du-thao.html>.

99 C. Hoàng, M. Thăng, Đ. Yên, and H. Duyên, "97,59% ấn nút thông qua Hiến pháp" ["97.59% Vote for the Constitution"] (*Vietnamnet*, November 28, 2013) <http://vietnamnet.vn/vn/chinh-tri/151344/97-59--an-nut-thong-qua-hien-phap.html>.

100 The other is still a mystery as at the time of writing.

101 "Tại sao Đại biểu Dương Trung Quốc Không Bấm Nút?" ["Why Didn't Delegate Dương Trung Quốc Vote?"] (translated by author) (*Tuổi Trẻ*, November 30, 2013) <http://tuoitre.vn/Chinh-tri-Xa-hoi/582847/tai-sao-dai-bieu-duongtrung-quoc-khong-bam-nut.html>.

102 Nhóm 72 (72 Group), "Tuyên bố về Hiến pháp sửa đổi" ["Declaration on the Revised Constitution"] (*Bauxite Việt Nam*, November 30, 2013) <http://boxitvn.blogspot.com/2013/11/tuyen-bo-ve-hien-phap-sua-oi.html#more>.

103 Cùng Viết Hiến Pháp, "Lời Tạm Biệt" ["Farewell Statement"] (translated by author) (*Cùng viết Hiến pháp*, November 28, 2013) <http://hienphap.net/2013/11/28/loi-tam-biet-cung-viet-hien-phap/>.

104 Nguyễn Sinh Hùng, "The Revised Constitution Is the Firm Legal and Political Guarantee for the Entire Party, the People, and the Army to Join Forces in the March Toward a New Period" (*Tạp chí Cộng Sản*, May 8, 2014) <http://english.tapchicongsan.org.vn/Home/Building-the-Law-governed-Socialist-State/2014/408/The-revised-Constitution-is-the-firm-legal-and-political-guarantee-for-the.aspx>. For a collection of essays written by constitution makers and political leaders which extol the new Constitution in this manner, see Nguyễn Văn Hùng (ed.), *Hiến pháp nước CHXHCN Việt Nam—nền tảng chính trị, pháp lý cho công cuộc đổi mới toàn diện đất nước trong thời kỳ mới* [*The Constitution of the Socialist Republic of Vietnam: The Legal Political Foundation for Comprehensive Renovation of the Nation in the New Period*] (2014).

Civil Code, and the law on religion) to make them consistent with the new constitutional provisions. According to an official report by the Ministry of Justice, by 2016, to enforce the Constitution, the legislature revised thirty-five laws, and enacted several new laws.[105] The following are major constitutional legislations which were revised or newly enacted to implement the new Constitution:

- Law on Organization of The National Assembly (2014)
- Law on Organization of People's Courts (2014)
- Law on Organization of People's Procuracies (2014)
- Law on Election of Deputies to The National Assembly and People's Councils (2015)
- Law on Supervisory Activities of The National Assembly and People's Councils (2015)
- Law Organization of the Government (2015)
- Law on Organization of the Local Government (2015)
- Law on State Audit Office of Vietnam (2015)
- Law on Promulgation of Legislative Documents (2015).

III. Explaining the Law of Change

1. Implict Replacement through Amendment

The form of socialist constitutional change in Vietnam can be called *implicit replacement through amendment*. The project of constitutional change was initiated as an amendment project: the *Proposal for Amending and Supplementing the 1992 Constitution*. The process of constitutional change followed the amendment rules established by the 1992 Constitution: constitutional amendments are adopted by the legislature with the requirement of two-thirds majority vote.[106] At the time of its adoption, the 2013 version was labeled by the NA as the Constitution of the Socialist Republic of Vietnam (Amended). But, the document was nowhere officially declared as the amendments to the 1992 Constitution. However, as at the time of this writing, the charter is officially and popularly referred to as the "2013 Constitution." Formally, the 2013 Constitution is comprised of 120 articles divided into eleven chapters, retains only seven articles and amended 101 articles of the 1992 Constitution, and introduced twelve new articles. With its official name and these formal changes, the 2013 charter is a new Constitution and a replacement

[105] Thanh Hà, "5 năm thực hiện Hiến pháp 2013—Những thành tựu lập pháp Tạo nền móng sáng tạo, phát triển và bảo vệ đất nước" ["Five Years Implementing the 2013 Constitution- Achievements foundational to the Innovation and Development of the country"], (*Trung Tâm Tư Vấn Pháp Luật Tp.Hồ Chí Minh—Trung Ương Hội Luật Gia Việt Nam*, Janurary 16, 2019) <www.nguoibaovequyenloi.com/User/ThongTin_ChiTiet.aspx?MaTT=171201952513934849&MaMT=23>

[106] 1992 Constiution (n 19) 147.

rather than an amendment of the 1992 Constitution. But, the replacement is nowhere declared officially. This may be because the party-state needs to emphasize the stable continuity of the socialist constitutional regime. In addition, as the 1992 Constitution enjoyed the reputation as the charter for *Đổi Mới* (Renovation), the major economic reform program in the last three decades, the party-state might hesitate to explicitly declare its replacement.

The amendment process is highly demanding and follows several universal norms of constitution-making, particularly public participation and international engagement. Despite formal replacement, the cores of the socialist constitutional order remain (the leadership of the communist party, the centralized constitutional structure, citizens' rights regulated by the state, the state's control over the economy), although there are progressive changes to be explored in greater detail later.

B. Constituent Power

The global return of constituent power is resonated in Vietnam. In fact, constituent power of the people is espoused by not only younger constitutionalists but also senior soviet-trained constitutional law scholars.[107] To illustrate, criticizing the class understanding of constitution as flawed, Professor Đào Trí Úc, a senior legal scholar, opines that the constitution is the "legal contract of different social forces," and "the legal foundation of the entire society which recognizes and embodies the interests of the entire society, the general interests of the people and the nation, although it always counts for the interests and the will of the leading class of the society in different historical periods."[108] Professor Nguyễn Đăng Dung presents a more radical shift to constituent power, evident in his numerous writings during the constitution-making process. To cite an example, invoking Rousseau and Thomas Paine, he suggested that the future Constitution in Vietnam should be conceived as a social contract reflecting the general will of the people, and a product of the people, not the government.[109] This idea of constituent power also informs the constitutional commentaries of other soviet-trained legal scholars.[110] The people's constitution was ardently hailed by the Vietnamese public.

[107] This is based on my many exchanges with them.

[108] Đào Trí Úc, "Hiến pháp trong Đời sống Xã hội và Quốc gia" ["Constitution in the Life of Society and Nation"] in *Bàn về lập hiến* [*Discussions on Constitution-Making*] (Phạm Văn Hùng (ed.), 2010) 12–13.

[109] Nguyễn Đăng Dung, "Hãy tìm cho mình một chỗ đứng trong Dự thảo Hiến pháp" ["Find Your Place in the Draft Revised Constitution"] (*Báo Lao Động* [*Labor Newspaper*], March 29, 2013) <http://laodong.com.vn/lao-dong-cuoi-tuan/hay-tim-cho-minh-mot-cho-dung-trong-du-thao-hien-phap-108088.bld> accessed April 21, 2015.

[110] Trần Ngọc Đường, "Mô hình Hiến pháp với việc Sửa đổi Hiến pháp 1992" ["Model of Constitution and Amending the 1992 Constitution"], in *Discussions on Constitution-Making* 13; Lê Văn Cảm and Vũ Văn Huân, "Hiến pháp với việc Tổ chức Bộ máy Nhà nước trong Gia đoạn Xây dựng Nhà nước pháp

Official mass media enlivened the idea of the people's constitution by approvingly disseminating it from the academic to popular fora.[111] Furthermore, popular constitutional petitions were strongly influenced by the idea of a constitution made by the people's constituent power. [112]

As the consequence of the concept of people's constitution, legal scholars, lawyers, senior officials, legislators, members of the government, retired politicians, and members of civil society, activists, and dissidents, vehemently called for the people as the constitutional author and popular ratification of a new Constitution. [113] According to a reporter, "*despite in different fora and in different time, there is a convergence among many comments on the draft amendments to the 1992 Constitution on vesting the constitution-making power to the people*."[114] To illustrate, in a public meeting, a commentator named Nguyễn Hữu Chót stated: "The nature of our state is the state of the people, by the people, and for the people, confirmed in Article 2 of the [1992] Constitution ... The practice of constitution-making through indirect democracy (through the National Assembly) as the current practice somewhat limits the people's power and does not reflects the will and the desire of the people. Therefore, the Constitution must be amended to make the constituent power belonging to the people through referendum."[115]

It can be seen that the intellectual community and the society understood the nature of the constitution in the new contractual line. Intellectuals do realize that this is a new understanding. To illustrate, a senior intellectual named Phan Hữu Dật comments: "Formerly, there were people who understood that the National Assembly is the supreme organ in our country which possesses all legislative, executive, and judicial powers. Nowadays, there is a deeper and wider understanding that the people are the supreme organ, which stemmed from the recognition of the force of the people and the people as the base of every enterprise ... That means

quyền Việt Nam" ["The Constitution and the Organization of State Machinery in the Period of Building Vietnam's Socialist Rule of Law State"], in *Discussions on Constitution-Making* 194.

[111] Viễn Sự and Mai Hương, "Hiến pháp phải là Khế ước Xã hội" ["The Constitution Must be a Social Contract"] (*Báo Tuổi Trẻ* [*Youth Newspaper*], February 2, 2013) <http://tuoitre.vn/tin/chinh-tri-xa-hoi/20130223/hien-phap-phai-la-ban-khe-uoc-xa-hoi/535009.html22>; Hồ Tấn Sáng, "*Xây dựng Hiến pháp là tạo ra 'khế ước xã hội'*" ["*Constitutional Building is to create a Social Contract*"], (*Báo Đà Nẵng* [*Daning Newspaper*], April 3, 2013) <http://baodanang.vn/channel/5399/201304/xay-dung-hien-phap-la-tao-ra-khe-uoc-xa-hoi-2231287/>.

[112] Interview with Mr. Lê Quang Bình, in Hanoi on January 16, 2017. Mr. Bình together with other lead people submitted three constitutional petitions by civil society's organizations and groups to the Constitutional Amendment Committee. See also Bui and Nicholson, "Activism and Popular Constitutionalism" (n 72).

[113] See, e.g., Nguyên Lê, "Lập hiến là Quyền trực tiếp của Nhân dân" ["Constitution-making is the Direct Right of the People"] (*VnEconomy*, February 20, 2013) <http://vneconomy.vn/thoi-su/lap-hien-la-quyen-truc-tiep-cua-nhan-dan-20130219030752355.htm>.

[114] Nguyên Lê, "Quyền Lập hiến phải thuộc về Nhân dân" ["The constituent Power Must Belong to the People"] (*VnEconomy*, Janurary 21, 2013) <http://vneconomy.vn/thoi-su/quyen-lap-hien-phai-thuoc-ve-nhan-dan-20130121111546767.htm>.

[115] Ibid.

the new Constitution must guarantee the people's right to vote in referendum. Actually, this understanding is just a return to the spirit and words of the 1946 Constitution of our country."[116]

It is reported that: "During the deliberation at the National Assembly in late 2012, some delegates suggested that after being approved by the National Assembly, the Constitution must be voted in a referendum to be valid. Referendum must be determined in the Constitution as a citizen's fundamental rights."[117] My interviews indicate that constitution-makers also adopted the new understanding that the nature of the constitution is the expression of the popular will, not merely the party's creed.[118] The Government also agrees: "*It is necessary to determine that the constituent power is the expression of the people's supreme power, including the powers to initiate constitution-making, to participate in the constitutional drafting process, and finally to ratify [the constitution] in a referendum.*"[119]

The call for a referendum as a mandatory step in the constitution-making process was also informed by the discourse and practice of constitutional referendums around the globe.[120] It also resonated with the contractual conception of the nature of constitutions derived from the writings of Enlightenment political thinkers.[121] At the same time, the Vietnamese discourse on referendums in the constitution-making process was motivated by local concerns. The call for the people's ratification of the Constitution implied advocacy for popular redetermination of the nature of the political system and the Party's leadership. Different forces may have had different political reasons to support a constitutional referendum. Establishment constitutionalists, legislators, and officials may have supported popular approval of the Constitution as a means for the people to formally constitute the current polity and affirm the Party's leadership, thereby giving the socialist system and the Party's leadership a legitimate basis. Meanwhile, radical liberals and dissidents may have mobilized in favor of a constitutional referendum as a peaceful means to downplay the current socialist system and the role of the CPV and

116 Ibid.
117 Ibid.
118 Interviews.
119 "Chính Phủ Kiến nghị Quyền Lập hiến Thuộc về Nhân dân" ["The Government Suggests: Constituent Power Belonging to the People"] (*VietNamNet*, January 4, 2013) <http://vietnamnet.vn/vn/thoi-su/116712/chinh-phu-kien-nghi-quyen-lap-hien-thuoc-ve-nhan-dan.html>.
120 The references to other countries' experiences of constitutional referendum are numerous. *See*, e.g., the proceedings of the Institute of Legislative Studies Conference entitled *Quy trình lập hiến của một số nước trên thế giới—Những kinh nghiệm có thể kế thừa và phát triển* ["The Constitution-Making Process in Some Nations of the World: Experiences for Reference and Developments"] held in Vũng Tàu, Vietnam (September 16–17, 2010).
121 Vietnamese constitutional commentators often make reference to the social contract theories of John Locke (1632–1704), Montesquieu (1689–1775), and Jean-Jacques Rousseau (1712–1778) to argue for constituent power and referendum. See e.g., Nguyễn Sĩ Dũng, "Khế ước xã hội" ["Social Contract"] (*Tạp chí Tia sáng*, January 3, 2013) <http://tuanhsl.blogspot.sg/2013/01/khe-uoc-xa-hoi.html>; Viễn Sử and Mai Hương, "Hiến pháp phải là bản khế ước xã hội" ["The Constitution Must Be a Social Contract"] (*Tuổi trẻ*, February 23, 2013) <http://tuoitre.vn/tin/chinh-tri-xa-hoi/20130223/hien-phap-phai-la-ban-khe-uoc-xa-hoi/535009.html>.

transform Vietnam into a liberal constitutional democracy. In other words, they mobilized in favor of a change in the constitutional process as a means to change the constitutional substance.

C. Public Participation

1. Controlled Participation

The call for constituent power in Vietnam failed to result in its actual practice by the people but was consequential to the participatory constitution-making. The 2013 constitution-making process has encouraged the most participation and has been the most open process in country. The process of making Vietnam's 2013 Constitution reflects to a considerable extent the global trend of involving the public. Even before the draft Constitution had been officially released for public consultation, it was published on the NA's website[122] and the public had in fact already been engaged in the early stages of the constitution-making process. This website also collected and published constitutional commentaries publicly. The NA's debates on the draft Constitution were also highly publicized: all of these debates were televised live and the transcripts were then published on its website. This helped the public to follow the NA's debates and engage in the public dialogue, which put pressure on the NA's forum. In addition, before the official release of the draft constitution to the public, there had already been a proliferation of articles published in national law journals, popular media, and books, as well as workshops and conferences discussing constitutional revision issues.[123]

The people's participation was prominent when the second draft of the constitution was released for public consultation in early 2013. This was the most participatory constitution-making process ever to have happened in Vietnam, and as such was consistent with the international norm of public participation in constitution making. The political leadership allowed a "no taboo" public constitutional deliberation. The public touched on virtually all substantial constitutional questions without fear of punishment, including the sensitive issues that challenged the current socialist polity, such as the Party's leadership, the holding of a constitutional referendum, the establishment of a constitutional court, and a change to the nation's name.[124] The striking rise of constitutional mobilization was permitted by political elites. Even such radical figures as the members of the 72 Group were not

[122] Dự thảo Online [Online Drafts] <http://duthaoonline.quochoi.vn>.

[123] I attended most of these workshops and conferences. It should be noted that most Vietnamese law journals publish monthly, which allows for the timely publication of constitutional commentaries. In particular, the National Assembly's *Tạp chí Nghiên cứu Lập pháp* (*Journal of Legislative Studies*)—the journal most referred to by the constitutional commentators—is published twice a month both in print and online at http://www.nclp.org.vn/. Many articles appearing here are then republished on other popular websites, which helps to widely disseminate constitutional commentaries.

[124] Compare the 2001 constitutional debate, in which discussion of the Party's leadership was taboo and constitutional review was still a very sensitive issue. See Sidel (n 19) at 82.

put in jail, although they petitioned for a radical transformation of the regime. This is an important observation in the authoritarian context of Vietnam, where the call for change of the regime is normally criminalized.

While the international norm of public participation was adopted, it was contextualized by local attempts to impose political controls over the process of public constitutional consultation. The particular process of constitutional consultation as well as the constitution-making process as a whole was under the Party's orchestration. The Party managed, controlled, and directed the constitutional discussions to achieve possible reforms and to preclude radical change. The Constitutional Amendment Committee was an instrument for the Party to control the constitution-making process. This explains the fact that its membership was made up of senior and influential Party members. In theory, this body was responsible for constitutional drafting. However, in reality, given its overwhelming number of senior politicians, its role was more likely to manage and control the constitution-making process. Instead, the constitutional drafting was put in the hands of the Editorial Board of Constitutional Amendment. This Editorial Board, however, did not merely edit, but actually drafted the Constitution under the control of the Committee, which—as noted—was in turn controlled by the Party. These constitution-making bodies lacked substantial participation from the people and were employed as instruments to control the constitution-making process.

The Party's effort to control the popular constitutional debate was obvious during the public consultation. The Politburo's *Instruction on Organizing the Collection of People's Opinions on the Draft Amendment to the 1992 Constitution* was not merely intended to instruct, but also to direct the discussions to certain vectors. Party bodies like the Central Military Commission and the Central Party Committee of Public Security were employed to guarantee these directed discussions.

The Party also employed the official mass media to control public constitutional discussions, particularly the television news, the *People's Newspaper* (*Báo Nhân dân*), the *People's Military Newspaper* (*Báo Quân đội Nhân dân*), and the *Great Solidarity Newspaper* (*Báo Đại Đoàn Kết*). The official mass media were summoned to defend the state and the Party's constitutional options, and to again counter such liberal proposals as a multiparty system, the separation of powers, and a civil military. The advocates of such liberal proposals, including the 72 Group, were excluded or restricted from expressing their voices in the official media. Instead, they could communicate with the public, the state, and the Party mainly through unofficial media on the internet.

Finally, public participation was combined with confidential meetings of the constitution makers and political leaders. The public was informed about the meetings of the Constitutional Amendment Committee [125] and of the Party's

[125] The sessions of the Constitutional Amendment Committee were reported on the website of the National Assembly, at "Uỷ ban Dự thảo sửa đổi Hiến pháp họp phiên thứ 2" ["Constitutional

Central Committee where political leaders considered constitutional questions.[126] However, what was discussed behind closed doors was secret. Tushnet states:

> Public discussions by drafters might produce agreement on a few items, but many others are likely to be intractable without hard bargaining of the sort that is difficult to do in public. Instead, the drafters will retreat to the back rooms, or to dinner tables, where the important work will be done.[127]

The confidential meetings allowed the Vietnamese constitution makers and political leaders to negotiate and perhaps come to conclusions on hard constitutional questions that had caused serious divisions in the public and between NA delegates, such as constitutional review, land ownership, and the position of state-owned enterprises.

Why did Vietnamese leaders attempt to both conform to the international norm of public participation and at the same time put political controls on the constitution-making process? David Law and Mila Versteeg point out that nations conform to global constitutional norms to gain acceptance and support from domestic and international audiences.[128] As public participation is recognized as an international norm, Vietnamese political leadership recognized the right to participate in constitution making, consistent with the global trend and the requirement of international law, so as to gain more international legitimacy. This explains the fact that, in the aforementioned report, produced for the Universal Periodic Review, the Vietnamese government presented to the United Nations Human Rights Council the country's experience of public participation in the constitution-making process as a national achievement of human rights practice.[129]

Public participation may also have enhanced the domestic legitimacy of the Vietnamese political leadership. Involving the public in the constitution-making process may have helped increase the legitimacy of the constitution, which was concurrently instrumental to the Vietnamese communist leadership and Vietnamese socialism, whose legitimacy is confirmed by the constitution. Furthermore, the pressure exerted by the call for popular constitution-making

Amendment Committee Held the Second Session"] (*Dự thảo Online* [*Online Draft*]) <http://duthaoonline.quochoi.vn/DuThao/Lists/TT_TINLAPPHAP/View_Detail.aspx?ItemID=203>.

[126] See, eg, "Thông báo Hội nghị BCH Trung ương Đảng lần thứ 8" ["Announcement of the 8th Meeting of the Central Committee of the Party"] (Vietnam+, October 9, 2013) <www.vietnamplus.vn/thong-bao-hoi-nghi-bch-trung-uong-dang-lan-thu-8/224578.vnp>.

[127] Mark Tushnet, "Some Skepticism About Normative Constitutional Advice" (n 12) 1996.

[128] David S. Law and Mila Versteeg, "The Evolution and Ideology of Global Constitutionalism" (2011) 99 California Law Review 1163, 1178.

[129] Universal Periodic Review National Report 3.

was truly consequential. The political leadership could have aggregated its legitimacy by simply neglecting the public demand for a referendum unless it mollified the public with an alternative remedy. Widely consulting the people on the draft constitution was one such remedy. Public consultation then became the basis for the constitution makers and political leaders to claim the legitimacy of the constitution, on the ground that it expressed the people's will because their opinions had been collected during the constitution-making process, even though there was no referendum.[130] The meaning of the process of constitutional consultation thus turns out to be complex. In some sense, the process was appropriated as a sort of political expediency to legitimize the existing political leadership and regime.[131]

Yet, the Party did not abandon political control of the constitution-making process. Its logic lay in the political interest in maintaining the existing socialist regime. This is more obvious in context, when the public mobilized for substantial changes that challenged the socialist regime, such as changing the nation's name, removing the Party's leadership, and curtailing state power in the national economy and land. In particular, the rise of constitutional movements was so forceful that they had the potential to lead to a "constitutional moment."[132] The retention of political control was meant to avoid such a moment. This also explains the rejection of the call for a constitutional referendum: a referendum supported by activists and popular mobilization could have resulted in a moment of reconstituting the polity. But the Party did not control the constitution-making process in a completely authoritarian manner. Strict authoritarian control would sow dragon's teeth in the legitimization of the Vietnamese socialist leadership. Therefore, there was an interplay of the global norm and local concerns, and public participation and political control were combined.

2. Constitutional Mobilization

The constitution-making process offers the particular constitutional opportunity for social actors to mobilize for constitutional change in Vietnam. Especially, the

[130] See Nguyễn Sinh Hùng (n 104); H Vũ, "Tổng Bí thư Nguyễn Phú Trọng: Hiến pháp mới là sự đồng lòng, đồng sức của toàn Đảng, toàn dân" ["General Secretary Nguyễn Phú Trọng: The New Constitution Is the Consensus of the Entire Party and the Entire People"] (*Báo mới*, December 27, 2013) <www.baomoi.com/tong-bi-thu-nguyen-phu-trong-hien-phap-moi-la-su-dong-long-dong-suc-cua-toan-dang-toan-dan/c/12767624.epi>

[131] This is not an exception that is unique to Vietnam, but happens elsewhere too, illustrating the phenomenon of "abusive constitutionalism" and the "dangers of popular constitution-making." See generally David Landau, "Abusive Constitutionalism" (2013) 47 UC Davis Law Review 189 (arguing that popular mechanisms of constitutional change were used by would-be autocrats to undermine democracy in Hungary, Egypt, and Venezuela); William Partlett, "The Dangers of Popular Constitution-Making" (2012) 38 Brooklyn Journal of International Law 193 (arguing that popular mechanisms of constitution making have been appropriated to legitimize dictatorships in Russia, Kazakhstan, and Belarus).

[132] The idea of constitutional moments was proposed by Bruce Ackerman. See generally Bruce Ackerman, *We the People*, vol 2 (Harvard University Press 1998).

state's commitments to "comprehensive constitutional revision" and "no taboo"[133] constitutional discussion during the constitutional consultation process allows constitutional activists and intellectuals to launch constitutional proposals and mobilize public support without apprehension of political sanctions.

That particular constitutional opportunity is underpinned by the general environment. To illustrate, despite international criticisms,[134] commentators on Vietnamese politics have demonstrated "the proliferation of non-governmental organizations and associations, the increasing freedom of the press and media due to the declining salience of state ideology, and the loosening of the state's political control over society."[135] In addition, although under political control in paper, civil society in Vietnam is vibrant in reality and the space for its activity has been increasingly extended.[136] This allows the civil society to involve in constitutional mobilization.

Moreover, the booming of the Internet and social media and the state's soft control of them create the environment for constitutional mobilization in Vietnam. As Zachary Abuza documents: "Forty-four percent of the population, over 39 million people, are now online, making Vietnam the 14th-largest Internet market in the world . . . It is estimated that over 60 percent of urbanites and suburbanites are connected."[137] Importantly, "the Internet is surprisingly freewheeling in Vietnam," mainly because its growth "far outpaced the government's ability to contain it technologically."[138] Actors that involve in the Petition 72, for example, had created its blog which was blocked by the authorities, but they then quickly created other different blogs where the Petition 72 was publicized, beyond the technological control of the authorities. So, due to technological reasons, the authorities are unable to put a strong control on the Internet, especially Youtube and social media like Facebook and blogs where the social mobilization operates. Social actors have employed online media to mobilize for social changes in Vietnam,[139] and when the regime undertook constitution-making, they seized this opportunity and utilized the cyberspace to mobilize for constitutional change.

At the root of the constitutional environment is economic development in Vietnam. Constitutional Economics suggests the connection between

[133] Chung Hồng, "Không có Cấm kỵ trong Góp ý Sửa Hiến pháp" ["There is no Taboo in Commenting on Constitutional Amendment"] (*VietnamNet*, December 29, 2012) <https://vietnamnet.vn/vn/thoi-su/khong-co-cam-ky-khi-gop-y-sua-hien-phap-103205.html>.

[134] See, for example, "World Report 2014: Vietnam" (*Human Rights Watch*, 2014) <www.hrw.org/world-report/2014/country-chapters/vietnam>.

[135] Thiem Bui, "*Vietnam's Civil Society*" (*EastAsiaForum*, September 5, 2013) <www.eastasiaforum.org/2013/09/05/vietnams-civil-society-undergoing-vital-changes/>.

[136] Andrew Wells-Dang, "The Political Influence of Civil Society in Vietnam" in *Politics in Contemporary Vietnam* (Jonathan D. London (ed.), Palgrave Macmillan 2014).

[137] Zachary Abuza, "Vietnam" in *Stifling the Public Sphere: Media and Civil Society in Egypt, Russia, and Vietnam* (Report of International Forum for Democratic Studies 2015) 6.

[138] Ibid. 7.

[139] Jason Morris-Jung, "Vietnam's Online Petition Movement" (2015) Southeast Asia Affairs 401.

constitutional arrangement and economic performance.[140] Particularly, economic liberalization pushes pressure on constitutional liberalization. Nearly three decades of *Renovation* has resulted in speed economic development in Vietnam and the authoritarian constitutional institutions borrowing from the former Soviet Union presents an impediment for continued economic development.[141] Consequently, the economy was stagnated around the 2010s, corruption was increasingly serious, government's mismanagement of the economy was disclosed, which challenges the sociological foundation of legitimacy of communist rule in Vietnam.[142] This compels Vietnamese political leaders to initiate a project of constitutional reform so that they and the public can engage in a constitutional dialogue to exchange ideas and discuss reforming institutional questions.

Economic development also explains the regime's appeased control of the civil society, freedom of speech, and freedom of press. Economic growth creates new social groups and diversifies social interests in Vietnam. The new middle class has emerged in Vietnam as the consequence of urbanization brought about by economic liberalization and industrialization.[143] They are adaptive to globalization, competent in foreign languages (especially English), receptive to global ideas, and skillful in using technological products and the Internet. In response to social dynamics and pluralism, the regime is compelled to tolerate the autonomy of the civil society and their pluralist voices to a certain extent that the regime can guarantee that the civil society and their pluralist discourse will not go so far to destroy the regime. In this line, the regime also accommodates constitutional mobilization to the extent that the regime is confident to put a firm stop when necessary.

On constitutional framing, Vietnamese constitutional activists and intellectuals use the 1992 Constitution as a frame to address and to draw the public attention to the problems internal to the existing communist regime. Despite different expression, social actors have identified common constitutional problems rooted in the exclusive leadership of communist party, the concentration of state power, and the control of the state over human rights and economic resources, which are embodied in the 1992 Constitution. So, the authoritarian constitution operates as the frame for the society to identify constitutional problems.

To develop arguments for constitutional change, mobilizing actors refer to alternative sources. *First*, they refer to international and transnational ideas, norms, discourses, or symbols. For example, they resort to international human rights law, such as Universal Declaration of Human Rights, the International Covenant on Civil and Political Rights, and the Convention on the Elimination of all Forms of

[140] Ames M. Buchanan and Gordon Tullock, *The Calculus of Consent, Logical Foundations of Constitutional Democracy* (University of Michigan Press 1962).
[141] Khuong (n 30).
[142] For more details, see Bui and Nicholson, "Activism and Popular Constitutionalism in Vietnam" (n 72).
[143] See generally, Catherine Earl, *Vietnam's New Middle Classes* (NIAS Press 2014).

Discrimination Against Women. They also invoke the amorphous pool of global constitutional ideas and institutions like social contract, limited government, human rights, and constitutional review. In addition, they vindicate foreign constitutional experiences (e.g., constitutional convention, constitutional referendum, and same-sex marriage). To gain wider acceptance and support, social actors connect their arguments to general values of the civilizing world rather than specify experiences of a particular foreign nation. *Second*, the constitutional framing is situated within the national cultural richness, the local social diversity, and the popular aspiration of the Vietnamese people. This kind of nationalism helps consolidate the legitimacy of the constitutional arguments and draw public support. Consequently, there is a dialogical interaction between global and local sources in framing constitutional arguments.

Despite different expression, reasoning, and level of concern, mobilizing actors share common proposals for constitutional changes as a response to their identification of common problems, including: popular sovereignty, democratic elections, constitutional referendum, universalist human rights, specific institutions to protect human rights (such as a constitutional court or council and a human right committee), clear distribution of state power, market economy without the "leading role" of the SOEs, and multi-ownership of land.

To engage in a dialogue with authoritarian leaders, mobilizing actors *align* their constitutional arguments to the official constitutional language. The 1992 Constitution and party's constitutional rhetoric include ambiguous and contradictory language which lacks substantive meanings. This allows social actors to construct substantive constitutional meanings and align them to the florid constitutional language, by which they challenge those in power in a dialogical way. To illustrate, the 1992 text includes the ambiguous and broad language of "socialist rule of law state." Social actors align to this language and call for its substantive elements, such as human rights and constitutional review. Moreover, they refer to the constitution's provision that all powers belong to the people to mobilize for constitutional referendum. In addition, they invoke the contradictory constitutional confirmation of both the supreme position of the National Assembly and the leading role of the Party to call for curtailing the party power in favor of parliamentary supremacy. Apart from the existing constitution, social actors also align to constitutional rhetoric expressed in the party's documents and constitution-makers' discourse. For example, the rhetoric of "controlling the state power" adopted by the Party in the Eleventh Convention in 2011[144] and repeated by the

[144] "Báo cáo chính của Ban Chấp hành Trung Ương Đảng Tại Đại hội lần thứ 11 của Đảng Cộng Sản Việt Nam" ["Political Report of Central Committee of the Party in the 11th Convention of the Vietnamese Communist Party"] <http://chinhphu.vn/portal/page/portal/chinhphu/NuocCHXHCNVietNam/ThongTinTongHop/noidungvankiendaihoidang?categoryId=10000716&articleId=10038382>

constitution-makers allows social actors to frame argument about checks and balances and constitutional review.

Even when framing constitutional arguments basing on transnational sources, social actors also align to official constitutional language. In fact, Vietnamese leaders and constitution-makers also support revising the constitutional human rights provision in consistence with international human rights treaties Vietnam has signed.[145] Social actors adjust to this official commitment in framing their reformist constitutional arguments informed by transnational sources. By that, they engage in a dialogue with the government to articulate the meaning of international law in domestic context. This helps enhance the legitimacy of their arguments and avoid political sanction.

Some groups have specific constitutional concerns and they *amplify* particular constitutional arguments. The CVHP group, for example, includes mainly educators, which explains why they are specifically concerned with the constitutional provisions of schooling fee or official language. The catholic bishops focus on freedom of thought and freedom of religion. The vulnerable groups underline the constitutional protection of diversity and equality among different social groups. The NGOs petition features the call for constitutional protection of freedom of association. The LGBT group emphasizes the constitutional recognition of gender and sex equality and freedom of marriage. The amplification of constitutional frames reflects the collective identity of the mobilizing groups.

On the other hand, mobilizing groups *extend* to general national concerns, by which they engage in the wider national constitutional dialogue. Consequently, social actors share the same national concerns beyond their collective identity. Even when they underline specific constitutional arguments reflecting their collective identity, they are not demanding for constitutional recognition of their specific identity but connect their specific concern to a general constitutional recognition. The LGBT group, for example, does not argue for specific rights of the gay people but for the constitutional rights sufficient to include the gays' rights.

The resources for constitutional mobilization in Vietnam are the communist political elites rather than judges. This stems from both the nature of the communist authoritarian regime in Vietnam and the Confucian tradition of meritocracy which leads to the public conceiving of political elites as the resource of social change.[146] Therefore, social actors approach communist elites as mobilization resource, most of whom are members of the Constitutional Amendment Committee. Social actors seek to mobilize the Vietnamese communist elites to engage in a national constitutional dialogue to change the communist constitutional system dialogically. They do not call for violent revolution to overthrow the communist regime and to

[145] Interviews. See also Nguyễn Sinh Hùng (n 104).

[146] For a most recent account, see Daniel A. Bell, *The China Model: Political Meritocracy and the Limits of Democracy* (Princeton University Press 2015).

establish a fundamentally new constitutional system. Even the social actors who mobilize for multi-party system also place the Communist Party in the dialogical process of constitutional change. They suggest that the Communist Party should participate in the free elections to compete for political power. Vietnamese activists and intellectuals have also tried to avoid a confrontational approach to the existing power-holders. They avoid holding demonstrations or marches, as these can be considered crimes concerning subversion of the regime or destroying the social order according to the Criminal Code.[147] Instead, they use different dialogical methods to communicate and exchange with the political leaders and constitution-makers, such as letter, suggestion, declaration, and petition.

To maintain a dialogue with political elites they avoid creation of well-organized oppositional bodies because this would invite strong political suppression. They instead employ a wide range of dialogical methods to connect with each other and with the public. To illustrate, they organize conferences, consultation, interviews, and surveys which involve the public participation; create online fora for the public to engage in national dialogue on constitutional questions; and collect thousands of online signatures. They maintain amorphous networks, sometimes online, sometimes offline. In particular, in addition do discursive platforms, the website of the CVHP group operates as a shared cyberspace in which the works of all social actors are presented. Although all of the constitutional activists and intellectuals are not connected as a single body, they are mostly aware of their fellow works, they know that they are mobilizing for relatively similar things, and they inspire and consolidate each other.

D. International Involvement

Twenty-first century constitution making is not an exclusively domestic affair, but rather features the involvement of the international community.[148] This was also evident in Vietnam. To illustrate, the United Nations and foreign organizations were also involved in the Vietnamese constitution-making process through aid programs supporting constitutional discussions. To illustrate, the United Nations Development Programme (UNDP) in Hanoi supported the NA's Institute of Legislative Studies in organizing a number of conferences and workshops on the issues of constitutional reform during the constitution-making process.[149] The Rosa Luxemburg Foundation also supported the organization of conferences and workshops[150] and the publication of their proceedings and other books on

[147] Vietnam Penal Code (2015) art. 109.
[148] Saunders (n 11) 3.
[149] I attended some of them.
[150] For example, "Hội thảo 'Sửa đổi, bổ sung Hiến pháp 1992: Đề xuất và lập luận'" ["Workshop on Amending the 1992 Constitution: Recommendations and Reasons"] (*Vietnam National University Law*

constitutional revision issues, which were then distributed to constitution makers and legislators.[151]

International experts also travelled to Vietnam, attending and presenting at domestic conferences and workshops on constitutional revision issues. Most notable was a conference jointly held by the Vietnam National University–Hanoi Law School and the Institute of Legislative Studies, which was attended by international scholars from the United States, the United Kingdom, Canada, France, Germany, Switzerland, China, Japan, Korea, Indonesia, and India.[152] In addition, Professor Tom Ginsburg, a world-renowned international expert in comparative constitutional law from the University of Chicago Law School, also travelled to Vietnam and co-operated with the Institute of Legislative Studies to organize a workshop on "Experiences in Constitution Making in Vietnam and the United States."[153] In this workshop, Professor Ginsburg shared the U.S. experience of judicial review and provided general guidance on how to make a durable constitution.[154] There was also a special workshop organized by Vietnam's Constitutional Amendment Committee in which Japanese scholars engaged in discussions on constitution-making issues with Vietnamese scholars and constitution makers.[155]

It should also be added that, from the United States, the Indiana University's Center for Constitutional Democracy was involved in the constitution-making process in Vietnam in certain activities. According to its website,

> Center personnel have advised the Democratic Party of Vietnam on proposing a platform for democratic constitutional reforms … Working within the context of

School, held July 2, 2012) <http://law.vnu.edu.vn/abipoly_32/542/content-hoi-thao-sua-doi-bo-sung-hien-phap-1992-de-xuat-va-lap-luan. I attended this workshop>

151 The Rosa Luxemburg Foundation has sponsored the publication and distribution of the proceedings of this workshop. Other volumes published and distributed under the auspices of the Foundation include: Sửa đổi, *Bổ sung Hiến pháp 1992 những vấn đề lý luận và thực tiễn* [*Amending the 1992 Constitution: Practical and Theoretical Issues*] (Phạm Hồng Thái (ed.), Hồng Đức Publishing House, 2012) 1–2; Nguyễn (n 62); Đào Trí Úc et al. (eds), *Sự tham gia của nhân dân vào Quy trình Lập hiến lý luận, thực tiễn trên thế giới và ở việt na* [*People's Participatino in the Constition-making Process: Theory and Practice Around the World and in Vietnam*] (VNU Press 2013) 252.

152 This conference was "Hội thảo 'Sửa đổi Hiến pháp: Kinh nghiệm từ một số nước và viễn cảnh của Việt Nam" ["Conference on Amending the Constitution: Experiences from Some Nations and the Prospects of Vietnam"] (*Vietnam National University Law School*, held September 28–30, 2011) <http://law.vnu.edu.vn/abipoly_32/370/content-hoi-thao-sua-doi-hien-phap-kinh-nghiem-tu-mot-so-nuoc-va-vien-canh-cua-viet>.

153 Thu Hằng, "Hội thảo 'Kinh nghiệm lập hiến của Việt Nam và Hoa Kỳ'" ["Workshop on 'Experiences in Constitution-Making in Vietnam and the United States'"] (*Báo điện tử—Đảng cộng sản Việt Nam*, December 19, 2012) <http://www.cpv.org.vn/cpv/Modules/Preview/PrintPreview.aspx?co_id=0&cn_id=561184>.

154 This is drawn from his and others' theory on the endurance of national constitutions. See Zachary Elkins, Tom Ginsburg, and James Melton, *The Endurance of National Constitutions* (Cambridge University Press 2009).

155 See "Hội thảo Hiến pháp với sự ổn định và phát triển của quốc gia—từ kinh nghiệm của Nhật Bản" ["Workshop on the Constitution and the Stability and Development of a Nation: Experiences from Japan"] (*Sài Gòn Giải Phóng*, September 20, 2012) <www.sggp.org.vn/phapluat/2012/9/299468/>.

the current situation in Vietnam, the Center has also published short papers on constitutionalism, individual rights, and democracy, which have been translated and published inside Vietnam.[156]

Moreover, international NGOs such as Human Rights Watch and Article 19 involved in the Vietnamese constitution-making process to a certain degree. To illustrate, after the consultation process ended, Human Rights Watch addressed a letter to NA President Nguyễn Sinh Hùng, urging "the National Assembly to ensure that the amendment process brings the Constitution into conformity with Vietnam's obligations under international law so that it fully protects the rights and liberties of all people in Vietnam."[157] In addition, Article 19 recognized the positive changes in the preamble and rights provisions in the draft constitution but criticized it for "fail[ing] to specify the legal status of international human rights treaties that Vietnam has signed and ratified and is obliged to implement through domestic law;"[158] it then offered detailed recommendations to revise the rights provisions so as to be consistent with international human rights standards from Article 19's universal perspective.[159]

But, international involvement in the Vietnamese constitution-making process was constrained by local concerns. The Vietnamese government is more open to United Nations institutions like the UNDP but much more cautious with respect to other potential programs from foreign governments that would support discussion on constitutional reform. The conferences and workshops on constitutional reform where foreign attendees were present were always accompanied by officials from the Ministry of Public Security. The Vietnamese government was cautious about international involvement and tried to limit the infiltration of Western, liberal constitutional ideas into domestic constitutional thinking. More importantly, as the Vietnamese constitutional debate touched on substantial issues regarding the nature of the socialist regime, the political elites understandably sought to limit interferences from the non-socialist world in order to protect the regime. Consequently, the impact of international involvement was relatively limited.

[156] See Center for Constitutional Democracy, "The Center in Vietnam" (*Indiana University Bloomington*) <http://ccd.indiana.edu/projects/vietnam>. The Center's papers have been translated and published in Vietnam in *Tạp chí Tia Sáng*, a magazine of the Ministry of Science and Technology. See e.g., David Williams, "Kiểm soát và cân bằng quyền lực" ["Checks and Balances"] (subscription required) (*Tạp chí Tia Sáng*, February 27, 2012) <http://tiasang.com.vn/Default.aspx?tabid=62&News=4941&CategoryID=42>.

[157] "Letter from Brad Adams, Exec Dir, Asia Div, Human Rights Watch, to Nguyen Sinh Hung, Chairman of the Nat'l Assembly of Viet, Re: Amended Vietnam Constitution" (*Human Rights Watch*, October 22, 2013) <www.hrw.org/news/2013/10/22/letter-chairman-nguyen-sinh-hung-re-amended-vietnam-constitution>.

[158] "Vietnam: Proposed Constitutional Amendments Go Against International Law" (*Article 19*, March 25, 2013) <www.article19.org/resources.php/resource/3680/en/vietnam:-les-propositions-d%E2%80%99amendements-%E3%A0-la-constitution-sont-contraires-au-droit-international>.

[159] Ibid.

The toleration of international involvement in the Vietnamese constitution-making can be explained by the logic of *diplomatic constitution-making*.[160] As Vietnam has been deeply integrated into the global community, it allowed international actors to be involved in its constitution making to a certain extent to win the political recognition of international diplomacy rather than to improve the contents of constitutional text. This explains the limited impact of international involvement in Vietnamese constitution-making.

E. Global Diffusion

In addition to the involvement of international actors, the global constitutional ideas have been diffused in Vietnam via various channels. One such channel has been the translation of enlightenment thinkers' work into Vietnamese. Jean-Jacques Rousseau's *The Social Contract* and Montesquieu's *The Spirit of The Laws* have been republished and referenced more often in the 2010s.[161] In addition, the new century features for the first time the publication inVietnamese of works by other western liberal thinkers, such as John Locke's *Two Treatises of Government*, John Stuart Mill's *Considerations on Representative Government* and *On Liberty*.[162] Particularly, the publication of these books in the Vietnamese language is instrumental to Soviet-trained senior constitutional scholars and Vietnamese-trained scholars to gain access to western liberalist ideas, which inspires them to envisage new ideas on the constitution, rights, and the public power. Consequently, as will be discussed below, the constitutional intellectuals advocate for a contractual constitution, constitutional referendum, natural rights, and the separation of power, which are characteristically predicated on European enlightenment liberalism, which challenges the established socialist constitutional understanding.

Translation work has also resulted in the impact of American liberal constitutionalism on the Vietnamese constitutional intellectual life. The Vietnamese version of the *Federalist Papers* has been increasingly referenced.[163] Additionally, the twenty-first century witnessed publications in Vietnamese of Tocqueville's

[160] For diplomatic constitutional adjudication, see David S. Law, "Judicial Comparativism and Judicial Diplomacy" (2015) 163 University of Pennsylvania Law Review 927.

[161] Ch S. Montesquieu, *Bàn về tinh thần pháp luật* (Hoàng Thanh Đạm tr, Political Theory Publishing House 2004); J J Rousseau, *Khế Ước Xã Hội* [*The Social Contract*] (Hoàng Thanh Đạm (tr.) (Political Theory Publishing House 2004).

[162] John Locke, *Khảo luận Thứ hai về Chính quyền* [*Two Treaties of Government*] (Lê Tuấn Huy (tr.)) (Knowledge Publishing House 2007); John Stuart Hill, *Bàn về tự do* [On Library] (Nguyễn Văn Trọng (tr.)) (Knowledge Publishing House 2009); John Stuart Mill, *Chính Thể Đại Diện* [*Considerations on Representative Government*] (Nguyễn Văn Trọng and Bùi Văn Nam Sơn (tr.) (Knowledge Publishing House 2009).

[163] See *Hiến pháp Hoa Kỳ* [*On the US Constitution*] (Nguyễn Hưng Vượng tr, Như Nguyện Publishing House 1959) (The Vietnamese selective translation of the *Federalist Papers* was first published in Saigon prior to the 1975 unification.).

Democracy in America[164] and James Madison's *Notes On the Constitutional Convention of 1787*.[165] The Embassy of The United States in Hanoi also publishes Vietnamese translations of informational work on modern constitutionalism and American constitutional system.[166] The particular consequences of the influence of American constitutionalism in Vietnamese constitutional intellectual life are the constitutional proposals of constitutional limitations, constitutional endurance, constituent power and constitutional convention, and judicial review. American constitutionalism is also referenced in other constitutional discourse regarding the separation of power, human rights, and judicial independence.

In addition to legal translation, the development of legal education is another factor conducive to the diffusion of generic constitutional ideas in Vietnam. Young Vietnamese constitutionalists and lawyers trained either in European universities (such as France, Germany, and the Netherlands) and American law schools play an especially important role in diffusion of new constitutional ideas in Vietnam.[167] They are competent in foreign languages, particularly English, which is instrumental to their imbibing and disseminating western and global ideas. Their exchanges and publications in Vietnamese buttress senior constitutionalists' support of western and global ideas. As Mark Sidel states, Vietnamese constitutional scholars "have also explored theory and constitutional development in Europe, North America, Asia, and elsewhere."[168] The publications of constitutionalists and lawyers in Vietnam have helped spread the constitutional government ideas and practices of major nations in the West.[169] Western liberal constitutionalism informs new discourse in Vietnam on popular sovereignty, separation of power, checks and balances, constitutional review, human rights, and judicial independence. Many Vietnamese constitutional intellectuals invoke western liberal constitutional experiences in different ways. Importantly, the Vietnamese constitutional intellectuals have now no longer worked purely within the four walls of academia. They have engaged in constitutional dialogues with local legislators and constitution-makers, which precipitates the pluralization of their constitutional thinking. Workshops and conferences on constitutional issues have not been

[164] Alexis De Tocqueville, *Nền Dân Trị Mỹ* [*Democracy in America*] (Phạn Toàn (tr.)) (Tri thức Publishing House 2008).

[165] Nguyễn Cảnh Bình (ed.) (tr.), *Hiến Pháp Mỹ Được Làm Ra Như Thế Nào* [*How was the US Constitution Made*] (Thế Giới Publishers 2009).

[166] See, e.g., Leslie High (ed.), "Chủ nghĩa Hợp hiến và các Nền Dân chủ đang Nổi lên" ["Constitutionalism and Emerging Democracies"] (2014) 9(1) Tạp chí điện tử của Bộ Ngoại giao Hoa Kỳ; US Dept of St, *Hiến pháp Hợp chủng quốc Hoa Kỳ và chú thích* [*About America: The Constitution of the United States with Explanatory Notes*] (Bureau of Int'l Info. Program tr, 2004).

[167] I met and exchanged with many of them.

[168] Sidel (n 69) 25.

[169] See, e.g., Nguyễn Đăng Dung (ed.), *Hiến pháp: Những vấn đề lý luận và thực tiễn* [*Constitution: Theory and Practice*] (VNU Press 2011) (containing a large collection of constitutional writings by Vietnamese scholars).

purely academic: law-makers and constitution-makers have been often invited to attend these fora and exchanged ideas with scholars.[170]

Global constitutional ideas have been also diffused in Vietnam through transnational dialogues, especially the dialogues on human rights. International human rights laws (particularly, the Universal Declaration of Human Rights, the International Covenant on Civil and Political Rights, and the International Covenant on Economic, Social, and Cultural Rights) are important to the change of Vietnamese comprehension of human rights from specific to more cosmopolitan posture. Both constitution-makers and public intellectuals accept the idea that constitutional rights in Vietnam must be consistent with international human rights treaties that Vietnam has signed.[171] The Vietnamese government has also engaged in transnational human rights dialogues with international bodies like the UN Human Rights Committee and with the United States, the European Community, Australia, and Canada.[172] The dialogical interactions with foreign leaders in transitional fora have further engendered disharmonic visions on human rights: the socialist specific and the universalist understandings of human rights.

International legal aid programs also contribute to the diffusion of global constitutional ideas in Vietnam. As evidence of the new movement of "law and development,"[173] the United Nations Development Programme in Vietnam and some European governments have supported organizing a numbers of workshops on constitutional revision issues which have created the platform for Vietnamese legislators, constitution-makers, domestic scholars, and international scholars to exchange constitutional ideas. Through this dialogical platform, global constitutional ideas have affected the thinking of local legislators, constitution-makers, and intellectuals, facilitating the emergence of alternative constitutional ideas.

Jacobsohn contends that disharmonies within the constitution and between it and the surrounding society creates "the incentives, opportunities, and costs inhering in the practice of looking abroad for interpretive inspiration."[174] In addition to this, the gap between national constitutions and global standards of constitutionalism creates the incentives and opportunities for looking abroad for constitution-making or constitutional amendment. While the global spread of constitutional ideas is inevitable, these ideas are situated within the local context and balanced with local ideas. The gap between the Vietnamese socialist constitution and social reality, and especially the gap between this charter and normative

[170] I attended many such workshops and conferences.

[171] Interviews.

[172] John Gillespie, "Human Rights as a Larger Loyalty: The Evolution of *Religious Freedom* in Vietnam" (2014) 27 Harvard Human Rights Journal 107, 138.

[173] Carol V. Rose, "The 'New' Law and Development Movement in the Post-Cold War Era: A Vietnam Case Study" (1998) 32 Law & Society Review 93–140.

[174] Jacobsohn, *Constitutional Identity* (n 13) 142.

requirements of global constitutionalism create incentives, spaces, and chances for different actors to turn to global sources for constitution-making inspirations.

IV. Progressive Change

A. The Dynamic Constitution

Drawing from the data of the 2001 Vietnamese constitutional amendment, Professor Mark Sidel has persuasively argued that the Vietnamese Constitution and its amendment process have become "a forum for dialogue—albeit moderated, bounded and controlled dialogue—as well as a framework for management and mobilization."[175] The 2013 constitution-making process can support this argument and illustrate another dimension. The constitution-making process has become a platform for the Party-state in Vietnam to communicate with not only domestic people but also the global community. Accordingly, two local and global dimensions of the constitutional dialogue in Vietnam can be observed.

First, the constitution-making process has become a platform for a domestic constitutional dialogue. The constitutional dialogue serves as the forum for local actors to deliberate, exchange, and even compromise on substantial issues regarding the construction of modern constitutionalism in Vietnam, such as constraints of the public power, democracy, judicial review, and human rights protection. This dialogue involves a wide range of local actors, namely Party leaders, constitution makers, legislators, legal scholars, lawyers, retired politicians, intellectuals from other fields, members of civil society, dissidents, and ordinary people. They each play different roles in the dialogue. Party leaders decide the rules, the contents, and the outcome of the dialogue. Constitution makers draft the constitution. Public actors deliberate on it. The legislators deliberate and finally approve the constitution.

Although the entire constitution-making process is moderated and controlled by Party leaders, it is not a monologue, as the Party leaders do not decide the process on their own and ignore alternative voices. Consequently, constitutional dialogue among different actors really does happen. Popular fora (such as the mass media, the internet, and social media) are important for constitutional dialogue. The Party moderates and controls these fora but does engage in the dialogue with the public. In particular, the Party has accommodated the striking rise of collective activism which has exceeded its expectations, and engages in a dialogue with constitutional activists rather than suppressing them outright. Moreover, the Party allows the public to debate sensitive issues that have substantially challenged the existing socialist regime, such as changing of the nation's name. Concerning

[175] Sidel, "Constitutional Dialogue" (n 1) 47.

constitutional questions that do not radically threaten the current polity or promise possible changes, the Party allows more open discussions. In this respect, the Party and the public engage in more balanced conversations on constitutional proposals, which, interestingly, have been initiated by the Party and the state themselves, such as institutionalized restraints on state powers, the Party's responsibility to the public, popular sovereignty, constitutional review, human rights protection, and judicial independence. Certainly, however, the political leadership decide the outcomes of these constitutional conversations.

The legislature is another important forum for constitutional dialogue. It remains true that the NA in Vietnam is an instrument for the institutionalization of the Party and operates under the Party's control. Given the fact that around 90 percent of NA delegates are Party members, the Party could effectively control the NA's role in the constitution-making process. Its voice is expressed within the parameters established by the Party. It approves what the Party has chosen on the constitutional menu. Yet, the legislature is no longer the puppet of the Party. Although the NA's final authority to approve the Constitution is tempered by the fact that its approval must be consistent with the Party's direction, its deliberations are highly active and open. The Party can only impose its position on the NA after allowing open and active deliberation. Notably, the NA is relatively divided on the substantial questions of constitutional review, constitutional referendum, the role of the state-owned enterprises, and local government. Assembly delegates may agree on essential issues which they find unchangeable within the current polity (like the Party's leadership and the nation's name), but on other issues which promise possible reforms, they engage in a more open dialogue and present their conflicting positions. The NA is no longer a platform of united interests as it was in previous eras. The deputies come from different areas, have different backgrounds, and represent different interests of constituencies in a more pluralist Vietnamese society. Consequently, although the legislative platform is under the control of the Party, legislators' positions on constitutional questions are very different and may even conflict. In addition, "competition among elite members of the Communist Party of Vietnam"[176] is another factor generating active legislative constitutional debate. Different delegates express the varied views of the elite Party members.

The pluralist feature of the Vietnamese constitutional dialogue should be examined in particular. Actors in the Vietnamese constitutional dialogue emphasize different and even conflicting interests and preferred values, adopt various perspectives, and advocate varying constitutional options. Generally speaking, constitutional disagreements are indispensable in liberal societies, because, to paraphrase John Rawls,[177] when people who deliberate about fundamental constitutional issues emphasize different aspects of questions and employ different

[176] Jonathan D. London, "Politics in Contemporary Vietnam" in *Politics in Contemporary Vietnam* (Jonathan D. London (ed.)) (Palgrave Macmillan 2014) 1.

[177] John Rawls, *Political Liberalism* (Columbia University Press 1993) 54–8.

methods of investigation, they will come to different constitutional answers. Although Vietnam has not been a liberal society, the impact of globalization (including constitutional globalization) and the domestic liberalization of the economy have considerably diversified social interests and made the society more pluralist, which in turn has engendered reasonable disagreements in an increasingly pluralist constitutional dialogue. For example, the forces that emphasize socialist values would defend more conservative positions, while the forces that are more concerned with the development of a market economy and global integration would adopt more progressive positions.

We now turn to consider the global aspects of the Vietnamese constitutional dialogue. In this regard, the constitution-making process operates as a platform for the Vietnamese government to engage in a dialogue with the global community. The constitution-making process is the forum for the Vietnamese government to engage in transnational constitutional discourse. Through the platform of constitution making, the government responds to international pressures on domestic socialist reforms, deliberates on global constitutional questions, practices the global rules of the constitution-making process to the greatest possible extent, and involves the participation of different sectors of the global community to a certain extent.

What is the meaning of the Vietnamese constitutional dialogue, given that its outcome is ultimately decided by political leaders? Two procedural and substantial points can be offered. First, the dialogue among different local actors and between the Vietnamese government and the global community does constrain the arbitrariness of political control of the constitution-making process. Second, the content of the dialogue involves substantial issues of modern constitutionalism, such as democracy, judicial review, and human rights protection. The dialogue therefore envisages options for constitutionalism in Vietnam. Ruti Teitel's theory of "transitional constitutionalism" suggests that the constitutional dialogue is constructive to the incremental move towards modern constitutionalism in Vietnam.[178]

Another consequence of the interplay of local and global factors is a less authoritarian paradigm of constitutional imposition. The Vietnamese Constitution is formally new but does not include radical changes. In the latest episode of constitution making, the Party successfully managed the process and imposed its constitutional preferences. Yet, the interaction between global and local factors has made the paradigm of political control and imposition in the Vietnamese constitution-making process less authoritarian. For local concerns, the Party imposes its constitutional options pertaining to issues essential to the current polity, such as the Party's leadership, unity of power, the nation's name, and the state's exclusive ownership of land, all of which are still features of the 2013 constitution. However, the

[178] Ruti Teitel, "Transitional Jurisprudence: The Role of Law in Political Transformation" (1997) 106 Yale Law Journal 2009.

imposition of the Party's will can now only be achieved after holding relatively pluralist deliberations on universal constitutional questions, broadly involving the public in the constitutional deliberation process, and allowing international involvement to a certain degree.

B. Constitutionalizing the Party

Article 4 of the 1992 Constitution which provided for the communist party leadership was described as the sacrosanct gospel and was the taboo in constitutional discussion in Vietnam for many years. However, during the 2013 Constitution-making process, the party-state, public intellectuals, dissidents, and others, and the senior members of the Party participated in a critical dialogue on the vanguard role of the communist party. At the extreme level, radical liberals, dissidents, and even retired Party's members imputed the shortcoming of the communist party's leadership to the lack of political competitions and the checks and balances among different political forces. They, therefore, called for a radical change in constitutional identity by establishing a multi-party system. To illustrate, a petition initiated by seventy-two intellectuals many of whom are party-members, called for free elections and political competition, implying a multi-party system.[179]

In a public letter, Lê Hiếu Đằng, a lawyer and party member, who worked for a long time in the Vietnam Father Front, the political organization closely tied to the Communist Party, eventually called for the creation of a "Democratic and Social Party" to compete with the Communist Party, which triggered wide attention.[180] He reasoned that economic development will create different social groups who will form different organizations to protect their interests.[181] "This is natural trend, and therefore multi-party system is indisputable, and the Article 4 of the Constitution is senseless."[182] He also commented on the legal base for creating an alternative party: "The policy of no multi-party system is the policy of the Communist Party. There is no any law prohibiting this."[183] He then suggests that the party members who have no longer wanted to be the party's members can "declare the abandonment of the [Communist] Party and create a new party, like the Democratic and Social Party."[184] Lê Hiếu Đằng publicly

[179] Nhóm 72 [72 Group] (n 75).

[180] "Kêu Gọi Thành Lập Chính Đảng Mới Ở VN" ["Call for Creation of a new Party in Vietnam"] (*BBC Vietnamese*, August 16, 2013) <www.bbc.com/vietnamese/mobile/vietnam/2013/08/130816_vietnam_new_party.shtml>.

[181] Ibid.

[182] Ibid.

[183] Ibid.

[184] Ibid.

declared himself to be an apostate in December 2013, shortly before he passed away.[185]

The proponents of a multi-party system do not repudiate the role of the Communist Party but insist that if the Party aspires to lead the state and the society on the legitimate base, it must participate in equal political competitions through free elections and will be checked and balanced by other parties. An incumbent senior official agreed with the creation of the new party, but stated that the new party will not oppose, but co-operate with, the Communist Party "to build democracy for Vietnam."[186]

However, the mainstream trend is not to radically change the constitutional identity regarding the Communist Party but to modify it by reconciling the disharmony between party leadership and people's sovereignty. To illustrate, consider the notable comment by the former President of the National Assembly, Nguyễn Văn An. He boldly points out that the party has interfered into state governance and even violated the Constitution. He stated that the reality that the General Secretary of the Party heads the Central Military Commission, the highest party organ on military issues in Vietnam, is unconstitutional because the 1992 Constitution provides that the President of State is the commander of the military force. He then suggested that a law pertaining to the party should be enacted to separate party leadership from state governance and to ensure the constitutionality and legality in the party's action.[187]

Many party scholars share the view that the new Constitution should mandate the enactment of law pertaining to party. This is meant to reconcile the disharmony between the principle of popular sovereignty and the principle of party leadership. The idea is that the leadership of the Communist Party must be constrained by law to avoid party arbitrariness and to make the Party accountable to the people. Consider, for example, the debate on the draft Constitution in a meeting of the Vietnam Father Front. [188] A senior member named Phạm Xuân Hằng agrees on the constitutional mandate of the party leadership but suggests that this leadership must be "guaranteed by law and defined by law" to ensure that the Party "is under the people's supervision" and "is accountable to the people in its decisions."[189] He

[185] An Nguyen and Joshua Lipes, "Two Veteran Members Quit Vietnamese Communist Party" (*Radio Free Asia*, December 6, 2013) <www.rfa.org/english/news/vietnam/party-12062013165627.html>.

[186] Đào Trí Úc, "Hiến pháp năm 2013 và việc phát triển nhận thức về Hiến pháp" ["The 2013 Constitution and The Development of the Understanding about the Constitution"] (*Nghiên cứu Lập pháp*) <www.nclp.org.vn/nha_nuoc_va_phap_luat/hien-phap-nam-2013-va-viec-phat-trien-nhan-thuc-ve-hien-phap>.

[187] Nguyễn Văn An, "Nguyên Chủ tịch Quốc hội bàn về phương thức cầm quyền của Đảng" ["Ex-President of the National Assembly Comments on Party's Leadership"] (*Tuan Vietnam*, December 6, 2010) <http://tuanvietnam.vietnamnet.vn/2010-12-05-nguyen-chu-tich-quoc-hoi-ban-ve-phuong-thuc-cam-quyen-cua-dang>.

[188] Lê Nhung, "Cần có luật về Đảng" ["There Should be a Law on the Party"] (*BÁO Vietnamnet*, February 19, 2013) <http://vietnamnet.vn/vn/chinh-tri/109512/can-co-luat-ve-dang.html>.

[189] Ibid.

further underlines that: "This is not a new issue. Many cadres and party members have expressed this thought. In the trend of perfecting the socialist rule of law state, we think that this is the fundamental issue of political transparency."[190] Another senior member, Hoàng Thái, concedes, stating that: "Every organ has a law to regulate it. The Party is the core of the political system but there is no law about it. This is unacceptable. There should be such law so that the Party will operate publicly and transparently, avoiding arbitrariness."[191] In an article published in official media, Bùi Đức Lại, who used to work as a senior specialist for the Party, suggests that the class nature and the ideological foundation of the Communist Party should be removed from the Constitution, because these issues should be provided in the party's Constitution rather than the state's Constitution.[192] This is actually meant to abolish the constitutional establishment of Marxist ideology as the dominant ideology of the polity.

Constitution-makers did receive radical suggestions, but their debates focused on the accountability of the party.[193] Consequently, the 2013 Constitution rejects the call for a multi-party system and re-confirms the party's leadership and vanguard role in Article 4.[194] But in order to enhance the legitimacy of this controversial Article and assuage the forces which sought to introduce greater disharmonies and challenged the party leadership, it adopts new ambiguous commitments. First, it stipulates the party's accountability to the public in this way: "The Communist Party of Vietnam maintains a close tie with the People, serves the People, submits to People's supervision and is accountable to the People in its decisions."[195] Second, the Constitution is committed to the constitutionality and legality in the party's actions, providing that: "All organisations and members of the Communist Party of Vietnam operate within the framework of the Constitution and the law."[196] However, the Constitution does not articulate mechanisms to hold the party accountable to the public and check the constitutionality and legality of the party's power. So, the commitments to the party's accountability and constitutionality, which reflected the public criticism and demand, are ambiguous and discordant with the persistent mandate of the party's leadership. In particular, the constitutional aspirations of popular and legal checks on the party's power contradict the constitutional mandate that party leads over the society and the state.

[190] Ibid.

[191] Ibid.

[192] Bùi Đức Lại, "Hiến pháp nên đề cập về Đảng thế nào?" [How should the Constitution Provide for the Party?] (*BÁO Vietnamnet*, January 23, 2013) <http://vietnamnet.vn/vn/chinh-tri/106462/hien-phap-nen-de-cap-ve-dang-the-nao-.html>.

[193] Interview with a member of the Constitutional Amendment Committee (Hanoi, Vietnam, January 13, 2017).

[194] Hiến pháp [Constitution] art. 4 (November 28, 2013) (Viet).

[195] Ibid.

[196] Ibid.

Another important development concerns Article 6 of the Constitution, which provides that: "The people practice the state power under the forms of direct democracy and indirect democracy through the National Assembly, the People's Councils and other state agencies."[197] This commitment to democracy is dissonant with the constitutionally established monopolist power of the Party. However, this commitment in theory allows the people to check the party's policies embodied in the law through their representatives and forms of direct democracy like referendum.

The constitutional debate on the party is conditioned by constitutional disharmonies surrounding party vanguardism. First, the fact that the 1992 Constitution entrenched the leadership of the communist party is at odds with the requirement of constitutional government created by democratic process, like free and equal elections. Second, the constitutional condition for emergence of the dialogue about Article 4 on the leadership of the communist party is in disharmony with the preceding Article 2 which confirms the principle of popular sovereignty: "All power belongs to the people."[198] Third, the gap between constitutional commitment on party vanguardism and the social reality creates the opportunity for the dialogue about the legitimacy and meaning of Article 4. The 1992 Constitution removed the confirmation of the "exclusive leadership" communist party, but the single domination of the communist party is the living constitutional norm in Vietnam as there is no any party that is allowed to be established. This has also generated alternative understandings of political competition and multiparty elections which emerged during the constitutional consultation process. Moreover, while the Constitution confirms the party as a vanguard force, the social reality reveals a discordant picture. In its 2011 Eleventh National Congress, the Party itself realized the gravity of its actual leadership: "Our nation has still confronted with numerous great challenges … The risk of further lagging behind economically compared to many nations in the region and in the world is apparent. The situation of degradation in political ideology, morality, and life-style of an ineligible part of officials and party members is serious, which is closely related to the evils of authoritativeness, corruption, and extravagance."[199] This opened the door for critical discussion on the legitimacy of Article 4. In addition, in reality, the Party does not merely "lead" the state but interferes in the state's affairs, which engenders rethinking about the meaning of party leadership.[200]

[197] Ibid. art. 8.

[198] Hiến pháp [Constitution] art. 2 (April 15, 1992) (Viet.).

[199] Communist Party of Vietnam Online Newspaper, "Báo cáo chính trị của Ban Chấp hành Trung ương Đảng khoá X tại Đại hội đại biểu toàn quốc lần thứ XI của Đảng" ["Political Report of The 10th Party Central Committee at the 11th Party National Congress"] (*Viet Nam Gov't Portal*) <http://chinhphu.vn/portal/page/portal/chinhphu/NuocCHXHCNVietNam/ThongTinTongHop/noidungvankiendaihoidang?categoryId=10000716&articleId=10038382accessed April 8, 2017.

[200] Nguyễn Hữu Đổng, "Đổi mới mô hình "Đảng lãnh đạo Nhà nước" ở nước ta hiện nay" ["Reforming The Model 'The Party Leading the State' in Our Country Today"] (Viên nghiên cứu Lập

These problems inspire domestic actors to look at global sources for solutions. Several global ideas regarding democratic government, political accountability, and free and equal elections have been diffused in Vietnam and have complicated the constitutional discussions on the Party. However, these global ideas are balanced with local conditions and intellectual sources. To illustrate, domestic corruptions among party members are important local factors that drive the discourse of constitutional restraints on the party's power. Moreover, the call for free elections and even a multi-party system are justified by both global norms and the local constitutional legacy concerning the 1946 Constitution which embodied these norms.[201]

Constitution-making operates as the mechanism for the party, the state, and the people to engage in a constitutional dialogue to redefine the meaning of party leadership. There is a dialogical interaction between the socialist specific principle of party vanguardism and the generic ideas of democracy, free elections, and accountability. Consequently, the identity of party vanguardism remains but is modified by new commitments to the Party's accountability and constitutional restraints on the Party. This adaption to the identity of party vanguardism is reflective of the emerging new understanding about the party's leadership within party intellectuals and society. Practically, this is instrumental to reinforcing the legitimacy of the party's leadership. The continued disharmony internal to Article 4 and the continued gap between the commitment to the party's vanguard and the social reality (especially serious corruption among party members) creates continually shifting dynamics regarding the identity of constitutional vanguardism in Vietnam.

C. Distributing Power

The 2013 constitutional dialogue features the debate on "distribution of state power" conceived as "the reasonable element"[202] of the Western theory of the separation of power. Constitutional law scholars call for clearer definition of the National Assembly as the holder of the legislative power, the Government as the holder of the executive power, and the courts as the holders of the judicial power, *à la* Montesquieu.[203] This is actually the call for eliminating the concentration of

Pháp, March 12, 2012) <http://vnclp.gov.vn/ct/cms/tintuc/Lists/NhaNuocVaPhapLuat/View_detail.aspx?ItemID=191>.

[201] See Bui Ngoc Son, "Restoration Constitutionalism and Socialist Asia" (2015) 37 Loyola of Los Angeles International and Comparative Law Review 67.

[202] Đào Duy Tùng, *quá trình hình thành con đường đi lên CNXH ở Việt Nam* [*The Formation Process of the Path to Socialism in Vietnam*] (2004) 209.

[203] Nguyễn Như Phát, "Đánh giá về Tổ chức Quyền lực Nhà nước theo Hiến pháp 1992 (Sửa đổi, bổ sung năm 2001)" ["Assements on Organization of State Power According to 1992 Constitution (amended in 2001)"] (2012) 8 Tạp chí Nhà nước và Pháp luật 5–6; Bùi Xuân Đức, "Các Quy định về Bộ máy Nhà nước Trung ương Trong Dự thảo Sửa đổi Hiến pháp 1992 Cần Thể hiện Đầy đủ hơn sự

powers (including the executive and judicial powers) in the hands of the National Assembly and ensuring the independence of state institutions in exercising their allocated powers. It bears noting the particular implication of this constitutional proposal for judicial independence, which is motivated by the global discourse and practice of judicial power and judicial review. The mobilization for the real judicial power practiced by the courts implies that the functions of constitutional supervision and constitutional interpretation have been misallocated to the National Assembly and its Standing Committee, and should be reallocated to the judicial site.[204]

But the most important thing in the 2013 constitutional dialogue on state power is the call for a new principle of "controlling the state power," which resonated with the western principle of checks and balances.[205] In the 2000s, Vietnam saw special concerns of "restraining state powers" or "controlling state power."[206] As the reflection of the practical and academic demands, the Communist Party in the Eleventh Convention in 2011 has remarkably introduced the new principle that: "State power is unitary with distribution, co-ordination, and *control* among state organs in exercising legislative, executive and judicial powers."[207] The Party has accepted the constitutionalist idea of inter-control of the public powers, an intriguing development of constitutional ideology in a single party polity like Vietnam. In reflection of the party's orientation, the Constitutional Proposal suggests that the future Constitution should clearly define the mechanism of control among state bodies in exercising legislative, executive, and judicial powers.[208] During the time of the constitution-making processes, various members of the citizenry were inspired by the endorsement of mechanisms for controlling state bodies by the party and constitution-makers. Particularly when the draft constitution was released for public comments, scholars, National Assembly delegates, and citizens vehemently discussed different mechanisms for mutual control among the three branches of the state.[209]

Phân công, Phối hợp và Kiểm soát Giữa các Cơ quan Nhà nước" ["The Provisions on Central State Machinery in the Draft Amendment to the 1992 Constitution Need More Elaboration of Distribution, Cooperation, and Control Among State Bodies"] (2013) 4 Tạp chí Nhà nước và Pháp luật 11–13.

204 Ngo Duc Manh, "Giai thich phap luat la bao dam tinh toi cao cua hien phap" ["Legal Interpretation and the Supremacy of the Constitution"] (2008) 11 Tạp chí Nghiên cứu Lập pháp 5.

205 In comparative constitutional law literature the language of "controlling" is also employed to describe the nature of constitutionalism. See, e.g., Scott Gordon, *Controlling the State: Constitutionalism From Ancient Athens to Today* (1999).

206 See Nguyễn Đăng Dung, *Sự hạn chế quyền lực nhà nước* [*Restraining State Power*] (2004); Trịnh Thị Xuyến, *Kiểm soát quyền lực nhà nước: một số vấn đề lý luận và thực tiễn ở Việt Nam hiện nay* [*Controlling State Power: Some Theoretical and Practical Issues*] (2008).

207 See Communist Party of Vietnam Online Newspaper (n 199).

208 Nguyễn Sinh Hùng (n 29).

209 See, e.g., Nguyễn Đăng Dung, "Hiến pháp Phải là Văn bản Kiểm soát quyền lực Nhà nước" ["The Constitution Must be the Document to Control the State Power"] (*Tạp chí Kiểm sát*) <http://vks.hagiang.gov.vn/viewtopic/phap-luat-58/GS-TS-18.html> accessed October 11, 2014; Bảo Linh, "Ba câu hỏi về Kiểm soát Quyền lực" ["Three Questions on Controlling the State Power"] (*BÁO

To justify the controlling of the state power, some liberal constitutionalists such as Nguyễn Đăng Dung underlined the imperative to limit arbitrary power generated by human nature's inclination to abuse power and to ensure government accountability.[210] Other scholars, such as Trần Ngọc Đường, Đinh Xuân Thảo, and Đào Trí Úc, however, explain that controlling the state power stems from both negative and positive impetuses: to limit misuse of power and to promote effective and efficient state functions.[211] This kind of discourse resonated with the international debate on negative and positive constitutionalism.[212]

The purpose of controlling state power has been canvassed. Some liberal constitutionalists emphasized the necessity of protecting individuals' rights.[213] Others are more concerned with the public interests, rationalizing that to ensure that the state will practice the delegated power for their interests, the state power must be controlled.[214]

Alternative mechanisms for controlling the state power have been discussed. The legal mechanism for controlling the state power by a special body of judicial review has been hotly debated.[215] In addition, a number of political mechanisms have been proposed, including internal mutual control among state bodies and external popular controls through election, removal of representatives, referendum, and press. This Vietnamese discourse on controlling the state power has resonated with the international debate on political and legal constitutionalism.[216]

Vietnamnet, March 6, 2013) <http://vietnamnet.vn/vn/chinh-tri/111469/3-cau-hoi-ve-kiem-soat-quyen-luc.html>; "Dự thảo Hiến pháp sửa đổi: Vẫn chưa rõ cơ chế kiểm soát quyền lực" ["Draft Revised Constitution: Mechanisms for Controlling the Power are not Clear"] (*Dự thảo Online*) <http://duthaoonline.quochoi.vn/DuThao/Lists/TT_TINLAPPHAP/View_Detail.aspx?ItemID=977>.

[210] See Nguyễn Đăng Dung, "Hiến pháp phải là Văn bản Kiểm soát Quyền lực Nhà nước" ["The Constitution Must be a Document to Control the State Power"] (2012) 4 Tạp chí Nhà nước và Pháp luật 10; Đoàn Loan, "Kiểm soát quyền lực nhà nước để hạn chế lạm quyền" ["Controlling the State Power To Limit Misuse of Power"] (VnExpress, 5 November 2013) <http://vnexpress.net/tin-tuc/thoi-su/kiem-soat-quyen-luc-nha-nuoc-de-han-che-lam-quyen-2905648.html> accessed June 24, 2015.

[211] See Đinh Xuân Thảo, "Vấn đề Kiểm soát Quyền lực trong Dự thảo sửa đổi Hiến pháp 1992" ["The Issue of Controlling Power in the Draft Amendments to the 1992 Constitution"] (2013) 6 Tạp chí Nhà nước và Pháp luật 3–4; Trần Ngọc Đường, "Kiểm soát quyền lực nhà nước trong xây dựng Nhà nước pháp quyền xã hội chủ nghĩa Việt Nam" ["Controlling the State Power in the Construction of the Vietnam's Socialist Rule of Law State"] (2011) 16 Tạp chí Nghiên cứu Lập pháp 5–9.

[212] For the distinction of negative and positive constitutionalism in general, see Stephen Holmes, *Passions and Constraint: On the Theory of Liberal Democracy* (University of Chicago Press 1997).

[213] See Nguyễn (n 210) 13.

[214] *See* Trần Ngọc Đường, "Kiểm soát quyền lực nhà nước trong xây dựng Nhà nước pháp quyền xã hội chủ nghĩa Việt Nam" ["Controlling the State Power in the Construction of the Vietnam's Socialist Rule of Law State"] (2011) 16 Tạp chí Nghiên cứu Lập pháp 5, 5–9; Đào Trí Úc, *Sửa đổi Hiến pháp năm 1992 và cơ chế kiểm soát quyền lực ở Việt Nam* [*Amending the 1992 Constitution and Mechanisms for Controlling the Power in Vietnam*]; Lê Văn Cảm and Vũ Văn Huân, "Cơ chế Kiểm soát Quyền lực Nhà nước và Một số Kiến giải Lập hiến trong Giai đoạn Xây dựng Nhà nước Pháp quyền Việt Nam" ["Mechanisms for Controlling the State Power and Some Constitutional Suggestions in the Period of Construction of Vietnam's Rule of Law State"] (2012) 6 Tạp chí Nhà nước và Pháp luật 14.

[215] See Bui, (n 55) (examining this debate in detail).

[216] For the distinction between legal and political constitutionalism, see generally Richard Bellamy, Political Constitutionalism (CUP 2007).

Members of the National Assembly also strongly supported the new principle of controlling state power but were confused about how to materialize it in the new constitution.[217] A delegate agreed that the incorporation of the new principle of controlling state power is necessary, but he stated "to control whom" and "how to control" are still open questions.[218] On these questions, another delegate distinguishes internal and external controls: "We understand that internal control is the control practiced by state organs and external control is the control practiced by the people and the society. Basically, the contents of the draft Constitution have properly expressed this principle."[219] But according to another delegate, controlling state power means control among the three state powers: the legislative, executive, and judicial powers.[220]

Consequently, the new Constitution continues but modifies the Leninist centralized constitutional structure. On the one hand, it continues to reject the Montesquieu principle of separation of power. This is due to the ideological reason that the party-state adheres to the principle of unity to maintain the socialist identity of the polity. Moreover, that rejection also has a practical reason. Although the Communist Party can also play the leading role in the separationist polity, it rejects the separation of power because of the practical concern that separation of power will invite greater political conflicts which may lead to political maelstrom. This is complicated by rumors about internal conflicts among top political leaders.[221] In addition, the separation of power may not deprive the party power as a whole, but may threaten it in some aspects. For example, the party may lose control of the judiciary in a separationist polity.

On the other hand, the Constitution introduces new changes to Leninist unitary constitutional structure. First, although the Constitution rejects the doctrine of the separation of power, it continues the principle of "distribution of power" established by the 1992 Constitution and goes further to employ Montesquieu's language to clearly define the public power. For the first time, the Constitution clearly vests legislative power to the National Assembly, executive power to the Government, and judicial power to the courts.[222] Courts also feature, for the first time, the constitutional function of protecting human rights and justice.[223] Moreover, judicial independence is stipulated in the provision

[217] Lam Nguyên, "Đại biểu băn khoăn về kiểm soát quyền lực Nhà nước" ["Delegates Are Confused about Controlling the State Power"] (*Vietstock*, November 18, 2012) <http://vietstock.vn/PrintView.aspx?ArticleID=248571>.

[218] Ibid.

[219] Ibid.

[220] Ibid.

[221] Le Hong Hiep, "Power Shifts In Vietnam's Political System" (*East Asia Forum*, March 5, 2015) <www.eastasiaforum.org/2015/03/05/power-shifts-in-vietnams-political-system/>(noting "the ongoing power struggle within Vietnam's top political elites").

[222] Hiến pháp [Constitution] arts 69, 94, 102 (November 28, 2013) (Viet.).

[223] Ibid. art. 102.

that: "The judges and assessors are independent and shall only obey the law; interference with the trials of the judges and assessors by bodies, organisations, and individuals is strictly prohibited."[224] Second, the Constitution introduces the new principle of mutual control among the three branches of power: "The state power is unified and distributed to state agencies which coordinate with and control one another in the exercise of the legislative, executive and judicial powers."[225] Third, two independent institutions, namely the National Election Council and the State Audit Office, are newly introduced. The National Election Council established by the National Assembly is in charge with organizing the national and local elections.[226] The State Audit Office established by the National Assembly, is responsible for auditing the management and use of public finance and assets.[227]

The debates on distributed and controlled power is animated by disharmonies related to constitutional principle on centralized and unitary power. First, the principle of unitary power adopted in this Constitution and its lack of institutional checks and balances is discordant with the normative requirement of constitutionalist polity in which power is separated and checked to prevent arbitrariness, which triggers the debate on distributed and controlled power. Second, this Constitution adopted competing organizational principles: the principle of unity of power informed by socialist constitutional thinking and distribution of powers informed by western doctrine of separation of power. Yet, distribution of state power has only been enshrined in the revised 1992 Constitution as a principle and has not yet been reified in concrete institutional designs. This internal disharmony resulted in constitutional dialogue in the 2010s on clearer definition and allocation of the powers of the three state branches. Furthermore, the fact that the Constitution adopted competing commitments to the rule of law (which implies the legal restraints on the public power) and unified state power and party leadership (which conversely implies consolidating power) provides space for dialogue on distributed and controlled power.

Third, the gap between organizational commitment and reality encourages dialogue on distributed and controlled power. To illustrate, while the 1992 Constitution stipulated to distributed power, in reality, the power is concentrated in the hands of the Party, and the National Assembly is the forum for the Party to centralize power. This reality triggers the debate on distributed power, which is in fact meant to separate the party power from the state power. The logic is that when the powers of different state branches are clearly defined, the intervention of the Party into state activities will be limited, as state agencies will operate

[224] Ibid. art. 103.
[225] Ibid. art. 2.
[226] Ibid. art. 117.
[227] Ibid. art. 118.

according to their autonomous constitutionally defined spheres. In addition, the increasing number of serious corruption cases and similar public power abuses caused considerable popular dissatisfaction,[228] which is disharmonic with the constitutional commitment to "combating against corruption, misspending and all manifestations of bureaucratism, arrogance, and authoritarianism."[229] The call for controlled power reflects this social malaise.

Those constitutional disharmonies incentivize different actors to seek inspiration from global sources. The global ideas of separation of powers and limited government have been diffused in Vietnam and induce disharmonic constitutional debates. However, these global ideas are situated in the local context. The ideas of the separation of powers and limited power are balanced with the local ideas of unity of powers and co-operation of powers. Consequently, the public power is both distributed and concentrated. The National Assembly remains the supreme body, and independence among the state bodies, including judicial independence, is not encouraged. The state bodies can mutually check, but they must co-operate with each other, and such aggressive mechanisms of checks and balances, such as the ability to veto, impeachment, and judicial review are not provided.

The constitution-making process allows different actors within the polity to not only discuss detailed issues pertaining to institutional design, but also to critically rethink, redefine, and adapt constitutional postulates fundamental to the overall constitutional structure. The socialist principle of unitary power remains the hegemonic feature of the regime, but is balanced with generic ideas of separated and limited government. The new Constitution is reflective of the ideational adjustment to constitutional structure and includes disharmonic commitments to unitary, distributed, and controlled power, giving rise to the continuous evolution of the identity of the socialist constitutional structure.

In addition to the horizontal distribution, there were controversial debates on local government during the constitution-making process. The debates focused on local autonomy and democratization of local government through direct election of local leaders.[230] Reflecting these debates, the Constitution, for the first time in Vietnamese constitutional history, includes a separate article on the principle of decentralization in central-local relation. The provision is as follows:

1. Local governments organize and ensure the implementation of the Constitution and the law at localities; decide on local issues according to

[228] Dien Luong, "Vietnam's Corruption Problem" (*The Diplomat*, February 29, 2016) <http://thediplomat.com/2016/02/vietnams-corruption-problem/>

[229] 1992 Constitution (n 19) art. 8.

[230] On these debates, see Bui Ngoc Son, "Central-Local Relation and the Constitutional Discourse on Political Decentralization in Twenty First Century Vietnam" in *Central-Local Relations in Asian Constitutional Systems* (Andrew Harding and Mark Sidel (eds), Hart Publishing 2015) 57–84.

the law; and are subject to the examination and supervision of the superior state organs.

2. The duties and competences of local governments shall be determined on the ground of differentiating authorities between central and local state organs and between different levels of local governments.
3. In case of need, local governments are allocated to exercise some duties of superior state organs with guaranteed necessary conditions to exercise those duties.[231]

Three important points should be noted in this provision. First, the Constitution on one hand attempts to centralize powers as it requires the local governments to be supervised by central authorities (by conventional political-administrative mechanisms), but, on the other hand, it empowers the local governments to decide their own affairs in consistence with the law. The call for local self-government is resonated to a certain degree here. Second, the Constitution provides that authorities of central and local governments and of different levels of local governments are different and shall be clearly defined by law. This actually opens the door for the practice of political devolution. These two points together indicate the constitutional base for political decentralization. The third point means that administrative allocation which has been practiced in Vietnam for several decades now becomes a constitutional principle.[232]

Local government is the issue that engendered serious division among the constitution-makers and legislators. So, conclusive answers at constitutional level, which implies long-term consequences, to concrete questions such as whether to remove the district people's councils or whether to allow popular election of local leaders may aggravate the political division. A more affordable alternative to the political leadership is to leave these issues to further deliberation at legislative level, which allows political leadership to reach to more flexible and less consequential solutions. This explains why the Constitution just includes general principles of local government which on one hand tends to support political decentralization to meet the reforming aspirations but on the other hand does not articulate any institutions of political decentralization with concrete consequences so as to appease the conservatives. Consequently, local-central relations in Vietnam now can potentially move in both reforming and conservative directions (political decentralization and political centralization) without constitutional difficulty.[233]

[231] 2013 Constitution (n 222) art. 112.
[232] Bui, "Central-Local" (n 230) 76.
[233] Ibid. 81.

D. Universalizing Rights

In the Vietnamese constitutional dialogue in the 2010s, the alternative vision of naturalist human rights emerged, challenging the statist regime of human rights.[234] Constitutional law scholars share the universalist position that human rights are natural rights recognized and protected by the state, not rights the state has granted to the citizens.[235] Social actors also strongly mobilized for a new human rights regime consistent with universal standards.[236]

Importantly, political leadership and constitution-makers also adopted a universal outlook toward human rights. A member of the Constitutional Amendment Committee told me that the enactment of the new Constitution is necessary to reflect the state's new understanding about human rights, which is that human rights are no longer sensitive issues and that human rights are different from citizen's rights.[237] Political leaders and constitution-makers agreed that constitutional rights provisions must be revised in concordance with international human rights laws.[238] The group of constitutional drafters responsible for drafting the bill of rights even compared word for word to ensure the Vietnamese bill of rights is consistent with international human rights treaties Vietnam signed.[239] When the proposed bill of rights was presented to the Constitutional Amendment Committee, it was quickly adopted.[240] On January 1, 2013, during the online dialogue between the Government and the people on the revised draft constitution, which was released to the public for comments, Vietnamese constitution-makers explained the universalist view adopted to write new constitutional rights provisions, stating that: "Sixteen provisions on human rights are supplemented and applied to everybody residing the territory of Vietnam ... Previously, to talk about human rights was sensitive. Now, the state considers human rights universal

234 Gillespie (n 172) at 112; Bui Hai Thiem, "Deconstructing the 'Socialist' Rule of Law in Vietnam: The Changing Discourse on Human Rights in Vietnam's Constitutional Reform Process" (2014) 36 Contemporary Southeast Asia 77.

235 Phạm Hữu Nghị, "Về Định hướng Sửa đổi, Bổ sung các quy định của Hiến pháp năm 1992 về Quyền con người, Quyền và Nghĩa vụ Cơ bản của Công dân" ["On the Orientations to Amend the 1992 Constitution's Provisions on Human Rights and Citizen's Fundamental Rights and Duties"] (2012) 10 Tạp chí Nhà nước và Pháp luật 12; Nguyễn Như Phát, "Một số Định hướng và Phương pháp ghi nhận Quyền Cơ bản của Công dân, Quyền Con người trong Hiến pháp sửa đổi" ["Some Orientations and Methods to Provide for Citizens' Fundamental Rights and Human Rights in the Revised Constitution"] (2012) 2 Tạp chí Nhà nước và Pháp luật 3; Thanh Lưu, "Hiến pháp Không phải để Ban ơn cho Nhân dân" ["The Constitution is not Used to Bestow Honor to the People"] (*Báo Pháp Luật TP HCM*, September 3, 2012) <http://phapluattp.vn/thoi-su/chinh-tri/hien-phap-khong-phai-de-ban-on-cho-nhan-dan-39991.html>.

236 Interviews.

237 Interview (n 193).

238 Interviews.

239 Interview with a National Assembly officer (Hanoi, Vietnam, January 13, 2017).

240 Interviews.

values naturally inherent to human, which the Vietnamese people have the right to enjoy."[241]

Consequently, the 2013 Constitution modified the identity of rights statism. The Constitution attempts to establish a human rights regime in concordance with universal human rights standards. To illustrate, Article 14 attempts to dispel the image of statist rights by providing that human rights in Vietnam "are acknowledged, respected, and protected in accordance with the Constitution and the law."[242] This provision tries to demonstrate a cosmopolitan vision of human rights as natural rights respected by the state, not the rights "provided for" by the state as in the previous 1992 Constitution.[243] Moreover, in a number of provisions concerning specific individual rights, the subjects of rights are referred to as "everyone" rather than "citizens" as in the previous constitutions, indicating that rights are valid not because the subject is a member of the state but because he or she is a member of the *Homo sapiens* community. The Constitution also includes new rights in accordance with international human rights laws, such as the right to life, the right to presumption of innocence, and the right to live in a healthy environment.[244]

The 2013 Constitution also established for the first time the principle of balancing, "an inherent part of the near-universal general conception of a constitutional right as an important prima facie claim that nonetheless can, in principle, be limited or overridden by non-constitutional rights claims premised on conflicting public policy objectives."[245] Article 14 provides that: "Human rights and citizens' rights shall only be restricted when prescribed by statute in imperative circumstances for the reasons of national defence, national security, social order and security, social morality and community's well-being."[246] The adoption of this near-universal principle of constitutional balancing attempts to limit the arbitrary restrictions of human rights by administrative authorities, which have been subject to domestic and international criticisms, by mandating that only legislative statutes can legitimately establish restrictions on human rights for public interests.[247]

However, this new view contradicts other provisions that stipulated to a more statist vision of human rights. To illustrate, in contrast to Article 14 mentioned above, Article 15 tries to establish a statist human rights regime which reflects local values, providing that: "(1). Citizens' rights are inseparable from citizens' duties; (2). Everyone has the duty to respect the rights of others; (3). Citizens are

[241] Chung Hoàng, "Quyền Con người Không còn là Chuyện Nhạy cảm" ["Human Rights have no longer been a Sensitive Issue"] (*Vietnamnet*, January 23, 2013) <http://vietnamnet.vn/vn/chinh-tri/106613/quyen-con-nguoi-khong-con-la-chuyen-nhay-cam.html>.

[242] Hiến pháp [Constitution] (n 222) art. 14.

[243] Hiến pháp [Constitution] (n 19) art. 50. ("In the Socialist Republic of Vietnam, human rights . . . are provided for by the Constitution and the law.")

[244] Ibid. arts 19, 31, 43.

[245] Stephen Gardbaum, "A Democratic Defense of Constitutional Balancing" (2010) 4 Law & Ethics of Human Rights 79.

[246] Hiến pháp [Constitution] (n 222) art. 14.

[247] Interviews.

responsible to practice their duties to the State and society; (4). The practice of human rights and citizens' rights cannot infringe national interests and legal and legitimate rights and interests of others."[248] The Constitution also requires citizens to be responsible to the state and prohibits the abuse of rights to infringe upon the state's interests.[249] Provisions on specific rights often stipulate that rights must be in accordance with the law, indicating that the rights are provided and practiced under the state's regulations.[250]

So, the identity of right statism remains but is modified by the incorporation of a more universalist outlook on human rights: human rights of everyone (not only citizens) are acknowledged (not provided) by the state. This dynamic is animated by the disharmonic human rights regime established by the 1992 Constitution. To begin with, normatively, this human rights regime is discordant with international human rights standards. Constitution-makers did realize that this document failed to meet international human rights standards.[251] This gap is because the document adopted the statist conception of rights and lacked several human rights recognized in international human rights law, such as the right to life. Second, the human rights regime created by the 1992 Constitution included internal contradictions and ambiguity. The 1992 Constitution introduced the concept of human rights for the first time: "In the Socialist Republic of Vietnam, human rights in all respects, political, civic, economic, cultural and social are respected, find their expression in the rights of citizens and are regulated by the Constitution and the law."[252] The ambiguity is that human rights are equated to citizens' rights regulated by the state.[253] The phrase "in concordance with the law" appeared in most constitutional provisions on citizens' particular rights. The Constitution also stipulated inseparability of rights from duties, and the citizen's fulfilment of their obligations towards the State and society.[254] So the citizens' statist rights are discordant with the constitutional aspiration of human rights. Third, the constitutional commitment to human rights is discordant with the actual restriction of human rights, which has been strongly criticized by domestic activists, foreign governments, and international organizations.[255]

The gaps between the national human rights regime and international standards, the ambiguity and contradiction internal to this regime, and the gap between formal human rights commitments and actual human rights practices create the conditions for different actors to seek solutions from global sources. Consequently,

248 1992 Constitution (n 19) art. 15.
249 Ibid.
250 Ibid. arts 22, 23, 25, 27.
251 Interview (n 193).
252 1992 Constitution (n 19) art. 50.
253 My interviews indicate that constitution-makers did realize this ambiguity.
254 1992 Constitution (n 19) art. 51.
255 See, e.g., "World Report 2013: Vietnam" (*Human Rights Watch*, Janurary 2013) <www.hrw.org/world-report/2013/country-chapters/vietnam>.

the globalization of human rights impacts Vietnamese constitutional identity. Constitution-makers and social actors resort to international human rights treaties to redefine the meaning of human rights in Vietnam. However, international human rights are situated within the Vietnamese condition and local specific human rights vision. This generates the continuously ambiguous human rights regime which mixes both universal and statist human rights commitments.

The constitution-making process operates as the mechanism for different actors in the polity to engage in a dialogue to redefine the rights identity. In this dialogical forum, the socialist statist principle of rights and the universal human rights value are disharmoniously interacted. The consequence is the modification of the statist principle of rights. Public intellectuals and political leaders expressly state that the new Constitution indicates a regime's new self-understanding and commitment about human rights, which is more universalist.[256] The new Constitution continues to establish a discordant human rights regime, the condition for the continuous evolution of the identity of constitutional rights in Vietnam.

E. Marketizing the Economy

Although the 1992 Constitution abandoned the centrally-planned economy, it confirmed the "leading role" of state-owned enterprises (SOEs) in the economy to ensure its "socialist orientation."[257] But, in reality, losses and corruption at state corporations were significant.[258] In addition, the contribution of the state economic sector has considerably declined. To illustrate, within ten years (2000–2010), the contribution of the state economic sector to the national budget was less than 20 percent, significantly lower than that of the private sectors. Also, state enterprises' contribution to GDP declined to 19 percent in the period 2006–2009, a half of that of the private sectors. Moreover, the rate of creating new jobs

[256] Interviews. See also Nguyễn Sinh Hùng (n 104); Trần Ngọc Đường, "Hiến pháp năm 2013: Nhận Thức Mới Về Quyền Con Người Và Một Bước Tiến Về Kỹ Thuật Lập Hiến" ["The 2013 Constitution: New Understanding about Human Rights and A new Progress in constitutional Drafting Methods"] (*Tạp chí Tổ chức nhà nước*) <http://tcnn.vn/Plus.aspx/vi/News/125/0/1010067/0/6598/Hien_phap_nam_2013_Nhan_thuc_moi_ve_quyen_con_nguoi_va_mot_buoc_tien_ve_ky_thuat_lap_hien>; Nguyễn Phú Hưng, "Sự Thống Nhất Giữa Quyền Con Người Của Hiến pháp năm 2013 với 'Bộ luật quốc tế về Quyền con người'" ["The Consistence of Human rights Provided in the 2013 Constitution with 'The International Human Rights Law'"] (*Tạp chí Quốc phòng toàn dân*) <http://tapchiqptd.vn/vi/lam-that-bai-chien-luoc-dbhb/su-thong-nhat-giua-quyen-con-nguoi-cua-hien-phap-nam-2013-voi-bo-luat-quoc-te-ve-quyen-con-nguoi/8514.html>.

[257] 1992 Constitution (n 19) art. 15.

[258] Vietnamese Government, *Báo cáo Thực trạng Hoạt động của Tập đoàn, Tổng công ty Nhà nước Giai đoạn 2006–2010 và Phương hướng, Nhiệm vụ, Giải pháp Giai đoạn 2011 – 2015* [*Report on the Real Situation of the Activities of the State Groups and Corporations in the Period 2006–2010 and the Directions, Duties, and Measures in the Period 2011–2015*].

in state economic sectors decreased to minus 22 percent, which means that state enterprises have cut jobs down rather than created new labors.[259]

Due to the gap between constitutional stipulation and reality, the provision on the "leading role" of the SOEs was subjected to critical debate during the constitution-making process.[260] To illustrate, in the National Assembly constitutional debate, some delegates argued that the confirmation of the leading role of the state economic sectors contradicts the provision that every economic sector is equal.[261] While many delegates agreed on the leading role of the SOEs,

> Many opinions held that, during the last years, the state economic sectors have received many preferences but have operated ineffectively. Meanwhile, the private and other economic sectors are developing robustly, contributing to the economy, but have been not properly considered. Therefore, the provision that every economic sector is equal with the same legal framework will create better development to the country, create more wealth, jobs, and contribute more to the national budget.[262]

A delegate argued that the party's resolution confirms the leading role of the SOEs is only valid within five years, while the Constitution has a "higher value."[263] She then concludes: "Whatever we want, the state economic sectors cannot play the leading role because this is the rule of development and a reality."[264] Another delegate concurs, stating that the Constitution has durable effect, and hence should provide for the equality of every economic sector.[265]

In addition to the SOEs, land ownership is subject to contentious debate in the constitution-making process due to its social, economic, and political consequences.[266] The 1992 Constitution introduced the principle of "the people's ownership" of land, which actually means the state is the owner of all land.[267] While the constitutional aspiration is benevolent (to prevent capitalists' agglomeration of

[259] Vũ Thành Tự Anh, "Doanh Nghiệp Nhà nước Không đủ Năng lực đóng Vai trò Chủ đạo" ["State Enterprises are not Capable to Play the Leading Role"] (*The Saigon Times*, October 21, 2010) <www.thesaigontimes.vn/Home/thoisu/sukien/42114/>.

[260] Interviews.

[261] Vũ Hạnh, "*Hiến pháp: 'Kinh tế Nhà nước giữ Vai trò Chủ đạo'*" ["*The Constitution: 'State-Owned Enterprises Play the Leading Role'*"] (*Vov VN*, November 5, 2013 <http://vov.vn/kinh-te/hien-phap-kinh-te-nha-nuoc-giu-vai-tro-chu-dao-289652.vov>.

[262] Nguyên Thảo, "Sửa Hiến pháp: Kinh tế nhà nước không thể chủ đạo?" ["Amending the Constitution: State Economy's Impossibility of the Leading Role?"] (*VNEconomy*, November 6, 2012) <http://vneconomy.vn/thoi-su/sua-hien-phap-kinh-te-nha-nuoc-khong-the-chu-dao-20121106021629108.htm>.

[263] Ibid.

[264] Ibid.

[265] Ibid.

[266] Interviews.

[267] Nguyễn Minh Đoan, "Sở hữu Đất đai trong Hiến pháp Việt Nam" ["Land Ownership in Vietnamese Constitutions"] (2012) 7 State and Law Review 13.

lands and to ensure the use of lands for socialist collective goals), the reality is different. Commentators have pointed out that the state, under the name of public goals, has expropriated people's fields to benefit individual authorities without offering sufficient compensation. The corruption in land acquisition and land allocation, other types of mismanagement of land, and the limits of the courts in dealing with land disputes have resulted in mass demonstrations, numerous collective petitions, and violent clashes between the farmers and the authorities.[268]

Consequently, this principle of "the people's ownership" of land was subject to critical debate. The most radical proposal—mobilized by liberal intellectuals, businessmen, and ordinary people—established a multi-form of land ownership, including both state and private ownership. Two other moderate proposals focused on the constraints of the state prerogative powers over land without adopting private property.[269] One proposal called for acquisition with compensation according to the market price.[270] The other petitioned for eliminating the government's powers to acquire land for projects of socioeconomic developments so as to extinguish the root of corruption in land management of provincial authorities.

The call for privatization of land radically challenges important instruments of socialist management in Vietnam. It is understandable that the political leaders have denied the proposal of private property of land. However, the party and state's commitment to the constraint of the state's authority over land and the enhancement of the quality of the land-use right presents a more liberal movement unconventional to the Soviet thinking. John Gillespie observes: "The debate so far suggests that party thinking about land law has continued its incremental shift from the socialist notion of 'people's ownership and state management' to a more individualized conception of private proprietary rights."[271]

The 2013 Constitution continues to confirm "socialist-oriented market economy" as a distinctive attribute of socialist Vietnam.[272] To promote the market economy, the Constitution continues to include the commitments to multi-forms of ownership and multi-sectors of economic structure; equality, co-operation, and competition among all economic sectors; the protection of private property; and global economic integration.[273] The Constitution includes new commitments to

[268] Danish Embassy, the World Bank and the Swedish Embassy, *Recognizing and Reducing Corruption Risks in Land Management in Vietnam* (2011). For limits of courts in land disputes, see John Gillespie, "Exploring the Limits of the Judicialization of Urban Land Disputes in Vietnam" (2011) 45 Law & Society Review 241.

[269] John Gillespie, "Vietnam's Land Law Reforms: Radical Changes or Minor Tinkering?" (*East Asia Forum*, May 14, 2013) <www.eastasiaforum.org/2013/05/14/vietnams-land-law-reforms-radical-changes-or-minor-tinkering/>.

[270] The price of compensation is around 20 percent of the market price. In major cities, the number is around 30–60 percent. Phan Trung Hiền, "Kiến nghị Hoàn thiện Cơ sở Hiến định về Thu hồi đất, Bồi thường, Hỗ trợ và Tái định cư" ["Recommendations to Perfect the Constitutional Basis for Land Acquisition, Compensation, Support and Resettlement"] (2013) 3 Tạp chí Nghiên cứu Lập pháp 46.

[271] Gillespie (n 227).

[272] 1992 Constitution (n 19) art. 50.

[273] Ibid. art. 51.

the encouragement of investment and protection of investors' capital from nationalization.[274] At the same time, to ensure the "socialist orientation" of the economy, the Constitution continues to confirm the "leading role" of the state economic sector, the state's co-ordination of the economy, the state's ownership of all lands, and the state's recovery of land used by organizations and individuals for developmental projects.[275]

The debates on constitutional economy are conditioned by the disharmonies surrounding the statist economy. First, the fact that the Constitution provided for the dominant role of the state over economic resources is discordant with the normative ideals of free market and private ownership. Second, the 1992 Constitution already included competing socialist and market commitments: market economy but under socialist direction, equal competition but under the leading role of the SOEs, private property rights but state ownership of all lands. Particularly, the constitutional provision of the "leading role" of the state's economic sector is conceived as contradictory to the constitutional commitment of economic equality and fair corporation and competition, and this has triggered the call for its elimination. Third, there is a significant gap between the constitutional economic commitments and practices. While the Constitution established the SOEs as the leading force of the economy, losses and corruption at state corporations were significant.[276] Besides that, the contribution of the state economic sector has considerably declined. To illustrate, within ten years (2000–2010), the contribution of the state economic sector to the national budget was less than 20 percent, significantly lower than that of the private sectors. In addition, state enterprises' contribution to GDP declined to 19 percent in the period 2006–2009, a half of that of the private sectors. Moreover, the rate of creating new jobs in state economic sectors decreased to minus 22 percent, which means that state enterprises have cut jobs down rather than created new labors.[277]

Similarly, while the constitutional aspiration of "people's ownership of lands" is benevolent, to prevent capitalists' agglomeration of lands and to ensure the use of lands for socialist collective goals, the reality is different. Commentators have pointed out that the state, under the name of public goals, has expropriated people's fields to benefit individual authorities without offering sufficient compensation. The corruption in land acquisition and land allocation, other types of mismanagement of land, and the limits of the courts in dealing with land disputes have resulted in mass demonstrations, numerous collective petitions, and violent clashes between the farmers and the authorities.[278]

[274] Ibid.
[275] Ibid. arts 51, 52, 53, 53.
[276] Vietnamese Government (n 258).
[277] Vũ (n 259).
[278] Danish Embassy, the World Bank, and the Swedish Embassy (n 268).

The ambiguity and disharmony of the socialist constitutional economy, both internally and externally, have created the opportunity of solutions through the use of global sources. A member of the Constitutional Amendment Committee and of the group of constitutional drafters responsible for drafting the Constitution's chapter on economic and social principles told me that their intention is to create a chapter meeting with the (global) "standards of a market economy."[279] The global ideas of market economy and private property have been diffused in Vietnam and are balanced with the Vietnamese reality and local statist economic vision, which results in the mixture of both market and socialist elements in the constitutional economy. Similarly, the party and state's thinking about land ownership also presents a shift to a more individualist conception of private proprietary rights but seeks to balance it with the conventional collective conception.

The state-owned economy remains essential to the Vietnamese constitutional polity, but is adapted by adopting new liberal and market ideas. The socialist identity of economic statism is modified by the commitment to "socialist market economy" in which the state still controls the economy, but private property rights are guaranteed, private enterprises can develop, and some limits on the state economic power are possible. Examples include privatization of the state-owned enterprises, and the transparent process of acquisition and compensation of lands. Thus, the 2013 Constitution establishes an ambiguous constitutional economy, facilitative to the continuous dynamics of the Vietnamese constitutional economy.

F. Implementation

A member of the Constitutional Amendment Committee told me that in the new Constitution substantial principles remain but are understood with "new ways and new spirit" suitable to the "new context."[280] This captures the epistemological adaption to socialist constitutional order in Vietnam.

Moreover, the new constitutional commitments have begun to inform constitutional practices. To illustrate, following the commitment to constitutional referendum and direct democracy, the National Assembly enacted the Law on Referendum on November 25, 2015, finalizing the restraints on the party-state and amendments to the Constitution.[281] But how this law is implemented remains to be seen. In addition, consistent with the commitment to state constitutionality, constitutional oaths have been taken twice in Vietnam since the passage of the new

[279] Interview (n 76).

[280] Interview (n 193).

[281] "Vietnam Legislature Adopts Law on Referendum, among Others" (*Tuoi Tre News*, November 26, 2015) <http://tuoitrenews.vn/society/31875/vietnams-legislature-adopts-law-on-referendum-among-others>.

Constitution.[282] Constitutional oaths may raise the political leaders' awareness of the relevance of the Constitution to their activities.

In addition, new constitutional commitments to distributed and controlled power have been realized to some extent. As mentioned above, the National Assembly has revised a number of organic laws to make them consistent with the new Constitution, including the laws on major branches of the state. These laws do not merely repeat the constitutional provisions but go on to further clarify the distribution of power. Moreover, these constitutional laws have some developments regarding controlling state power, such as: strengthening the deputies' right to interpellate government's members, and the role of the National Assembly's Legal Committee in constitutional supervision;[283] emphasizing the independence of the government to practice its executive power and clarifying the personal authorities and responsibility of the Prime Minister and ministers;[284] strengthening judicial independence by, for example, extending the judges' terms to ten years, stipulating to adversarial trials, and establishing the role of the Supreme Court in developing precedents, which reflects the influence of the common law tradition;[285] and stipulating the mutual checks between the courts and the procuracies.[286]

Similarly, following the new constitutional commitments to human rights, a number of legislative acts regarding human rights have been revised. The Minister of Justice states that there are thirty-six legislative acts needing revision or replacement in concordance with the new Constitution.[287] The new requirement that human rights can only be limited by statutes puts strong pressure on the government's regulations.[288] This means the government cannot issue decrees that limit human rights. The Constitution also puts pressure on the National Assembly's law-making activities. National Assembly deputies now have a strong concern for

282 See, Nguyễn Lê, "Các nhà lãnh đạo tuyên thệ đều phải đặt tay lên Hiến pháp" ["Political Leaders take oath, Putting Their Hands on the Constitution"] (*VnEconomy*, March 31, 2016) <http://vneconomy.vn/thoi-su/cac-nha-lanh-dao-tuyen-the-deu-phai-dat-tay-len-hien-phap-20160331050257461.htm>.

283 "Một số điểm mới của Luật Tổ chức Quốc hội năm 2014" ["Some New Points of the 2014 Law on Organization of the National Assembly"] (*Vientam Ministry of Justice*, December 16, 2014) <www.moj.gov.vn/ct/tintuc/Pages/van-ban-chinh-sach-moi.aspx?ItemID=5866>.

284 Nguyễn Phước Thọ, "Một số điểm mới của Luật Tổ chức Chính phủ 2015" ["Some New Points of the 2015 Law on Organization of the Government"] (August 1, 2015) <http://baochinhphu.vn/Hoat-dong-Bo-nganh/Mot-so-diem-moi-cua-Luat-To-chuc-Chinh-phu-2015/233022.vgp>.

285 Nguyễn Hà Thanh, "Một số nội dung cơ bản của Luật Tổ chức tòa án nhân dân năm 2014" ["Some Fundamental Points of the 2014 Law on Organization of the People's Courts"] (January 26, 2015) <http://noichinh.vn/ho-so-tu-lieu/201501/mot-so-noi-dung-co-ban-cua-luat-to-chuc-toa-an-nhan-dan-nam-2014-296789/>.

286 Văn Tình, "Những nội dung mới của Luật tổ chức Viện kiểm sát nhân dân (sửa đổi)" ["Some New Points of the Law on Organization of the People's Procucracies (Revised)"] <http://duthaoonline.quochoi.vn/DuThao/Lists/TT_TINLAPPHAP/View_Detail.aspx?ItemID=2223>.

287 Nguyễn Vũ, "Sửa đổi, bổ sung thay thế 36 luật, pháp lệnh về quyền con người" ["Revising and Replacing 36 Laws and Ordinances on Human Rights"] (*VnEconomy*, May 25, 2015) <http://vneconomy.vn/thoi-su/sua-doi-bo-sung-thay-the-36-luat-phap-lenh-ve-quyen-con-nguoi-20150524045653252.htm>.

288 Interviews.

how to make sure their legislations are consistent with new constitutional rights provisions.[289]

That has some positive impacts. For example, the new Civil Code, Penal Code, and Criminal Procedure Code have been revised with new developments regarding human rights, which somewhat indicates the universalist vision. To illustrate, the new Civil Code adopted in 2015 recognizes transgender rights, minimalizes the intervention of administrative authorities in civil transactions, and forces the courts to hear civil complaints even in case of absence of applicable law.[290] The Penal Code excludes the application of death penalty to "under-18 offenders, pregnant women and women who are nursing children under 36 months or those who are more than 75 years old when they commit a crime or are put into trial."[291] The Code also abolishes the death penalty for seven crimes: surrendering to the enemy, opposing order, destruction of projects of national security importance, robbery, drug possession, drug appropriation and the production and trade of fake food.[292] This development is consistent with the Constitution's new recognition of the right to life. The Criminal Procedure Code recognizes the right to silence, the detainees' "right to have legal assistance of lawyers before making any statement," and requires "audio and video recording during interrogation" to prevent "torture and other cruel treatments by police investigators."[293]

Yet, the above codes also echo the constitutional disharmony regarding human rights. The Civil Code continues the communitarian-statist vision of rights, evident by its emphasis on its role in protecting not only the interests of the individuals but also the interests of the state and the community.[294] The Penal Code more clearly shows its statist vision when it "maintains controversial articles with severe punishments against government critics and human rights activists."[295] Dissidents had petitioned for removing the offence of "propaganda against the state," as this violates the constitutionally protected right to freedom of speech.[296] This offence continues to feature in the new Penal Code.

[289] Interview with an Assembly deputy (Hanoi, Vietnam, January 2, 2017).

[290] "Revising Civil Code to better protect citizens' rights" (*Vietnam breaking News*, November 1, 2015) <www.vietnambreakingnews.com/2015/11/revising-civil-code-to-better-protect-citizens-rights/>.

[291] "National Assembly Adopts Draft Revised Penal Code" (*Vietnam Breaking News*, 27 November 2015) <www.vietnambreakingnews.com/2015/11/national-assembly-adopts-draft-revised-penal-code>.

[292] "Vietnam Abolishes Death Penalty for 7 Crimes" (*AlJazeera America*, November 27, 2015) <http://america.aljazeera.com/articles/2015/11/27/new-law-in-vietnam-abolishes-death-penalty-for-7-crimes.html>.

[293] Vu Quoc Ngu, "Vietnam Adopts Criminal Procedure Code, Human Rights May Be Enhanced" (*Vietnam Human Rights Defenders*, December 1, 2015 <www.vietnamhumanrightsdefenders.net/2015/12/01/vietnam-adopts-criminal-procedure-code-human-rights-may-enhanced>.

[294] Vietnamese Civil Code (December 25, 2001), art I (Vietnam).

[295] Vu Quoc Ngu, "Vietnam Adopts Criminal Procedure Code" (n 293).

[296] Cu Huy Ha Vu, "Standing up for Human Rights in Vietnam" (*The Washington Post*, May 16, 2014)<www.washingtonpost.com/opinions/standing-up-for-human-rights-in-vietnam/2014/05/16/cd040826-d7b6-11e3-8a78-8fe50322a72c_story.html>.

Last but not least, new economic constitutional commitments have begun to inform the reality. For example, the Government has implemented the policies of equitization or privatization of the state-owned enterprises.[297] The new Land Law, effective July 2014, has some developments respecting the larger right to use land and a more transparent process of acquisition and compensation.[298]

New constitutional commitments and principles in the 2013 Constitution shape the scope, potential, and constraints of political, legal, and economic reforms in Vietnam. But, the constraints are not very strict, and there is ample space for the continuing dynamics of socialist constitutional identity in Vietnam. First, this is because the 2013 Constitution is a disharmonic constitution. Many ideas and principles newly introduced in the Constitution are very broad and ambiguous, such as constituent power by the people, constitutional referendum, controlling the state power, and legislative constitutional review, thus opening the door for alternative constructions. Moreover, the disharmonic gap between the Constitution and global constitutionalism (for example, party leadership vs. free election, unitary vs. separated power, statist vs. universal rights, the legislative vs. judicial constitutional review) creates the condition for continuous change in the socialist constitutional identity. In addition, the disharmony between the Constitution and the social reality is facilitative of the continuing evolution of the socialist constitutional identity. Most notably, constitutional aspirations to "prosperous people" and "that all people enjoy an abundant, free, and happy life with conditions for comprehensive development,"[299] are discordant with the fact that Vietnam is still a middle income country,[300] replete with serious social problems, such as a polluted environment, social inequality, an underdeveloped education system, terrible transportation system, and the like. The aspiration to the "socialist rule of law state" has been discordant with the social reality of corruption, miscarriages of justice, and ineffectiveness of law enforcement.[301] Also, the constitutional commitment to protect universal human rights is disharmonic with the functional human rights regime in which rights are constricted for statist purposes. These constitutional disharmonies continue to offer space for, and incentives to, looking at global sources and animate the continuing shifts in constitutional identity in Vietnam.

[297] See a series of papers on equitization of state-owned enterprises at the website of Prime Minister Nguyễn Tấn Dũng <http://nguyentandung.org/tag/co-phan-hoa-doanh-nghiep-nha-nuoc>.

[298] Phạm Thị Bích Hảo, "Điểm mới trong thu hồi và bồi thường của Luật đất đai" ["New Points on Acquisition and Compensation in the Land Law"] (VietnamNet, July 1, 2014) <http://vietnamnet.vn/vn/ban-doc-phap-luat/183557/diem-moi-trong-thu-hoi-va-boi-thuong-cua-luat-dat-dai.html>.

[299] Hiến Pháp [Constitution] art. 3.

[300] United Nations Development Programme in Vietnam, "About Viet Nam" <www.vn.undp.org/content/vietnam/en/home/countryinfo.html>.

[301] Vietnam is ranked 64th in the Rule of Law Index by the World Justice Project. *See* Vietnam is ranked 64th in the Rule of Law Index by the World Justice Project. See The World Justice Project, "The WJP Rule of Law Index 2015 Report" <http://worldjusticeproject.org/sites/default/files/roli_2015_0.pdf>.

In the near future, as judicial review is absent and constitution-making process is not available, constitutional dynamics in Vietnam may be limited, but can also proceed in popular and political forums. In fact, in these popular and legislative platforms, social and institutional actors have continued to engage in dialogues on the constitutional referendum, the popular checks of the party power, mechanisms to control the state powers, the protection of human rights, and the constraints of the state power over the economy.[302] Global constitutional ideas still inform this dialogue and are situated with the local reality and interact with local ideas.

V. Conclusion

Constitutional change in Vietnam facilitates the active role of the government in improving the material well-being of living conditions of the local people. Progressive constitutional changes include: the dynamic constitutional dialogue, constitutionalization of the party, distribution of power, universalization of human rights, and markertization of the national economy. The attachment to universal, global values is one of the prominent elements legitimatizing the process and substances of constitutional change in Vietnam. This presents a kind of constitutional universalism in Vietnam.

Vietnamese constitution-makers and political leaders adopt an instrumentalist approach to global constitutionalism to enhance the legitimacy of constitution-making process, the substantive contents of the Constitution. To be sure, Vietnam's Constitution also refers to Marxism-Leninism and Ho Chi Minh's Thought as general dominant ideology of the Communist Party. Officials and establishment constitutionalists refer to Ho Chi Minh's "constitutional thought" to argue for constitutional reform. But, the ideas explored and restored from Ho Chi Minh's prerevolutionary constitutional statements are global ideas like constitutional referendum, popular sovereignty, and private property rights.[303] Post-Renovation

[302] See generally, Võ Hải, "Luật Trưng cầu Ý Dân gây Nhiều e Ngại" ["The Law on Referendum Causes many Worries"] (*VnExpress*, February 25, 2015) <http://vnexpress.net/tin-tuc/phap-luat/luat-trung-cau-y-dan-gay-nhieu-e-ngai-3150655.html> accessed June 6, 2015; Hòa An, "Cần có cơ chế để dân giám sát hoạt động của Đảng" ["There Should be Mechanisms to Supervise the Party"] (*Voice of Vietnam*, December 27, 2013) <http://vov.vn/chinh-tri/can-co-co-che-de-dan-giam-sat-hoat-dong-cua-dang-301892.vov>; Tuần Việt Nam, "Kiểm soát quyền lực bằng cách nào?" ["How to Control the State Power?"] (*Tuần Việt Nam*, August 7, 2015) <http://vietnamnet.vn/vn/tuanvietnam/254919/kiem-soat-quyen-luc-bang-cach-nao-.html>; Vũ Ngọc Hoàng, "Tham vọng quyền lực và Sự tha hóa" [Desire for and Misuse of Power] (Thanh Niên, August 11, 2015) <www.thanhnien.com.vn/chinh-tri-xa-hoi/tham-vong-quyen-luc-va-su-tha-hoa-595496.html>; Bùi Tiến Đạt, "Hiến pháp hóa Nguyên tắc Giới hạn Quyền con người: Cần nhưng chưa đủ" ["Constitutionalizing the Principle of Human Rights Restrictions: Necessary But Not Enough"] (2015) 6 Tap Chi Nghien Cul Lap Phap [J Leg Studies] 3; Trần Du Lịch, "Vai trò của Nhà nước và kinh tế nhà nước trong nền kinh tế thị trường ở nước ta" ["The Role of the State and State's Economic Sector in Our Market Economy"] (*Tạp chí Kinh tế và Dự báo*) <http://svec.org.vn/index.php/nghien-cuu/Nghien-cuu-Trao-doi/Vai-tro-cua-Nha-nuoc-va-kinh-te-nha-nuoc-trong-nen-kinh-te-thi-truong-o-nuoc-ta-37/>.

[303] See Bui (n 201).

Vietnamese political leaders do not articulate distinctive constitutional "theories" or ideology like the Chinese leaders. The rhetoric of "socialist rule of law state" adopted by the Vietnamese political leaders is not a concrete theory or vision but a vague language in which both distinctive socialist ideas and global ideas can be filled. Especially, "socialist rule of law state" is the base for public intellectuals to argue for global ideas. Importantly, in 2013, Vietnamese communist leaders and constitution-makers were committed themselves to revising the nation's constitution in consistence with "the development trend of the age."[304] In particular, as mentioned above, constitution-makers underlined the necessity of the domestic constitution's conformity to the international human rights treaties Vietnam signed.

The fact that Vietnamese leaders allow the discourse of global constitutionalism enables not only the discussion of global constitutional ideas among the officials and establishment constitutionalists but also the social mobilization for global constitutional values by constitutional activists and dissidents. The consequence is the national constitutional dialogue. Why do communist leaders in Vietnam allow discussions of ideas of global constitutionalism and engage in a national constitutional dialogue? Vietnam is neither a global economic power nor global political power, and it therefore does not long to be an alternative to the Western power. Instead, socializing the socialist regime to the global community is an important strategy to consolidate the international recognition of the legitimacy of the socialist regime and the reformist model of socio-economic development in the country. However, the dilemma is that global integration is both instrumental to the domestic legitimacy but also has the potential risk of destroying the communist regime by alternative values. To deal with this, the communist government in Vietnam adopts an instrumentalist approach to global constitutionalism. Global values of constitutionalism are supported not because of their intrinsic virtue but because they are instrumental to the Vietnamese communist resilience. From this instrumentalism, social actors are allowed to mobilize global constitutionalism, political leaders agree to engage in a dialogue with the global voices to consolidate the legitimacy of the existing regime. But, due to complex dynamics, the consequence of Vietnamese constitutional universalism is unpredictable. The regime may use global constitutionalism in an instrumental way, but once its language and ideas spread in the society, social actors may work (through mobilization, for example) to demand for its realization.

304 Biên Tập Viên, "Chủ tịch Quốc hội Nguyễn Sinh Hùng chủ trì phiên họp Ủy ban dự thảo sửa đổi Hiến pháp" ["President of the National Assembly Nguyễn Sinh Hùng Presides the Meeting of the Constitutional Amendment Commission"] (*Nguyen Sinh Hung*, August 7, 2011) <https://nguyensinhhungvip.wordpress.com/tag/thay-doi-hien-phap/>

5
The Integration Model
Laos

Introduction

On December 8, 2015, the National Assembly of the Lao People's Democratic Republic (LPDR) (or Laos) approved a new Constitution, replacing the 2003 one.[1] This chapter focuses on this change, but some background of recent dynamics is helpful. The introduction of market reform to transform the Soviet-style planned economy in 1986 has been instrumental to the socio-economic transition in Laos in the last three decades.[2] The political dynamics are also evident,[3] including the recent "critical moments of leadership renewal and transition" following the Tenth Congress of the Party and subsequently the National Assembly elections in 2016.[4] Laos has recently drawn international attention on several issues, e.g. the Lao-China railway project, human right controversies, the rotating chair of ASEAN (Association of Southeast Asian Nations) in 2016, and the visits of former American President Barack Obama in 2016 and President Xi Jinping of China in 2017.[5]

In addition to economic and political dynamics, constitutional change was vibrant before the 2015 replacement. In 2003, the 1991 Constitution of Laos was amended but eventually replaced by a new Constitution, formally called "Amended Constitution of the Lao People's Democratic Republic." Stuart-Fox considers it "the better to reflect the political and economic reality of contemporary Laos."[6] The new draft constitution was first endorsed by the Politburo, then enacted by the National Assembly, and formally promulgated on May 6, 2003, by the President of State

[1] Constitution of the Lao People's Democratic Republic (revised 2015).

[2] For transition in Laos, see generally Vanina Bouté and Vatthana Pholsena (eds), *Changing Lives in Laos: Society, Politics and Culture in a Post-Socialist State* (NUS Press Singapore 2017); Jonathan Rigg, *Living with Transition in Laos: Marker Integration in Southeast Asia* (Routledge 2005); Yves Bourdet, *The Economics of Transition in Laos: From Socialism to Asean Integration* (Edward Elgar Pub 2000).

[3] Aurel Croissant and Philip Lorenz, *Comparative Politics of Southeast Asia* (1st edn, Springer 2018) 113–39.

[4] Soulatha Sayalath and Simon Creak, "Regime Renewal in Laos: The Tenth Congress of the Lao People's Revolutionary Party" (2017) Southeast Asian Affairs 179, 179–80.

[5] Simon Creak and Keith Barney, "Conceptualizing Party-State Governance and Rule in Laos" (2018) 48 Journal of Contemporary Asia 693, 698.

[6] Martin Stuart-Fox, "Laos" in *Countries at the Crossroads: A Survey of Democratic Governance* (Sanja Kelly et al (eds), Rowman & Littlefield Publishers 2008) 371.

Constitutional Change in the Contemporary Socialist World. Bui Ngoc Son, Oxford University Press (2020). © Bui Ngoc Son.
DOI: 10.1093/oso/9780198851349.001.0001.

which was concurrently the President of the Politburo.[7] Article 98 provides that "this Constitution enters into force on the date of the promulgating decree issued by the President of the Lao People's Democratic Republic."[8] That means the 1991 Constitution expired, and constitutional replacement was in place.

The 2003 text included ninety-eight articles compared to eighty articles in the previous text. Some fifty articles were revised or newly added to the 2003 version. Despite formal replacement, the 2003 Constitution retained substantive contents (including the party provision, the overall centralized constitutional structure with slight modification, and statist rights) and the structure of the 1991 document. The most important changes focused on Chapter II on socio-economic regime. The old chapter had eight articles, while the new one had eighteen articles. The changes responded to the domestic socio-economic transition after several decades of reform and to the impact of globalization. Consequently, the new constitutional economy featured the emphasis on regional and global integration (Article 13); the principles of market economy such as enterprises' equality under the law, competition, and co-operation (Article 13); the state's commitment to promoting domestic and foreign investments (Articles 14 and 15); the state's commitment to implement open policies on economic co-operation with foreign countries; and the importance of human resource development (Article 21). The new chapter also encouraged private investment in education and (Article 22) and stipulated the state's commitment to promote scientific and technological development and protect intellectual property (Article 24).

The 2003 Constitution was replaced by a new Constitution in 2015. Although the process of constitutional change was conducted as an amendment project according to the amendment rules established by the 2003 Constitution and relevant law, Article 119 of the new 2015 Constitution explicitly stipulates: "This Constitution and its contents shall replace the previous version of the Lao People's Democratic Republic Constitution of No. 25/NA dated 6 May 2003." That means the form of change is a constitutional replacement.

This chapter focuses on that constitutional replacement through amendment. It demonstrates that Laos introduces progressive constitutional change—notably, the redefinition of the position, structure, and functions of state institutions, including the imposition of term limits on executive power holders; strengthened commitment to a market economy; new commitments to human rights protection, judicial independence, and adversarial trials; and the creation of new institutions, namely, the local people's councils, the state audit, and the election committee—to facilitate the improvement of the socialist constitutional system which in turn promotes the improvement of the material well-being of the living conditions of the Lao multi-ethnic people.

[7] Ibid.

[8] Amended Constitution of the Lao People's Democratic Republic 2003, art. 98.

The adherence to the integration of the Lao multi-ethnic people legitimatizes the process and substance of constitutional change in this country. The Lao story, therefore, indicates the integration model of socialist constitutional change. Compared with the other four socialist countries, Laos is marked by the high level of ethnic diversity. Laos is perhaps the "most ethnically diverse" [9] in Southeast Asia. The country is the home of some 6.5 million people[10] divided into four main linguistic groups, which is in turn further divided into forty-nine ethnic groups.[11] "These multi-ethnic people are scattered across the country each with their own unique traditions, culture and language."[12] The Lao ethnic group is the largest group, occupying 50 percent of the country's population.[13]

That ethnic plurality necessarily invites constitutional response. Theorists of constitutional designs for pluralist societies have identified two competing models called accommodation and integration.[14] While integrationists promote a single public identity, accommodationists advocates for dual or multiple public identities.[15] Lao constitution-makers adopt the integration model. The Constitution attempts to establish a united whole at the public sphere while recognizing ethnic diversity at the private sphere. Three important factors explain why Laos adopts this integration model. First, this model is more acceptable to the communist party in Laos. Within the integrationist framework, the communist party can maintain its monopolist, centralized, and unitary power. Second, the history of regional division in Laos makes integration more favorable than accommodation as the latter may exacerbate conflicts and divisions. Third, ethnic diversity in Laos does not engender serious ethnic divisions and does not present as a significant threat to the communist power. Therefore, constitutional design can transcend ethnic plurality by creating a framework for public unity while recognizing ethnic diversity at the private sphere.

McGarry, O'Leary, and Simeon distinguish three forms of integrationism: republican, socialist, and liberal.[16] Accordingly, "Socialist integrationists regard social classes as the key component of social thought and practice, and regard the promotion of distributive justice as the appropriate public priority ... Socialist integrationism is popular with European left and Marxists everywhere, including

[9] Elizabeth M. King and Dominique van de Walle, "Laos" in *Indigenous Peoples, Poverty, And Development* (Gillette H Hall and Harry Anthony Patrinos (eds), Cambridge University Press 2012) 249.

[10] Lao Statistics Bureau, "Results of Population and Housing Census 2015" (2016) 21 <http://lao.unfpa.org/en/publications/results-population-and-housing-census-2015-english-version>.

[11] Jeffrey Hays, "Minorities in Laos, Facts and Details" (2014) <http://factsanddetails.com/southeast-asia/Laos/sub5_3c/entry-2962.html>.

[12] Ibid.

[13] Lao Statistics Bureau, "Results of Population and Housing Census" (n 10) 36.

[14] See John McGarry, Brendan O'Leary, and Richard Simeon, "Integration or accommodation? The enduring debate in conflict regulation" in *Constitutional Design for Divided Societies: Integration or Accommodation?* (Sujit Choudhry (ed.), Oxford University Press 2008), 42.

[15] Ibid.

[16] McGarry, Brendan O'Leary, and Simeon, "Integration or accommodation?" (n 14) 46.

in the South African Communist Party."[17] Laos provides an additional example of socialist integrationism. The Constitution clearly defines the three social classes (working, peasants, and intellectuals) as the key component of the united people. Constitutional politics is based on social classes led by the nuclear of the working class, namely the communist party. The Constitution has a strong emphasis on the material base (e.g., economic development) for the unity of ethnic groups and other interest groups. In line with the socialist perspective, the source of conflicts of communities in Laos would come from material causes rather than ethnic diversity. This will be the case when the communist elite exploit the market for their material benefits rather than national interests. So, the most significant challenge to constitutional politics in Laos is how the "socialist market economy" can provide the material base for the state's redistribution, which contributes to consolidating the public unity and recognizing ethnic plurality at the same time.

The ethnic integration informs and legitimizes the process and substance of socialist constitutional change in Laos. The imperative to improve the material well-being of the Lao multi-ethnic people is the key factor of constitutional change. The process of constitutional change features efforts to engage different ethnic groups in the public consultation on the draft constitution. The integration of "multi-ethnic Lao people" informs the substances of the new Constitution in five aspects. First, the Constitution refers to one people, namely the "multi-ethnic Lao people," not different peoples, and provides for one official language: the Lao language and Lao script. Second, the Constitution establishes the vanguard role of one single party, the communist party (no ethnic-based parties). Third, ethnic integration informs the distribution of power according to the principle of democratic centralism: the non-ethnics-based legislature as representatives of individuals and administrative regions; the single executive leader as representative of one united people, parliament-based cabinet, no power-sharing coalitions; no substantive specific institutional arrangements for minority groups; central–local relations predominantly centralized, albeit some degree of decentralization. Fourth, the bill of rights predominantly includes the rights of individuals applied nation-wide. Finally, the national economy aims to "improve the material and spiritual living conditions of the multi-ethnic people."[18]

This chapter is supported by a qualitative empirical methodology. In October 2017, I conducted fieldwork in Vientiane, the capital of Laos. I visited the Lao Ministry of Justice and the National Assembly and conducted extensive formal interviews with two political incumbents who had directly participated in the formal process of constitutional amendment. The first interview was with Inthananya Khieovongphachanh, the Director General of the Department of

[17] Ibid. 47.
[18] Laos Constitution 2015 (n 1) art. 13.

Legislation of the Lao Ministry of Justice.[19] He participated in the formal process of constitutional amendment as a member of a subcommittee responsible for drafting amendments to the Constitution's chapters on the executive branch and local government. The second interview was with Amphay Chitmanonh, the Vice Chairman of the Law Committee of the Lao National Assembly.[20] He was involved in the formal process of constitution-making as the head of the secretariat board of the National Committee for Amending the Constitution, and in this position he attended all meetings of this committee. This secretariat board was responsible for collecting proposals for constitutional amendments from different subcommittees and from the people and reporting to the National Committee for Amending the Constitution. The interviews were conducted at the offices of the interviewees.[21]

These formal interviews are contrasted with other sources. To begin with, I engaged in extensive informal conversations about Lao constitutional amendment and other legal issues with a Lao lawyer and three Lao legal scholars (one constitutional law scholar, one civil law scholar, and one scholar on international law and international relations) at the Faculty of Law and Politics of the Lao National University which I visited during my fieldwork. Because of the sensitive nature of the issues, the informal engagements inform this chapter but can be contextual only. In addition to interviews and conversations, this study is supported by written sources: official documents regarding the amendment process and the amended Constitution.[22] The first document is the Lao National Assembly Standing Committee's *Proposal for Amending the 2013 Constitution of Laos in the 10th Congress of the National Assembly termed VII, 2015*.[23] Another document is the Lao Ministry of Home Affairs' *Summary of the Contents of the Amended Constitution of Lao People's Democratic Republic of 2015*.[24]

I have relied on two unofficial translations of the Lao amended Constitution of 2015, the English and Vietnamese versions. The English translation is by a Lao lawyer in Vientiane, and the Vietnamese translation is by a Lao officer studying in a law school in Hanoi. The citation of provisions in the Laos Constitution in this

[19] Interview with Inthananya Khieovongphachanh (Vientaine, Laos, October 4, 2017) [hereinafter Interview I].

[20] Interview with Amphay Chitmanonh (Vientaine, Laos, October 5, 2017) [hereinafter Interview II].

[21] I communicated directly with Inthananya Khieovongphachanh in English. Amphay Chitmanonh mainly spoke Lao and some English. When he spoke Lao, we had an English translator.

[22] Scholarly writings in Lao language on the Lao amended Constitution of 2015 are virtually absent. Personal communication with a Lao lawyer (November 13, 2018).

[23] I rely on a thesis by a Lao student written in Vietnamese, which substantively cites this document. Vilayvieng Thoumma, "Những Điểm Mới Về Bộ Máy Nhà Nước CHDCND Lào Theo Hiến Pháp Lào Năm 2015" ["New Points on the State Apparatus in the 2015 Constitution of the Lao People's Democratic Republic 2015"] (2017) Unpublished master's thesis, Hanoi University of Law (on file with author).

[24] Lao PDR's Ministry of Home Affairs, Summary of the Contents of the Amended Constitution of Lao People's Democratic Republic of 2015 (2015) 2 (on file with author). This document is translated into Vietnamese by Vilayvieng Thoumma. I thank her for sharing this document.

study is mainly based on the English version but is occasionally modified on the basis of comparison with the Vietnamese version.

The remainder of this chapter is structured as follows: Section I considers the factors of Laos' constitutional change. Section II describes and analysis the legal process of the Lao constitutional amendment in 2015. Section III analyzes substantive constitutional change. Section IV concludes with further reflections.

I. Factors

Constitutional change in Laos is animated by a top-down dynamic: the change to socio-economic programs. This is reflected in the Proposal for Amending the 2013 Constitution of Laos submitted to the Tenth Congress of the National Assembly termed VII in 2015, which provides official justifications for constitutional amendments. First, it proposed that amending the Constitution is necessary to implement the communist party's strategy for socio-economic development from 2016 to 2026.[25] In addition, the government believes that constitutional amendments are necessary to correct the shortcomings of the current Constitution and more generally to provide a framework for long-term socio-economic development. To begin with, constitutional amendment is necessary to rectify the limits of the current Constitution. Constitutional amenders explained that the Constitution of 2003 was implemented to foster domestic social and economic changes, to extend international relations, to structure the state institutions, and to protect people's rights. But, it had important limitations that required constitutional amendments. First, important state institutions, such as the state audit, had not yet been provided in the Constitution. Second, some important institutional reforms had been implemented but not yet reflected in the Constitution, such as the creation of the regional courts and regional procuracies. Third, the people's rights in several regions had not yet been strongly promoted. Fourth, the people and officers in different levels had failed to respect the Constitution as expected.[26]

In addition, Lao constitutional amendment is driven by the bottom-up pressure to improve the material well-being of the living conditions of the multi-ethnic people. The socio-economic context in Laos explains why material well-being matters for constitutional amenders. Although the Lao People's Democratic Republic created in 1975 is committed to transition to socialism without moving toward the capitalist path, several factors in other socialist countries effect Lao's post-1975 developmental policy: the *Perestroika* (reconstructing the political

[25] Lao National Assembly Standing Committee, *Proposal for Amending the 2013 Constitution of Laos* (2015), cited in Thoumma (n 23) 25.

[26] Ibid.

and economic systems) in the Soviet Union and Eastern European countries in the 1980s, China's *Gǎigé kāifàng* ("Reform & Opening up") policy in 1979, and Vietnam's reform policy in 1979 culminating in the comprehensive economic reform program called *Đổi Mới* (Renovation) in 1986.[27] Consequently, Kaysone Phomvihane, conceived as the founding father of LPDR, advocated a slogan called *Chintanakan Mai* (New Thinking) in 1986, stating that "we think that changing the ownership of the means of production is the key to develop forces of production, which will automatically lead to the improvement of the people's lives."[28] The slogan was used to promote "New Economic Management Mechanism," a major market-oriented reform to improve the people's material living conditions, including the multi-ownership and multisector economy, recognized in the 1991 Constitution.[29] A new national goal was set by the Party in 1993: to "graduate" from the United Nation's list of least-developed countries. The Sixth Party Congress in 1996 set the year of 2020 as the deadline for this graduation.[30] One standard to judge the Party action created by the Party itself is "improving living standards and creating benefits for the people."[31] When it seemed likely that Laos would achieve the "graduation" goal, at the Tenth Congress in 2016, the Party announced Vision 2030, targeting a new goal of becoming an upper-middle-income state by 2030.[32] One scholar summarized the national goals in the Lao development trajectory as "includ[ing] the post-war normalization of people's lives during the 1970s and 1980s, graduation from least-developed country status and becoming an upper-middle-income state by 2030."[33]

Why has the improvement of the living conditions of the people been the preoccupation of the socialist regime in Laos in the last three decades? The reason is to consolidate the sociological legitimacy[34] of the single-party rule. As the legal foundation of the legitimacy of this regime is limited (the absence of multiparty democratic and fair elections, corruption, the limits of rule of law and human rights),[35] the regime has to depend on the actual acceptance of the relevant public of its rule as justified and appropriate, which in turn significantly depends on how the regime can actually work to improve the living conditions of the population.

[27] Norihiko Yamada, "Legitimation of the Lao People's Revolutionary Party: Socialism, Chintanakan Mai (New Thinking) and Reform" (2018) 48 Journal of Contemporary Asia 717, 722.

[28] Ibid. 725 (slightly modified translation).

[29] Ibid. 727.

[30] Ibid. 730.

[31] Ibid. 731.

[32] Ibid. 732.

[33] Ibid. 933.

[34] For legitimacy as a sociological concept, *see* Richard H Fallon, Jr., "Legitimacy and the Constitution" (2005) 118 Harvard Law Review 1787, 1795.

[35] Creak and Barney, "Conceptualizing Party-State Governance" (n 5) 698–700; Martin Stuart-Fox, "Politics and Reforms in the Lao People's Democratic Republic" (2005) 126 Murdoch University's Asia Research Centre 1, 23–8 [hereinafter Stuart-Fox, "Politics and Reforms"]; Martin Stuart-Fox, "The Political Culture of Corruption in the Lao PDR" (2006) 30 Asian Studies Review 59.

Despite speedy economic development and social transition, Laos remains a country with a low ratio of poverty reduction per unit of gross domestic product growth.[36] Lao transition is fragile because "there are structural factors which limit the ability of Laos to capitalize on recoveries and translate these into longer-term stability."[37] These constraints include "low industrial competitiveness, high corruption, and under-performance in the areas of education, rule-of-law and human rights."[38]

The structural constraints on continuing socio-economic progress are constitutionally relevant. Consequently, the need to modify these impediments to ease the continuing improvement of the living conditions of the local people creates a need to improve the constitutional system. This explains why the official agenda of constitutional amendment and the amended constitutional preamble clearly indicate that constitutional amendments are driven by the pressures to boost socio-economic progress. In a constitutional consultation meeting, Dr. Sonexay Siphandone, the chairman of the NCAC, said that "Legislative changes influence the government's development vision until 2030 and the socio-economic development plans for 2016–25, so it has become necessary to amend the Constitution."[39] The expectation is that constitutional amendment will facilitate socio-economic progress. He said: "One of the expected outcomes of amendments to the Constitution is that it will enable the government to implement socio-economic development from 2016–25 more effectively."[40] In addition, after the amended Constitution was adopted, the Ministry of Home Affairs prepared a report on the Constitution in the occasion of the socialist country's fortieth anniversary, stating that the enactment of the amended Constitution presents "the strong determination of the nation to altogether combat against difficulties" and especially to help the country "escape the fate of an underdeveloped country in 2020."[41] The regime's hope is that the amended Constitution will provide a new fundamental framework to implement the long-term plan and vision of socio-economic development to improve the material well-being of the local people, which is instrumental to the consolidation of the sociological foundation of the regime's legitimacy.

In addition to internal factors, constitutional amendment in Laos is also driven by external factors. The country has actively integrated into the regional and international community. To illustrate, Laos joined the World Trade Organization (WTO) on February 2, 2013, and hosted the Seventh Asia–Europe Parliamentary

[36] Creak and Barney, "Conceptualizing Party-State Governance" (n 5) 700.

[37] David Carment et al, "Towards a Theory of Fragile State Transitions: Evidence from Yemen, Bangladesh and Laos" (2015) 36(7) Third World Quarterly 1316, 1325.

[38] Creak and Barney, "Conceptualizing Party-State Governance" (n 5) 700.

[39] "Constitutional Amendments to Boost Economic Growth" (RightsLinkLao, April 2, 2009) <http://rightslinklao.org/?p=5978&lang=en>

[40] Ibid.

[41] Laos PDR's Ministry of Home Affairs, Summary of the Contents of the Amended Constitution (n 24) 2.

Meeting and the Ninth Asia–Europe Summit in October and November 2012, respectively; the Sixth Cambodia–Lao PDR–Myanmar–Vietnam (CLMV) Summit; and the Fourth Aryavady Chaophaya–Mekong Economic Cooperation Summit (ACMECS), March 12–13, 2013; and the Thirty-fifth ASEAN Parliamentary Meeting in 2014.[42] In the view of the government, "all of these events have underpinned development and facilitated business investment, production, and services."[43] Moreover, while Laos retains important relationships with its neighbor countries, the country is adroit in diplomatic relations, which can be seen in the capital's infrastructure: the construction of the National Assembly building is funded by Vietnam;[44] "airports built by Japan; an international conference hall built by China; and the Mekong riverbank redeveloped by Korea."[45] Laos also established the "Comprehensive Partnership" with the United States in 2016.[46]

With these international dynamics, it becomes imperative for Laos to have a new constitutional framework to further regional and international integration by adopting similar constitutional norms and institutions to those of the global community (such as human rights and judicial independence) and dropping the unfamiliar ones (e.g. regulating the economy in the direction of socialism) to gain more international legitimacy and attract foreign investments.[47] This is, in turn, conducive to domestic legitimacy and the improvement of domestic living conditions.

II. The Law of Change

A. Descriptive Exploration

1. Setting Agenda

The Proposal for Amending the 2013 Constitution of Laos articulates five basic "principles" for amending the constitution:[48,49]

42 "The Government of Lao PDR's 8th Five-Year National Socio-economic Development Plan (2016–2020)" (*Ministry of Planning and Investment*, June 2016) <www.la.one.un.org/images/publications/8th_NSEDP_2016-2020.pdf>

43 Ibid.

44 News Desk, "Laos, Vietnam Break Ground for New National Assembly Building" (*Asia News Network*, November 2, 2017) <http://annx.asianews.network/content/laos-vietnam-break-ground-new-national-assembly-building-59904>

45 Sayalath and Creak, "Regime Renewal in Laos" (n 4) 192.

46 Athitc, "United States and Lao PDR Unveil Comprehensive Partnership" (*US Embassy in Laos*, September 7, 2016) <https://la.usembassy.gov/united-states-and-lao-pdr-unveil-comprehensive-partnership/>

47 David Law, "Globalization and the Future of Constitutional Rights" (2008) 102 Northwestern University Law Review 1277, 1281–2 (constitutional rights are used to attract foreign investments).

48 The following description of the constitutional amendment procedure is drawn on Interview I, Interview II, and Thoumma (n 23) 27.

49 Lao National Assembly Standing Committee, *Proposal for Amending the 2013 Constitution of Laos* (2015), cited in Thoumma (n 23) 25.

First, constitutional amendments must continue to confirm that the nature of Laos is a country of "people's democracy," that the communist party is the leading force, and that the state power is unified but there are distribution and co-operation of the powers and the mutual supervisions among the legislature, executive, and judiciary.[50]

Second, fundamental contents of the Ninth Congress of the Party must be incorporated into the constitution. The National Committee of Constitutional Amendment will co-operate with the subcommittees to prepare the political report to be presented at the Tenth Congress of the Party, and the strategy on the national socioeconomic development.[51]

Third, constitutional amendments must be based on the reality of the implementation of the 2003 Constitution, retain the "correct contents" that are consistent with the reality, amend "inappropriate contents," and supplement important and necessary contents based on the consultation of the whole country.[52]

Fourth, subcommittees are responsible for studying amendments of constitutional provisions in their respective areas to improve the whole Constitution, but the supplementation of the new contents or the abolition of certain contents must be collected and reported to the Politburo and the Secretary board of the Party for their guiding opinion.[53]

Fifth, consultation meetings "with oriented direction" will be held in six regions of the country to collect opinions and comments on the draft constitutional amendments; the results of these meetings will be referenced in the Eighth Congress of the National Assembly and reported to the plenary congress of the central committee of the communist party.[54]

2. Amendment Body

Constitutional amendment rules used in the 2015 circle are provided in the amended Constitution of 2003 and the related legislation called Law on Making Legislation of 2012. Accordingly, the National Assembly, the ordinary legislature, enjoys the exclusive power to amend the constitution. Article 53 of the Constitution provides for the powers of the National Assembly, including the power "to prepare, adopt or amend the Constitution."[55] Article 79 of the Constitution underlines that this is the exclusive power of the National Assembly: "Only the National Assembly session of the Lao People's Democratic Republic has the right to amend the Constitution."[56] The adoption of constitutional amendments "requires the

50 Ibid. 26–7.
51 Ibid.
52 Ibid.
53 Ibid. 26.
54 Ibid.
55 Constitution of the Lao People's Democratic Republic 2003, art. 53.
56 Ibid. art. 79.

affirmative votes of at least two-thirds of the total number of the National Assembly members."[57] After the National Assembly's approval, constitutional amendments will be promulgated by the President of State.[58]

The Law on Making Legislation of 2012 stipulates the creation of a "National Committee for Making or Amendment of the Constitution" vested with the functions to "collect information and conduct public consultations in a broader manner than making and amending of laws."[59] This law does not provide more details on the procedure of constitutional amendment but allows the National Assembly to "determine[s] the detailed regulations on the procedures for making and amending the Constitution."[60]

On August 15, 2014 (the Constitution Day), the President of State issued a decision to create the National Committee for Amending the Constitution (NCAC). Presided by Sonexay Siphandone, the head of the Government Office, the NCAC was comprised of seventeen members, which was later extended to more than twenty members.[61] These members are key state persons from major branches of the state. They included the president of the National Assembly, vice president of the National Assembly, the heads of six National Assembly's specific committees,[62] the president of the supreme people's courts, the president of the supreme procuracy, and the chairman of the presidential office. The NCAC also included the heads of mass organizations, such as Lao Front for National Construction, the Lao Federation of Trade Unions, the Lao People's Revolutionary Youth Union, and the Lao Women's Union.[63]

The NCAC created specific subcommittees under the direct control of the former. These subcommittees were responsible for discussing and proposing amendments to different chapters of the Constitution. These subcommittees are consistent with the functions of the respective state institutions. For example, the Minister of Home Affair was in charge of issues relating to local government, and therefore is responsible for discussing and proposing amendments to the Constitution's chapter on local government. The heads of the state institutions are also the heads of the subcommittees.[64] The NCAC also created a secretariat responsible for collecting and synthesizing opinions of different subcommittees.[65]

[57] Ibid.
[58] Ibid. art. 67.
[59] Law on Making Legislation of the Lao People's Democratic Republic 2012, art. 15.
[60] Ibid.
[61] Interview II.
[62] At the time of constitutional amendment, Laos had six National Assembly committees. Now it has two more committees: justice, and finance and audit. Interview II.
[63] Interview II.
[64] Interview I.
[65] Interview II.

3. Drafting and Deliberation

The subcommittees studied the constitutional contents needing amendments. Proposals for constitutional amendments from different subcommittees were synthesized and reported to the National Assembly. The National Assembly discussed the proposals of constitutional amendments in its eighth session. The National Assembly discussions were lively televised. Official media also spread the discussions. On the basis of the National Assembly's constitutional discussions, the NCAC prepared the first draft of constitutional amendments.

The constitutional drafting process in Lao involved transnational materials and actors. Constitutional amenders actively engage with international and foreign constitutional materials, especially the ones of the neighboring countries. The deliberation among constitutional amenders is informed by foreign constitutional experience and international law. They consulted the constitutions of all ASEAN countries, China, Japan, Russia, and Germany, and international treaties on human rights.[66]

Particularly, the transnational engagement with Vietnamese constitutional experience is notable. The member of the Ministry of Justice told me that among foreign constitutions Laos consulted Vietnam's Constitution first.[67] The member of the National Assembly also said to me that "we looked at all contents of Vietnam [2013] Constitution."[68] There were in fact constitutional dialogues between members of the two governments. To illustrate, on July 30, 2014, in his visit to Laos, the Vietnamese Minister of Justice, Mr. Hà Hùng Cường, delivered a speech on the process of making Vietnam's 2013 Constitution and its substantial contents, attended by some 400 Lao senior cadres.[69] The Lao Minister of Justice said to the reporters before the speech: "This is a valuable occasion for Laos to learn from Vietnam in building the constitution, especially from the new points in the 2013 Constitution of Vietnam."[70] The President of Laos National Assembly, Mr. Pany Yathotou, stated that "Laos always follows closely the development of Vietnam and is pleased with Vietnam's achievements," informed that Laos is considering amending its Constitution, and "wanted Vietnam to share valuable experience in building the Constitution with Laos."[71] In addition, a member of the Vietnamese National Assembly's Legal Committee also delivered a speech in Vientiane introducing Vietnam's 2013 Constitution to the Lao legislators.[72] I have

[66] Interview I and Interview II.

[67] Interview I.

[68] Interview II.

[69] Thu Hằng, "Bộ trưởng Hà Hùng Cường giới thiệu Hiến pháp 2013 cho các cán bộ cao cấp Lào" ["Minister Hà Hùng Cường Introduces the 2013 Constitution to Lao Senior Cadres"] (*Bao Phap Luat*, July 31, 2014) <http://baophapluat.vn/tu-phap/bo-truong-ha-hung-cuong-gioi-thieu-hien-phap-2013-cho-cac-can-bo-cao-cap-lao-191805.html>

[70] Ibid.

[71] Ibid.

[72] Interview II.

interviewed the members of the Lao Ministry of Justice and National Assembly about the two above speeches. They said that the Vietnamese officers were invited to share Vietnamese constitutional experience because Vietnam had similar constitutional system with Laos.[73] There were no such speeches by experts or officials from other countries.[74]

4. Public Consultation

The next step is public consultation. The NCAC conducted two rounds of public consultations on the draft amended constitution in June 2014 and October 2015. In each round, a consultation meeting was concurrently undertaken on the same day in different regions. Participants of the meetings were major officials of the provinces, experts, academics, and retired officials. Approximately 400 to 500 participants attended the consultation meetings in Vientiane.

The focus of each of the two rounds of public consultations was rather different. The first round focused on the rationales and proposals of the constitutional amendments, while the second one was more concerned with the expected outcomes of the constitutional amendments. In the meetings, people also asked many questions. Especially, the retired officials had many comments on the draft constitutional amendments. One of the important questions that was subject to vibrant discussion during consultation meetings concerned the proposal for creating a new body, the "people's council," at the local government level. People discussed who should be the head of the council. Should it be the secretary or vice secretary of the Party at the parallel local government? Although this is not a constitutional question, people were concerned because the secretary is the most powerful figure in a locality. People also discussed the name of this institution: some suggested that it should be called "provincial council" rather than "people's council" because it was only proposed to be created at the provincial level.

In addition to the general public consultations, the NCAC held more specific workshops. It organized more than twenty workshops to consult the opinions of different sectors of society, including the private sector, such as private companies, mainly in Vientiane.[75] Especially, it also held a workshop at the Faculty of Law and Politics of Lao National University, attended by faculty members and students. On October 28–29, 2015, NCAC also organized a workshop on exchanging experience of constitutional amendment with Vietnam's National Assembly, entitled "Theory and Practice in Building and Amending the Constitution."[76] In addition,

[73] Interview I and Interview II.
[74] Interview I.
[75] Thoumma (n 23) 27.
[76] Ibid.

the NCAC also held meetings with subcommittees to discuss and resolve questions that were still the subject of disagreement.

5. Legislative Approval

On the basis of the consultations, the NCAC revised the draft of the amended Constitution and submitted it to the National Assembly for further discussion and approval. Like the first round, the second round of the national Assembly discussions of constitutional amendment were televised. Retired officials closely followed the discussions to consider whether their comments had been reflected in the Constitution. The Constitution was approved by the National Assembly on December 8, 2015, ratified by the President of State on December 15, 2015, and went into effect on February 4, 2016. The Constitution is officially known as the Amended Constitution of the Lao People's Democratic Republic of 2015.[77]

6. Legislative Implementation

After the adoption of the amended Constitution, assembly deputies propagandized its new elements to their constituencies.[78] In addition, the National Assembly has amended or passed new organic laws. Major organic laws on the government, the National Assembly, the courts and procuracy, and elections have been amended.[79] The law on local government has been amended to create the people's councils. The provincial people's councils have been created through elections by the local people.[80] The following laws have been amended or enacted after the promulgation of the amended 2015 Constitution:

- State Audit Law No. 09/NA dated November 11, 2016;
- Law on Government No. 04/NA dated November 8, 2016;
- Amended Law on Election of members of National Assembly and People's Council of Provinces No. 66/NA dated December 14, 2015;
- Amended Article 41 and 42 of the Law on Election of members of National Assembly and People's Council of Provinces No. 01/NA dated May 12, 2016;
- Law on People's Council of Provinces No. 65/NA dated December 10, 2015;
- Amended some Articles of Law on People's Council of Provinces No. 11/NA dated November 14, 2016;
- Amended Law on National Assembly 64/NA dated December 9, 2015;

[77] Laos PDR's Ministry of Home Affairs, Summary of the Contents of the Amended Constitution (n 24).
[78] Interview II.
[79] Ibid.
[80] Ibid.

- Amended some Articles of Law on National Assembly No. 10/NA dated November 14, 2016;
- Amended Law on Oversight by the National Assembly and People's Council of Provinces No. 12/NA dated November 15, 2016;
- Amended Law on Local Administrative No. 68/NA dated December 14, 2015.
- The Amended Law on People's Court No. 22/NA, dated May 10, 2017.[81]

B. Explanation

1. Explicit Replacement through Amendment

The project of constitutional change in Laos is called "Proposal for Amending the 2013 Constitution of Laos." The project follows the rules laid down by the 2003 amended Constitution. A body in charge with this project is called the "National Committee for Amending the Constitution." The new Constitution is officially addressed as the "amended Constitution" of 2015.[82] But, Article 119 of this Constitution provides that "This Constitution and its contents shall replace the previous version of the Lao People's Democratic Republic Constitution of No. 25/NA dated 6 May 2003."[83] This experience suggests a complicated story: a project of constitutional change is in line with the existing constitution but ends up with promulgation of a new constitution replacing the existing one without significant change to the existing constitutional order.

The form of constitutional change in Laos can be conceptualized as *explicit constitutional replacement through amendment.* The new charter expressly indicates that it replaces the former one. In fact, the process and the substances of constitutional change have features of constitution-making rather than amendment. For example, the process featured public participation and transnational involvement, which are normally practiced in constitution-making rather than amendment projects. In terms of substance, the Constitution of 2015 has many new contents. It is comprised of the preamble and fourteen chapters divided into 119 articles. Compared with the 2003 version, the 2015 version has three more chapters and twenty-one more articles.[84] The preamble has been amended to set down new constitutional goals, stating that the amended Constitution of 2015 is meant to improve "the high efficiency" of the state, "to create a new phrase for protecting and constructing the nation," and "to integrate into economy into the region and the international community in the new era."[85] Turning to the body of the constitution,

[81] I thank Khamphaeng Phochanthilath for updating the information about these new laws. Khamphaeng Phochanthilath, personal communication, December 26, 2017.
[82] Interview II.
[83] Laos Constitution 2015 (n 1) art. 119.
[84] Ibid.
[85] Ibid.

nearly all chapters of the Constitution have new contents. Constitutional changes touch on fundamental principles of the regime, constitutional rights and duties, and the nature and functions of state institutions. The government underlines that the important constitutional amendments focus on major central state institutions and local government.[86]

But, the formal replacement of the constitutional document does not result in the functional replacement of the constitutional system. Formal constitutional change enables the constitutional system incrementally and continuingly evolve into a better stage (e.g. the evolution from a repressive system into more responsive one) without destroying the existing system. Constitutional amenders may end up with enacting a new constitution, officially replacing the existing one, but the new Constitution only practically improves rather than replaces the existing constitutional system. Although the amended Constitution of 2015 includes progressive amendments, it retains the overall structure, major principles, and many provisions of the preceding constitution, and consequentially, the existing socialist constitutional order basically remains intact. In addition, the whole project of constitutional alternation modifies rather than dismember the socialist constitutional identity: the leadership of the community party, the Leninist constitutional structure, the statist rights, and the statist economy are only adapted, not dismantled. The regime may need to house old and new constitutional ideas, institutions, and principles in a new formal provenance to signal[87] to the local and international audiences the regime's commitment to continuing reform in the new globalizing era.

2. Replacement Power

The existing Constitution in Laos allows the National Assembly to assume three powers: constitution-making power, amendment power, and law-making power. This ordinary legislature is in fact the locus of both constitutional amendment power and legislative power. The fact that the Law on Making Legislation defines constitutional amendment rules indicates that legislative power can even define how the constitutional amendment power is practiced. Laos'Constitution does not have explicit provisions limiting the amendment power.[88]

In theory, as the National Assembly enjoys both constituent and constitutional amendment powers, and it is free to amend the constitution. Neither does Laos have implicit constitutional unamendability since judicial review of constitutionality is absent as the consequence of authoritarian arrangement. However, this does not means that there are no constraints on the amendment power in Laos

[86] Laos PDR's Ministry of Home Affairs, Summary of the Contents of the Amended Constitution (n 24).

[87] For the signaling function of authoritarian constitutions, see Tom Ginsburg and Alberto Simpser (eds), *Introduction to Constitutions in Authoritarian Regimes* (CUP 2013) 8.

[88] For the difference between implicit and explicit constitutional unamendability, see Yaniv Ronzai, *Unconstitutional Constitutional Amendments: The Limits of Amendment Powers* (OUP 2017) 15, 39.

in practice. The regime established "principles" constraining constitutional reform. The communist party ensures that constitutional reform is within the established principles. The conjunction of the party-state (*phak-lat*), the term used in Laos in everyday conversation, indicates that the party "is, if not synonymous with the state."[89] In such a political environment, the state's amendment power is constrained by the Party. The Party establishes and ensures the scope within which constitutional amendment is possible. Thus, the amendment power is unlimited formally but limited functionally.

3. Popular Participation

The process of constitutional amendment in Laos includes public consultations which allow the multi-ethnic people in different regions of the country to have a say. Within Lao's constitutional history, the public constitutional discussion is not new as this was carried out in the previous circle of constitutional change.[90] The 2015 circle continues this practice, which provides the base for the continued claim in the constitutional preamble that: "This Constitution is the fruit of the process of the people's discussion throughout the country."[91]

To compare the constitutional amendment process with other two socialist countries, the Lao process is more progressive than in China albeit less so than in Vietnam. The 2018 constitutional amendment process in China lacked public discussion, and critical comments on the amendment proposals were banned.[92] The Lao story presents a better practice: constitutional consultations are extended to private sectors and academic forum as happened in the National University of Laos. Yet, the Lao constitutional consultation is less open than the Vietnamese practice in 2013,[93] such as the lack of the publication of the draft amendments for the public debates in mass media and other public fora.[94] Unlike the Vietnamese citizens,[95] the Laotian citizens did not actively engage in constitutional debate, activism, mobilization, and paid less attention to constitutional amendment.[96] This is explained by the broader context in Laos: the weakness of civil society,[97] the virtual

[89] Creak and Barney, "Conceptualizing Party-State" (n 5) 698. See also, Martin Stuart-Fox, "Laos: Politics in a Single-Party State" (2007) Southeast Asian Affairs 161 (discussing the party congress as the platform to determine the leadership of the country).

[90] Martin Stuart-Fox, "The Constitution of the Lao People's Democratic Republic" (1991) 17 Review of Socialist Law 299, 299.

[91] Amended Constitution 2015 (n 1).

[92] Salvatore Babones, "China's Constitutional Amendments Are All about The Party, Not The President" (Forbes, March 11, 2018) <www.forbes.com/sites/salvatorebabones/2018/03/11/chinas-constitutional-amendments-are-all-about-the-party-not-the-president/>

[93] For the Vietnamese case, see chapter 5.

[94] Interview II.

[95] Bui Ngoc Son and Pip Nicholson, "Activism and Popular Constitutionalism in Contemporary Vietnam" (2017) 42 Law & Social Inquiry 677.

[96] Interview II.

[97] Gretchen Kunze, "Laos" in *Routledge Handbook on Civil Society in Asia* (Akihiro Ogawa (ed.), Routledge 2018) 204 ("although some kind of civil society will continue to exist and constructively

absence of social mobilization and activism,[98] "the absence of alternative political organizations and attendant political constraints,"[99] and the regime's control of information.[100]

What is the meaning of the constitutional consultation after all? From an instrumentalist perspective, one may argue that the populist leaders may employ the constitutional consultation as a mechanism to legitimize their power and the constitution. From a consequentialist perspective, one may insist that the public participation may not help produce a better constitution. Instrumentalism and consequentialism have their own virtues but do not exhaust the way to conceptualize the meaning of constitutional consultation. The third way is essentialism: the meaning of the constitutional consultation must be understood in its own term. The constitutional consultation indicates a better relationship between the government and the people even under an authoritarian setting: the government allows the multi-ethnic people from rural to urban areas to have a constitutional say and engages in a dialogue with them.

4. International Involvement

Laos' engagement with Vietnamese constitutional experience is due to several channels of deliberative constitutional learning, namely common legal origin, geographic proximity, trade relationship, and military alliances.[101] First, Laos has practical reasons to consult recent constitutional changes from the country sharing the socialist legal system, the socialist political regime, the socialist constitutional system.[102] Second, Lao is bordered by Vietnam with 2,069 km to the East. Geographic proximity enables easy interaction and exchange of constitutional experience between the two countries. Third, after China, Vietnam is the second biggest foreign investor in Laos.[103] The Minister of Planning and Investment of Vietnam reported that "Vietnam currently has 408 investment projects in Laos with a total registered investment capital of US$3.7 billion."[104] Laos may adjust the

contribute to the nation's development, it will be limited to complementing the state's policies and plans rather than being an activist force.")

[98] Creak and Barney, "Conceptualizing Party-State Governance" (n 5) 700.
[99] Kyaw Yin Hlaing, "Laos: The State of the State" (2006) Southeast Asian Affairs 129, 144.
[100] Ian G Baird, "Party, State and the Control of Information in the Lao People's Democratic Republic: Secrecy, Falsification and Denial" (2018) 48 Journal of Contemporary Asia 739, 741.
[101] Benedikt Goderis and Mila Versteeg, "The Diffusion of Constitutional Rights" (2014) 39 International Review of Law and Economics 1, 3.
[102] My interviews confirm that Laos consulted Vietnamese constitutional experience because of the shared socialist political regime. Interview I and Interview II.
[103] VTV 4, "Vietnam now Laos' 2nd biggest foreign investor" (VTV News, August 22, 2015) <http://english.vtv.vn/news/vietnam-now-laos-2nd-biggest-foreign-investor-20150926201118154.htm>
[104] Anh Phuong, "Vietnam, Laos Intensifying Investment Cooperation" (Vietnam Business Forum magazine of Vietnam Chamber of Commerce and Industry, August 15, 2017) <http://vccinews.com/news_detail.asp?news_id=34987>

constitutional arrangement along the line of those of their trade partners so as to ease cross-border transactions.[105]

Finally, military alliance is an important factor for Lao's consulting the Vietnamese constitutional experience. Martin Stuart-Fox indicates that "the course of the Lao revolution has been closely tied to events in Vietnam."[106] He further explains that "The ruling parties in Vietnam and Laos share a single origin in the Indochinese Communist Party, and stood shoulder to shoulder throughout the 'thirty-year struggle' from 1945 to 1975. During that time the military of both states forged especially close bonds, and in both countries military leaders of this revolutionary generation still wield considerable power."[107] In addition, the *Lao-Vietnamese Treaty of Friendship and Cooperation* was signed in July 18, 1977, "affirming the consistent solidarity, cooperation and support for each other in national construction and defence in either country."[108] The military closeness facilitates exchange of constitutional information between Laos and Vietnam.

As the consequence of transnational engagement, Lao's amended Constitution of 2015 and Vietnam's Constitution of 2013 share several new features, such as human right provision, independent judicial power, and adversarial trials. Another prominent example is the two independent institutions, the state audit and the election committee, which are introduced into the two constitutions for the first time. One Lao officer writes: "The supplementation of the two institutions, the state audit and election committee, in the Lao People's Democratic Republic is based on learning the Vietnamese experience of constitution-making. Therefore, the provisions on the structure, duties, and authorities of these independent constitutional institutions in the 2015 Constitution of Lao People's Democratic Republic are completely similar to those in the 2013 Constitution of Socialist Republic of Vietnam."[109]

In addition, Lao constitutional amendments have several new contents which have been established in Vietnamese constitutional history and reconfirmed in the 2013 Constitution, such as the creation of the people's councils. The two constitutions in Laos and Vietnam have similar definition on the nature of this local institution. One Lao officer writes that constitutional change regarding local government in Laos "is based on learning experience of constitution-making in socialist countries, especially Vietnam."[110] My interviews confirm that the

[105] After this Treaty, Vietnam sent army troops in Laos "for its protection against hostile or counterrevolutionary neighbors." MacAlister Brown and Joseph J Zasloff, "Chapter 4. Government and Politics" in *Laos: A Country Study* (Andrea Matles Savada and Donald P. Whitaker (eds), Federal Research Division, Library of Congress 1995) 245.

[106] Martin Stuart-Fox, "LAOS: The Vietnamese Connection" (1980) Southeast Asian Affairs 191, 191.

[107] Stuart-Fox, "Politics and Reforms" (n 35) 44.

[108] "Lao Defence Ministry Celebrates Vietnam-Laos Relationship" (Nhan Dan Online, July 20, 2017) <http://en.nhandan.com.vn/politics/external-relations/item/5360502-lao-defence-ministry-celebrates-vietnam-laos-relationship.html>

[109] Thoumma (n 23) 89.

[110] Ibid. 86.

creation of the people's councils is based on consulting the Vietnamese experience and the experiences of China and Japan.[111] After the adoption of the amended Constitution, Laos has created the provincial people's councils, and Vietnam and Laos have shared experience in People's Councils activities. For example, in his visit to Vietnam in August 2016, Mr. Bountone Chanthaphone, Chairman of the People's Council of Xieng Khouang province of Laos, said that his visit is "to learn from Vietnam's experience in organizing the activities of the People's Councils, and wished that the Vietnamese legislature and localities will continue assisting Laos in this field."[112] More recently, on September 25, 2017, in Ho Chi Minh City, leaders of the Champassak province of Laos and of Ho Chi Minh City also shared the experience of operating people's councils: "The two sides discussed their practices in managing people's councils, communicating with people and informing them about results of the council conferences, implementing regulations and supervision, and training human resources."[113]

However, Laos deliberately learns from, not simply copies transnational experience. The creation of the people's council is an example. The Lao amended Constitution of 2015 does not copy the three-level structure of people councils established by the Vietnamese counterpart. It only establishes the institution at the provincial level and allows flexible room for the legislature to decide on the details of local government by statutes. In addition, Lao's amended Constitution of 2015 has many distinctive contents reflecting the Lao pluralist society, such as the recurrent references to the "multi-ethnic Lao people" throughout the Constitution and the provision on Buddhism.[114] Finally, Laos' Constitution includes features more progressive than Vietnam's Constitution, such as constitutional term limits, parliamentary vote of no confidence, and the stronger emphasis on the independence of the judicial power.

III. Progressive Change

1. The Dynamic Constitution

The Constitution in Laos remains an instrument for political control. But it has become dynamic in three dimensions: juridification, pluralization, and political implementation.

[111] Interview I and Interview II.

[112] "Vietnam, Laos Share Experience in People's Councils Activities" (*Vietnamnet*, August 20, 2016) <http://english.vietnamnet.vn/fms/government/162396/vietnam--laos-share-experience-in-people-s-councils-activities.html>

[113] "HCM City, Lao province share experience in people's council work" (*Vietnam Plus*, September 26, 2017) <https://en.vietnamplus.vn/hcm-city-lao-province-share-experience-in-peoples-council-work/118433.vnp>

[114] Laos Constitution 2015 (n 1) art. 9.

On juridification, the amended Constitution of 2003 and its early 1991 Constitution already stipulated that state bodies "must function within the bounds of the Constitution and the laws."[115] The amended Constitution of 2015 continues this provision.[116] This provision suggests understanding that the constitution is not only the instrument for the state to control the society; the state must be also legally bounded by the constitution. The aspiration to constitutionality and legality in the practice of the public power is a modification to constitutional instrumentalism.

Apart from juridification, the Laos Constitution has been increasingly pluralized as the consequence of its response to ethnic diversity in the integration manner. The pluralization of the Constitution means that although the document remains predominantly an instrument for political control, it also expresses the reality of ethnic diversity and the concern of multi-ethnic Lao people. This is evident in the consistent expression of the idea of "multi-ethnic Lao people" in the constitution. Stuart-Fox comments that the careful reference to the "multi-ethnic Lao people" throughout the 1991 Constitution is meant "to the sensitivity of minority groups to ethnic Lao domination, though nowhere does it designate separate or special bodies to administer or represent them."[117] Some explain that the frequent use of the "multi-ethnic Lao people" is "a clear rhetorical attempt to promote unity within an ethnically diverse society."[118] The concept of "multi-ethnic Lao people" is an axiological expression of constitutional aspiration. Given the reality that the society is ethnically diverse, and the dynastic and modern history of division, the "unity" of the multi-ethnic groups is the central aspirational goal that the socialist regime in Laos attempts to achieve.[119]

The 2015 Constitution continues to express the idea of "multi-ethnic Lao people" in its preamble, political principles, and state structure. The first sentence of the constitutional preamble reads: "The multi-ethnic Lao people have existed and developed on this beloved land for thousands of years."[120] The "multi-ethnic Lao people" denotes the idea of "unity in diversity."[121] The idea is that the Lao people are a united community of diverse ethnic groups. The tradition of "multi-ethnic Lao people" is said to have emerged with the reign of Chao Fa Ngum, who is founder of the united Lane Xang kingdom.[122] Therefore, the constitutional preamble further underlines this legacy: "Starting from the middle of the 14th century,

[115] Constitution of the Lao People's Democratic Republic 1991, art. 10; Laos Constitution 2003 (n 8) art. 10.

[116] Laos Constitution 2015 (n 1) art. 10.

[117] Stuart-Fox "The Constitution" (n 90) 306.

[118] Brown and Zasloff "Chapter 4" (n 105) 224.

[119] For more details, see Bui Ngoc Son, "Constitution in Ethnically Plural Societies: Vietnam and Laos" in *Pluralist Constitutions in Southeast Asia* (Jaclyn Neo and Bui Ngoc Son (eds), Hart Publishing 2019) 203–24

[120] Laos Constitution 2015 (n 1) preamble.

[121] Vatthana Pholsena, *Post-war Laos: The Politics of Culture, History, and Identity* (Silkworm Books 2006) 59.

[122] Ibid.

during the time of Chao Fa Ngum, our ancestors founded the unified Lane Xang country and built it into a prosperous land."[123]

The idea of "multi-ethnic Lao people" is not only mentioned in the preamble but is frequently referred to throughout the body of the constitutional text. This expresses the regime's central constitutional aspiration to "unity." The preamble establishes "unity" as one of "the long-standing aspirations and strong determination of the national community."[124] Article 1 defines that the Lao People's Democratic Republic is "a unified country belonging to all multi-ethnic people and is indivisible."[125] Article 2 provides that the all powers belong to the people and are exercised for "the interests of the multi-ethnic people."[126] Article 3 ensures "the rights of the multi-ethnic people to be the masters of the country."[127] Article 8 details the state's commitment to promotion of unity among ethnic groups, protection of their rights, and prohibition of ethnical discrimination.[128]

The structure of state institutions is also responsive to the concern of the integration of ethnic plurality. To illustrate, the Constitution defines the unicameral National Assembly as "the representative of the rights, powers and interests of the multi-ethnic people."[129] The Constitution also confirms that this body is created through the principle of *universal suffrage*.[130] In the last election on March 20, 2016, some 3.66 million voters elected 149 deputies from 210 candidates. Among them, 144 are members of the communist party, and five independents.[131] The new legislature is headed by Sapha Heng Xat, and selected Bounnyang Vorachit as the president of state, and Thongloun Sisoulit as prime minister.[132] There is a specific committee in National Assembly responsible for ethnic affairs, called Ethnic Affairs Committee.[133]

The idea of multi-ethnic Lao people is also expressed in the executive structure. The executive branch is comprised of the President of State and the Government. The President of the State is also constitutionally defined as "the representative of the multi-ethnic Lao people both within the country and abroad."[134] The presidential position is not merely ceremonial. The real constitutional powers of the

123 Laos Constitution 2015 (n 1) preamble.
124 Ibid.
125 Ibid. art. 1.
126 Ibid. art. 2.
127 Ibid. art. 3.
128 Ibid. art. 8.
129 Ibid. art. 52.
130 Ibid. art. 4.
131 "Lao People's Democratic Republic" (*Electronic Guide*, March 20, 2016) <www.electionguide.org/elections/id/2963/>
132 Ibid.
133 "National Assembly of the Lao People's Democratic Republic" (*National Assembly of Lao PDR*) <www.na.gov.la/index.php?option=com_content&view=article&id=72&Itemid=107&lang=en>
134 Laos Constitution 2015 (n 1) art. 65.

president include: to issue presidential edicts and decrees; to convene and preside at the government's special meetings; and to negotiate or sign treaties and international agreements on behalf of the State.[135] In the reality of constitutional politics, the president of state is a powerful figure as he is also currently the president of the communist party or General Secretary of the Lao People's Revolutionary Party.[136] In addition to the president, the Government forms part of the executive branch, consisting of the Prime Minister, Deputy Prime Ministers, Ministers and chairmen of the ministry-equivalent organizations, selected by the National Assembly with the same term as the latter, who can only hold the position for two consecutive terms.[137] The design of the executive branch in Laos is a response to at least three different concerns: ethnical diversity, party leadership, and national administration. The presidency is more closed to the concerns of ethnical diversity and party leadership, while the Government is mainly designed for national administration.

The third aspect of constitutional dynamics in Laos concerns political implementation of the constitution. The Laos' Law on Making Legislation lists the following sources of legal norms in the country:

1) Constitution;
2) Law;
3) Resolution of the National Assembly;
4) Resolution of the National Assembly Standing Committee;
5) Presidential Decree;
6) Decree of the Government;
7) Resolution of the Government;
8) Order or Decision of the Prime Minister;
9) Order, Decision or Guideline of the Minister or head of the organization under the supervision of the Government;
10) Order, Decision or Guideline of the Provincial Governor or Mayor;
11) Order, Decision or Instruction of the District Governor or Head of municipality;
12) Regulation of the village.[138]

The Constitution is not the exclusive source of constitutional norms. Beyond that, constitutional norms can be found in legislations of the national assembly. To implement the constitution, the National Assembly has passed several organic laws regarding major state institutions, which constitutes the sources of constitutional norms. These constitutional laws include the laws on the National Assembly, the

[135] Ibid. art. 67.
[136] Benjamin Elisha Sawe, "Presidents of Laos Since 1975" (*Worldsatlas*, April 25, 2017) <http://www.worldatlas.com/articles/presidents-of-laos-since-1975.html>
[137] Laos Constitution 2015 (n 1) art. 71.
[138] Laos' Law on Making Legislation (2012) art. 4.

Government, the Courts, and the public prosecutors, local administration, and the oversight of the national assembly. Moreover, constitutional norms are not merely available in the legislation. The Constitution authorizes the Government to "implement the Constitution, the laws and resolutions of the National Assembly."[139] In addition, the Constitution also mandates the governors of provinces and cities and the mayors of districts "to ensure the implementation of the Constitution and the laws."[140] To implement the Constitution and constitutional laws, the central government and local government have the power to enact different types of regulations, and these regulations may also contain constitutional norms in the sense that the regulations may interpret the meaning of constitutional provisions.

C. Constitutionalizing the Party

The communist party is the essential element of the Lao's constitutional structure, not a political organization of the civil society created to compete for power through free and equal elections as in liberal democracy. Stuart-Fox captures this feature in these words:

> The Party permeates and controls the four key institutions in the country: the government, the bureaucracy, mass organizations, and the military. In all four it is virtually *de rigueur* for leading figures to be Party members. In fact they would not be in those positions unless they were members of the Party. Party cells operate in all institutions, and there is active recruitment of promising young personnel into the Party, membership of which is by invitation only.[141]

Given its essential role in the constitutional structure, the Party's role is defined in the constitution. But, the way the Constitution defines the party role is informed by the concern of integration of ethnic diversity in Laos. Unlike Vietnam's counterpart, the Laos Constitution does not firmly establish the leadership of the communist party over the state and the society. This has a historical reason relevant to concern of integration of ethnic diversity. This is traced back to the process of making the 1991 Constitution. In the first draft of the constitution presented to the Politburo on April 4, 1990, and published for discussed in the Party journal on June 4, the role of the communist party was mentioned in the first article, which defines the Lao People's Democratic Republic as "a people's democratic state under the leadership of the Lao People's Revolutionary Party."[142] This provision triggered

139 Laos Constitution 2015 (n 1) art. 70.
140 Ibid. art. 76.
141 Stuart-Fox, "Politics and Reforms" (n 35) 12.
142 Stuart-Fox, "The Constitution of the Lao People's Democratic Republic" (n 90) 302.

criticism and social mobilization. Unofficially organized as "Social Democratic Club," a group of some forty government officials and intellectuals through a series of letters and meetings criticized the Article for maintaining the monopolist power of the communist party and called for a multi-party system.[143] One critic accused the communist party in Laos as a "communist monarchy" and insisted that "only a multiparty system could ensure democracy, freedom, and prosperity."[144] The criticism was further strengthened and broadened with the joining of Laotian students oversea (in Paris, Farague, and Warsaw), and "a group of young, educated party cadres associated with non-party bureaucrats-many educated in France and Canada-targeted veteran party leaders."[145] The movement was continued until October 1990 when three leading figures were arrested and then sentenced for fourteen years.[146]

The public criticism was not meaningless. In response, in the final version of the constitution adopted on August 14, 1991, the article on the party moved from first to third and removed the formal confirmation of the "leading role" of the communist party. In Article 3, the Marxist ideology of party vanguard was confirmed as the expression of the concern of the dominant communist elite. But in response to the reality of ethnic plurality and the popular mobilization for multiparty democracy which is informed by political liberalism, this Article is committed to the rights of the multi-ethnic people as the sovereignty of the country practiced by a political system in which the communist party is the center. In addition, in the party's view, "there are too many ethnic groups, and open political participation would lead to disunity and chaos."[147]

The amended Constitution of 2015 continues the lasting concern of ethnic integration in its statement and provision in the party. It confirms in the preamble "the correct leadership of the former Indochinese Communist Party and the present Lao People's Revolutionary Party."[148] But, the body of the Constitution does not explicitly establish the leadership of the communist party over the state and the society. Rather, Article 3 reads: "The rights of the multi-ethnic people to be the masters of the country are exercised and ensured through the functioning of the political system with the Lao People's Revolutionary Party as its leading nucleus."[149] This constitutional provision on the communist party in the political system is not merely expressive of the Marxist orthodoxy of party vanguard but also responsive to the local concern of integration of ethnic diversity. This is an ambiguous constitutional commitment as a response to ethnic plurality.

[143] Brown and Zasloff, "Chapter 4. Government and Politics" (n 105) 220.
[144] Stuart-Fox, "The Constitution of the Lao People's Democratic Republic" (n 90) 302.
[145] Brown and Zasloff, "Chapter 4. Government and Politics" (n 105) 221.
[146] Gerald Leather, "Laos: A Constitution in Search of Constitutionalism" in *Constitutionalism in Southeast Asia* (Clauspeter Hill and Jörg Menzel (eds), Konrad Adenauer Stiftung 2008) 136.
[147] Brown and Zasloff, "Chapter 4. Government and Politics" (n 105) 236.
[148] Laos Constitution 2015 (n 1) preamble.
[149] Ibid. art. 3.

The party constitutional provision may also respond to ideational plurality. Unlike other socialist constitutions of Vietnam, China, and Cuba, Laos' Constitution makes no explicit preference to Marxism-Leninism as the guiding ideology of the communist party. In response to ideational plurality, this ideological pragmatism enables the co-existence of Marxism-Leninism with traditional values (e.g. Buddhism) and universal and liberal values (e.g. human rights and market institutions) which are adopted in the Constitution as discussed latter.

The amended Constitution of 2015 retains a provision (Article 10), which requires that the Party, like the state, "must function within the bounds of the Constitution and the laws." This provision stipulates the aspirational commitment to constitutionality and legality in the Party actions.

D. Distributing Power

The principle of "democratic centralism" is confirmed in Article 5 of the 2015 Constitution: "The National Assembly, the Local People's Assemblies and other state organizations are established and function in accordance with the principle of democratic centralism."[150] However, important constitutional amendments redefine positions, structure, and the functions of the state institutions and create new institutions, which indicates clear distribution and independence of powers. These amendments can be classified as: positional, functional, and structural amendments.

Consider first the positional amendments. These amendments redefine the nature of the position of the three branches. The Constitution clearly defines the National Assembly as the legislative branch,[151] the government as the executive branch,[152] and for the first time defines that "the people's courts are the judicial organs; only courts have the power to adjudicate and judge cases."[153] While the two formers have already featured the previous versions of the constitution, the latter is a significant amendment as it provides the constitutional foundation for judicial independence and prevents the interference of other political institutions into the work of the judicial branch.

Next are functional amendments. Many amendments are introduced to clearly define, adjust, delete, and supplement the functions of the major state institutions. These functional constitutional amendments have the general trend to make the state functions clearer, less concentrated, and more responsible. To begin with, several amendments define in more details the functions of the national assembly

150 Laos Constitution 2015 (n 1) art. 5.
151 Ibid. art. 52.
152 Ibid. art. 69.
153 Ibid. art. 90.

in deciding important socio-economic affairs and government formation.[154] One amendment gives the national assembly the function to void legal regulations issued by other state institutions found as unconstitutional.[155] Another amendment allows this institution to appoint and dismiss the Prime Minister.[156] One amendment removes the function of the National Assembly's Standing Committee to supervise the activities of the executive bodies, courts, and the public prosecutors.[157] This allows independence of powers to some extent, especially, judicial independence.

On the President of State, the Constitution also defines more specifically its functions. In addition, the Constitution removes the function to appoint the prime minister which has been transferred to the National Assembly.[158] At the same time, the Constitution adds the presidential powers to grant political asylum to persons of other nationalities, and to negotiate or sign international treaties and agreements on behalf of the State.[159]

On the Government, one amendment requires this institution to be accountable to the National Assembly and President of State.[160] The Parliamentary vote of no confidence is the mechanism for the National Assembly to hold the Government accountable, the mechanism established in the previous Constitution and reconfirmed in the amended Constitution of 2015: "The National Assembly may pass a vote of no confidence in any member or all members of the government if the National Assembly Standing Committee or one-fourth of the total number of National Assembly members raises the issue. In the event that the National Assembly has no confidence on any member or all members of the government the President has the right to request to the National Assembly for reconsideration or decides to terminate the member of the government."[161]

The Constitution also defines in more details the executive functions.[162] In addition, it vests the Government with more functions to: "decide the establish or liquidate of districts, municipalities, city and determine the boundaries of the districts, municipalities, city after approval by the People Assembly of the provinces;" "establish or liquidate of Special and Specific Economic Zone;" "decide on conferment, withdrawal, relinquishment and re-acquisition of Lao nationality"; and "decide on granting a foreigner to become a honorary person.[163]

154 Ibid. art. 53.
155 Ibid. art. 53.
156 Ibid. art. 53.
157 Ibid. art. 56.
158 Ibid. art. 67.
159 Ibid.
160 Ibid. art. 69.
161 Ibid. art. 75.
162 Ibid. art. 70.
163 Ibid.

The amended Constitution does not have many changes to the judicial functions. However, a new article is added to stipulate adversarial trials, providing that: "Litigants shall have the right to argue and debate at court-room and to participate in all stages of the case proceedings. Accused persons shall have the right to defend the case raised against them, either by themselves or by their guardians or lawyers."[164]

The third type is structural amendments. These structural amendments are introduced to make the power structure less concentrated and more accountable. For example, one important amendment limits the presidential term to two consecutive terms.[165] Another amendment provides that Government members cannot hold two consecutive terms.[166] These provisions aim to hold the power holders accountable. In addition, the courts structure has a significant constitutional change. The 2003 amended Constitution created a court system in which local courts are based on local administrative units at provincial and district levels.[167] The amended Constitution of 2015 removed this administration-based court system, stipulating that the court system includes the supreme people's court, local people's courts, and military courts.[168] This allows the creation of local courts independent from administrative units, which can prevent the interference of local administrators into the judicial adjudication of local courts. The amended Constitution also changes the procuracy structure in the same manner.[169]

On the local government, the most important change is the creation of the "local people's councils" which is detailed in a new chapter of the Constitution, Chapter VIII divided into nine articles.[170] The local people's council is defined as "the representative of the rights and interests of the multi-people" and "the organ of state power at locality."[171] Its general functions are to adopt "important legislations," decide on "fundamental issues" of the local level, and to supervise the activities of other state organs at the same local level.[172] The amended Constitution stipulates that the local people's council shall be created at the three local levels: provinces, districts, and villages. The Constitution, however, defines the position, functions, and structure of the local people's councils at the provincial level, and authorizes the legislation to detail the creation of the local people's councils at the district and village levels. Article 4 of the Constitution provides that members of the local people's councils, like those of the National Assembly, are elected by the people through universal, equal, direct, and secret suffrage.[173]

164 Ibid. art. 96.
165 Ibid.
166 Ibid. art. 71.
167 Ibid. art. 79.
168 Ibid. art. 90.
169 Ibid. art. 100.
170 Ibid. Chapter VIII.
171 Ibid. art. 76.
172 Ibid.
173 Ibid. art. 4.

The creation of the local people's councils is a significant departure from the socialist principle of "democratic centralism" which also requires vertical centralization of power. My interviews suggest that one of the motives to create the local people's councils is to facilitate the decentralization policy called the Sam Sang ("Three Builds") Directive detailed in Prime Minister's Instruction Number 16/PM on July 15, 2012.[174] "The Directive proposes villages as the development unit, districts as the integration unit, and provinces as the strategic unit."[175] The creation of the local people's councils allows local government to have more autonomy to legislate at the local level and to decide their own local affairs. To illustrate, the amended Constitution authorizes the provincial people's council to: adopt plans for socio-economic development and state budget; adopt "important legislations at that provincial level; and appoint and remove the provincial governors.[176] In addition, local people's councils are also an institution to check the local administrative authority. In this regard, they are vested with the powers to null regulations issued by administrative authority found as inconsistent with the law, and to interpellate the governor at their sessions.[177] This pragmatic practice of political decentralization allows local government to enjoy great autonomy. The local need of autonomy and economic betterment is dissonant with the Marxist orthodoxy of "democratic centralism."

In addition to the structure of the local government, the amended Constitution creates two new independent institutions, namely, the state audit and the election committee. These institutions are detailed in the two new chapters.[178] My interview suggests that the motive to create the state audit office is to make it independent from the Government.[179] The state audit includes the audit authorities at central and regional levels. The President of the State Audit is selected and removed by the National Assembly and is responsible to the latter.[180] The Constitution provides that the State Audit Authorities have to the right "to conduct the audit independently in accordance with the law in order to certify the correctness of the financial reports, their legality and consequence of their implementation."[181] The Election Committee includes the National Election Committee and Election committees at the local levels, responsible for "leading and directing" the elections of the National Assembly and the local people's councils respectively. The National Election Committee shall be established by the National Assembly Committee.[182] The creation of the local election committees shall be provided by a law.[183]

174 Interview I and Interview II.
175 Adam Smith International, *Report: Sam Sang in Practice: Early Lessons From Pilot Implementation* iv (December 2015).
176 Laos Constitution 2015 (n 1) art. 77.
177 Ibid. art. 83.
178 Ibid. Chapter XI and XII.
179 Interview I.
180 Laos Constitution 2015 (n 1) arts 53 and 106.
181 Ibid. art. 107.
182 Ibid. art. 108.
183 Ibid.

E. Universalizing Rights

The 2015 Constitution continues the spirit of rights statism, which allows the state to regulate the practice of citizens' rights. But it also confirms universal rights protected in the initial Constitution of 1991 and additional rights newly introduced in the amended 2003 Constitution.[184] The original 1991 Constitution already required the state to protect "the freedom and democratic rights of the people which cannot be violated by anyone."[185] Stuart-Fox explains this clause is considered by Marxists as the product of "bourgeois," but it was adopted perhaps as a sop to the expectations of Western democracies or in response to recommendations by foreign legal experts.[186] The 2003 amended Constitution moved further to provide that: "The right of Lao citizens in their bodies, honor and houses are inviolable. Lao citizens cannot be arrested or searched without the order of the Public Prosecutor or the people's courts, except if otherwise provided by the laws."[187] the Constitution also prohibits "all forms of bureaucratic threats and actions that undermine the physical and mental wellbeing or the dignity of the people," and "actions that cause damage to their rightful assets," ensures "solidarity and equal rights among the multiethnic people," and protects intellectual property rights and the rights of foreign nationals in Laos and of those who have no nationality.[188]

In addition to continuing those rights, one of the most important changes is that the 2015 Constitution explicitly recognizes "human rights" for the first time. The following provision is added to the amended Constitution: "The State recognizes, respects, protects, and guarantees human rights and fundamental rights of citizens in accordance with the law."[189] My interviews indicate that the constitutional insertion of human rights is motivated by two concerns. First, this is a response to the international criticism[190] of human rights restrictions in Laos.[191] Second, the constitutional provision on human rights is to implement international treaties on human rights that Laos has recently ratified before the enactment of the amended Constitution.[192] Laos ratified the International Covenant on Civil and Political Rights (ICCPR) in 2009, the Convention on the Rights of Persons with Disabilities (CRPD) in 2009, and International Covenant on Economic, Social, and Cultural

[184] Laos Constitution 2003 (n 8) arts 36, 39, 41, and 42.

[185] Ibid. art. 6.

[186] Stuart-Fox "The Constitution" (n 90) 305.

[187] Laos Constitution 2015 (n 1) art. 42.

[188] "Amended Constitution Creates Provincial Assemblies, Gives President Two Terms" (*Vietiane Times*, December 29, 2015) <www.vientianetimes.org.la/FreeContent/FreeConten_Amended constitution.htm>

[189] Laos Constitution 2015 (n 1) art. 34.

[190] See for example, United States Department of State, "Laos 2016 Human Rights Report" (June 3, 2019) <www.state.gov/documents/organization/265560.pdf>

[191] Interview II.

[192] Interview I.

Rights in 2007, and the Convention against Torture and Other Cruel Inhuman or Degrading Treatment or Punishment in 2012.[193]

Constitutional rights in Laos are a response not only to the state's dominant concern of regulating and controlling individual rights but also the competing concerns of the domestic society and external pressures. The state needs to control rights practices to protect the regime, but it is also compelled to response to the need of attracting foreign investment, which requires the protection of individual rights. Moreover, the international criticism and international advisors may be also a factor compelling constitution-makers to adopt inviolable rights. Consequently, the human rights regime is pluralist, reflecting the mixture of both statist and universal rights. Particularly, the new constitutional provision on human rights indicates both universalist and statist positions of human rights. On the one hand, human rights are considered something not granted but acknowledged, respected, protected by the state. On the other hand, the provision allows the practice of human rights to be regulated by the state law. Despite that, the new constitutional provision on human rights expresses a modification to the socialist, statist conception of rights.

F. Marketizing the Economy

The initial 1991 Constitution and the 2003 amended Constitution confirmed this socialist feature but already modified it by introducing liberal elements of market economy. These market elements include the constitutional commitments to: the multi-sector economy;[194] the state's promotion of foreign investment and protection of investors' lawful assets and capitals;[195] economic co-operation with foreign countries;[196] protection of property rights,[197] and the state's promotion of "knowledge and invention in scientific and technological research and application" and protection of intellectual property.[198]

The commitment to these socialist and market features is continued and strengthened in the amended Constitution of 2015. One important constitutional amendment is the removal of the provision stipulating that the economy is "regulated by the state in the direction of socialism."[199] The new constitutional provision defines the nature of Lao economy as "the economic system that follows the

[193] For Lao status of ratification of international human rights treaties, see "Ratification Status for Lao People's Democratic Republic" (United Nation Human Rights Office of the High Commissioner) <http://tbinternet.ohchr.org/_layouts/TreatyBodyExternal/Treaty.aspx?CountryID=94&Lang=EN>

[194] Laos Constitution 2003 (n 8) art. 13.

[195] Ibid. art. 15.

[196] Ibid. art. 20.

[197] Ibid. art. 16.

[198] Ibid. art. 24.

[199] Laos Constitution 2015 (n 1) art. 13.

socialist economic theory which consists of divergent forms of economy, and various forms of enterprises."[200] The economy is grounded on the socialist economic theory, but the commitment to socialism is no longer a feature of the constitutional economy. This is connected to the constitutional provisions on the promotion of foreign investment and economic co-operation with foreign countries. The firm commitment to the direction towards socialism may limit the investment from and economic co-operation with the non-socialist world.

The Constitution stipulates a "socialist market economy." The competing aspirations to both market and socialism is expressed in this provision: "All types of enterprises are equal before the laws and operate according to the principle of the market economy, competing and cooperating with each other to expand production and business while regulated by the State in the direction of socialism."[201] To ensure the direction of socialism, the Constitution stipulates that: "The State manages the economy in accordance with the mechanism of the market economy regulated by the State, to implement the principle of combining centralized management through the consensus of central authorities with the delegation of responsibilities to local authorities in accordance with the laws and regulations."[202] In addition, for the state to manage the economy, the state must be the owner of major resources, such as lands. The Constitution therefore establishes the state's ownership of all lands while allowing the citizens enjoy the right to use the land granted by the state.[203] As the reflection of the socialist policy, the Constitution provides that: "The State attaches great importance to the development of the economy in conjunction with cultural and social development by giving priority to human resource development."[204]

But, the constitutional provisions on the economy focus more on promoting the market economy by commitments to multi-sectoral economy, promotion of foreign investments, creation of the favorable conditions for foreign investments, protection of property rights of the investors, protection of all forms of property rights, and economic co-operation with foreign countries. These commitments are illustrated by the following provisions:

- The national economy of the Lao People's Democratic Republic relies on a stable multi-sectoral economy (Article 13).
- The State promotes the investment by all domestic economic sectors in production, businesses, and services, to contribute to the industrial transformation and modernization of, and to develop and strengthen, the national economy (Article 14).

200 Ibid. art. 13.
201 Laos Constitution 2015 (n 1) art. 13.
202 Ibid. art. 18.
203 Ibid. art. 17.
204 Ibid. art. 21.

- The State promotes foreign investment in the Lao People's Democratic Republic, [and] creates favorable conditions for the injection of capital, for the use of technology and for introducing modern types of management into production, businesses and services. The lawful assets and capital of investors in the Lao People's Democratic Republic shall not be confiscated, seized or nationalized by the State (Article 15).
- The State protects and promotes all forms of property rights: State, collective, private domestic and foreign investment in the Lao People's Democratic Republic (Article 16).
- The State protects the property rights (such as the rights of possession, use, usufruct, and disposition) and the inheritance rights of organizations and individuals (Article 17).
- The Lao People's Democratic Republic implements open policies on economic cooperation with foreign countries in different ways, on a multilateral basis and in different forms on the basis of the [following] principles: respect for each other's independence, sovereignty, equality and mutual benefit (Article 20).

It can be seen that the constitutional economy reflects the competing commitments to socialism and market values. While constitution-makers do not abandon socialist economic theory, they are more concerned with the local actual need, namely economic amelioration. The main goal of the national economy is realistic: to "transform the natural economy into a trading and manufacturing economy" so as to "improve the material and spiritual living conditions of the multi-ethnic people."[205] The consequence is the competing constitutional economic commitments to both socialism and market values. These commitments are dissonant and contradictory, but do not radically negate each other. Within the pluralist constitutional economic framework, the state still remain the power to control the economy to achieve its goals and interests. In addition, the practice of market policy, which aims to attract domestic foreign investment to improve the economic condition, can confer more legitimacy to the communist leadership.

IV. Conclusion

The Laos Constitution is an instrument for political control, but its making process and substance also express the concern of integration of ethnic diversity. The attachment to the commitment to a unified Lao multi-ethnic people informs and legitimizes the process and contents of constitutional change. The adherence to

[205] Ibid. art. 13.

ethnic integration generates unique features of the socialist constitution in Laos compared with other socialist constitutions. Particularly, the idea of multi-ethnic people informs constitutional provisions on the party, centralized institutional structure, individual rights, and the economy.

The Lao constitutional change under the form of replacement through amendment is progressive in substantial and directional ways. In a substantial sense, constitutional amendment aims to improve the material well-being of living conditions of the Lao multi-ethnic people. Because of the socio-economic circumstances of the country, its preoccupation is the material betterment of the living conditions of the local people. In a directional sense, constitutional amendment facilitates the movement of the constitutional system to a better stage. Although the authoritarian regime remains (the single leadership of the communist party, centralized power, rights regulated by the state), constitutional amendments soften and modify the authoritarian arrangement and introduce elements which facilitate constitutional term limits, the creation of the state audit, accountable government, human rights, local autonomy, judicial independence, and adversarial trials. Particularly, the creation of the people's council allows local government to address the developmental concerns of the local people.

Many of these contents of constitutional amendment are aspirational. A constitution includes not only legalistic rules but also a community's aspirations for the future.[206] Lao constitutional amendment includes aspirational contents that the government cannot achieve immediately, but these contents are normative constitutional values, principles, and hopes to which the Lao people are committed and which they will attempt to realize in the long-term future throughout many generations. For example, the commitment to human rights, judicial independence, and adversarial trials are not prescriptions that the regime can implement immediately but aspirations the regime hopes to realize in the future. The initial constitutional amendment may include aspirational provisions which would be realized by generations over time, and new generations will come up with new aspirations that would be supplemented in the Constitution, which generates further constitutional amendments.[207]

Prospectively, political scientists believe that although Laos remains an authoritarian regime, it "is less authoritarian than it used to be."[208] The political elite monopolizes power for their interests,[209] but they are also compelled to work to improve the living standards of the local people, which is essential to the sociological

[206] Kim Lane Scheppele, "Aspirational and Aversive Constitutionalism: The Case for Studying Cross-Constitutional Influence Through Negative Models" (2003) 1(2) International Journal of Constitutional Law 296, 299.

[207] I thank Mark Tushnet for suggesting this idea. Personal communication, Mark Tushnet (November 3, 2017).

[208] Hlaing, "Laos" (n 99) 135. See also, Creak and Barney, "Conceptualizing Party-State Governance" (n 5) 698.

[209] Stuart-Fox, "Laos" (n 89) 178.

legitimacy of their rule. Recent constitutional amendment indicates the improvement in its authoritarian constitution, which enables us to situate Laos within comparative study of authoritarian constitutionalism to some extent. The authoritarian leaders in the country may be less interested in imposing constitutional constraints on their power in the name of individuals' liberty. But, for the sake of sociological legitimacy, constitutional amendment establishes the state's positive constitutional duty to improve the material well-being of living conditions. The achievement of this aspirational goal requires empowering rather than negatively limiting the state. On the mechanism of constitutional enforcement, because authoritarian constitutional arrangements in Laos lack judicial review, the political (legislative) form may be relevant. The Lao parliament "is typically dismissed as a 'rubber-stamp' parliament," but "as one of the only institutions where concerns over development projects and other controversies can formally be raised, the parliament has played an increasingly prominent oversight function, even if this does not extend to the role of the Party itself."[210] It also enacted many legislations to implement the amended constitution. The Lao legislature may operate as the platform to put pressure on the enforcement of the state's positive constitutional duty to improve the living conditions of the local people.

210 Sayalath and Creak, "Regime Renewal in Laos" (n 4) 188.

6
The Reservation Model
Cuba

Introduction

A decade after its amendment in 1992 in response to the collapse of the Soviet bloc, Cuba's first socialist Constitution was amended a second time in 2002 to definitively reserve the socialist identity of the regime. Amendments were introduced to Articles 3, 11, and 137. The amended Article 3 asserts that "Socialism . . . is irrevocable: Cuba will never revert to capitalism." The amended Article 11 provides that "economic, diplomatic or political relations with other states shall never be negotiated under aggression, threat or coercion by a foreign power." Article 137, which deals with constitutional amendment rules, makes the above two provisions unamendable.

The 2002 amendments were an aversive/resistant reaction to external and internal demands for fundamental change. First, they were resistant to the external call for fundamental reform. On May 20, 2002, in his remark at the White House on the occasion of the 100th anniversary of Cuba's Independence, US President George W. Bush demanded that Cuba introduce far-reaching political and economic reforms as a condition for the US's incremental easing of the economic embargo against the country. The Cuban government interpreted this as a demand for regime change in Cuba. In response, the Cuban government held mass marches around the country mobilizing support for an amendment to the Constitution, to confirm the irrevocable socialist nature of the regime.[1]

Second, the 2002 amendments were a constitutional resistance to the internal demand for fundamental political change. The dissident petition, known as the Varela Project *(Proyecto Varela),* collected more than 10,000 signatures to support a referendum on democratic reform (e.g. freedom of expression, association, and press, a right to free enterprise, and electoral reforms). It was submitted to the National Assembly in May of 2002. Former U.S. President Jimmy Carter made an approving reference to the Varela Project in a speech at the University of Havana.

[1] Michael B. Wise, "Cuban Constitutionalism: Will There Be Changes?" (2013) 51(2) Duquesne Law Review 467, 484–5; "Thousands March in Support of Cuban Constitutional Amendment – 2002-06-12" (*VOA*, October 26, 2009) <https://www.voanews.com/a/a-13-a-2002-06-12-51-thousands-66287357/541037.html> accessed December 22, 2019.

Constitutional Change in the Contemporary Socialist World. Bui Ngoc Son, Oxford University Press (2020). © Bui Ngoc Son.
DOI: 10.1093/oso/9780198851349.001.0001.

The Cuba government rejected the petition without explanation, initiated its own referendum on constitutional amendments to reserve the irrevocable commitment to socialism, and repressed dissidents throughout the country.[2]

Therefore, in addition to the above changes, the 2002 amendment added, following a Special Provision at the end of the Constitution: "Between June 15 and 18, 2002, almost the whole of the Cuban people expressed their unconditional support for amendments to the Constitution proposed by an Extraordinary Assembly of all the national headquarters of the mass organizations, held on the 10th of that month. This ratified the entire Constitution of the Republic and proposed that the socialist nature and political and social system it contains be declared irrevocable, as a fitting and categorical response to the demands and threats made by the United States imperialist administration on May 20, 2002. The proposal was approved by the unanimous passing of Resolution No. V-74 at an Extraordinary Session of the Fifth Legislature, held between June 24 and 26, 2002." This statement is not merely an explanation of constitutional amendment. At a deeper level, it is a vehement and populist expression of resistance to external pressure: vehement in the sense that the constitutional form is used for this resistant expression; and populist in the sense that this constitutional resistance arguably received the people's support, campaigned by the government.

After the 2002 amendment, no further amendment was introduced to the 1976 Constitution. This charter remained in force for more than four decades. In a national referendum on February 24, 2019, Cubans overwhelmingly ratified a new constitution after an extensive process of public constitutional debates and consultation. This second socialist constitution in Cuba was formally proclaimed on April 10, 2019, effectively replacing the 1976 document. This chapter focuses on the process and substances of the 2019 constitution-making. It demonstrates that the 2019 Constitution introduces progressive change to improve the socialist constitutional system and material wellbeing of the living conditions of the local people. Compared with the four other socialist countries I consider, Cuba is characterized by the reservation model of socialist constitutional change. Constitutional change reserves unique features of Cuban Caribbean Marxism: the revolutionary commitment to communism and the praxis of "socialist democracy" in the form of mass rallies, consultations, and referenda. The adherence to Cuban Caribbean Marxism informs and legitimatizes the process and substances of constitutional change in this country.

The research for this chapter was supported by my field trip to Havana, Cuba's capital, in 2019, shortly after the new Constitution was proclaimed. This fieldwork helped me to obtain an empirical sense of the changing society which would inform constitutional change. My field research also enabled me to exchange ideas with

[2] Erik Luna, "Cuban Criminal Justice and the Ideal of Good Governance" (2004) 14(2) Transnational Law & Contemporary Problems 529, 559, 560.

local citizens and jurists, including attending two individual lectures delivered by an international law scholar at Cuba's National Union of Jurists (Unión Nacional de Juristas de Cuba), and a constitutional law scholar at University of Havana Law School. This engagement has informed my thinking about Cuba's new Constitution but only in a contextual sense.

I. Factors

Cuba's 2019 constitution-making was a response to leadership change. Raúl Castro succeeded his brother Fidel Castro as the country's President in February 2008. Raúl has been often described "as a pragmatic leader who, unlike Fidel, does not make policy decisions based on ideological convictions."[3] He believed that substantive changes to the economy were crucial to the survival of the political regime and to the survival of Cuba as an independent state. He said: "We are facing really unpleasant realities, but we do not close our eyes to them. We are convinced that we need to break away from dogma and assume firmly and confidently the ongoing upgrading of our economic model in order to set the foundations of the irreversibility of the Cuban socialism and its development, which we know are the guarantee of our national sovereignty and independence."[4] In April 2018, Raúl was succeeded by Miguel Díaz-Canel, the first president born after the 1959 Revolution and the first president of the Cuban socialist state since 1979 who was not a member of the Castro family. Although Raúl was no longer president, he was still a powerful figure as the First Secretary of the Cuban Communist Party, which played the leading role in the state.[5] Under socialist authoritarianism, despite its institutionalization, leadership change was important for constitutional change. Constitutional change had to be supported by the top leaders. In addition, the leaders may have needed constitutional reform to institutionalize their new policy. Raúl and Díaz-Canel were both supportive of constitutional reform to respond to the party's changing policy and to a changing society.

[3] "Cuba's New Leadership" (*Freedom House*) <https://freedomhouse.org/report/another-special-period-cuba-how-citizens-view-their-countrys-future/cubas-new-leadership> accessed December 22, 2019.

[4] "Key Address by Army General Raul Castro Ruz, President of the State Council and the Council of Ministers and Second Secretary of the Communist Party of Cuba Central Committee, at the Closing Session of the 9th Congress of The Young Communist League, Havana, April 4, 2010, Year 52 of the Revolution" (*Cuba.cu*, April 4, 2010) <http://www.cuba.cu/gobierno/rauldiscursos/2010/ing/r030410i.html> accessed December 22, 2019.

[5] Larry Catá Backer, "Transitions to Entertain and Distract the West: A Harder Review at a New Era that Changes little as Raúl Castro Remains First Secretary of the Cuban Communist Party and Diaz Canel Assumes the Presidency Under the Leadership of the PCC" (*Law at the End of the Day*, April 19, 2018) <http://lcbackerblog.blogspot.com/2018/04/transitions-to-entertain-and-distract.html> accessed December 22, 2019.

That brings us to the second internal factor of constitution-making: the party's changing policy. Constitutional change responded to the party's three important political documents: the *Lineamientos De La Política Económica Y Social Del Partido Y La Revolución* (hereafter *Lineamientos*), *Conceptualización Del Modelo Económico Y Social Cubano De Desarrollo Socialista* (hereinafter *Conceptualización*), and the *Plan Nacional De Desarrollo Económico Y Social Hasta 2030: Propuesta De Vision De La Nación, Ejes Y Sectores Estratégicos* (hereinafter Plan). The *Lineamientos,* adopted in the Party's Sixth Congress in 2011, outlined the strategy for social economic development in Cuba for the years 2016–2021. Based on the revised version of the *Lineamientos,* the Seventh Congress in April 2016 discussed the *Conceptualización,* which articulated principles for "updating" Cuba's economic model, and the *Plan,* which provided more concrete guidance for medium-term economic and social development. These two documents were approved in the Third Plenum of the Central Committee of the Party in May 2017.[6]

Consequently, the three political documents altogether provided blueprints for constitutional reform. An empirical survey demonstrates the textual similarities between the draft constitution and the party's documents: Of the 224 articles in the Constitution Project, 175 are based on the principles and the policy priorities articulated in the *Conceptualización*, the *Lineamientos*, and the *Plan*.[7] In particular, the *Lineamientos* transformed the Soviet-style centralized planned economy into a mixed economy featuring a combination of the state, private, co-operative, and joint venture economic sectors. This dramatic reform reflected the new leadership's pragmatic approach to socialism. In particular, it articulated 274 measures for reform, including the dismissal of around a million government employees and an opening up to private entrepreneurship. The *Lineamientos* can be considered as a living "constitutional" law in some ways. Notably, it introduced a fundamental norm for the mixed economy, which contradicted the planned economy established by the existing 1976 Constitution. Yet, such informal constitutional change may not have been useful for the legitimacy and sustainability of the long-term and more far-reaching social, economic, and political reform. Formal constitutional change became necessary.

The two above internal factors are political, but the third internal factor is sociological: the change of the Cuban society and economy. Constitutional change was necessary to both reflect and facilitate social and economic change. After the *Lineamientos* was introduced, both the society and economy of Cuba changed dramatically. This change has attracted extensive academic analysis.[8] One of the

6 On these documents, see Larry Catá Backer, Flora Sapio, and James Korman, "Popular Participation in the Constitution of the Illiberal State—An Empirical Study of Popular Engagement and Constitutional Reform in Cuba and the Contours of Cuban Socialist Democracy 2.0" (2019) 34 Emory International Law Review.

7 Ibid. 33.

8 C. Mesa-Lago and J. Pérez-López, *Cuba Under Raúl Castro: Assessing the Reforms* (Lynne Rienner Publishers 2013); J. I. Domínguez, O. E. P. Villanueva, M. E. Prieto, and L. Barberia (eds),

most important changes was the dissonant emergence of the private economic sectors within the socialist economic structure. The government granted some 250,000 new licenses for self-employed private businesses in various areas, such as restaurants, retail trade, and tenancy. Consequently, within six months, the number of private entrepreneurs had increased from 157,000 to over 320,000.[9] The incremental transformation of the economy and the society put pressure on constitutional reform. Particularly, the continuing development of the economy with the emergence of the private sector required change to the constitution, in which private ownership of property was not recognized.

Constitutional change became necessary, not only to reflect the existing practice but also to facilitate social-economic engineering. Despite dramatic changes, the island was confronted with serious social and economic problems: a lazy and incompetent bureaucracy, corruption (particularly among the state's middle management level), discrimination, poor economic productivity, overemployment among the public sector, the weakness of the production infrastructure, and an aging population.[10] These social and economic problems were not independent from the institutional setting under which they emerged and would be handled. To tackle these difficulties in the long-term, therefore, meant dealing with institutional questions at a fundamental level. Consequently, social and economic malaise put pressure on constitutional reform.

Cuba's constitutional reform was not only driven internally. Several external factors, which had been animated by globalization, generated the need for making a new constitution. First, due to globalization, Cuba was widely integrated into regional and international orders. Under the new leadership of Raúl Castro, Cuba's policy for international relations had three main aims, as described by William M. LeoGrande: "first, to diversify Cuba's international economic relations so that the disruption of ties with any one country will not throw the economy into chaos; second, to build diplomatic support both regionally and globally through active participation in a wide range of international organizations; and third, to pursue normal relations with the United States, reducing the threat Washington poses to Cuba's security and opening the doors to expanded trade and investment."[11] This

Cuban Economic and Social Development: Policy Reforms and Challenges in the 21st Century (Harvard University Press 2012); C. Brundenius and R. T. Pérez (eds), *No More Free Lunch: Reflections on the Cuban Economic Reform Process and Challenges for Transformation* (Springer 2013); and Alberto Gabriele (ed.), *The Economy of Cuba after the VI Party Congress* (Nova Publishers 2012); A. R. M. Ritter, "Revolution in the Revolution: Recent Developments in the Cuban Economy" (2014) 49 Latin American Research Review 3, 246–55 (reviewing scholarship in Cuban economic reform).

[9] Salim Lamrani, "Reforming the Cuban Economic Model: Causes and Prospects" (2012) 4 International Journal of Cuban Studies 1, 27.

[10] Ibid. 19–26.

[11] William M. LeoGrande, "The Danger of Dependence: Cuba's Foreign Policy After Chavez" (*World Politics Review*, April 2, 2013) <https://www.worldpoliticsreview.com/articles/12840/the-danger-of-dependence-cubas-foreign-policy-after-chavez> accessed December 22, 2019.

change required a constitutional response. For example, days after Raúl Castro assumed the presidency in 2008, the Cuban government signed two major international human rights treaties—the Covenant on Civil and Political Rights, and the International Covenant on Economic, Social, and Cultural Rights—that the preceding president Fidel Castro had long opposed.[12] Signing international human rights law provided an impetus for the constitutional incorporation of human rights. In addition, constitutional change might have been necessary to support foreign investment. Finally, globalization resulted in increased interaction between people in Cuba, particularly the presence of foreigners on the island, immigration, and emigration.[13] This transnational interaction may have required a constitutional adjustment regarding international travel and citizenship to allow insiders to leave and outsiders to enter.

II. The 2019 Constitution-Making Process

A. Agenda Setting

Once the Party had articulated a new direction for social progress, constitutional change became necessary to institutionalize its vision. Therefore, shortly after the adoption of *Lineamientos*, at the 2012 meeting, the Party contemplated whether the implementation of the *Lineamientos* required changes to the constitutional system. Subsequently, in 2013, the Political Bureau created a working group for constitutional change. In the sixth Congress in 2016, in which the *Conceptualización* and the *Plan* were discussed, Raúl Castro explicitly called for constitutional reform to respond to a changing society and the Party's new development policies. After Miguel Díaz-Canel was selected by the National Assembly in April 2018 to succeed Raúl as President, Raúl mentioned in his farewell speech that in its next regular session in July, the Assembly would be proposing a commission of deputies to launch a constitutional project. Yet, an extraordinary session of the National Assembly convened on June 2, 2018 and created the Commission for the Drafting of the Draft Project of the Constitution of the Republic (hereinafter, the Commission) made up of thirty-three members from different sectors of the government and society. Díaz-Canel designated Raúl, who still served as first secretary of the Communist Party, as the commission's president, while he was its vice-president.[14] Cuba's

[12] James C. McKinley Jr, "Cuba Signs 2 Human Rights Treaties" (*New York Times*, Feburary 29, 2008) <https://www.nytimes.com/2008/02/29/world/americas/29iht-cuba.4.10589148.html> accessed December 22, 2019.

[13] Catherine Krull, "Introduction: Cuba in a Global Context" in *Cuba in a Global Context: International Relations, Internationalism, and Transnationalism* (C. Krull (ed.), University Press of Florida 2014).

[14] Granma, "Díaz-Canel: La nueva Constitución tendrá en cuenta los principios de nuestro sistema politico, Granma" [Díaz-Canel: The new Constitution will take into account the principles of our political system] (*Granma*, June 2, 2018) <http://www.granma.cu/cuba/2018-06-02/

constitution-making body was, in fact, constituted by influential features in the Party, the government, and mass organizations under the Party's control. The function of this body, therefore, was not merely to draft a constitution: it was also a body to control the constitution-making process to make sure that the process would move forward to the referred directions.

The Cuban regime deliberately designed the project of constitutional change as constitution-making (or constitutional replacement) rather than amendment. Díaz-Canel reported that: "During the studies we conducted, we came to the conclusion that more than a reform, a new constitution was required, one that would not be limited to updating the economic and social order, but would deepen the principles of our state structure, the extension of citizen rights and guarantees, and other relevant issues; thinking not only of the present, but, above all, the future of the nation."[15] The formal process was clearly designed as a constitution-making one. Díaz-Canel said that the fundamental mission of the Commission was to draft a new constitution, which would be submitted to popular consultation, and eventually approved by the people as the constituent body in a national referendum. However, Díaz-Canel also insisted that the new Constitution must confirm the irrevocability of the socialist system, and "irremovable pillars," including the role of the Communist Party of Cuba as an organized vanguard and superior leading force of society and the State.[16] Constitution-makers, in fact, pursued a dissonant project: constitution-making in formal terms while reserving socialist identities as the substance of the constitutional order.

B. Drafting

After its creation, in several sessions from June 10–15, 2018, the Commission discussed a range of constitutional issues.[17] To prepare the first draft of the constitution, members of the Commission studied three kinds of sources: political sources, national constitutional experience, and transnational constitutional experience. First, the political sources, the "obligatory references," refers to national

diaz-canel-la-nueva-constitucion-tendra-en-cuenta-los-principios-de-nuestro-sistema-politico> accessed December 22, 2019; W. T. Whitney Jr., "Constitutional Change Underway in Cuba, People's World" (*People's World*, June 12, 2018) <https://www.peoplesworld.org/article/constitutional-change-underway-in-cuba/> accessed December 22, 2019.

15 Raúl Castro Ruz, "The Constitution We Proclaim Today Guarantees the Continuity of the Revolution and the Irrevocability of Our Socialism" (*Granma*, April 11, 2019) < http://en.granma.cu/cuba/2019-04-11/raul-the-constitution-we-proclaim-today-guarantees-the-continuity-of-the-revolution-and-the-irrevocability-of-our-socialism> accessed December 22, 2019.

16 Granma, "Díaz-Canel" (n 14).

17 Granma, "First Draft of Proposed New Constitution Progressing, Granma" (*Granma*, June 15, 2018) <http://en.granma.cu/cuba/2018-06-15/first-draft-of-proposed-new-constitution-progressing> accessed December 22, 2019.

ideological guidance, and political documents, including: Fidel Castro Ruz's political thought; Raúl Castro Ruz's speeches and directives; The Conceptualization of Cuba's Economic and Social Model of Socialist Development; The National Plan for Economic and Social Development through 2030: Vision of the Nation, Axes, and Strategic Sectors, The Economic and Social Policy Guidelines of the Party and the Revolution, and The Party Work Objectives approved by the First Party Congress.[18] Given that constitution-making was animated by the pressure to institutionalize the new political directions of social progress, these political documents understandably provided normative sources for constitutional design. The second sources were national constitutional experience, particularly the 1940 Constitution, the 1959 Fundamental Law, and the current 1976 Constitution.[19] Despite Cuba's rich constitutional history, socialist constitutional documents were underlined as the sources guiding the new constitution-making. The elite's attempts to reserve the socialist constitutional fundamental values explain the particular reference to the socialist constitutional history. The third sources included transnational constitutional experience, especially in Latin American countries and socialist countries.

C. Deliberation

On July 2 and 3, 2018, the first draft of the Constitution was presented by Cuba's Commission to the Party Central Committee for consideration.[20] Subsequently, on July 21 and 22, 2018, the draft was discussed and approved by the National Assembly.[21] Major new issues in the draft, which received international attention, included: the abolition of the goal to build a "communist society," the restoration of the position of prime minister, the definition of marriage as a voluntary union of two persons, thereby opening the door for same-sex marriage, the recognition of the presumption of innocence, the recognition of the right to own private property, and the encouragement of foreign investment.[22] In particular, the constitutional recognition of homosexual marriage was campaigned for by Mariela Castro Espín, a Cuba lawmaker and Raul Castro's daughter.[23] In her speech at the plenary session

[18] Homero Acosta, "A New Constitution With Transformational Purpose" (*Granma*, August 2, 2018) http://en.granma.cu/cuba/2018-08-02/a-new-constitution-with-transformational-purpose accessed December 22, 2019.

[19] Ibid.

[20] Ibid.

[21] Lissy Rodríguez Guerrero and Susana Antón, "A Constitution With All" (*Granma*, July 20, 2018) <http://en.granma.cu/cuba/2018-07-30/a-constitution-with-all> accessed December 22, 2019.

[22] Kirk Semple, "New Cuba Constitution, Recognizing Private Property, Approved by Lawmakers" (*New York Times*, July 22, 2018) <https://www.nytimes.com/2018/07/22/world/americas/cuba-constitution.html> accessed December 22, 2019.

[23] Calvin Freiburger, "Cuba's New Constitution May Open Door to Gay 'Marriage': Castro's Daughter" (*LiftSiteNews*, June 25, 2018) <https://www.lifesitenews.com/news/raul-castros-daughter-new-cuban-constitution-may-open-door-to-gay-marriage> accessed December 22, 2019.

of the National Assembly, she stated that the new provision of marriage "would be in the vanguard of countries recognizing and guaranteeing human rights."[24] Thus, she situated the argument for same-sex marriage within the general constitutional protection of human rights regardless of sexual orientation and gender identity.

Deputies also debated on a range of constitutional reforms related to non-discrimination; childhood, adolescence, and youth; education, culture, and science; environmental protection; and local government.[25] While the general concepts (e.g. human rights) informed the debates, Marxist ideas and concepts (e.g. "dialectical," "revolutionary," and "socialism") were used to justify several constitutional proposals. For example, the deputy Miguel Barnet justified non-discrimination in this manner: "This is a dialectical, modern Constitution, if breaking with tradition is required, let it be done, because breaking with tradition is also a revolutionary act, and there is no place for any kind of discrimination against human beings within socialism. Love does not have a sex."[26]

D. Consultation

From August 13 to November 15, 2018, the draft constitution was released to the public for consultation. This process was characterized by the institutionalized format; constitutional dialogue; and impactful outcome.

To begin with, the formal format of constitutional consultation was highly institutionalized by the state. This format is described below:

> The format adopted involves the publication of draft documents, and their distribution in both printed and electronic versions. The next step is the convening of meetings held at grass-roots levels—in schools, hospitals, factories, neighborhoods. At meetings, the content of documents is explained to those in attendance, and a discussion then ensues. During the discussion participants can suggest modification to documents, express their doubts, or raise questions about them. The comments, and the general content of discussions are then summarized by the conveners of the meetings, and transmitted to the bureaucracies responsible for their selection, collection, and analysis. Once processed, data is then presented to the Central Committee of the PCC [the Communist Party of Cuba], or to the ANPP [the National Assembly of People's Power]. Based on information provided by the public consultation, documents are then revised, and submitted to formal approval by the PCC or the ANPP.[27]

24 Guerrero and Antón, "A Constitution With All" (n 21).
25 Ibid.
26 Ibid.
27 Backer and others, "Popular Participation in the Constitution of the Illiberal State" (n 6) 35.

The consultation process generated a controlled popular constitutional dialogue. There are two dimensions of this constitutional dialogue: the dialogue among the citizens and the dialogue between the citizens and the government. In the first instance, the three-month consultation process triggered "unusual" popular constitutional debates under a socialist institutional setting which lacks campaigns and independent mass media.[28] In official venues, one controversial issue in the debates concerned the nature of constitutional change: constitutional amendment or replacement. Opponents of replacement argued that this would alter the nature of "the revolutionary Cuban political and social system," while its supporters believed that a new constitution was needed to introduce "profound shifts in the structure of the state" and broaden "the range of rights" "without losing its socialist nature and essence" as this change was a "break from the past" but "within political and social continuity."[29] Turning to the substance of the draft constitution, these issues attracted considerable attention in public debates in official venues: the role of the communist party, same-sex marriage, and private property.[30]

As in the case of Vietnam, constitutional mobilization during the consultation process in Cuba was vibrant. The Cuban constitutional petitioners, like the Vietnamese seventy-two petitioners, demanded radical democratization. To illustrate this, consider a letter promoted by the Cuban Observatory of Human Rights (OCDH) and the Damas de Blanco Association and signed by intellectuals and leaders of Cuban civil society.[31] The letter criticized the fact that the draft constitution "does not respond to democratic principles or to the political and social plurality of Cuban society, because it has been designed exclusively by the Communist Party and only responds to its will and interests."[32] The letter also criticized the way in which the draft "does not include respect for several fundamental rights, including the existence of political parties, freedom of the press, assembly and association."[33] Constitutional petitioners then called on "democratic governments, international organizations, parties and good citizens from all over the world" to "continue working to encourage a true transition to democracy in Cuba," and urged the Cuban government "not to miss this historic opportunity."[34]

[28] Andrea Rodriguez, "Cuban Constitutional Reform Spawns Unusual Public Debate" (*Fox News*, October 11, 2018) <https://www.foxnews.com/world/cuban-constitutional-reform-spawns-unusual-public-debate> accessed December 22, 2019.

[29] Homero Acosta, "Cuba's Future Constitution is a Collective Work" (*Granma*, October 24, 2018) <http://en.granma.cu/cuba/2018-10-24/cubas-future-constitution-is-a-collective-work> accessed December 22, 2019.

[30] Andrea Rodriguez, "Cuban Constitutional Reform Spawns Unusual Public Debate" (n 28).

[31] The full text and signatures are available at: "On the Constitutional Reform in Cuba" (*Cuban Observatory of Human Rights*, November 12, 2018) <https://us11.campaign-archive.com/?e=854a8765dd&u=92a02330088b38b34d642c70e&id=6ed4257bbb> accessed December 22, 2019.

[32] Ibid.

[33] Ibid.

[34] Ibid.

The second dimension is the dialogue between the citizens and the government. This involved the citizens' articulation of their doubts, questions, and disagreement and the government's acceptance of their political responsiveness. The latter is manifested in the government's "appreciation of disagreement, and a faithful collection and transmission of all the input provided by the people."[35] Notably, the government employed advanced technologies to analyze the outcomes of the popular constitutional consultation to avoid data corruption.[36]

That said, the popular constitutional dialogue was politically controlled. A commentary in an unofficial venue stated that critics of the constitutional reform "had no opportunity to make their arguments during the 'popular consultation' process, overseen by the Communist Party. Nor have they been able to do so through the [official] media."[37]

The popular constitutional dialogue induced an impactful outcome. The Secretary of the Council of State, Homero Acosta, presented on December 21, 2018, a detailed report to the National Assembly on the results of the popular consultation process, most debated issues, and significant changes to the new draft. Accordingly, there were 133,681 meetings (79,947 held among the general population, 45,452 among groups of workers, 3,441 among campesinos, 1,585 among university students, and 3,256 among high school students); 8,945,521 people attended these meetings; and there were 1,706,872 comments (783,174 proposals, 666,995 modifications, 32,149 additions, 45,548 deletions, and 38,482 requests for clarification). The constitutional proposals focused on six issues: marriage, particularly same-sex marriage; the presidency (term limits, age limit, and direct election), work, the provincial government, the right to legal assistance in one's defense, and the right to decent housing. A working group, divided into seven subgroups, was created to analyze these proposals, using information technology support. The result of the analysis was presented to the Constitution Drafting Commission. After extensive debates on each issue, the Commission prepared a new Draft Constitution, which included around 760 changes to its predecessor.[38] Changes that received considerable international attention included: the reinsertion of the goal to build "communism" in response to the call of thousands of citizens at community-level meetings,[39] and the deletion of the language promoting

[35] Backer and others, "Popular Participation in the Constitution of the Illiberal State" (n 6) 34.
[36] Ibid. 36.
[37] Madrid, "CubaData Poll Reveals Widespread Rejection of the Regime's New Constitution" (*Diario de Cuba*, December 21, 2019) <http://www.diariodecuba.com/cuba/1550742259_44754.html> accessed December 22, 2019.
[38] Granma news staff, "A Text Enriched by the Contributions of the Cuban People" (*Granma*, January 3, 2019) <http://en.granma.cu/cuba/2019-01-03/a-text-enriched-by-the-contributions-of-the-cuban-people> accessed December 22, 2019.
[39] Acosta Nelson, "Cuba Reinserts 'Communism' in Draft of New Constitution" (*Reuters*, December 21, 2018) <https://www.reuters.com/article/us-cuba-constitution-communism/cuba-reinserts-communism-in-draft-of-new-constitution-idUSKCN1OJ2YB> accessed December 22, 2019.

same-sex marriage in response to the protests from evangelical churches.[40] The new draft constitution was then presented to the Party Central Committee for consideration and then discussed by the National Assembly in December 2018.[41] The new draft constitution indicates that, at least in the Cuban experience, public participation does matter. This exercise generated substantive changes to the draft constitution.

E. Ratification

The new draft constitution was unanimously approved by the National Assembly on December 23, 2018.[42] The regime then prepared for the ratification of the Constitution in a national referendum, which would be "a democratic exercise"[43] according to the regime's anticipation. But, in an unofficial venue, nineteen independent Cuban organizations (including opposition parties, civil society groups, and human rights organizations) criticized the draft constitution as "undemocratic" in a statement, and added that they had come together to campaign to say "No" in the coming constitutional referendum as they believed that the new draft constitution was "undemocratic."[44] The signatories anticipated that "the Cuban government will not allow equal opportunities between the campaigns for YES and NO, in terms of resources, participation in communication media and public events."[45]

On February 24, 2019, the draft constitution was overwhelmingly ratified by the Cuban people in a national referendum with 86.85 percent "Yes" votes, 9 percent opposing votes, and 4.5 percent spoiling or leaving ballot papers blank.[46]

[40] "Cuba Removes Support for Gay Marriage in New Constitution After Protests" (*The Guardian*, December 19, 2018) <https://www.theguardian.com/world/2018/dec/19/cuba-removes-support-for-gay-marriage-in-new-constitution-after-protests> accessed December 22, 2019.

[41] Granma, "Party Central Committee Plenum considers draft Constitution of the Republic of Cuba" (*Granma*, December 13, 2018) <http://en.granma.cu/cuba/2018-12-13/party-central-committee-plenum-considers-draft-constitution-of-the-republic-of-cuba> accessed December 22, 2019; Yudy Castro Morales, "Deputies study proposed Constitution reflecting input from the popular consultation" (*Granma*, December 19, 2018) <http://en.granma.cu/cuba/2018-12-19/deputies-study-proposed-constitution-reflecting-input-from-the-popular-consultation> accessed December 22, 2019.

[42] "Cuba: Legislature Unanimously Approves Draft Constitution for Referendum" (*Havana Times*, December 23, 2018) <https://havanatimes.org/?p=145929> accessed December 22, 2019.

[43] Granma news staff, "Referendum: A Democratic Exercise" (*Granma*, January 9, 2019) <http://en.granma.cu/cuba/2019-01-09/referendum-a-democratic-exercise> accessed December 22, 2019.

[44] "Nineteen Independent Cuban Organizations Campaign for a 'No' Vote on the Constitution" (*Translating Cuba*, December 25, 2018) <https://translatingcuba.com/nineteen-independent-cuban-organizations-campaign-for-a-no-vote-on-the-constitution-14ymedio/> accessed December 22, 2019.

[45] "Nineteen Independent Cuban Organizations Campaign for a 'No' Vote on the Constitution" (n 44).

[46] Marc Frank and Nelson Acosta, "Cubans Overwhelmingly Ratify New Socialist Constitution" (*Reuters*, February 26, 2019) https://www.reuters.com/article/us-cuba-constitution-referendum/

This provided the base for the regime's claim of the "democratic mechanism" of constitution-making and the "strength and continuity" of the principles of the socialist system self-determined by the Cuban people.[47] It is, however, said that "the government had campaigned heavily for ratification" through radio and television programming, and billboards, while there was "little open opposition."[48] In the online media, some Cuban people expressed opposition to the dominant role of the Communist Party over state institutions and the socialist economic model.[49]

On April 10, 2019, the new Constitution was officially proclaimed by the National Assembly. Speaking at the Assembly's meeting, Raúl Castro Ruz stated that "The Constitution we proclaim today represents the continuity of this first one [the 1976 Constitution], as it preserves the unity of all Cubans and the independence and sovereignty of the homeland, as fundamental pillars of the nation."[50] This statement captures the reservational nature of the new Constitution.

F. Implementation

Raúl Castro Ruz articulated a plan to implement the Constitution, including the creation of the National Electoral Council, the Assembly's selection of major state leaders, and the election of provincial governors and vice-governors.[51] In addition, to implement the new Constitution, the Cuban government planned to enact or revise some seventy laws over the next two years. Several working groups were created to be in charge of drafting laws. In particular, to implement the above new constitutional provisions, the regime planned to enact a new electoral law, a new business law, a new family code, and a new criminal code.[52] Given that judicial constitutional review was absent in Cuba, constitutional implementation definitely took the legislative form.

cubans-overwhelmingly-ratify-new-socialist-constitution-idUSKCN1QE22Y> accessed December 22, 2019.

47 Raúl Castro Ruz, "The Constitution We Proclaim Today..." (n 15).

48 Elisabeth Malkin, "Cubans Approve a Constitution, but Opponents Speak Out" (*New York Times*, February 25, 2019) <https://www.nytimes.com/2019/02/25/world/americas/cuba-constitution-vote-referendum.html> accessed December 22, 2019.

49 Ibid.

50 Raúl Castro Ruz, "The Constitution We Proclaim Today..." (n 15).

51 Ibid.

52 National News Staff, "May the Constitution Have the Laws Needed for its Implementation" (*Granma*, May 7, 2019) <http:/en.granma.cu/cuba/2019-05-07/may-the-constitution-have-the-laws-needed-for-its-implementation> accessed December 22, 2019; "Cuba Planning Major Changes to State and Legal System" (*Learning English*, March 21, 2019) <https://learningenglish.voanews.com/a/cuba-planning-major-changes-to-state-and-legal-system/4831072.html> accessed December 22, 2019.

III. Explaining the Law of Change

A. Replacement

The constitutional process in Vietnam, Laos, and Cuba all resulted in the enactment of a new constitution. However, in contrast to Vietnam and Laos, Cuba deliberately created a new constitution rather than amending the existing constitution. This constitutional replacement presents a dissonant project: legal rupture and substantive continuity.

As far as the first feature is concerned, the enactment of the 2019 Constitution signifies a legal rupture. This legal rupture has three manifestations: the "constitution project," the unbounded process, and the new form. As an issue of agenda setting, constitution-makers deliberately designed a "constitution project" to replace the existing constitution. In addition, the procedure of constitutional change was not bounded by the existing constitution as the existing constitution only anticipated procedures for amending,[53] not replacing it. Rather, the constitutional framers deliberately designed rules which aimed to vest the constituent power in the people, particularly the rules governing the processes of public consultation and referendum. Finally, as the consequence of this process, the new charter is formally addressed as a new constitution.

However, continuity was preserved, as the new Constitution had much in common with its predecessor. Although Constitution-makers introduced many substantive changes, ranging from socio-economic principles and fundamental rights to state structures, thanks to the form of replacement, they deliberately reserved the core features of the socialist economic and political system. Consequently, as explored in greater detail later, the 2019 Constitution adapted but retained the constitutional identities established by the 1976 Constitution, particularly the planned economy and the centralized political order with the communist party as the exclusive leading force. Thus, despite legal, procedural rupture, the substantive continuity was guaranteed. In other words, rupture and continuity happened at the same time.

Cuba's choice of constitutional replacement is a function of constitutional legitimacy and political economy. First, constitutional replacement is due to the concern of two types of constitutional legitimacy: sociological and legal. The 1976 Constitution was only amended twice with minor changes and, therefore, failed to reflect the socio-economic changes that occurred over four decades, especially after the Party's introduction of reform policy. The fact that the Constitution had left society far behind would undermine its social acceptance. Its replacement became the choice to ensure the sociological foundation of the nation's constitution.

[53] 1976 Constitution, art. 137.

In addition, the legal foundation of constitutional legitimacy is the explanation for the constitutional replacement. To make a new constitution would involve the wider public in the process of constitutional change and return the constituent power to the people as the authors, and this would boost the legal foundation of the Constitution.

Apart from legitimacy, Cuba's choice of constitutional replacement was also shaped by political economy. The regime chose to make a new constitution to signal a new program for incremental political, economic, and social progress. This program is both retrospective and prospective. Retrospectively, this constitutional program reflected existing social changes. Prospectively, the program deals with *principles* that will guide the party, government, and society's activities during a long-term future. These fundamental issues include the principles of state structure, the principles of human rights, and the principles of the economy. These issues are not policies and technical institutions that can be handled by amendments. They are significant enough to render replacement a choice.

The choice of replacement is consequential. This allowed Cuban constitution-framers to design a more flexible process of constitutional change as they were not limited by the existing constitution. They therefore had more freedom to create a constitution-making body, to repeatedly deliberate the constitutional drafts in the legislative platform, to consult the public, and to carry out a constitutional referendum. Replacement also gave the constitutional framers the freedom to design the substantive constitutional menus: they were free to put on the table what can and cannot be changed. Consequently, apart from the self-restrained socialist pillars, a range of changeable principled issues were placed on the constitutional agenda.

B. Constituent Power

Cuba is the only one of the five current socialist countries to make a new Constitution with the people's constituent power manifested in their exercise of constitutional referendum. This is due to both legal and historical reasons. Legally, a deliberate decision of constitutional replacement opened the door for returning the constituent power to the people. Historically, this practice of constituent power is underpinned by the Cuban tradition of constituent power and popular engagement in deciding significant national affairs.

Cuban-American constitutionalist Larry Catá Backer and his collaborators traced the 2019 exercise of the people's constituent power to two mass rallies in Havana in the 1960s, the 1976 constitution-making, and popular consultation on political documents. First, following the Cuba Revolution, the two Havana mass rallies in 1960 and 1962 which formed the National General Assembly of the People of Cuba enabled the people to express their agreement with the revolutionary government. In addition, the 1976 Constitution was created through the popular consultation and then referendum processes. Moreover, the three political documents (the *Conceptualización*, the *Lineamientos*, and the *Plan*) were also made with extensive public consultations albeit not engaging the entire Cuban people as the constitution-making process. So, the popular exercise of the constituent power did not happen in a vacuum but was the continuing development of the Cuban tradition which involved popular affirmation of sovereignty, constituent power, and popular debates on national affairs.[54]

During the period between the end of the Second World War and the dissolution of the Soviet Union, except for the case of the East German Constitution of 1968 which had different reasons,[55] Cuba was the only country in the socialist camp to practice the people's constituent power through a popular referendum. During the post-Soviet area, Cuba was the only country to exercise the people's constituent power. The exercise of the constituent power is, therefore, considered the unique feature of Cuban Caribbean Marxism. This is manifested in its form of "socialist democracy." The Cuban model of "socialist democracy" has two distinctive characters: the revolutionary emphasis on direct democracy and praxis. Before Cuba adopted the Soviet constitutional model, the Cuba Revolution rejected the notion of representative democracy though competitive elections due to concerns about fictitious and manipulated votes, and therefore favored a direct democracy with the potential to empower the citizens to decide their own destiny. The Soviet constitutional model borrowed but was contextualized by this revolutionary aspiration of direct democracy: the 1976 Constitution infused with Soviet ideas and institutions (e.g. vanguardism and democratic centralism) could only be conceived as being legitimate with the popular approval through referendum, the embodiment of the people's constituent power. The second feature of Cuban Caribbean Marxism is the constitutional praxis of "socialist democracy." In contrast to China where the elite's constitutional theory precedes and informs institutional design, Cuba's "socialist democracy" is not deliberately theorized but manifested through the people's mobilizing, deliberative, and affirmative actions: mass rally, consultation, and referendum.[56]

The general practice of constituent power is not unique to Cuba as this practice is a common feature of modern constitutionalism and witnesses a global return in twenty-first century constitution-making. However, Cuba is distinctive in its exercise of the constituent power under a socialist regime. A socialist state essentially lacks theoretical, institutional, practical underpinnings of the people's constituent power. Socialist constitutional theory underlines class dictatorship rather than

[54] Backer and others, "Popular Participation in the Constitution of the Illiberal State" (n 6) 24–34.
[55] Michael Bothe, "The 1968 Constitution of East Germany: A Codification of Marxist-Leninist Ideas on State and Government" (1969) 17 American Journal of Comparative Law 268.
[56] Backer and others, "Popular Participation in the Constitution of the Illiberal State" (n 6) 24–5.

popular sovereignty and direct democracy. The institutionalization of "democratic centralism" results in the concentration of all constitution-making, amendment, and legislative powers in the national legislature. As a practical issue, constituent power is normally exercised by the legislature despite the vehement social mobilization for the people's constituent power as the case of Vietnam. Yet, Cuba is able to exercise the people's constituent power thanks to its continued revolutionary aspiration to direct democracy and its unique constitutional praxis as opposed to constitutional theory.

The practice of constituent power indicates the reservational nature of Cuba's constitution-making. This practice is justified not by the invocation of the western contractual constitutional theory (as the discourse on this power in Vietnam) but by the local principle of "socialist democracy." In fact, the practice of the constituent power by the people is informed by the attitude of reserving the aspiration and achievements of the revolutionary moment: the aspiration to direct democracy and the popular affirmation of sovereignty.

C. Participation

The popular participation through consultation in the constitutional drafting and through referendum in the constitutional ratification was the consequence of the deliberate decision of constitutional replacement and the embodiment of the popular constituent power.

Backer and his collaborators argue that participation in Cuba's constitution-making process does not simply involve making a dichotomic decision on a negative or affirmative decision on the socio-economic program institutionalized by the Constitution. Participation through consultation process created the informed discussions among citizens about the reformist model of social and economic development, and the "fidelity of a Marxist-Leninist party to the people" or the party's responsive reaction to the popular constitutional comments.[57] Participation through the referendum process did not aim at approving or rejecting the Constitution. Rather, constitutional referendum sought to test the correctness of the prior process of consultation: how the individual and collective views were taken into account in substantive constitutional choice. Another important object of the constitutional referendum is the party's political work in building mass consensus on the developmental model under its vanguard leadership. In this aspect, what is crucial to the party is not the affirmative votes but the entirety of the voting. With regard to the 2019 constitutional referendum, "the most important portion of the vote was not the 6.8 million votes cast to affirm, but rather the 857,000

[57] Ibid. 34–5.

people who failed to vote, the 706,000 no votes and the roughly 330,000 blank and annulled votes. Having given the masses the authority to approve or not to approve the final outcome of a consultation they took part in, it is incumbent on the vanguard to understand how the people failed to be convinced of the value of the object of the plebiscite."[58]

The above exposition is germane in that participation in the Cuban context is not merely about a "yes" saying or a gainsaying on the Constitution. The extensive constitutional consultation aimed to inform the citizens about the reformist constitutionalized model for social, economic, and political progress. This process also sought to build popular agreement on this model. The exercise of constitutional consultation is also important for the subsequent informed constitutional referendum: thanks to consultation, citizens are knowledgeable about the document that they are going to ratify in the referendum. It is also apt that what is crucial to the party is not the affirmative votes. Since the process is managed by the party and without institutionalized opposition campaigns, to obtain a popular affirmation in the referendum surely did not present a problem for the party.

Yet, the non-binary exposition of participation in Cuba's constitutional process seems to underestimate the instrumental nature of the participatory processes. It does not sufficiently account for the meaning of the party-state's control of the consultation process and its overwhelming campaign in referendum. From an instrumentalist perspective, the party-state's seeking for a totality of voting in constitutional referendum aims to both achieve a political consensus and consolidate the legitimacy of the existing socialist political regime and the reformist socialist economy articulated in the Constitution. This explains the fact that popular views opposing core values of socialism could be virtually expressed in unofficial venues. The marginalization or dismissal of opposition views was instrumental to the regime's seeking of total voting.

Another instrumental purpose of the total voting in Cuba's 2019 constitutional referendum was to signal an authoritative support and resistance to the external competing audiences. This external instrumental function must be situated within the fragmentation of Cuba's diplomatic relations between Latin America and Washington.[59] The US Government has consistently implemented democracy promotion programs to encourage regime change in Cuba.[60] In particular, shortly before Cuba's constitutional referendum was held on February 24, 2019, US President Donald Trump commented on the Venezuela turmoil in front of the Venezuelan American community in Miami on February 18, 2019, and remarked that "in Venezuela and across the Western Hemisphere, socialism is dying, and

[58] Ibid. 37.

[59] India Birrell, "Cuba Reforms Cold War Constitution" (*The Organization for World Peace*, March 9, 2019) <https://theowp.org/cuba-reforms-cold-war-constitution/> accessed December 22, 2019.

[60] See Alessandro Badella, "American Hýbris: US Democracy Promotion in Cuba after the Cold War (Part 1)" (2014) 6 International Journal of Cuban Studies 157.

liberty, prosperity, and democracy are being reborn."[61] Cuba's 2019 constitutional reference is a response to the Venezuela events and the US President's statement. Cuba's President Miguel Diaz-Canel said "We Cubans are voting for our new constitution, we're voting for Latin America and the Caribbean."[62] The referendum with an overwhelming confirmative vote on the Constitution institutionalizing the open-up social economy program while confirming socialism sent two strong signals to the outsiders: a supportive message to Venezuela's socialist system and a resistant message to the United States' programs promoting democracy in Cuba generally and Trump's statement about socialism particularly. As to the latter, like the 2002 amendment, Cuba's 2019 constitutional change was an aversive response to the United States.

D. Transnational Engagement

Council of State Secretary Homero Acosta reported to the National Assembly that members of the Commission consulted "several constitutions, first from Latin American countries, among them Venezuela, Bolivia, and Ecuador, which represent the most advanced constitutional works in the region, as well as other constitutional models like those of Vietnam and China, nations which are constructing socialist societies with their own characteristics, as well as constitutional texts from other countries."[63] Specifically, as in the case of Laos, the transnational constitutional engagement between Cuba and Vietnam was notable. In October 2013, Homero Acosta led a delegation from the Cuban Council of State to visit Vietnam when the latter was in the final stage of creating the 2013 Constitution. Homero Acosta met Vietnam's National Assembly Vice-Chairman Uong Chu Luu, who was also Vice-Chairman of Vietnam Constitutional Amendment Committee, and the two leaders "discussed a wide range of issues related to constitutional amendments."[64] There was a more recent engagement when Cuba's Commission was preparing the first draft of the Constitution: on July 6, 2018, the General Secretary of the Confederation of Cuban Workers Ulises Guilarte Nacimiento met Uong Chu Luu in Hanoi, and they also discussed their experience of constitutional

[61] "The White House, Remarks by President Trump to the Venezuelan American Community" (*The White House*, February 18, 2019) <https://www.whitehouse.gov/briefings-statements/remarks-president-trump-venezuelan-american-community/> accessed December 22, 2019.

[62] "Cuba Votes in Referendum on New Constitution that President Miguel Diaz-Canel Says is Also a 'Vote for Venezuela'" (*South China Morning Post*, February 25, 2019) <https://www.scmp.com/news/world/americas/article/2187517/cuba-votes-referendum-new-constitution-president-miguel-diaz> accessed December 22, 2019.

[63] Acosta, "A New Constitution with Transformational Purpose" (n 18).

[64] "Vietnam, Cuba Exchange Experiences on Constitutional Amendments" (*Nhan Dan Online*, October 16, 2013) <http://en.nhandan.com.vn/politics/external-relations/item/2082302-vietnam-cuba-exchange-experiences-on-constitutional-amendments.html> accessed December 22, 2019.

amendment.[65] After the Constitution's adoption, in June 2019, Council of State Secretary Homero Acosta Alvarez led a Cuban delegation to Ho Chi Minh City, gave a briefing about Cuba's new Constitution and stated that underlined learning from Vietnamese experience in drafting the Constitution resulted in many similarities with Vietnam regarding the state structure and local government's financial and administrative autonomy.[66]

Cuba's transnational engagement with the constitutional experience in Latin American and socialist countries can be explained by the logic of constitutional learning: countries tend to reference the constitutional experience of the neighboring countries and countries sharing the same political regime. In addition, as Cuba's constitution-maker tried to reserve the core values of socialist constitutional order, they refused to refer to the constitutional experience of western liberal democracies.

One distinctive feature in Cuba's 2019 constitution-making process is the external engagement of the Cuban diaspora community. This engagement is both formal and informal. Two formal mechanisms are available: virtual and physical. In the first instance, an online platform managed by the Ministry of Foreign Affairs provided the forum for some 1.4 million Cubans living in some 120 countries and the Cuban diaspora to comment on the draft Constitution during the consultation process. They could also engage in constitutional debates through the official website called *Cuba.Debate* created by the Association of Cuban Journalist Against Terrorism. As a physical mechanism, Cubans abroad could present and discuss hundreds of proposals and comments on the draft constitution in the meetings of state missions. Such meetings were held in Panama, Spain, Angola, Ecuador, El Salvador, Uruguay, and elsewhere.[67]

This formal external engagement in the constitution-making process is due to two factors. First, the Cuban government extended the extraterritorial constitutional consultation to consolidate the external legitimacy of the Constitution: the acceptance of the Constitution by the Cuban community abroad. Second, many substantial constitutional issues are international: principles of international relations, universal human rights, climate change, foreign investment, dual citizenship, and the rights of foreigners. Notably, the issue of dual citizenship and

[65] VNA, "Cuba Looks to Learn From Vietnam's Constitutional Amendment" (Vietnam Plus, 6 July 2018) <https://en.vietnamplus.vn/cuba-looks-to-learn-from-vietnams-constitutional-amendment/134198.vnp> accessed December 22, 2019.

[66] "Cuba học hỏi kinh nghiệm cải cách tư pháp của Việt Nam" [Cuba learns from Vietnamese Experience in Judicial Reform] (*Báo ảnh Việt Nam*, June 15, 2019) <https://vietnam.vnanet.vn/vietnamese/cuba-hoc-hoi-kinh-nghiem-cai-cach-tu-phap-cua-viet-nam/420266.html> accessed December 22, 2019.

[67] Backer and others, "Popular Participation in the Constitution of the Illiberal State" (n 6) 43; PL, "Cubans Abroad Continue Discussing Draft Constitution" (*PERIODICO*, September 18, 2018) <http://www.periodico26.cu/index.php/en/culture/item/11997-cubans-abroad-continue-discussing-draft-constitution> accessed December 22, 2019.

foreign investments are highly relevant to the Cuban diaspora community, and this explained the external dimension of the constitutional consultation process.

However, one of the most intriguing external aspects of Cuba's constitution-making process is the engagement of Cuban residents overseas and the Cuban diaspora in the consultation process through informal digital platforms outside the state structure. Since the cost of internet accession (USD $2 per hour) considerably outruns the average salary,[68] online engagement in the constitutional debates is affordable only to a limited number of wealthy local citizens and the Cuban diaspora. Cuban citizens residing overseas and members of the Cuban diaspora were able to engage in constitutional debates through unofficial platforms, such as the *Postdata.club* website created by four University of Havana academics, and its Facebook group called *Reforma Constitucional de la República de Cuba* followed by 2,154 members. [69] Outside the state's control, comments in the informal platforms were highly critical, e.g. the calls for a no vote in the referendum and the elimination of socialism in the Constitution, although such comments also echoed controversial issues discussed in formal venues, such as gay marriage.[70]

The informal mechanisms, despite radical comments leading to no substantive constitutional changes, should not be dismissed as irrelevant. The government may rely on the informal comments to gauge the extent to which their reformist model of political, social, and economic development is supported or resisted externally. The availability of the informal mechanism also "allowed non-governmental organizations based in the West to conduct advocacy campaigns on the Cuban constitutional referendum" and "avoid or at least reduced the use of government-approved websites by human rights groups based outside Cuba."[71] In addition, the informal online mechanisms generated an extraterritorial constitutional dialogue between the internal and external Cubans. This dialogue may have fostered a connection of the external Cubans to their home or lineage and may have induced a nostalgic sentiment which may have affected their positive views and actions related to substantive constitutional choices of dual citizenship and foreign investment.

IV. Progressive Change

Formally, the 2019 Constitution replaces the 1976 Constitution. Therefore, the formal structure of the Constitution is considerably reconstructed. While the previous charter was divided into chapters, the new one is comprised of larger

[68] Personal experience in Havana and personal conversations with local citizens, June, Havana, 2019.
[69] Backer and others, "Popular Participation in the Constitution of the Illiberal State" (n 6) 41–4.
[70] Ibid. 70–1.
[71] Ibid. 46.

"titles" many of which are constituted by chapters. In addition to the last "special provisions" and "transitionary provisions" dealing with constitutional implementation, the text includes eleven titles as below:

- Title I: Political Foundations, divided into Chapter 1—Political Principles and Chapter II—International Relations
- Title II: Economic Foundations
- Title III: Foundations of Educational, Scientific, and Cultural Policy
- Title IV: Citizenship
- Title V: Rights, Duties, and Guarantees, divided into Chapter I—General Provisions, Chapter II—Rights, Chapter III—Family, Chapter IV—Duties, and Chapter VI—Guarantees of the Rights
- Title VI: Structure of State, divided into Chapter I—Principles of Organization and Functioning of the Organs of the State, Chapter II—National Assembly of the People's Power and Council of State, Chapter III—President and Vice President of the Republic, Chapter IV—Government of the Republic, Chapter V—Tribunals of Justice, Chapter VI—Office of the Attorney General of the Republic, Chapter VII—Office of the Controller General of the Republic, and Chapter VIII—Of the Normative Provisions.
- Title VII—Territorial Organization of the State.
- Title VIII—Local Organs of the People's Power, divided into Chapter I—Provincial Government of the People's Power, and Chapter II—Municipal Organs of the People's Power,
- Title IX—Election System, divided into Chapter I—General Provisions, and Chapter II—National Electoral Council
- Title X—Defense and National Security, divided into Chapter I—General Provisions, Chapter II—Council of National Defense, Chapter III—Armed Institutions of the State, and Chapter IV—Exceptional Situations and Situations of Disaster
- Title XI—Reform of the Constitution.

Substantively, the general impression tends to be that the Constitution seeks to advance the country economically and socially while reserving socialism politically and ideologically.[72] In particular, constitutional changes that received considerable international and local attention concern private ownership, market economy, foreign investment, and the new definition of family.[73] The constitutional

[72] James A. Baer, "Cuban Constitution of 2019" (*CoHA*, April 11, 2019) <http://www.coha.org/cuban-constitution-of-2019/> accessed December 22, 2019; Cuba's New Constitution: Socialism Preserved, Private Property Approved (*People's World*, February 27, 2019) <https://www.peoplesworld.org/article/cubas-new-constitution-socialism-preserved-private-property-approved/> accessed December 22, 2019.

[73] My conversations with local lawyers and ordinary citizens during my field trip confirm the local attentions on these issues. For international attention, see, for example, E. McKirdy, "Cubans

liberalization of the economy is obviously significant. However, all five socialist constitutional cores are adapted despite the constitutional reservation of socialism. The following sections examine these adaptive changes in detail.

A. The Dynamic Constitution

Cuba's Constitution remains an instrument for political control, but the process of changing the Constitution creates an opportunity for a national and transnational constitutional dialogue. The dynamic national constitutional dialogue is between the party-state and the public. Consequently, the substantive changes in the new Constitution are not merely the consequence of authoritarian imposition but also reflect the outcome of public discourse, evidenced by the changes to constitutional text after the consultation process. In addition, the Constitution-making process also engenders a transnational constitutional dialogue between the internal and external Cubans, and between the Cuban states and other socialist states and the neighboring states. As the consequence of national and transnational constitutional dialogue, the Constitution changes to reflect not only the party's instrumental interests but also to address the local citizens' concerns to improve their living conditions. This is particularly evident in some notable changes to empower citizens and liberalize the economy.

The Constitution remains an instrument to institutionalize the party's new policy for social progress, but the juridification of the Constitution is evident to some extent. Technically, while the Constitution is largely a programmatic document replete with political and ideological jargon, it employs more legalistic terms and expressions. The substantive changes are more important. The first article defines Cuba as "a socialist state of law" (Article 1). Like China and Vietnam, Cuba now aspires to implement a socialist version of the rule of law. This signals a commitment to legality in the structure and the use of state power while retaining the socialist nature of the legal and political systems.

The commitment to the socialist state of law yields consequence for the legalistic nature of the Constitution. Several new articles are introduced to underline the legal nature of the Constitution and constitutional supremacy. To illustrate, Article 3 provides that the people's power is exercised through their representatives according to the forms created by the Constitution. Article 7 establishes that "the Constitution is the supreme juridical norms of state" and mandates that all state bodies must observe constitutional provisions. While these provisions are not necessarily a commitment to constitutionalism, the regime attempts to subject

Overwhelmingly Vote in Favor of New Constitution" (*CNN*, February 26, 2019) <https://edition.cnn.com/2019/02/25/americas/cuba-votes-new-constitution-intl/index.html> accessed December 22, 2019.

the use of political power to constitutional norms. Article 8 creates the primacy of the Constitution over the international treaties that Cuba had signed. Article 10 stipulates that state organs must subject themselves to the people's control according to the constitutional rules. In an institutional setting when judicial review of constitutionality is absent, this provision potentially enables the political control of constitutionality of the state actions via mechanisms deployed by the public, such as referendums, popular initiatives of legal reform and constitutional amendment, and other forms of public participation (Article 80).

B. Constitutionalizing the Party

Party vanguardism remains the identity of the socialist constitutional order in Cuba but is adaptive to local contexts. The new provision on the party leadership reads: "The Communist Party of Cuba, sole, *martiano* [of Marti], *fidelista* [of Fidel], Marxist and Leninist, organized vanguard of the Cuban nation, based on [*sustentado*] its democratic character and the permanent link with the people, is the superior directive political force of society and of the State. It organizes and it orients the common efforts in the construction of socialism and the progress towards the communist society. It works to preserve and to strengthen the patriotic unity of Cubans and to develop ethical, moral and civic values" (Article 5).

Therefore, like the previous Constitution, party vanguardism together with its communist ideology—Marxism and Leninism—is constitutionalized. This constitutionalization of party leadership aims to ensure the social progress toward socialism and ultimately communism in the country. While the constitutional mandate of the party's monopolist power is the identity shared with the four other socialist countries, Cuba is unique in the continued commitment to achieving communism. The reservation of revolution's commitment to communism is due mainly to public support during the constitutional consultation process.

The party constitutionalization, however, has several new features. First, in addition to Marxism-Leninism and *martiano*, Fidel Castro's ideology is now constitutionally confirmed as the official ideology of the party. Apart from the aforementioned Article 5, the new constitutional preamble considers Fidel Castro's ideology (along with other communist and nationalist ideologies) the guiding ideology of the regime. Fidel now joins Ho Chi Minh, Mao Zedong, Deng Xiaoping, Xi Jinping, Kim Il-sung, and Kim Jong-il to have his ideology inserted in the constitutional preamble. The second feature of constitutional vanguardism concerns the relationship between the party and the people: the party's "democratic character" and its "permanent link with the people." The Constitution aims to legitimize the party's vanguard role in the populist base. Populism is expressed in formal constitutional design. Finally, party vanguardism blends communist and nationalist commitments. The party's leadership aims not only to achieve the socialist and communist goal but also to consolidate patriotism, national unity, and nationalist moral and civic values. The attachment to nationalist grounds would lend more legitimacy to party vanguardism.

C. Distributing Power

Like the previous Constitution, the 2019 charter stipulates that the state structure is organized and functions according to the principle of "socialist democracy," which is, in fact, the Cuban version of "democratic centralism." Article 101 articulates eight points about the substantial aspects of "socialist democracy." On the "democratic" side, the representatives are elected by the people; the people control the work of state institutions; elected persons are accountable and can be removed from their offices; state institutions perform their work transparently; and the freedom of discussion and the exercise of criticism and self-criticism in state institutions (Article 101). On the socialist or centralist sides, the regulations of the superior state institutions are obligatory for the inferior ones; the inferior state institutions are responsible to the superior ones and rend accounts to them in their administration; and the minority is subordinate to the majority (Article 101).

In consistence with that principle of "socialist democracy," the overall centralized constitutional structure has basically remained intact despite the formal constitutional replacement. The National Assembly of the People's Power is the supreme state institution, exercising constituent power, legislative power, and the supreme supervisory power over other state institutions (Articles 102, 103, and 108). The President, the Council of Ministers (the executive), the People's Supreme Tribunal (the highest court), and the Office of the Attorney General are created by the National Assembly and therefore report to it (Article 109).

Yet, the overall tendency is to make the power less concentrated and more accountable by distributing it to different central and local institutions. This is evident by the following new features in the Constitution regarding state institutions.

First, the Constitution creates a personal presidency (Title VI, Chapter III) independent from the Council of State. The preceding Constitution followed the Soviet model of Presidium to create the Council of the State with dual functions: the permanent body of the National Assembly and the head of the state with the President of the Council assuming the latter function. The 2019 Constitution distributes these two functions to two separate institutions: the President as the individual head of the state and the Council of the State as the permanent body of the National assembly, the equivalence of the legislature's standing committee in China, Vietnam, and Laos. Notably, the Constitution imposes term limits and age limit on the president (Articles 126, 127). A president can only hold office for two consecutive terms (Article 126). In contrast to the trend of presidential term limit evasion which China joined,[74] Cuba and Laos created term limits on their leaders. In addition, the president elected by the National Assembly must be a minimum age of thirty-five and a maximum age of sixty for the first term (Article 127). The age limit is a constitutional guarantee for the generational change of leadership in Cuba: any future president must be born after the 1959 Revolution.[75] The President is vested with the power to direct foreign policy and policy related to national defense security, to perform the Supreme Command of the armed institutions, and to preside over the Council of National Defense, among others (Article 128). Despite not being popularly elected, the president is not merely a symbol, but a chief executive leader in relation to international affairs, national defense, and national security. This position may reflect the actual influential role of the president in Cuban politics, particularly the role assumed by Fidel Castro for more than three decades. This powerful position explains the calls for direct presidential election during the popular constitutional consultation process. The public might want to attribute a powerful president's legitimacy to the public.

Second, the Constitution establishes the post of Prime Minister alongside the President. The Prime Minister is the Head of the Government in charge of its quotidian operation (Articles 140 and 144). According to the previous Constitution, the President was the head of both the State and the Government. This created a burden for the holder of this post. Therefore, the distribution of two separate functions (the president in charge of foreign affairs and the prime minister in charge of the domestic day-to-day operation of the administrative system) aims to make governance more efficient. After the Constitution was approved in April 2019, Miguel Díaz-Canel still assumed the two posts, as a new election had not yet been held, but the regime expected to have a new separate prime minister by the end of the year.[76]

Third, the Constitution has created several independent institutions with checking functions. The first is the Office of the Controller General whose chief leader is selected by the National Assembly. This office is organized vertically throughout the country. The functions of this office are to oversee the administration of public funds and control over the administrative management (Articles 160, 161, and 209). The Cuban Office of Controller General shares some features with China's Supervision Commissions created by the 2018 constitutional amendment: both are an institution to supervise the transparent operation of the administrative system. The second independent institution newly created by Cuba's 2019

[74] Mila Versteeg et al, "The Law and Politics of Presidential Term Limit Evasion" 120 Columbia Law Review 173 (2020).

[75] Mimi Whitefield, "Cuba Approves New Constitution Amid Unprecedented Opposition. What Changes?" (*Miami Herald*, February 25, 2019) <https://www.miamiherald.com/news/nation-world/world/americas/cuba/article226540775.html> accessed December 22, 2019.

[76] Ibid.; EFE, "New Constitution Proclaimed and Cuba Will Have a Prime Minister This Year" (*Cubanews*, April 11, 2019) <https://oncubanews.com/en/cuba/new-constitution-proclaimed-and-cuba-will-have-a-prime-minister-this-year/> accessed December 22, 2019.

Constitution is the National Election Council, a body to organize and supervise the elections, popular consultations, plebiscites, and referendums (Article 211). As mentioned before, this institution was also created in the new constitutions of Vietnam and Laos. The creation of the new independent institutions in Cuba's Constitution may in part be due to the country's transnational engagement in constitution-making, especially with socialist countries.

Fourth, in addition to the horizontal distribution of the central powers, the Constitution strengthens local autonomy through a vertical distribution. Local government includes the provincial and municipal levels. At the provincial level, two new institutions are created, namely the Governor and the Provincial Council. The Governor is the executive leader of the province, selected by the corresponding delegates of the municipal assemblies (Articles 174 and 195). The creation of this post aims to strengthen individual authority and responsibility in the local administration. The Provincial Council is a deliberative institution, presided over by the Governor and constituted by the vice-Governor, presidents and vice-presidents of the corresponding local assemblies and the municipal intendants (Article 182). This Council approves and supervises the economic plan and the budget of the province, and co-ordinates other local political, social, and cultural activities (Article 184). The creation of this Council aims to facilitate the autonomy of provinces in deciding and managing their local affairs.

D. Universalizing Human Rights

In the new Constitution, statism continues to dominate rights provisions but has been mitigated by the universalist discourse of human rights. The Title V on rights and duties is rather long, including sixty articles divided into six chapters: Chapter I on general principles of rights; Chapter II on particular rights; Chapter III on families; Chapter IV on particular duties; Chapter V on the rights and duties of foreigners; and Chapter VI is devoted to mechanisms of right protections.

On the one hand, rights remain strongly statist. Rights depend on the state for their realization. The Constitution provides that the state makes rights effective through its public policies and law (Article 44). Therefore, rights provisions are often accompanied by the articulation of the state policy to implement these rights. For example, the Constitution provides for the right to adequate housing, and stipulates that the state makes this right possible through its programs of construction, rehabilitation, and conservation of housing (Article 71). This right provision is, in fact, the articulation of the state's housing policy. The same can be said of other provisions on the rights to public health and education, among many others.

On the other hand, there are notable changes, indicating the influence of the universalist discourse of human rights evident in the principles of rights and particular rights provisions. In the first aspect, the Constitution adopts universal principles of human rights. To begin with, it recognizes human dignity as the "supreme value" foundational to the particular rights and duties enshrined in the Constitution (Article 40). Secondly, the document explicitly employs the universal language of human rights. Article 41 provides that: "The Cuban State recognizes and guarantees to the person the non-renounceable, non-prescriptible, indivisible, universal and interdependent enjoyment and exercise of human rights, in correspondence with the principals of progressivity, equality and non-discrimination. Their respect and guarantee is the obligatory fulfillment for all." This is the first time the phrase "human rights" has appeared in the socialist Constitution of Cuba.

Based on these principles, the chapter on particular individual rights features a new format and substances resonant with the universalist language of rights. In the first instance, while the 1976 Constitution began with the right (and duty) to work and then moved on to other social rights and then political rights, the 2019 document started off with personal rights and proceeds to political freedoms, and then social economic and cultural rights. While the previous structure of right provisions was shaped by the Marxist conception of the workers as the ruling class, the new structure of the rights chapter resonates with the structure of rights in international human rights treaties. In terms of substance, while the previous Constitution listed around nineteen rights, the chapter on individual rights in the new Constitution included thirty-four articles, not to mention right provisions in other chapters. Following Benedikt Goderis and Mila Versteeg,[77] I have divided these rights into seven categories below with a focus on newly introduced rights.

(1) On *life, liberty, physical integrity, and privacy*, new development includes the right to life (Article 46), free development of personality (Article 47), the right to family privacy (Article 48), prohibition of torture (Article 51), and freedom of movement (Article 52).

(2) On *political, democratic, and accountability rights*, the right to information about the government (Article 53), freedom of thought (Article 54), and the right to participation (Article 80) have been newly introduced. Notably, Cuba's Constitution is the only document among the five current socialist constitutions to include the freedom of thought. The recognition of freedom of thought is a disharmonic development given Marxism-Leninism was constitutionally established as the officially ideology of the party. This development is due in part to the constitutional incorporation of the nationalist, non-communist ideology (*martiano*) and in part to the emergence of plural values, concepts, and interests as the consequence of domestic social dynamics (e.g. the rise of private economic sectors) and the impact of global diffusion of ideas from the outside world into Cuba. Apart from the freedom

[77] Benedikt Goderis and Mila Versteeg, "The Diffusion of Constitutional Rights" (2014) 39 International Review of Law and Economics 6–7.

of thought, the Constitution stipulates the right to participate in the creation, exercise, and control of the state power (Article 80). The Constitution also stipulates the detailed mechanisms to practice this right, including: to be inscribed in the electoral register; to propose and appoint candidates; to elect and be elected; to participate in elections, plebiscites, referendums, popular consultations, and other forms of participation; to decide on the rendition of accounts that elected persons present to citizens; to revoke the mandate of the elected; to exercise legislative initiative and the initiative of constitutional amendment; to perform public functions and offices; and to be informed of the administration of the organs and authorities of the State (Article 80). Given the absence of judicial review, these are political mechanisms formally available for the citizens to oversee the use of the public power.

(3) On *fair trial*, the Constitution includes the right of access to court (habeas corpus) (Article 96), presumption of innocence (Article 95), and right to legal assistance from the initiation of the criminal process (Article 95).

(4) On *equality rights*, the Constitution continues the protection of equality under the law and newly includes a provision prohibiting any form of discrimination. Article 42 stipulates that: "All persons are equal before the law, receive the same protection and treatment from the authorities and enjoy the same rights, freedoms and opportunities, without any discrimination for reason of sex, gender, sexual orientation, identity of gender, age, ethnic origin, color of the skin, religious belief, disability, national or territorial origin, or any other personal condition or circumstance that implies [a] prejudicial [lesiva] distinction to human dignity. All have the right to enjoy the same public spaces and establishments of services. In the same way, they receive the same salary for the same work, without any discrimination. The violation of this principal of equality is proscribed and is sanctioned by the law."

(5) On *social-economic rights*, the Constitution is elaborate in this area given its socialist characters. Apart from the rights inherited from the previous Constitution (e.g. the right to work, education, social security, and health care), the 2019 document includes these new rights: the right to housing (Article 71), the right to water (Article 76), and the right to food security (Article 77).

(6) On *women, children, and family*, the chapter on families, a part of the rights Title, deals with eight fundamental rights regarding family formation, marriage, specific protection of women and children, and protection against family violence. Notably, the chapter provides for the right to establish a family, one among various forms of family is marriage defined as "a social and juridical institution" (Article 82). The constitutional definition of marriage was controversially debated during the constitution-making process. The new provision opens for the door for same-sex marriage, although it does not explicitly use that language in response to the resistance during the constitutional consultation episode.

(7) On *other rights*, new developments include the right to participate in cultural and artist activities (Article 79), the right to a healthy environment (Article 75), right of disabled people (Article 89), right of consumers (Article 78). Other developments in other right-related provisions (albeit not included in the rights Title) should be considered. In addition to the right to a healthy environment, the Constitution acknowledges the threat of climate change to "the survival of the human species" and hence stipulates that the state is committed to the promotion of environmental protection (Article 16). This provision echoes the global discourse of environmental protection and its relation to human rights protection.[78] Another new change is the constitutional recognition of dual citizenship. Article 33 provides that "The acquisition of another citizenship does not imply the loss of Cuban Citizenship." Dual citizenship, which becomes "a commonplace of globalization," is relevant to human rights, the right to acquire nationality.[79] Cuba's constitutional recognition of dual citizenship may be a response to the massive refugee flow to the United States in history[80] and the recent Cuban immigrants to Latin American and European countries.[81] The latter is mainly due to the impact of globalization, and the Constitution tends to encourage migrants to retain their Cuban citizenship while acquiring another nationality.

In short, while rights are statist and depend on the state for their implementation, the language of rights in Cuba's new Constitution is now more universalist. Human rights and their universal principles are formally adopted, and fundamental rights familiar in the international human right treaties are formally incorporated into the Constitution. Rights statism remains hegemonic but is modified by rights universalism.

E. Marketizing the Economy

While the constitutional economy remains predominantly statist, it incorporates market elements. This dual nature is captured in the first article of Title II on Economic Foundations, which provides for "a system of socialist economy" (Article 18). On the statist side, the system is based on: (1) state ownership of the fundamental means of production as the principal form of ownership; and (2) the

[78] "Human Rights and the Environment" (*United Nations Environment Program*) <http://web.unep.org/divisions/delc/human-rights-and-environment> accessed December 22, 2019.

[79] Peter J. Spiro, "Dual Citizenship as Human Right" (2010) 8 International Journal of Constitutional Law 111, 111–12.

[80] See generally, G. J. Grenier, L. Perez, and N. Foner, *The Legacy of Exile: Cubans in the United States* (Pearson 2002).

[81] Jorge Duany, "Cuban Migration: A Postrevolution Exodus Ebbs and Flows" (*Migration Policy Institute*, July 6, 2017) <https://www.migrationpolicy.org/article/cuban-migration-postrevolution-exodus-ebbs-and-flows> accessed December 22, 2019.

planned direction of the economy (Ibid.). At the same time, the state "considers, regulates and control the market as a function of the interests of society" (Ibid.). On that base, market elements are introduced into the Constitution.

The first is the constitutional recognition of private ownership. The Constitution provides for multiple forms of ownership, including: socialist ownership (or state's ownership), co-operative ownership; ownership of the mass organizations; the private ownership "with a complementary role in the economy"; the mixed ownership formed by two or more forms of ownership; ownership by institutions and associative forms; and personal ownership (Article 22). The recognition of private ownership is one of the most important constitutional changes as this facilitates the development of private economic sectors and enables citizens to conduct business to earn income, the practice traditionally condemned as capitalist evil in the communist view.

In addition to private ownership, the Constitution encourages foreign investment. Article 28 provides that "the State promotes and give guarantees to foreign investment, as an important element of the economic development of the country." Private ownership by foreigners is also recognized (Article 22). The Constitution in fact seeks to attract foreign investment to assist with domestic economic difficulties. These new provisions allow for the establishment of foreign enterprises in Cuba.

To support the development of the economy, the Constitution provides that "The State promotes the advancement of science, technology and innovation as essential elements for economic and social development" (Article 21). This provision intellectually reflects Marxist materialism which considers the advancement of science and technology the basis for social progress.

Thus, while the constitutional economy remains predominantly statist, it has incorporated market elements, particularly private ownership and foreign investment. Although private economic sectors and foreign investment have emerged in Cuba in recent years,[82] the constitutional protection provides a solid foundation for their further development.

V. Conclusion

The 2019 progressive constitutional change in Cuba improves the socialist constitutional system and facilitates the active role of the party-state in improving the material wellbeing of living conditions of the local citizens. Constitutional change reserves the revolutionary commitments to communism and "socialist

[82] Kevin J. Fandl, "Trading with the Enemy: Opening the Door to U.S. Investment in Cuba" (2018) 49 Georgetown Journal of International Law 563.

democracy." The adherence to Cuban Caribbean Marxism informs and legitimizes the process and substance of constitutional change.

While the core features of the socialist constitutional order are basically retained, they are considerably adapted to respond to the internal and external changing environment. Consequently, Cuba's 2019 Constitution is a dissonant document. Internally, the Constitution includes seemingly contradictory and ambiguous commitments: a socialist state of law and constitutional supremacy under party vanguardism; nationalist and communist ideologies; "socialist democracy" which both centralizes and distributes power and facilitates deliberation; universal human rights regulated by the state; a centrally planned economy promoting private ownership and foreign investment. In addition, the Constitution includes many aspirational socialist commitments (e.g. political freedom, equity, justice and social equality, well-being, and individual and collective prosperity)[83] disharmonic with the real society. Finally, there is a gap between the entrenched socialist constitutional norms (e.g. party vanguardism) and normative constitutionalist ideals (e.g. political pluralism) promoted by some sectors of the society in unofficial venues during the Constitution-making process.

These constitutional disharmonies provide the conditions for the continued constitutional dynamics in Cuba. The constitutional disharmonies matter because the party-state is committed to continued economic and legal reform within the new constitutional framework.[84] In addition, the disharmonies matter because the civil society in Cuba is becoming increasingly dynamic in engaging in public discourse,[85] including constitutional discourse as displayed during the constitutional consultation process. The gap between aspirational constitutional commitments and society may compel the party-state to incrementally bridge the gap through law-making and policy-making. The ambiguous constitutional language and the normative constitutional dissonance may create the space for public discourse and mobilization.

[83] Constitution of the Republic of Cuba (2019), art. 3.

[84] Associated Press, "Cuba's New Constitution Could Reshape Government, Economy, Rights" (*NBCNews*, March 14, 2019) <https://www.nbcnews.com/news/latino/cuba-s-new-constitution-could-reshape-government-economy-rights-n983136> accessed December 22, 2019.

[85] Lennier López, "Cuban Civil Society: Survival, Struggle, Defiance and Compliance" (*Civicus*) <https://www.civicus.org/index.php/re-imagining-democracy/stories-from-the-frontlines/3402-cuban-civil-society-survival-struggle-defiance-and-compliance> discussing recent works on civil society in Cuba, including: Marie Laure Geoffray, *Contester à Cuba* (Dalloz 2012); Marlene Azor, *Discursos de la resistencia: Los proyectos políticos emergentes en Cuba* (Editorial Hypermedia 2016); Velia C. Bobes, "Reformas en Cuba: ¿Actualización del socialismo o reconfiguración social?" (2016) 44 Cuban Studies 1.

7

The Exceptional Model

China

Introduction

On May 11, 2018, the National People's Congress of China adopted amendments to its 1982 Constitution which revoked its presidential term limit. While the amendments included several other substantive changes, they received wide domestic and international attention largely because of the revocation. In addition to national accounts,[1] several comparative constitutional law scholars have responded in a timely manner to these amendments in their academic research. China prominently features in Mila Versteeg and her co-authors' empirical account of the "global trend" of presidential term limit evasion.[2] The 2018 amendments are also the main topic in Taisu Zhang and Tom Ginsburg's treatment on legality in contemporary China.[3] Prior to 2018, China amended its 1982 Constitution several times, in 1988, 1993, 1999, and 2004, but these amendments have not been as substantively discussed in comparative constitutional law studies as the 2018 one. The international and comparative attention to the 2018 amendments is mainly due to the fact that these amendments respond to globalization or resonate with global phenomena. While the 1988 and 1993 amendments, explored in the previous chapter, responded to the fall of the Soviet bloc, the three amendments in 1999, 2004, and 2018 were a response to globalization, among other things. This chapter focuses on the latter: China's three constitutional amendments in the global era.

These amendments are basically progressive: they improve the socialist constitutional system and facilitate the role of the party-state in improving the living conditions of the local people. China's Constitution and its amendment processes are surrounded by controversial constitutional dynamics, including the *weiquan* (rights defense) movement, Charter 08, and the 2013 *xianzheng*

[1] Lin Feng, "The 2018 Constitutional Amendments: Significance and Impact on the Theories of Party-state Relationship in China" (2019) 1 China Perspectives 11; Keith J. Hand, "Constitutional Supervision in China after the 2018 Amendment of the PRC Constitution: Refining the Narrative of Constitutional Supremacy in a Socialist Legal System" [2019] UC Hastings Research Paper (forthcoming); available at SSRN: https://ssrn.com/abstract=3431293.

[2] Mila Versteeg et al, "The Law and Politics of Presidential Term Limit Evasion" (2020) 120 Columbia Law Review 173.

[3] Taisu Zhang and Tom Ginsburg, "China's Turn Toward Law" (2019) 59 Virginia Journal of International Law 278.

Constitutional Change in the Contemporary Socialist World. Bui Ngoc Son, Oxford University Press (2020). © Bui Ngoc Son.
DOI: 10.1093/oso/9780198851349.001.0001.

(constitutionalism) debate, which struggled for rights and constitutional change. This chapter examines the formal constitutional change and the functional constitutional dynamics. It demonstrates that, in the era of globalization, constitutional change in China is being shaped by Chinese constitutional exceptionalism: the country's confident attitude and belief in developing its own socialist constitutional model as a competitive alternative to those of the West.

Constitutional exceptionalism is a part of the broader picture of Chinese exceptionalism. The Chinese government is attempting to construct "socialism with Chinese characteristics," the national project of the sinolization of Marxist ideals of socialism, as an alternative model of social development to the West. Economically, China has practiced the "socialist market economy." The success of economic reform has resulted in China's "socialist market economy" becoming the world's second largest economy by normal GDP.[4] China has not only attempted to become the alternative economic power to the US in the global economic order, but the Chinese government has also supported the revitalization of the nation's cultural values, such as some elements of Confucianism deemed to be compatible with socialism, as an alternative to Western culture.[5] Technologically, China is also capable of creating alternatives to Western innovations like Google or Facebook.[6] Chinese exceptionalism is salient not only in the economic, technological, and cultural spheres, but also in the constitutional domain. China's emergence as a global economic power has given it the confidence to develop its own socialist constitutional model as a competitive alternative to Western constitutional models.

Chinese constitutional exceptionalism informs the motivations, process, and contents of formal constitutional amendments, and determines the outcomes of functional constitutional dynamics. Constitutional change is motivated by the incentive to incorporate local leaders' distinctive socialist constitutional ideologies and to counter the influence of constitutional globalization. The process of constitutional change is shaped by China's distinctive model of non-participatory, ordinary amendment under party-supremacy. Exceptionalism is also at the root of the party-state's resistance to constitutional mobilization and its aversive attitude toward Western models of constitutionalism. Finally, exceptionalism and resistant constitutionalism inform the progressive changes to the functions and contents of the Constitution. In particular, the 2018 constitutionalization of the party leadership, Xi Jinping's ideology, term limit removal, anti-corruption institutions, and

[4] Elana Holondy, "China's GDP is Expected to Surpass the US' in 11 years" (*Business Insider*, June 25, 2015) <http://www.businessinsider.sg/chinas-gdp-is-expected-to-surpass-the-us-in-11-years-2015-6/?r=US&IR=T#.V0UQ9eRUVBE> accessed December 14, 2019.

[5] Jeremy Page, "Why China Is Turning Back to Confucius" (*The Wall Street Journal*, September 20, 2015) <http://www.wsj.com/articles/why-china-is-turning-back-to-confucius-1442754000> accessed December 14, 2019.

[6] Sudhiir Krishnan, "Top 5 Alternative Social Networking websites in China!" (*GIZBO*, February 27, 2016) <http://www.gizbot.com/internet/features/top-5-alternative-social-networking-websites-china-031577.html> accessed December 14, 2019.

legislative constitutional review sends a strong, exceptional, and resistant signal to the domestic and international critics of China's moves in the opposite direction to Western constitutional models.

This chapter is structured as follows. Section I explains the factors of the constitutional amendments. Section II analyzes the legal and procedural features of the amendments and the surrounding dynamics. Section III examines the substantive contents of the progressive constitutional change. Section IV concludes.

I. Factors

The 1999 constitutional amendments were introduced after Chinese reformist Deng Xiaoping died in early 1997, and the Party's Fifteenth Congress in September of the year adopted "Deng Xiaoping's Theory" as the official ideology of the Party, along with Marxism-Leninism and Mao Zedong Thought. At that Congress, the Party articulated a new program for continuing reforms during the post-Deng era. Constitutional amendments became necessary to codify Dengism and the Party's post-Deng vision for social progress toward socialism.

Apart from the leadership and party policy changes, the 1999 amendments were driven by the larger process of globalization. By that time, China had joined most of the major international bodies except for the World Trade Organization (WTO).[7] The Constitution was amended in 1999 to facilitate China's accession to the WTO, which was eventually achieved in 2001. The accession was driven by both internal and international dynamics: the rapid domestic development of the national economy after two decades of Dengist reform; and its success in attracting considerable foreign investment (foreign trade accounting for 34 percent of GDP by 1998).[8] Accession to the WTO would benefit China politically and economically: the international prestige conferred by WTO membership, and accession to the global market.[9] The accession to this global economic community requires commitment to market institutions (non-discrimination and market opening) and the principles of the rule of law (transparency and predictability).[10] The amendments were introduced when China was entering the final stages of the process of accession to the WTO: conclusions of bilateral market-access negotiations and conclusions of multilateral negotiations in the Working Party.[11]

[7] Q. Kong, "China's WTO Accession: Commitments and Implications" (2000) 3 Journal of International Economic Law 34, 659.

[8] Ibid. 657.

[9] Ibid. 660–1.

[10] J.L. Gertler, "China's WTO Accession—the Final Countdown" in *China and the World Trading System: Entering the New Millennium* (Deborah Z. Cass, Brett G. Williams, and George Barker (eds), Cambridge University Press 2003) 55, 61–2.

[11] Ibid., 55, 56.

Understandably, to facilitate the negotiation process at this critical moment, the 1999 constitutional amendments signaled to the world China's commitment to the rule of law and market institutions at the most significant level.

Yet, by the time of the amendments, China had already emerged "as a regional power and even a potential world power."[12] In 1998, China's President Jiang Zeming pointed out one of the principles for China to adopt in its pursuit of WTO membership: WTO as a global trade organization "would be incomplete without the participation of China, the largest developing country in the world."[13] China longed to be an essential player in the global economic community, not one controlled by it. The amendments, therefore, signaled to the world that China was committed to the rule of law and market institutions, but would implement these commitments in its own way: the "socialist rule of law state" and the larger "socialism with Chinese characteristics."

Similar to the 1999 circle, the 2004 constitutional amendments were animated by the transfer of political leadership and a change in policy by the Party. Hu Jintao succeeded Jiang Zemin as the most senior political leader in 2002. The Sixteenth Party Congress took place in December 2002, and articulated a new program for socio-economic development. In March 2003, Wu Banguo, the new Chairman of the Standing Committee of the People's Congress, stated that it was necessary to amend the Constitution to be consistent with the policy adopted at the Party Congress.[14] Thus, constitutional amendment was driven by the need to incorporate the Party's new reformist policy. Besides responding to domestic factors, the 2004 amendments also responded to global pressures. The first concerned international human rights law. China ratified the International Covenant on Economic, Social, and Cultural Rights in 2001 and signed the International Covenant on Political and Civil Rights in 1998.[15] The international promotion of rights led to a need for the domestic constitutional incorporation of human rights. In addition, economic globalization generated "a stronger demand for a higher level of private property protection from both overseas investors and domestic citizens."[16] Consequently, three major amendments in 2004 included the incorporation of Jiang Zemin's ideology of Three Represents, the protection of human rights generally, and the protection of private property rights, in particular.

[12] Q. Kong, "China's WTO Accession: Commitments and Implications" (n 7) 659.

[13] Kong Qingjing, *China and the World Trade Organization: A Legal Perspective* (World Scientific 2002) 16.

[14] Albert Chen, *Introduction to the Legal System of the Peoples Republic of China* (5th edn, LexisNexis 2019) 52.

[15] Li Li, "China's Constitutional Amendments and Their Implications" (2005) 41(1) China Report 75, 80–1.

[16] Chuanhui Wang, *The Constitutional Protection of Private Property in China: Historical Evolution and Comparative Research* (Cambridge University Press 2016) 8.

After the 2004 amendment, China's Constitution remained without change for fourteen years, until 2018. The aforementioned rounds of formal amendments addressed two of China's major concerns following the fall of the Soviet bloc: institutions to promote economic development and global integration. With the codification of the grand aspiration of "socialism with Chinese characteristics," fundamental institutions of socialist market economy (multi-economic sectors, multi-forms of ownership, protection of private property) and fundamental commitments for international integration (the rule of law and human rights), it seems that China has achieved a stable constitutional framework for social progress toward socialism, in its own way.

However, the three prior amendments mainly addressed the issues of the constitutional economy and left the political constitutional structure largely intact. Economic development at some point will put pressure on political development. China's three decades of economic development and global integration have created new social groups, diverse social interests, and the diffusion into the country of new ideas about a legitimate constitutional structure. These dynamics brought pressure to bear for the constitutional reform of institutional structures. Consequently, China's 1982 Constitution was amended in 2018 to deal with structural issues. The 2018 amendments were introduced when China was strongly confident in pursuing its own way to socialism. President Xi Jinping stated in 2016 that the Chinese people "are fully confident in offering a China solution to humanity's search for better social systems."[17] Such confidence derives from domestic economic development and the country's emergence as a global power in the international political and economic order. The amendment was carried out after *Xi Jinping Thought on Socialism with Chinese Characteristics for a New Era* was incorporated into the party's constitution in the Nineteenth National Congress of the Communist Party in October 2017. As Xi Jinping was elevated to a status equal to that of Mao Zedong and Deng Xiaoping, it became necessary to amend the Constitution to project a new program of social progress toward socialism on the basis of his ideology. Xi's ideology embraces many structural issues (e.g. the supremacy of the Party, a people-centric approach, comprehensive reforms, representative institutions, rule of law-based governance, and Party discipline.)[18] Understandably, the Constitution was amended to address the corresponding structural issues: Xi's ideology, the party leadership, term limit removal, anti-corruption institutions, and legislative constitutional review.

[17] Jessica Chen Weiss, "A World Safe for Autocracy? China's Rise and the Future of Global Politics" (*Foreign Affairs*, July/August 2019) <https://www.foreignaffairs.com/articles/china/2019-06-11/world-safe-autocracy> accessed December 14, 2019.

[18] BBC Monitoring, "His Own Words: The 14 Principles of 'Xi Jinping Thought'" (*BBC*, October 24, 2017) <https://monitoring.bbc.co.uk/product/c1dmwn4r> accessed December 14, 2019.

II. The Law of Change

A. Ordinary Amendment

In theory, the constitutional amendment process in China follows the rules established by the 1982 Constitution. Accordingly, the legislature (the National People's Congress) enjoys the power of amendment as well as the legislative power.[19] Constitutional amendments can be proposed by its Standing Committee or by more than one-fifth of its delegates, and adopted by a two-third majority vote in the legislature.[20] In practice, the amendment process was under the Party's leadership. For example, in the 1999 amendment, the Party's Central Committee created a group in charge of drafting the amendments; in December 1998, the Party discussed internally the first draft of the amendments; in January, the Party submitted the amendment proposal to the National Assembly's Standing Committee for consideration and adoption; and finally, in March 1999, the National People's Congress approved the proposal "word for word."[21] There were twenty-one votes against the amendment proposal, but the dissenting views were not published by any of the public media in China.[22]

The 2004 amendment process was also placed under the Party's leadership, but this circle was considered more "democratic."[23] This was in part because the public consultation (of local government, corporate entities, and scholars) was conducted and digested before drafting the amendment recommendations to be submitted to the Party.[24] Yet, the Party quickly tied the constitutional debate: "A secret instruction was soon issued by the Party to stop all conferences and the publication of academic papers on constitutional reform, and leading economists and legal scholars actively involved in presenting their views were reported to have been harassed by the security forces."[25] The Central Committee of the Party adopted the Suggestions on amending the constitution, which was then converted verbatim into an Amendment Bill, and finally the Bill was adopted by the People's Congress in March 2004.[26]

The Party's initiative of constitutional amendment process is a norm, although this is nowhere specified in the Constitution. In 2014, this living constitutional norm achieved a more official status. In this year, the Party issued a policy document entitled "Central Committee Decision concerning Several Major Issues

[19] Constitution of the People's Republic of China (1982), art. 62 (hereinafter, China's Constitution)
[20] Ibid. art. 64.
[21] Jianfu Chen, *Chinese Law: Context and Transformation* (Brill 2016) 106.
[22] Ibid. 106.
[23] Qianfan Zhang, *The Constitution of China: A Contextual Analysis* (Hart Publishing 2012) 58.
[24] Ibid. 58.
[25] Chen Jianfu, "The Revision of the Constitution in the PRC" (2004) 53 China Perspectives 3.
[26] Ibid. 3–4. *See also* Hal Blanchard, "Constitutional Revisionism in the PRC: Seeking Truth from Facts" (2005) 17 Florida Journal of International Law 365.

in Comprehensively Advancing Governance According to Law," which explicitly states that: "The Party Centre puts suggestions for constitutional revision to the National People's Congress, and constitutional revision is conducted according to the procedure determined in the Constitution."[27] In practice, on January 26, 2018, the Central Committee adopted a proposal for constitutional amendments, which called for (among others) the removal of the term presidential limits and the incorporation of "Xi Jinping Thought" into the constitution, but the proposal was only made public a month later.[28] The practice of the amendment process has therefore been considered a "severe lack of transparency."[29] The amendment process also lacked public participation. "No governmental or Party entity is publicly soliciting comments" on the Party's amendment proposals.[30] Public discussions on the amendment proposal were strictly censored.[31] It is reported that "after the proposed amendments were made public, numerous Chinese people expressed their astonishment, discontent, and even distress through social media. However, such online comments were deleted instantly."[32] At the same time, the official media was employed to defend the amendment proposal: for example, the *Global Times* published this: "Out of rationality and faith, all Chinese people support the [constitutional] amendment and hope it can contribute to our well-being."[33]

The party's amendment proposal was approved by the National People's Congress's Standing Committee at its sessions on January 29 and 30, 2018. On March 11, 2018, the National People's Congress overwhelmingly adopted the final constitutional amendments which were virtually identical to the Party's proposal.[34] China's propaganda machine was then used to praise the constitutional amendments as being "of significance for ensuring the prosperity and lasting security of the Party and the country, and better embodying the aspirations of the people."[35]

[27] "CCP Central Committee Decision concerning Several Major Issues in Comprehensively Advancing Governance According to Law" (*China Law Translate*, October 28, 2014) <https://www.chinalawtranslate.com/fourth-plenum-decision/?lang=en> accessed December 15, 2019.

[28] Changhao Wei, "Translation: Communist Party's Proposals for Amending the P.R.C. Constitution" (*NPC Observer*, February 26, 2018) <https://npcobserver.com/2018/02/25/translation-communist-partys-proposals-for-amending-the-p-r-c-constitution-2018/> accessed December 15, 2019.

[29] Zhang and Ginsburg, "China's Turn Toward Law" (n 3) 328.

[30] Wei, "Translation: Communist Party's Proposals for Amending the P.R.C. Constitution" (n 28).

[31] "China censors in overdrive over possible Constitution amendment, International Federation of Journalists" (*International Federation of Journalist*, February 28, 2018) <https://www.ifj.org/media-centre/news/detail/category/press-releases/article/china-censors-in-overdrive-over-possible-constitution-amendment.html> accessed December 15, 2019.

[32] Charlotte Gao, "The CCP's Proposed Term Limit Change Shocks China" (*The Diplomat*, February 26, 2018) <https://thediplomat.com/2018/02/the-ccps-proposed-term-limit-change-shocks-china/> accessed December 15, 2019.

[33] Ibid.

[34] Wei, "Translation: Communist Party's Proposals for Amending the P.R.C. Constitution" (n 28).

[35] Huan Xiang, "China's Constitutional Revision Accords with the People's Will" (*People's Daily Online*, March 14, 2018) <http://en.people.cn/n3/2018/0314/c90000-9437065.html> accessed December 15, 2019.

The above examples indicate that the Chinese process of constitutional amendment is *ordinary*. The ordinary legislature under the political control of the Communist Party is the institutional platform for constitutional amendment. In addition, the ordinary model of constitutional amendment in China is *exceptional*: the Chinese party-state changed the Constitution in its own way without following the common norms (e.g. participation) of constitutional change.[36] To better understand this, it can be compared with other ordinary models of constitutional amendment. Donald S. Lutz theorizes about an ordinary model of constitutional amendment called *legislative supremacy*: one vote of a dominant legislature is sufficient to amend the constitution.[37] The countries listed as applying this model include Austria, Botswana, Brazil, Germany, India, Kenya, Malaysia, New Zealand, Papua New Guinea, Portugal, and Samoa.[38] China is not on the list, although in theory the legislative vote is sufficient to amend its Constitution. In practice, however, the Chinese amendment process was controlled by *party-supremacy* rather than legislative supremacy. The Chinese legislature is vested with the amendment power in theory, but in practice it adopted proposals and decisions on constitutional amendments made by the Party, and hence constitutional amendment became a part of the Party's ordinary politics. One may argue that the constitutional amendment process in Vietnam and Laos is also controlled by a communist party. This is true, but China is exceptional in the sense that *party-supremacy* dominates constitutional amendment without substantive public participation.

Another ordinary model of constitutional amendment is the *pragmatic model* theorized by Xenophon Contiades and Alkmene Fotiadou.[39] This model is characterized by smooth, efficient, and incremental formal change to the constitution as daily political practice, thanks to the easy amendment formula and/or political compromise.[40] Constitutional change, however, is within judicially protected limits (e.g. eternity clause).[41] This model is illustrated by the German, Austrian, and French experiences.[42] The Chinese model of constitutional amendment shares

[36] For non-participation as an example of exceptionalism in constitutional design, see Justin Blount and Tom Ginsburg, "Participation in Constitutional Design: Asian Exceptionalism" in *Comparative Constitutional Law in Asia* (Rosalind Dixon and Tom Ginsburg (eds), Edward Elgar 2015) 23. Participation is also a norm in constitutional amendment. See generally *Participatory Constitutional Change: The People as Amenders of the Constitution* (Xenophon Contiades and Alkmene Fotiadou (eds), Routledge 2017).

[37] Donald S. Lutz, *Principles of Constitutional Design* (Cambridge University Press 2006) 174. This model is applied in Austria, Botswana, Brazil, Germany, India, Kenya, Malaysia, New Zealand, Papua New Guinea, Portugal, and Samoa.

[38] Ibid.

[39] Xenophon Contiades and Alkmene Fotiadou, "Models of constitutional change" in *Engineering Constitutional Change: A Comparative Perspective on Europe, Canada and the USA* (Xenophon Contiades (ed.), Routledge 2013), 445.

[40] Ibid. 446.

[41] Ibid. 446.

[42] Ibid. 446–50.

some pragmatic features[43] (easy amendment formula and political consensus[44]) but does not fit with the pragmatic model: there are no formal limits for constitutional adaption, and no judicial review of amendments. The Party can propose any changes to the Constitution. The Party, however, may impose informal, implicit, political limits (e.g. the unamendable socialist directions of social and economic progress and the socialist political system under the party's leadership) for constitutional change ensured by the Party itself.

B. Amendment Culture

In theory, China's Constitution can be easily amended due to the lack of institutional barriers. The Constitution does not entrench the limits of constitutional amendment. Therefore, no constitutional amendments can be unconstitutional. In addition, the supermajority requirement can be easily achieved in a legislature dominated by a single party. The logical consequence of ordinary amendment seems to be the high amendment rate. The reality, however, is that China's 1982 Constitution is exceptionally endurable: it has lasted for nearly four decades with only five amendments. China's Constitution is seldom amended, unlike that of North Korea. Nor has it been replaced by a new constitution, as in the cases of Vietnam, Laos, and Cuba.

The source of China's constitutional endurance lies in what Tom Ginsburg and James Melton call "amendment culture," which they define as "the set of shared attitudes about the desirability of amendment, independent of the substantive issue under consideration and the degree of pressure for change."[45] Their empirical study indicates that the amendment rate is poorly correlated with procedural difficulty, and that the amendment culture displays "more important determinants of the level of resistance to constitutional amendments."[46] The Chinese experience confirms this theory.

China's amendment culture is shaped by the attitudes about the undesirability of formal amendment. Yan Lin demonstrates that the attitudes shared by the Communist Party and the legislature in China have modified over time, but the direction is to reduce the frequent use of formal constitutional amendment.[47] For

43 For the pragmatic approach to Chinese constitutional amendment, see Shiping Hua, *Chinese Legal Culture and Constitutional Order* (Routledge 2019) 3.

44 Zhang and Ginsburg, "China's Turn Toward Law" (n 3) (discussing Xi seeking support for the constitutional amendments).

45 Tom Ginsburg and James Melton, "Does the Constitutional Amendment Rule Matter at all? Amendment Cultures and the Challenges of Measuring Amendment Difficulty" (2015) 13(3) International Journal of Constitutional Law 699.

46 Ibid. 699.

47 Yan Lin, "Constitutional Evolution Through Legislation: The Quiet Transformation of China's Constitution" (2015) 13 International Journal of Constitutional Law 1, 81.

instance, the Party's 1990 report on constitutional amendment suggested that "the biggest state interest at present is stability, and *the stability of the Constitution is the basis for the stability of the nation*."[48] The report stated that "in several countries in Eastern Europe, the chaos that broke out starting last year *all started with amending the Constitution*."[49] In the same vein, a leader of the legislature said in 1992 that: "Both the peaceful evolution in Soviet Union and Eastern Europe and the turmoil we experienced between the Spring and Summer of 1989 have all taught us that maintaining the stability of the Constitution is not only the ultimate legal safeguard for the enduring stability of the nation, but also *a fundamental issue affecting the destiny of the party and the nation*. Although some specific rules of the Constitution may be amended, based on the development and necessity of the nation's practical situation, the fundamental institutions and missions of the nation prescribed in the Constitution *should never be revised rashly*."[50] Surveying further official statements about amendments in the early 2000s, Lin Yan concludes that "ensuring the stability of the Constitution and the regime has become a compelling principle to fence off 'unnecessary' requests for norm creation."[51]

China's hostile attitude to formal constitutional amendment explains why the Constitution was not amended often, even though it would have been procedurally easy to do so. This amendment culture is due to the concern of regime stability which depends on constitutional stability, as perceived by the party and the legislature. The source for this amendment culture is the perception of the anti-models of constitutional amendments. The fact that regime change in former socialist countries was accompanied by formal constitutional amendments has led to a resistant perception about the frequent use of formal amendments. In addition to the transnational constitutional past, domestic constitutional dynamics have resulted in an attitude about the undesirability of formal amendments. The party-state may worry that frequent amendments or constitutional replacement may open the platform for the public to mobilize for substantive constitutional change which challenges the regime stability and the party power. This concern can be anticipated due to the strong constitutional mobilization among Chinese citizens as discussed in the next part.

C. Constitutional Mobilization

Like their Vietnamese counterparts, Chinese citizens have been active in mobilizing constitutional change under the authoritarian condition in which the

[48] Ibid.
[49] Ibid. 82.
[50] Ibid.
[51] Ibid.

communist party holds monopoly over the public power. But, unlike the constitutional amendment process in Vietnam, the constitutional amendment process in China was not demanding, lacked participation, and therefore did not provide an opportunity for constitutional mobilization. Yet, Chinese citizens were able to appropriate other legal and political processes to mobilize constitutional change.

1. Weiquan Movement

The Chinese *weiquan* (rights defense) movement emerged in the early 2000s. The Chinese *weiquan* movement, which exemplifies what Louis Henkin calls "the age of rights"[52] even in a communist atmosphere, refers to a type of group action in which social actors (including lawyers, legal scholars, intellectuals, and other activists) use the legal process (including both litigation and non-judicial mechanisms like public protests) to mobilize for the protection and defense of civil rights against the government.[53]

The Sun Zhigang incident in 2003 is considered the starting point of the Chinese *weiquan* movement.[54] In April 2003, the public protested when the Chinese media reported that a young man named Sun Zhigang had died while in police custody. Taking this opportunity, three young legal scholars submitted a formal petition to China's Standing Committee of the National People's Congress, calling for this body's review of the legality and constitutionality of the Custody and Repatriation Measures, a legal instrument issued by the State Council in 1982. In addition to reasons concerning national legislative laws, the petitioners argued that the custody and repatriation system violated Article 37 of China's Constitution which prohibited "unlawful deprivation or restriction of citizens' freedom of person by detention or other means."[55] This legal mobilization effectively resulted in the repeal of China's custody and repatriation system, the result of the confluence of a number of factors, which according to Keith J. Hand's persuasive explanation, includes the political environment concerning China's leadership transition and the SARS crisis, the impact of online media, the institutional conflict between the National People Congress and the State Council, the flexibility in the government's policy concerning the issue and the effective work of legal intellectuals within the existing legal framework.[56]

The Sun Zhigang incident was the starting point of the Chinese *weiquan* movement, "a comprehensive movement involving all social strata throughout the

[52] Louis Henkin, *The Age of Rights* (Columbia University Press 1990).

[53] On this movement, see Feng Chongyi, "The Threat of Charter 08" in *Liu Xiaobo, Charter 08 and the Challenges of Political Reform in China* (Jean-Philippe Béja, Fu Hualing, and Eva Pils (eds), Hong Kong University Press 2012) 130.

[54] For particular examinations of this case, see Keith J. Hand, "Using Law for a Righteous Purpose: The Sun Zhigang Incident and Evolving Forms of Citizen Action in the People's Republic of China" (2006) 45 Columbia Journal of Transitional Law 114.

[55] China's Constitution, art. 37.

[56] Hand, "Using Law for a Righteous Purpose" (n 54) 114, 131–48.

country and covering every aspect of human rights."[57] One feature of the Chinese *weiquan* movement is the involvement of public interest lawyers and their use of litigation as a strategy of mobilization.[58] Importantly, there is a "small but growing body of constitutional case law" produced as the efforts of *Weiquan* movement lawyers in using courts as the mechanism for constitutional litigation.[59] One typical example is the Zhang Xianzhu case in 2003 which involved litigation against the hepatitis B discrimination law on a constitutional basis. Zhang passed the civil exam offered by a local bureaucracy but was denied the chance to take up the position, according to the provincial physical exam regulation because the physical text indicated that he was a hepatitis B carrier. The activist lawyer in this case argued that the local government's physical exam regulation violated Article 33 of China's Constitution which protects the citizen's right to equality.[60] The court ruled that Zhang symbolically won the case, not on a constitutional basis but on a factual basis.[61]

2. Charter 08

On December 10, 2008, 350 Chinese intellectuals and human right activists published a political manifesto, on the occasion of the hundredth anniversary of China's Constitution and the sixtieth anniversary of the Universal Declaration of Human Rights.[62] Adopting the name and style of Czechoslovakia's Charter 77, China's Charter 08, subsequently signed by more than 10,000 people inside and outside China, called for the substantive transformation of Chinese constitutional order. It is comprised of four parts: preamble, fundamental principles, basic positions, and conclusion. Its preamble establishes the rationale of its release, focusing the problems internal to the existing Chinese communist constitutional order, such as corruption, "absence of human rights," and other social, economic, moral, and environmental problems. It attributes these problems to "the political reality, which is plain for anyone to see, is that China has many laws but no rule of law; it has a constitution but no constitutional government."[63]

The charter then moves on to set out its underlying constitutional principles, namely freedom, human rights, equality, republicanism, democracy, and constitutionalism. On these grounds, the Charter articulates detailed constitutional proposals, namely amending the nation's Constitution; separation of powers and checks and balances; legislative democracy; judicial independence; civilization

[57] Feng Chongyi, "The Threat of Charter 08" in *Liu Xiaobo, Charter 08* (n 53) 129.
[58] See generally, Fu (n 34).
[59] Thomas E. Kellogg, Constitutionalism with Chinese Characteristics? Constitutional Development and Civil Litigation in China (2009) 7 International Journal of Constitutional Law 215, 218.
[60] Ibid. 239.
[61] The court held that it does not have the competence to offer remedy as the position has been filled. For more details, see Ibid. 240–1.
[62] The English translation is available at the Charter's website: http://www.charter08.com/.
[63] Ibid.

of the military; human rights protection; democratic elections with free competition and citizen participation; abolishing the household registration system to realize the constitutional rights to equality and freedom of movement; multi-party system; freedom of assembly; freedom of expression; freedom of religion; civic education; protection of private property rights; fiscal decentralization; social security; environmental protection; federal republic; and transitional justice. In its conclusion, the Charter calls for public support.[64]

The government's response to Charter 08 is described as "aggressively repressive"[65] with forty signatories being questioned in the first week of its release, more than a hundred being harassed or detained in the following year,[66] and Liu Xiaobo, one of the initiators of the Charter, being sentenced to eleven years in jail for "incitement to subversion of state power."[67] In 2010, Liu was awarded the Nobel Peace Prize, and the Chinese government's first reaction to this was to arrest several dissidents who gamely held a celebration party.[68]

In short, Charter 08 is a form of social mobilization directly aimed at constitutional change. The social elite worked collectively to release a manifesto and called for public support of a peaceful and dialogical transformation of the constitutional system in China. The authoritarian government, however, denied a constitutional dialogue and chose to oppress the mobilizing actors.

3. 2013 Xianzheng Debate

The authoritarian defeat of Charter 08 did not completely frustrate constitutional mobilization in China. The 2013 constitutionalism debate echoes some constitutionalist values mobilized by the Charter 08 actors. In this "nationwide debate that lasted for months," through the popular media, liberal intellectuals mobilized for the implementation of constitutionalism (*xianzheng*) in China, while its opponents operating in the party-state's constitutional line castigated constitutionalism as a Western concept inimical to China.[69]

The timing and political opportunity of the 2013 constitutionalism debate is relatively similar to that of Charter 08: the anniversary of China's Constitution. Speaking at the thirtieth anniversary of China's 1982 Constitution on December 4, Xi Jinping stated that: "The life and authority of the Constitution depend on its implementation."[70] Seizing this opportunity, seventy-one liberal intellectuals

64 Ibid.

65 Pitman B. Potter and Sophia Woodman, "Boundaries of Tolerance: Charter 08 and Debates over Political Reform" in Liu Xiaobo, *Charter 08* (n 53) 107.

66 Ibid.

67 "Introduction" in *Liu Xiaobo, Charter 08* (n 53) 1.

68 Willy Wo-Lap Lam, "The Politics of Liu Xiaobo's Trial" in *Liu Xiaobo, Charter 08* (n 53) 251.

69 Rogier Creemers, "China's Constitutionalism Debate: Content, Context and Implications" (2015) 73 The China Journal 91–2.

70 Heike Holbig, "China's Unwritten Constitution: Ideological Implications of a 'Non-ideological' Approach" (2014) 132 German Journal on Contemporary Asia 53, 54.

published online on Christmas Day an open letter called *A Proposal for a Consensus about Reform*.[71] Rather than calling for constitutional amendment or new constitution-making, these constitutionalists proposed reforms based on the existing 1982 Constitution.

The letter begins by suggesting that the Chinese citizenry can reach "a fundamental consensus on democracy, the rule of law, respect for human rights and other principles of constitutionalism demanded in a modern society."[72] On this ideational base, the intellectuals demonstrated many problems of the existing order, such as the lack of separation between the Party and the government, the symbolic position of the legislature, the restriction of freedom of expression, the monopoly position of State-owned enterprises, the lack of court independence, and the dormant constitutional supervision system.[73] They then proposed six reforms: governance according to the Constitution, implementing electoral democracy, respecting the freedom of expression, deepening the market economy, realizing judicial independence, and guaranteeing the effect of the Constitution.[74]

This open letter forms the basis of the New Year Greeting of the *Yanhuang Chunqiu [China Through the Ages]* (hereinafter, YHCQ) "a political journal associated with more liberal, pro-reform elements within the Chinese Communist Party."[75] Entitled "The Constitution is a Consensus for Political Reform,"[76] the Greeting called for the implementation of constitutionalism in China, which meant to implement the 1982 Constitution, with relatively similar proposals put forward in the seventy-one intellectuals' open letter. This greeting began the constitutionalism debate in China which lasted until August 2013. Articles mobilizing for constitutionalism were disseminated in such journals as the YHCQ, which published articles on constitutionalism in nearly every issue of 2013, the journal *Caijing*, and other official journals.[77] However, the cyberspace operated as the main medium for the mobilization for constitutionalism in China in 2013. As Creemers documents, "The original open letter advocating the implementation of the Constitution and many other writings were published, disseminated and shared via blogs, social media and intellectual websites such as *Love Thinking* (*Ai Sixiang* 爱思想) and *Consensus Net* (*Gongshiwang* 共识网). The debate aroused considerable interest online, outstripping interest in the Chinese moon probe launched at

[71] "A Proposal for a Consensus about Reform" (*China Copyright and Media*, May 3, 2014) <https://chinacopyrightandmedia.wordpress.com/2012/12/25/a-proposal-for-a-consensus-about-reform/> accessed December 15, 2019.

[72] Ibid.

[73] Ibid.

[74] Ibid.

[75] "A Consensus for Political Reform" <http://cmp.hku.hk/2013/01/02/30203/> accessed December 15, 2019.

[76] "The Constitution is a Consensus for Political Reform" <http://cmp.hku.hk/2013/01/02/30203/> accessed December 15, 2019.

[77] Creemers, "China's Constitutionalism Debate" (n 69) 96.

the same time. The vast majority of commentators demonstrated support for the pro-constitutionalist position."[78]

The popular attention compelled Party media to enter the affray. Three party media outlets, namely the *Red Flag Manuscripts*, *People's Daily*, and *Party Building*, published a number of anti-constitutionalist articles, conceiving constitutionalism as a Western product hostile to China, and accusing pro-constitutionalists as those who were attempting to Westernize the Chinese political system.[79] Pro-constitutionalist journals such as the YHCQ published a series of pieces which seemingly aimed to convince the leadership that constitutionalism should not be feared but was a logical stage in China's social-political development.[80] However, the party's response was strongly negative. By the middle of May 2013, a confidential document by the Party's Central Committee identified "constitutionalism" as one of seven ideological problems.[81] The document tended to consider the intellectual mobilization for constitutionalism as subversive. The Party considered constitutionalism as a "bourgeois concept of the State" which embraced the elements of "the tripartite separation of powers, the multi-Party system, universal suffrage, judicial independence, nationalization of the military and other such matters."[82] The party castigated this concept: "The danger of propagating Western constitutionalist democracy lies in setting the Party's leadership against the implementation of the Constitution and the law, denying Party leadership with Western constitutionalist democracy and abolishing the people's democracy, essentially, this aims to deny our country's Constitution and the system and principles determined in it, realize a change of banners in the end, and bring the Western political system and model to China."[83]

In August 2013, the party media continued to publish articles which were against constitutionalism, regarding it as "a US farce," a weapon of the "public opinion war."[84] These articles ended the constitutionalism debate in China in 2013. "Constitutionalism" had become taboo in Chinese public discourse.[85] A Chinese law professor was dismissed for teaching constitutionalism.[86] A recent response to the anti-constitutionalism movement was made by a constitutional law professor at

[78] Ibid. 96.
[79] Ibid. 95–6.
[80] Ibid. 98.
[81] The document was eventually made public and now is available in English translation at: "Communiqué on the Current State of the Ideological Sphere (Document No. 9)" (*China Copyright and Media*, May 4, 2014) <https://chinacopyrightandmedia.wordpress.com/2013/04/22/communique-on-the-current-state-of-the-ideological-sphere-document-no-9/> accessed December 15, 2019.
[82] Ibid.
[83] Ibid.
[84] Creemers, "China's Constitutionalism Debate" (n 69) 101.
[85] Qian Gang, "*China's Political Discourse in 2013*" (*China Media Project*) <http://cmp.hku.hk/2014/01/06/34866/> accessed December 15, 2019.
[86] "Chinese Professor Fired for Teaching 'Constitutionalism'" (*Epoch Times*, August 28, 2013) <http://www.theepochtimes.com/n3/268123-chinese-professor-fired-for-teaching-constitutionalism/> accessed December 15, 2019.

Peking University Law School, Zhang Qianfan, a prominent constitutionalist voice during the 2013 constitutionalism debate, who said that: "The anti-constitutional standpoint is ridiculous, because its essence is against humanity."[87]

China's 2013 constitutionalism debate is not merely a theoretical or ideological friction. It is a form of social mobilization for constitutionalism. In this case, constitutionalism is a socially mobilized value, evidenced by the social elite's address of an open letter calling for constitutionalism and the public attention and engagement of popular constitutional advocacy through the mass media. The constitutionalism movement is influential enough to force the party to engage in a limited conversation about constitutionalism.

4. Comparative Analysis

As Fu Hualing demonstrates, the opening policy initiated by Deng Xiaoping facilitated economic development, which put pressure on legal and political adaption by incorporating "democratic values and the rule of law."[88] Importantly, as mentioned above, China's constitutional amendments in 1999 and 2004 incorporated the ideas of "socialist rule of law state" and human rights respectively. This domestic legal and political reform was accompanied by China's greater integration into the global political economic community with China's sign of major international human rights treaties, such as the ICCPR and the ICECR and participation in major international economic institutions, like the WTO.[89] Domestic and international dynamic engendered the rise of civil society "characterized by the mushrooming of associations and non-governmental organizations (NGOs), along with a new wave of volunteerism, civil culture, and moral reasoning."[90] Fu Hualing also stresses that: "within the context of cultural and institutional changes, there is also a growth in demand for rights and the rule of law."[91] Moreover, like in Vietnam, the rise of social media and the Internet offered the cyberspace for a civil society to mobilize for rights and the rule of law.

Thus, China and Vietnam have offered a relatively similar political environment for the emergence of the social struggle for constitutional change. As in Vietnam, the social actors in China have appropriated the gap between political and legal commitment and social reality to mobilize for social changes, including constitutional change.[92] They have appropriated different legal and political processes to mobilize for constitutional construction, including litigation in the courtroom, petition to the legislative body, and violent protests.

[87] "Chinese Law Professor Offers Staunch Defense of Constitutionalism" (*Epoch Times*, January 11, 2015) <http://www.theepochtimes.com/n3/1191951-chinese-law-professor-offers-staunch-defense-of-constitutionalism/> accessed December 15, 2019.

[88] Fu, "Challenging Authoritarianism Though Law" in *Liu Xiaobo, Charter 08* (n 53) 187.

[89] Ibid. 189–90.

[90] Ibid. 190.

[91] Ibid.

[92] Ibid. 191.

Chinese and Vietnamese constitutional intellectuals and activists have framed similar constitutional arguments about the problems internal to the existing regime, and they have also framed similar constitutional proposals. This is particularly so when we compare China's Charter 08 and Vietnam's Petition 72. The identical constitutional problems identified the fact that social actors in the two countries are the monopoly of power of a single communist party, the concentration of power, the loyalty of the armed forces to the communist party, the restriction of human rights, the lack of judicial independence, the control of the SOEs, and state control of land. They also framed similar constitutional proposals: multiparty system, separation of power and checks and balances, human rights protection, judicial independence, the market economy, and private property rights. This convergence indicates that the communist authoritarianism in China and Vietnam has faced similar problems, and the social actors are aware of these, for which they have mobilized for constitutional transformation.

To mobilize constitutional change, social actors in China, like their counterparts in Vietnam, employ constitutional rhetoric like "socialist rule of law state," "human rights," "democracy," "equality," adopted in the existing constitutional text and repeatedly restated by political leaders to frame their substantive constitutional arguments. Even the most radical constitutional proposals are also framed in line with official constitutional rhetoric. To illustrate, the six principles of Charter 08, namely freedom, human rights, equality, republicanism, democracy, and constitutional rule, are all reflected in the 1982 Constitution.[93] Chinese constitutionalists in the 2013 debate also framed their arguments for reform, based on the existing constitutional text and political leadership's constitutional rhetoric. The dialogical connection to the official constitutional language allows social actors to avoid punishment and to gain more support from political leaders when they mobilize for substantive change under the hard conditions of communist authoritarianism.

However, like their Vietnamese counterparts, Chinese constitutional intellectuals and activists have constructed substantive meanings of the official constitutional language in a different line with the party-state's understanding. To frame substantive constitutional meanings, they, like the Vietnamese actors, draw on transnational sources or foreign constitutional experience. In particular, international human right laws operate as the frame for the social actors to develop reforming constitutional arguments. Importantly, Chinese constitutional intellectuals and activists construct the substantive constitutional meaning on the grounds of fundamental principles of Western liberal constitutionalism in contrast to the socialist construction adopted by political leaders. For example, the official language of "ruling the county according to the Constitution" is construed by the constitutionalists in the 2013 debate as "constitutionalism" with the

[93] Potter and Woodman, "Boundaries of Tolerance: Charter 08 and Debates over Political Reform" in *Liu Xiaobo, Charter 08* (n 53) 99.

liberal meaning of constraining the arbitrary power to protect fundamental rights. Similarly, the language of "human rights" is interpreted by the 08 Charter actors as universal rights inherent to everybody rather than rights bestowed by the state upon its subjects as a socialist construction of statist rights.[94]

Western liberal constitutionalism operates as the frame within which both Chinese and Vietnamese constitutional intellectuals and intellectuals can develop their constitutional arguments. "Constitutionalism" is an obvious principle of Charter 08, understood in the western liberal sense as limited government in the name of human rights protection. Its detailed proposals are framed, based on Western liberal constitutional ideals, such as the institutional separation of powers and judicial independence, and individual rights. The 2013 debate exclusively focuses on "constitutionalism" also understood in Western liberal meaning, for which it is accused by anti-constitutionalists of Westernizing the Chinese constitutional system. Although the mobilizing actors in Vietnam do not often use the term "constitutionalism" like their Chinese counterparts, they share a commonality in promoting fundamental ideals defined by Western liberal constitutionalism. This indicates the global appeal of Western constitutionalism. In the last three decades, Western liberal constitutionalism has provided the general framework for constitutional building around the world.[95] It also offers a frame for social mobilization for constitutional change in places where it has not been established, such as China and Vietnam.

As in Vietnam, mobilizing actors in China approach political leaders as the resources for dialogically mobilizing change in the Chinese legal political system. The nature of the communist authoritarian regime and the Confucian tradition of meritocracy have made the political elite become an attractive resource for mobilizing actors. The *weiquan* movement has included some violent protests but these protests focused on individual rights rather than substantive constitutional transformation. In other cases, such as the Sun Zhigang incident and the Zhang Xianzhu case, social actors engaged in a constitutional dialogue with legislative and judicial actors to define the meaning of some constitutional rights provisions.

Actors of Charter 08 and of the 2013 debate turned to political leaders as their mobilization resources. In the case of Charter 08, social actors attempted to convince political leaders to engage in a dialogue with society to challenge the political system peacefully. Similarly, the constitutionalists in the 2013 debate also hoped to engage in a dialogue with political leaders to exchange positions about detailed remedies for constitutional implementation. Like their Vietnamese counterparts, the Chinese mobilizing actors also used dialogical strategies and

[94] *Charter 08*, 287.

[95] See generally, David T. ButleRitchie, "Critiquing Modern Constitutionalism" (2004) 3 Appalachian Journal of Law 37; Jiunn-Rong Yeh and Wen-chen Chang, "The Changing Landscape of Modern Constitutionalism: Transitional Perspective" (2009) 4 National Taiwan University Law Review 145.

communicative methods to approach the political elite, such as releasing open letters, manifestos, and submitting constitutional petitions. The repressive nature of the authoritarian regime, the profile of dissidents in prison, the Tiananmen Square Massacre reminded social actors to avoid a confrontational approach in mobilizing for substantive constitutional change, like a well-organized opposition, or mass demonstrations.

In terms of consequence, constitutional mobilization in China, as in Vietnam, has failed to result in substantive constitutionalization but has contributed to the change of constitutional culture. The Chinese government remains repressive to the mobilizing actors and rejects the call for substantive constitutional change. However, the government has also engaged in a narrow constitutional dialogue with its citizens to define the meaning of the nation's existing constitution, as in the Sun Zhigang incident and the Zhang Xianzhu case, or the meaning of constitutionalism as in the 2013 debate. At least, this minimal constitutional dialogue is instrumental to fortifying a constitutional consciousness among the citizenry. Thanks to such dialogue, the people are becoming increasingly aware of the role of the constitution in their life, their fundamental rights embodied in the national constitution, the problems in the existing constitutional system, and the constitutional ideals. This constitutional awareness is conducive to a continued constitutional mobilization.

The aforementioned convergence in constitutional mobilization in China and Vietnam demonstrates that despite constitutional acclimation to the globalizing era, these countries have been confronted with similar constitutional problems, which mainly stemmed from the inherent nature of the communist authoritarianism. Social actors expose these problems to the public and draw on global sources to mobilize for new constitutional construction. To survive under these unfavorable conditions, they have to adopt a dialogical approach to the government. In response, the government adopts a mixture of both repressive and dialogical approach. The dance between repression and dialogue allows the government to consolidate its power without significantly undermining its sociological and moral legitimacy. Constitutional dialogue fails to result in substantive constitutionalization but is instrumental to the incremental flourishing of constitutional culture.

There are several important factors that have resulted from the convergence. First, the social complexity generated by nearly three decades of implementation of the reformist policy in the two nations has resulted in institutional adaption and social dynamics, including social mobilization for constitutional change. Second, the force of globalization is influential. Globalization compels the communist government to adjust their legal and political system which offers a more spacious environment for a civil society's constitutional mobilization. Globalization also offers new technology for the constitutional dynamics from below. In particular, the digital age allows social actors to operate widely in cyberspace. Globalization also includes constitutional globalization which diffuses Western constitutional ideas throughout the globe and motivates social actors living under authoritarianism to struggle for constitutional change. Third, despite the constitutional acclimation, communist authoritarianism retains its essential features, such as the exclusive leadership of the communist party, the political control of civil society and the judicial system. This authoritarian condition results in the convergence in social actors' adoption of the dialogical model in their constitutional mobilization, and the state's mixture of repressive and dialogical response.

Despite the convergence, there is a great divergence between China and Vietnam in terms of constitutional mobilization. The sharp divergence is that constitutional mobilization in Vietnam has generated a national constitutional dialogue with more vehement public engagement and the government's more dialogical and less repressive response, while constitutional mobilization in China failed to result in a national constitutional dialogue and met with the government's more vehement repressive response.

The lack of the momentum of constitution-making and the opportunity of public constitutional consultation in China is the key factor explaining that divergence. Compared to China, the constitutional environment in Vietnam is more conducive to constitutional mobilization. In addition, the institutional resource is also an important factor explaining the dramatic divergence in social mobilization for constitutional change in China and Vietnam. While Chinese social actors tend to use the judicial venue, their Vietnamese counterparts focus on the legislative platform. Fu Hualing argues that "without the opportunity to participate in political movements in China, [public interests] lawyers were virtually forced to use the courts as the *only* platform to achieve their objectives."[96] So, the lack of political opportunity compels mobilizing lawyers to turn to the judicial sites when some opportunities for constitutional litigation arise. However, the movement of "judicialization" of the China's Constitution is abortive.[97] China, like Vietnam, vests the constitutional supervision and interpretation power in the standing committee of the legislative body. After the *Qi Yuling* case in 2001, the judicial citation of the Constitution was officially prohibited.[98] This explains why in the Zhang Xianzhu case, the court refused to frame the rule in constitutional terms. The attempts to judicialize the China's Constitution failed because they challenged the constitutional role of political institutions. Political leaders were not ready to give

[96] Fu, "Challenging Authoritarianism Though Law" (n 88) 198.

[97] Kellogg, "Constitutionalism with Chinese Characteristics?" (n 59) 221–6.

[98] In *Qi Yuling*, comparatively rendered as "China's Marbury," for the first time in the constitutional history of China, the Supreme People's Court invoked the Constitution in order to render a decision protecting a fundamental right, but the decision has since been repealed. See Robert J. Morris, "China's Marbury: Qi Yuling v. Chen Xiaoqi—The Once and Future Trial of Both Education & Constitutionalization" (2010) 2 Tsinghua China Law Review 273.

up their prerogatives in the monopolization of constitutional meaning and to be bound by what courts stated about the Constitution.

Unlike China, Vietnam does not have a movement of judicialization of constitution, mainly because the social actors in Vietnam have alternative political institutional resources, especially the National Assembly. Like China's National People's Congress (NPC), Vietnam's National Assembly (NA) operates as both a constitution-making and law-making body. However, China's NPC meets only one time annually in around a half month, and hence most of its decisions are made by its Standing Committee.[99] By contrast, Vietnam's NA is the main legislative body and meets twice a year. Each session usually lasts from one to one and a half months. The NA's sessions are relatively transparent with live television and the direct observation of social groups and organizations. In addition, the NA's interpellation and vote of confidence on the Government's members was highly active and lively, when televised. The NA also rejected several bills and national projects proposed by the Government. Although under the party control, the NA is tied more to the public and operates as a forum for the public to check the use of public power.[100] Consequently, the NA offers an institutional resource for mobilizing actors to address their concerns. Public intellectuals who later constituted the 72 group had already addressed letters concerning national issues to the NA several times. Understandably, when the NA undertakes the task of constitution-making, it operates as the political site for the public intellectuals and other activists to mobilize for a national constitutional dialogue.

Without the necessary constitutional environment, political opportunity, and institutional resources, social actors in China, unlike their Vietnamese counterparts, were unable to initiate a national constitutional dialogue. They, however, can only initiate some limited constitutional dialogue like the 2013 *xianzheng* debate. However, this is not a constitutional dialogue at national level. Although the dialogue occurred nationwide through social media and led to the party-state concern and some engagement through the official media, substantial questions raised by Chinese constitutional intellectuals and activists were not debated on a national platform like the NPC. Unlike the story in Vietnam, the assembly delegates and political leaders in China have not appeared in public fora to discuss and exchange their views on substantial constitutional questions mobilized by social actors.

The Chinese government not only denies a national constitutional dialogue but also places serious sanctions on social actors mobilizing for constitutional change, like the punishment of Liu Xiaobo, harassment, or detainment of the Charter 08 signatories, the censorship and firm quell of the 2013 constitutionalism

[99] For general information about the NPC and its standing committee, see http://www.china.org.cn/english/27743.htm.

[100] For more details on the change of the NA, see Bui Ngoc Son, "Constitutional Developments in Vietnam in the First Decade of the Twenty First Century" in *Constitutionalism in Asia in the Twenty First Century* (Albert Chen (ed.), CUP 2014) 194–218.

debate. Unlike this story, the Vietnamese government did not punish initiators and signatories of such radial proposals like Petition 72 and the Declaration of Free Citizens, although it has a legal basis to do so.[101] Scholars have offered explanations to the Chinese government's repressive response to social mobilization for constitutional change, including the sensitive circumstances of leadership transition, the influence of dissidents like Liu Xiaobo, the threat of an Internet-based opposition movement, the danger of foreign interference, and so forth.[102] In fact, the Vietnamese government could have invoked relatively similar reasons to oppress constitutional activists like the seventy-two figures or the "free citizens" but they chose not to do so as they had committed themselves to a "no taboo" constitutional discussion.

Why does the Chinese government reject a national constitutional dialogue while the Vietnamese government allows this to happen? The key factors of this divergence are Chinese constitutional exceptionalism and Vietnamese constitutional universalism. Chinese constitutional exceptionalism explains the distinctive way of the government's reaction to constitutional mobilization. The Chinese government aims to advance a Chinese constitutional alternative to Western constitutionalism rather than copy Western ideas and institutions. The political consequence is the strong oppression of intellectuals and activists who mobilize for constitutional reform in China in line with Western constitutional standards. Charter 08 actors and constitutionalists of the 2013 debate are oppressed or opposed by political authorities as they violate Chinese constitutional exceptionalism endorsed by the political elite. The intrusion of Chinese constitutional exceptionalism undermines the ideological foundation of the Chinese constitutional legitimacy and challenges the power of the political elite. This explains the regime's serious sanctions of social actors who dare to mobilize for Western constitutionalism even when they use official constitutional language but with Western meanings. Skeptics may argue that when oppressing mobilizing actors to protect constitutional exceptionalism, Chinese political leaders may undermine their constitutional legitimacy. In fact, Chinese constitutional legitimacy mainly rested on sociological rather than a legal basis.[103] "Economic growth, social stability, strengthening national power, and 'good governance'" constitutes the sociological foundation for the popular acceptance of the Chinese communist political leadership.[104] This is the sociological base for the authorities to suppress social constitutional mobilization without substantially undermining its legitimacy.

[101] The Penal Code in Vietnam criminalizes those who make, store, and/or circulate documents and/or cultural products with contents against the Socialist Republic of Vietnam. Vietnam Penal Code (2015), art. 117. The last version of the Vietnam penal code has a similar article. See Vietnam Penal Code (1999), art. 88.

[102] Willy Wo-Lap Lam, "The Politics of Liu Xiaobo's Trial" in *Liu Xiaobo, Charter 08* (n 53) at 252–5.

[103] For distinction of sociological, legal, and moral standards of constitutional legitimacy, see Richard H. Fallon, Jr., "Legitimacy and the Constitution" (2005) 118 Harvard Law Review 1878.

[104] Yuchao Zhu, "Performance Legitimacy and China's Political Adaptation Strategy" (2011) 16 Journal of Chinese Political Science 123.

D. Resistant Constitutionalism

China resisted institutions of western-style constitutionalism as potential threats to the elite's power and the socialist regime. Exceptionalism is the root of China's resistant constitutionalism. China resisted Western-style constitutionalism in order to develop its own competing alternative constitutional model. The prohibition on judicial citation of the Constitution and the anti-constitutionalism campaign illustrate the Chinese model of resistant constitutionalism well.

Consider first the resistance to judicial review, a globally spread institution of Western constitutionalism.[105] Although China's Constitution stipulates legislative constitutional interpretation, in the *Qi Yuling v. Chen Xiaoqi* case in 2001, the Supreme People's Court (SPC) cited the Constitution for the first time, which was initially celebrated by the Court leadership as a "the major step" toward judicial constitutional interpretation.[106] In 2008, however, the Court repealed the *Qi Yuling* case.[107] According to Zhang Qianfan,

> It was rumored that the SPC circulated an internal directive forbidding following the Qi Yuling decision, which might have explained the de facto demise of the potential precedent. In any case, the new SPC president, who assumed the post in 2008, seemed to be dissatisfied with even Qi Yuling's dysfunctional existence and moved to explicitly delete the Qi Yuling case from the casebook. In December 2008, the SPC published a document that officially voided the legal effect of several outdated judicial explanations, among which the Qi Yuling case was the only one so voided without even a brief explanation.[108]

Consequently, the struggle for judicializing the Constitution "seemed to lose momentum," although a qualitative analysis of Chinese court cases from 2014 to 2016 indicates "that the use of the constitution in judicial decisions is actually fairly common in Chinese judicial practice."[109]

The repealing of the Qi Yuling decision exemplifies an anti-model of constitutional review. "Although the SPC itself did not refer to the 1803 US Supreme Court case of *Marbury v. Madison*, PRC [People's Republic of China] and other legal literature has frequently, sometimes uncritically, touted the Qi case as "China's Marbury."[110] The imagination of China's Marbury creates an imagination

[105] Tom Ginsburg, "The Global Spread of Constitutional Review" in *Oxford Handbook of Law and Politics* (Keith Whittington and Daniel Keleman (eds), OUP 2008) 81.

[106] Hua, *Chinese Legal Culture and Constitutional Order* (n 43) 110.

[107] Ibid.

[108] Zhang Qianfan, "Establishing Judicial Review in China: Impediments and Prospects" in *Constitutional Courts in Asia: A Comparative Perspective* (Albert H.Y. Chen and Andrew Harding (eds), Cambridge University Press 2018) 314.

[109] Daniel Sprick, "Judicialization of the Chinese Constitution Revisited" (2019) 19 China Review 2, 41–2.

[110] Morris, "China's Marbury" (n 98) 273, 275.

of potential threat: similar practices like the *Qi Yuling* case may lead to the incremental creation in China of a decentralized model of judicial review following the American model.[111] This judicial review model may threaten the Party's power.[112] If judicial review is established and hence the Constitution is professionally interpreted by judges, the Party may lose its political construction of constitutional meanings. More seriously, the American style of judicial review may threaten the broader socialist constitutional system in China. In places where it is established, judicial review institution is an integral part of the broader constitutional structure. Due to structural interdependence, the creation and function of judicial review does not merely affect the courts but may create structural changes (e.g. the demise of "democratic centralism" and legislative supremacy as its institutional embodiment), which may undermine the overall socialist constitutional order. This explains China's adverse reaction to the American model of judicial review. China did not merely reject the American model of judicial review for the reason that this model was not suitable for China. There is a more negative meaning here: China resisted the American model of judicial review because this model was a potential threat to the Party's power and the socialist regime.

China did not merely reject the Western (particularly American) model of judicial review. It also aspired to develop its own model of constitutional review. This is one aspect of Chinese constitutional exceptionalism, reflected in the discourse like "*constitutional review with Chinese characteristics*."[113] The Chinese way of constitutional review is legislative. Legislative constitutional review is common in the socialist world, but China's 2018 constitutional amendments indicated an exceptional move in this area. One amendment provided for the "Constitution and Law Committee" within the National People's Congress. This amendment added the constitutional component to the existing Law Committee to create a new legislative constitutional review body in charge of constitutional interpretation and constitutional review of legal norms and the proposal of recommendations to the Standing Committee in this regard.[114] This change reflects Xi's view in the Nineteenth Party Congress, which stresses the need to promote "the work of constitutional review."[115] The functions of this body are provided in detail by a legislative decision after the constitutional amendments, including: "implementation and interpretation of the Constitution, constitutional examination, strengthening

[111] In fact, this case created the base for some academic justifications for exporting the American model of judicial review to China. See Tahirih V. Lee, "Exporting Judicial Review from the United States to China" (2005) 19 Columbia Journal of Asian Law 152, 162.

[112] Zhang, "Establishing Judicial Review in China" (n 108) 314.

[113] Changhao Wei, "Recording & Review: An Introduction to Constitutional Review with Chinese Characteristics" (*NPC Observer*, January 18, 2018) <https://npcobserver.com/2018/01/19/recording-review-an-introduction-to-constitutional-review-with-chinese-characteristics/#Problems> accessed December 15, 2019.

[114] Chen, *Introduction to the Legal System of the Peoples Republic of China* (n 14) 318.

[115] Ibid. 318.

supervision, and coordinating with Constitution publicity."[116] The actual function of this body remains to be seen, but it seems to be an advisory specialist body of constitutional review. The final constitutional interpretation and decision on the constitutionality of the law and regulations remain the powers of the legislature. The legislature may practice these powers under the Constitution and Law Committee's recommendations. In any case, this unique arrangement indicates China's exceptional aspiration to develop its own model of constitutional review.

Apart from an anti-judicial review, the anti-constitutionalism campaign presents a broader dimension of resistant constitutionalism in China. "Constitutionalism" is among the most frequently censored words in China.[117] More recently, Xi Jinping penned an article for a Party's main theoretical periodical, stating: "The [2018] constitutional amendment has received very good response in all aspects," China "must never copy the models or practices of other countries," and "We must never follow the path of Western 'constitutionalism,' 'separation of powers,' or 'judicial independence.'"[118] This constitutional rhetoric indicates that China consistently resists Western constitutionalism and moves with its own socialist constitutional path, especially as reflected in the latest amendments. This section will explain the sources of resistant constitutionalism as manifested in the anti-constitutionalism campaign, while the next part will explain how resistant constitutionalism is reflected in the substantive content of the 2018 amendments.

The anti-constitutionalism campaign exemplifies the Chinese model of resistant constitutionalism. China does not merely reject Western-style constitutionalism for the reason that it will not work in China or that the country has another (socialist) constitutional option. Its forceful rejection of Western models of constitutionalism can be captured by a stronger negative sense of resistant constitutionalism. The party-state in China refuses Western models of constitutionalism to send two signals to the domestic audience as well as outsiders. The first signal is that Western-style constitutionalism is dangerous to the party leadership and to the socialist regime in China, and hence the party-state needs to counter its negative influence. China rejected Western-style constitutionalism not merely because this is a capitalist theory unsuitable for the socialist state in China. If China rejects Western-style constitutionalism for the unsuitability reason, the party-state does not need to attack it. There is a stronger negative sense here: the party-state perceives Western-style constitutionalism as a danger to its ruling. This perception is embodied in the several essays published in the Party's

116 ZX, "Duties of NPC constitution and law committee approved" (*Xinhua*, June 22, 2018) <http://www.xinhuanet.com/english/2018-06/22/c_137274151.htm> accessed December 15, 2019.

117 Bethany Allen-Ebrahimian, "On First Annual Constitution Day, China's Most Censored Word Was 'Constitution'" (*Foreign Policy*, December 5, 2014) <https://foreignpolicy.com/2014/12/05/china-constitution-censorship-rule-of-law/> accessed December 15, 2019.

118 Charlotte Gao, "Xi: China Must Never Adopt Constitutionalism, Separation of Powers, or Judicial Independence" (*The Diplomat*, February 19, 2019) <https://thediplomat.com/2019/02/xi-china-must-never-adopt-constitutionalism-separation-of-powers-or-judicial-independence/> accessed December 15, 2019.

main media, which "argued that constitutionalism is not only incompatible with Chinese socialism but also susceptible to a Western- principally US- plot to subvert the Communist Party."[119] This explains why the party-state censored constitutionalism debated to resist the influence of Western-style constitutionalism. The second signal is the resistance to the hegemony of western-style constitutionalism. One official line of the counter-constitutionalism argument is "that China's political system is unique and superior to Western democracies."[120] Such constitutional rhetoric does not simply indicate that China has another constitutional option. The party-state signaled a stronger message, particularly to the western world, that China's exceptional constitutional way even presents a better alternative to Western-style constitutionalism, and this indicates the resistance to the dominant influence of the latter.

The Chinese model of resistant constitutionalism is animated by a negative perception of a national and transnational constitutional past. To begin with, this is informed by the national constitutional past which can be traced back to Sun Yat-sen's constitutional doctrine.[121] In his Fundamentals of National Reconstruction (1923), Sun envisages three stages of national reconstruction: military government, political tutelage, and *xianzheng* (constitutional government or constitutionalism).[122] The Chinese Nationalist Party [KMT], which competed with the Communist Party of China, sought to materialize Sun's three-stage program of Chinese political transformation. The Constitution of the Republic of China, which remains in effect in Taiwan today, was promulgated in December 1946 to realize the final stage involving *xianzheng* construction as anticipated in Sun's theory.[123] China's contemporary attack on constitutionalism stemmed from the association of this concept with the competing republican nationalist ideology, political party, and political regime. The clues for this argument are the following historical narrative of the concept of constitutionalism in China put forward in an anti-constitutionalism article appearing in the *Party Building* (*Dangjian*),[124] which may express the Party's official view:

> Mr. Sun Yat-sen advocated that the "Five-Powers Constitution" was the concentrated reflection of the constitutional governance [*xianzheng*] standpoints of

[119] Samson Yuen, "Debating Constitutionalism in China: Dreaming of a Liberal Turn?" (2013) 4 China Perspectives 70.

[120] Ibid. 70.

[121] For more details on Sun's constitutional doctrine, see Bui Ngoc Son, "Sun Yat-Sen's Constitutionalism" (2016) 32 Giornale di storia costituzionale/Journal of Constitutional History 158; Eric Chiyeung Ip, "Building Constitutional Democracy on Oriental Foundations: An Anatomy of Sun Yat-sen's Constitutionalism" (2008) 9 Historia Constitucional 327.

[122] Sun Yat-sen, "Fundamentals of National Reconstruction," in Sources of World History (Mark A. Kishlansky (ed.)) Vol. 2 (Harper Collins 1995) 281–5.

[123] The constitution's preamble stated that it was enacted "in accordance with the teachings bequeathed by Dr. Sun Yat-sen in founding the Republic of China." The Constitution of the Republic of China, preamble.

[124] Creemers, "China's Constitutionalism Debate" (n 69) 100.

> China's bourgeoisie. The first generation of leaders of our Party also used the concept of "constitutional governance" at some point during the struggle with the authoritarian and dictatorial regime of the Guomindang. In 1930, Mao Zedong put forward: "What is the constitutional governance of the New Democracy? It is the revolutionary classes uniting to impose dictatorship over reactionaries." On the eve of victory for the New Democratic Revolution, our Party started to use the concept of the "People's Democratic Dictatorship". Afterwards, the constitutional governance concept that was used during the period of the bourgeois democratic revolution, as well as the constitutional governance concept that symbolized bourgeois rule of law and political system concepts, were not used by the Party.[125]

Such historical constitutional narrative deprecates constitutionalism as a defeated concept associated with the competing nationalist ideology, party, and regime. Sun's anticipation of constitutionalism as the final point in China's political development implies the substantive transformation of the existing socialist political regime in future. Understandably, the party-state in contemporary China was compelled to counter the liberals' rediscovery of this concept as the framework to debate on Chinese political reform. In addition, as the concept of constitutionalism was associated with the political program of the competing Party (Guomindang), its rejection by the Communist Party is comprehensible. Finally, the fact that the concept of constitutionalism is associated with and realized in the Western-style democracy in Taiwan may explain its resistance in mainland China, given the tensions between the island and the mainland.

In addition to the national constitutional past, resistant constitutionalism in China is informed by the transnational constitutional past. The transition from socialist regimes into Western-style constitutionalism in Europe after the collapse of the Soviet bloc necessarily generates the Chinese party-state's perplexity about the danger of constitutionalism as the weapon of regime-change. An anti-constitutionalism commentary published in the party's main newspaper, *People's Daily*, attributes the dissolution of the Soviet Union to the fact that Soviet leaders and scholars embraced constitutionalist theory as the theoretical weapon to abolish "the Socialist factors in the Soviet Constitution."[126] The construction of past transnational constitutional past in this way generates the presentiment that the spread

[125] The English translation is available at Zhengzhi Xue, "Clearly Understanding the Essence of 'Constitutional Governance'" (*China Copyright and Media*, May 29, 2013) <https://chinacopyrightandmedia.wordpress.com/2013/05/29/clearly-understanding-the-essence-of-constitutional-governance/> accessed December 15, 2019.

[126] The English translation is available at "'Constitutionalism' Essentially Is a Weapon of Public Opinion War" (*China Copyright and Media*, August 7, 2013) <https://chinacopyrightandmedia.wordpress.com/2013/08/07/constitutionalism-essentially-is-a-weapon-of-public-opinion-war/> accessed December 15, 2019.

of the idea of constitutionalism in the Chinese intellectual community and ultimately in the society may result in a similar effect—regime-change. This explains why the party-state was competed to halt its dissemination.

Apart from the national and transnational constitutional pasts, resistant constitutionalism in China also represents a negative response to contemporary transnational constitutional discourse: the national critical constitutional discourse that draws on transnational sources. Resistant constitutionalism is an aversive response to a relatively strong support to western-style constitutionalism among a considerable part of Chinese constitutional intellectuals and the public. Several Chinese scholars advocated for the application of institutions and ideas of western constitutionalism in China, evident in the discourse like "*The Path of Chinese Constitutionalism—With the American Constitution as the Background*," or "*What Can China Borrow from George Washington's Constitutional Thought in Building Chinese Constitutionalism*."[127] In addition to intellectual discourse, some empirical surveys indicate that a considerable part of the Chinese public supports Western models of constitutional democracy. On March 12, 2012, the party's main newspaper Global Times reported that "63 percent of those polled either favored or did not oppose Western democracy."[128] According to another online survey in 2012, for the Chinese public, "the most favored political systems are the United States (71.98 percent), Sweden (32.38 percent), Great Britain (30.76 percent), Germany (28.81 percent), and Singapore (27.51 percent). Over half of the respondents did not approve of China's political system."[129] Such intellectual and popular support of Western constitutional and political systems challenges the legitimacy of the existing socialist constitutional system in China and necessarily invites the party-state's aversive response.

Skeptics may argue that the party-state does the opposite to what a considerable part of the public favor which may undermine its legitimacy. The possible response is the Chinese party-state has an alternative, and perhaps a more important source of legitimacy: constitutional exceptionalism. The Chinese party-state does not bases its legitimacy on adherence to Western or universal standards of a constitutional government. Rather, the legitimacy of the Chinese socialist constitutional system depends more on the distinctive construction of local constitutional and political ideology declared in the constitutional preamble: Mao Zedong Thought, Deng Xiaoping Theory, Three Represents, the Scientific Outlook on Development, and the Xi Jinping Thought on Socialism with Chinese Characteristics for a New Era.[130] This constitutional exceptionalism provides an alternative source of constitutional legitimacy, because it signals to the public that the party-state is capable

[127] Hua, *Chinese Legal Culture and Constitutional Order* (n 43) 14, 119, 120.
[128] Ibid. 111–12.
[129] Ibid. 112.
[130] China's Constitution, Preamble.

enough to move the country constitutionally in a creative and distinctive way which may be considered superior to Western models.

III. The Progressive Change

A. The Dynamic Constitution

Instrumentalism remains the core of the Chinese socialist constitutional system, but is adapted by the legalization of the Constitution. China's Constitution now is not merely an instrument for political control but has increasingly become an important legal framework for the operation of political power. The constitutional amendment in 1999 incorporated a new principle called "Ruling the Country According to the Law," the Chinese version of socialist rule of law state.[131] Following this, at the Eighteenth Party Congress in 2012, the Party suggests a discordant understanding: "As the Constitution and laws are adopted by the Party and the people under its leadership," "the Party must act within the scope prescribed by the Constitution and laws."[132] One commentator said, "On the one hand, this passage seems to signal the willingness of the party to exercise its power only within the confines of the constitutional and legal framework, but on the other, the CCP is also clearly asserting its claim to be the originator of the constitution, and thus implicitly, the authority in control of the constitution."[133] On July 1, 2015, the nation's legislature adopted a bill requiring government officials to pledge allegiance to the nation's Constitution upon taking office.[134] This requirement was then incorporated into the 2018 constitutional amendment. China has begun to establish a culture of constitutional oath. These developments indicate the party-state's willingness to operate within the constitutional framework.

Recent developments further indicate the legalistic nature of the China's Constitution. In an important contribution, Taisu Zhang and Tom Ginsburg argue that China's Constitution "has become more instrumentally important: that is, emphasizing its authority now brings greater political benefits than in the not-so-distant past, whereas disregarding it now carries much greater political cost."[135] China's Constitution is already of political significance, and recent developments

[131] China's Constitution, art. 5.

[132] "Full text of Hu Jintao's report at 18th Party Congress" (*Xinhua*, November 17, 2012) <http://news.xinhuanet.com/english/special/18cpcnc/2012-11/17/c_131981259_6.htm> accessed December 15, 2019.

[133] Heike Holbig, "China's Unwritten Constitution: Ideological Implications of a 'Non-ideological' Approach" (2014) 132 German Journal on Contemporary Asia 53, 56.

[134] "China: Government Officials to Take Constitutional Oath" (*The Library of Congress*, July 27, 2015) <http://www.loc.gov/law/foreign-news/article/china-government-officials-to-take-constitutional-oath/> accessed December 15, 2019.

[135] Zhang and Ginsburg, "China's Turn Toward Law" (n 3) 347.

have further enhanced its significance in governmental rhetoric and actual political activity.[136] This is particularly substantiated by Xi's more frequent reference to Constitution in political discourse, and by the 2018 amendments which constitutionalize his ideology, the party's role, presidential term limit removal, and the party's anti-corruption institutions.[137] The Constitution's consolidated political weight is due to the government's response to the changing "social sentiment": the Chinese society now attaches more sociopolitical legitimacy to law and legality.[138]

That account indicates an important change in the foundation of political legitimacy in China. The Party-state has no longer merely relied on sociological legitimacy: the regime's actual performance through the achievement of economic development. Legal legitimacy has become more important. As society attaches more weight to legality, the party-state now greater adheres to constitutionality (the commitments or willing to operate within the Constitution) to gain more legal legitimacy.

As China's Constitution has become increasingly instrumentally important, it has become increasingly dynamic within the elite community. The defeated constitutionalism debate and the 2018 amendment indicate that the Constitution has consistently operated as an instrument for institutionalizing the Party's social and economic program and under the Party's control. But, these developments also indicate that the Constitution has become increasingly dynamic, which has occasionally generated unpredictable constitutional outcomes and rendered the centralized control of the constitutional process more difficult, albeit still possible. The unusual dynamics surrounding the 2018 amendments illustrate this well: the Party approved the amendment proposal without immediately publishing it, and then the Party held an unusual secret and urgent meeting, while the mass media published the amendment proposal.[139] The unusual circumstances surrounding the 2018 amendments led to the suspicion "that the amendment's passage was not entirely smooth sailing for Xi and his allies."[140] This observation suggests that the political control of the constitutional process is still possible but has become not easy due to the internal dynamics among the political leaders. When the Constitution has become more politically consequential, it will attract greater attention and concerns among different political leaders, and instigate more competing political views, which renders the single imposition of constitutional choices by a strong leader more difficult. The potential consequence tends to be that the process of constitutional change may generate greater internal dynamics within the elite community.

[136] Ibid. 346–7.
[137] Ibid. 347–63.
[138] Ibid. 357.
[139] Ibid. 355.
[140] Ibid. 356.

Another aspect of China's Constitution's dynamics concerns society. In addition to instrumental importance, the Constitution has become more socially important to Chinese citizens. The fact that the political elite adhere to the Constitution to gain more legal legitimacy suggests that the citizens have given the document more credit. If the Constitution is purely instrumental to the party-state or a symbolic document irrelevant to the society, it would not draw social attention and energy, as evident in the 2013 constitutionalism debate. Chinese citizens may realize that socioeconomic development would not be accomplished without certain necessary constitutional change. Their engagement in constitutional mobilization stemmed from the recognition that there are constraints to socioeconomic development which lie somewhere in the Constitution. Consequently, China's Constitution has not been merely an instrument for top-down control, but has operated as the frame for popular constitutional discourse and activity, including mobilization.

This dynamic is evident in both popular constitutional discourse and actual popular constitutional activity. Popular constitutional discourse has led to the construction of the meanings of the Constitution, as opposed to governmental wisdom. The 2013 constitutionalism debate illustrates this well. While governmental rhetoric only refers to "ruling the country according to the Constitution," intellectuals took this to mean constitutionalism and vehemently mobilized for it, leading to the moment of social constitutional attention and concerns[141] that the political elite might not have expected. The popular constitutional activity also indicates the dynamics of the Constitution. While the political elite may appropriate the constitution to legitimatize political ideology and policy, citizens may use it in a different way and for different social purposes beyond the party-state's anticipation. Popular constitutional petitions, as in the *Sun Zhigang* case, are employed to struggle for the judicial realization of constitutional rights.

The Constitution's dynamics lie in the competing difference between the document's instrumental importance for political elite and its social importance for the public.

B. Constitutionalizing the Party

Party vanguardism remains at the core of the Chinese constitutional polity, but is adapted. The original 1982 Constitution refers to the leadership of the CPC in its preamble, rather than expressly mandating this in a constitutional provision as in the 1975 and 1978 Constitutions.[142] Although this change does not alter the

[141] A 2017 *baidu* search of "宪政" (constitutionalism in Chinese) yielded 7,000,000 hits. H. Li, "Chinese Discourse on Constitutionalism and Its Impact on Reforms" (2017) 22 Journal of Chinese Political Science 3, 408.

[142] Chen, *Chinese Law* (n 21) 121.

nature of the party leadership, it moderates it and leaves space for a multiparty system. In fact, party vanguardism is adapted in a Chinese unique arrangement called "multi-party cooperation and political consultation system."[143] In China, there are eight democratic parties operating under the control of the CPC. They do not oppose the CPC and the regime. The basic principle is that "The CPC is the only party in power in the People's Republic of China while under the precondition of accepting the leadership of the CPC, the eight other political parties participate in the discussion and management of state affairs, in cooperation with the CPC."[144] The Constitution's preamble confirms the commitment that: "The system of multi-party cooperation and political consultation led by the Communist Party of China will exist and develop in China for a long time to come."[145] This commitment is embodied in practice by the Chinese People's Political Consultative Conferences through which the CPC consults other parties on national affairs.[146] Another practical embodiment is the appointment of members of democratic parties to government posts.[147] Thus, the essence of the vanguard role of the CPC remains but is adapted by the aspirational principle of multi-party cooperation and political consultation.

The 1999 constitutional amendments also indicate the adaption to party vanguardism. They articulate distinctive ideological and institutional features of "socialism with Chinese characteristics." The amended preamble incorporated "Deng Xiaoping's Theory" as the Party's official ideology and confirmed that China will be the primary stage of socialism "for a long period of time." The implication is that party vanguardism may incorporate capitalist legal concepts and economic institutions for a long time to come.

Another adaption to the Chinese constitutional vanguardism is related to Jiang Zemin's "three represents" doctrine. The Constitution's preamble was amended in 2004 to add "the important thought of Three Represents" to the party's official ideology. The Three Represents, introduced by Jiang Zemin in 2002 and officially adopted by the Party's Sixteenth Party Congress in 2002, which claims that the Party presents the development trend of China's advanced productive forces, the orientation of China's advanced culture, and fundamental interests of the overwhelming majority of the Chinese people.[148] This is a significant adaption to party vanguardism as a response to the transformation of social structure. Economic development triggered by reformist policy generated a new social elite (in particular, a professional and technical elite and private entrepreneurs) and diversified social

143 Ibid. 122.
144 "The System of Multi-Party Cooperation and Political Consultation" (*CHINA.ORG.CN*) <http://www.china.org.cn/english/Political/29034.htm> accessed December 15, 2019.
145 China's Constitution, preamble.
146 Chen, *Chinese Law* (n 21) 122.
147 Ibid. 126.
148 "Three Represents" (*News of the Communist Party of China*, June 23, 2006) <http://english.cpc.people.com.cn/66739/4521344.html> accessed December 15, 2019.

interests.[149] The Three Represents ideology was introduced to incorporate a new social elite and diverse interests into the party.[150] "In essence, the Three Represents slogan was intended to broaden the general character of the party, without abandoning its class foundation. The CCP replaced its claim of being the vanguard of the proletariat with a 'two vanguards' thesis: it represented the interests of both the working classes (comprising workers, farmers, intellectuals, party and government officials, and those in the military) and the vast majority of the people, especially entrepreneurs, professionals, and high-tech specialists."[151] The amendment confers a constitutional status to this adaptive vanguard ideology, signaling the fundamental commitment that capitalist forces are no longer considered "enemies" but are included within the Chinese path toward socialism.

The 2018 constitutional amendment illustrates the resistant and exceptional aspect of party vanguardism. Party vanguardism enjoyed a greater constitutional mandate in two ways. First, the party's new ideologies were written in the constitutional preamble: *Xi Jinping Thought on Socialism with Chinese Characteristics for a New Era,* and Hu Jintao's "*Scientific Concept of Development*"[152] without mentioning the latter's name. The second new aspect of party vanguardism is the confirmation of this identity in the first Article of the Constitution, which now reads: "The defining feature of socialism with Chinese characteristics is the leadership of the Communist Party of China" (Article 1).

This party constitutionalization is to emphatically formalize Chinese resistant constitutionalism and exceptionalism. The party constitutional provision sends a resistant and exceptional signal to both domestic citizens and outsiders: China has developed its own socialist constitutional system under the leadership of the communist party, and has rejected Western models of competitive multi-party constitutional democracy. The fact that the party provision appears in the most prominent place (Article 1) of the constitutional billboard may be a deliberate choice by the party-state to emphasize the exceptional and resistant message that China embraces the opposite of Western-style multiparty constitutional democracy. The emphatic party constitutionalization echoes the previous constitutionalism debate. As the call for "Western-style constitutionalism," which implies the denial of the legitimacy of the existing leadership of the communist party, was vehement and attracted social attention, this invited the party's formal constitutional resistance. Informal forms of constitutional resistance (e.g. party directives

[149] Bruce Dickson, "Whom Does the Party Represent? From 'three Revolutionary Classes' to 'three Represents'" (2003) 21 American Asian Review 1, 1, 11.

[150] Ibid. 16.

[151] Ibid. 14.

[152] The concept aims at three aspects of development: comprehensive (material, political, and spiritual); coordinated (a balanced growth between different areas and regions); and sustainable social harmony and environmental protection). "Scientific Concept of Development" (*China.org.cn*, May 13, 2011) <http://www.china.org.cn/china/CPC_90_anniversary/2011-05/13/content_22559237.htm> accessed December 15, 2019.

or media and academic censorship) may not be strong and legitimate enough. The formal confirmation of the Chinese socialism defined by the party leadership in the highest law of the land has become necessary to express and legitimatize Chinese resistant constitutionalism in its strongest form.

C. Distributing Powers

Democratic centralism remains the identity of the Chinese socialist constitutional system. Article 3 of the 1982 Constitution through the 2018 amendments confirms that: "The State organs of the People's Republic of China apply the principle of democratic centralism."[153] This provision suggests that the power is formally centralized in the legislature. The legislature is the supreme body, creating and supervising the rest of the central institutions. However, the centralized constitutional system is "democratic" in the sense that the legislature is created by the people, though elections and is subject to popular supervision. Another "democratic" aspect concerns central-local relations: local governments as inferior institutions are allowed to propose initiatives but this would be under the leadership of the central government. The centralized constitutional system, however, was adaptive through its distribution of powers.

One way for constitutional adaption is through the use of legislation. This is not unique to China but is a comparative practice, as reflected in William N. Eskridge Jr. and John Ferejohn's account of "Super-statutes,"[154] or Ernest A Young's account of "The Constitution outside the Constitution."[155] In China, prior to the 2018 amendments, due to a hostile attitude to formal amendments, the distribution of powers was undertaken though legislation. Yan Lin demonstrates that legislation facilitated the horizontal and vertical distribution of powers, which resulted in the Chinese constitutional structure becoming "more decentralized, diverse, and balanced."[156] In the same vein, Wen-chen Chang and David Law argue that to understand Chinese constitutional structure, "it is necessary to study the ways in which 'small-c' constitutional change has occurred in the statutory level."[157] To illustrate, on the horizontal distribution of powers, the governmental accountability has been strengthened in the Administrative Litigation Law (amended in 2014) and the principle of judicial independence is further clarified by the Judges Law (2001), the Lawyer's Law, and the Supervision Law.[158] In the vertical aspect, the 2010 Law

[153] China's Constitution, art. 3.

[154] William N. Jr. Eskridge and John Ferejohn, "Super-Statutes" (2001) 50 Duke Law Journal 1215.

[155] Ernest A. Young, "The Constitution Outside the Constitution" (2007) 117 Yale Law Journal 408

[156] Yan Lin, "Constitutional Evolution Through Legislation" (n 47) 82

[157] Wen-chen Chang and David Law, "Constitutional Dissonance in China" in *Comparative Constitutional Theory* (Gary Jacobsohn and Miguel Schor (eds), Edward Elgar Publishing 2018) 499.

[158] Yan Lin, "Constitutional Evolution Through Legislation" (n 47) 66–72; Chang and Law, "Constitutional Dissonance in China" (n 157) 498.

on Legislation distributed the legislative power between the central and local congresses.[159] Another adaption to the socialist principle of democratic centralism concerns the vertical governmental relations shaped by the concepts of regional autonomy, "Special Economic Zones," and Special "Administrative Region" or "one country, two system" (OCTS).[160] Such pragmatic adjustment creates discordant concepts and principles. For example, Albert Chen argues that: "The story of the debate on and struggle for universal suffrage in Hong Kong thus reveals such underlying tensions behind, and the contradictions inherent in, the very concept and practice of 'OCTS.'"[161] In other words, constitutional dynamics in Hong Kong is engendered by the disharmony internal to the aspiration of OCTS.

In addition to "small-c" constitutional change, "big-c" constitutional change contributes to the further distribution of power in China. The 2018 amendments introduce structural changes to the centralized constitutional framework. To begin with, Article 79 removed the two-term limit on the presidency. Prior to the 2018 amendments, the 1982 Constitution imposed two two-term limits on the president as well as the heads of the legislative and judiciary.[162] While the concept of a presidential term limit is not China's innovation,[163] this is based on local ideas and informed by past experience: Deng Xiaoping's idea which aimed to terminate one-man rule and constrain arbitrary power after the Mao era.[164] Constitutionally speaking, the Chinese presidency is a ceremonial office, whose incumbent promulgates statutes or confers state medals and titles of honor.[165] The more powerful position in Chinese politics is the Secretary of the Communist Party of China, which has no term limit, although no Party Secretary has served for more than two terms since Mao's death. In 1993, the two positions were merged in a single person.[166]

The official justification of the term limit removal is to make the state's Constitution consistent with the party's Constitution due to the constitutional convention of merging the unlimited term General Secretary of the Party with the Presidency.[167] Western media criticized this change as allowing Xi to rule for life.[168] At the same time, the official media defended the change, saying that the

[159] Yan Lin, "Constitutional Evolution Through Legislation" (n 47), 73.

[160] For more details, see Chen, *Chinese Law* (n 21), 142–5.

[161] Albert H.Y. Chen, "The Law and Politics of the Struggle for Universal Suffrage in Hong Kong" (2016) 3 Asian Journal of Law and Society 189, 205.

[162] China's Constitution, arts 79, 66, 120, and 130.

[163] For comparative practice, see Alexander Baturo and Robert Elgie, *The Politics of Presidential Term Limits* (Oxford University Press 2019).

[164] Lin Feng, "The 2018 Constitutional Amendments" (n 1).

[165] China's Constitution, art. 80.

[166] Zhang and Ginsburg, "China's Turn Toward Law" (n 3) 353.

[167] Chen, *Introduction to the Legal System of the Peoples Republic of China* (n 14) 316.

[168] "China's Xi allowed to remain 'president for life' as term limits removed" (*BBC News*, March 11, 2018) <https://www.bbc.com/news/world-asia-china-43361276> accessed December 15, 2019.

amendment did not "imply lifetime tenure for any leader" and that "Western political theories were of no use to China."[169]

Scholars hold different views about China's presidential term limit evasion. Lin Feng contends that the abolition of the presidential term limit, together with the entrenchment of the party leadership "will move China further away from the rule of law at the constitutional level."[170] This view echoes the accounts of China's turn against law.[171] However, for Zhang and Ginsburg, the term limit removal, as well as party constitutionalization exemplifies China's turn toward the law: "A society that attaches an increasing amount of political legitimacy to the law, however, is also likely to be one in which a constitutionally-sanctioned presidency is gaining sociopolitical stature relative to the essentially extra-legal office of Party Secretary."[172] The turn toward the law is not tantamount to a turn toward the rule of law. The adherence to the constitutionally-sanctioned presidency to consolidate the legal foundation of the legitimacy of this position is not equal to subjecting the public power to legal constraints.

Comparatively speaking, term limit removal is not distinctive to China.[173] Versteeg and her collaborators, in their empirical survey of 234 incumbents in 106 countries since 2000 (China prominently included), reveal that there were sixty attempts at overstay, forty of which involved constitutional amendments.[174] Formal constitutional amendment is the most common strategy for evading term limit because "it places the leader on solid legal footing."[175] The success in using this constitutional strategy is due to two elements: the president's power, and the ease of constitutional amendment.[176] The case of China and that of Rwanda are used to illustrate this theory: "In each case, Xi Jinping and Paul Kagame had the necessary ingredients of perceived mass popularity and support, as well as sufficient control over key aspects of government, notably the legislature and courts. Both leaders successfully changed term limits with essentially no opposition at all. Leaders with such powers can amend the constitution with ease."[177]

That observation is debatable in the case of China. Regarding the first element, that observation may overestimate the president's power. Drawing on the

[169] "China's state media defend changes to Constitution removing presidential term limits" (*Reuters*, March 12, 2018) <https://www.scmp.com/news/china/policies-politics/article/2136788/chinas-state-media-defend-changes-constitution-removing> accessed December 15, 2019.

[170] Lin Feng, "The 2018 Constitutional Amendments" (n 1).

[171] Carl Minzner, *End of an Era: How China's Authoritarian Revival is Undermining Its Rise* (OUP 2018).

[172] Zhang and Ginsburg, "China's Turn Toward Law" (n 29) 357.

[173] For comparative experience, see Versteeg and others, "The Law and Politics of Presidential Term Limit Evasion" (n 2); Tom Ginsburg, James Melton, and Zachary Elkins, "On the Evasion of Executive Term Limits" (2011) 52 Wm & Mary L Rev 1807.

[174] Versteeg and others (n 2) 199.

[175] Ibid. 19.

[176] Ibid. 23.

[177] Ibid. 23.

unusual secrecy and urgency surrounding the 2018 amendment process, Zhang and Ginsburg argue that "there is no evidence to suggest that the removal of constitutional term limits was, in fact, painless or easy. Instead, there is reason to suspect that Xi had actually encountered opposition that was only overcome with some difficulty."[178] The fact that the constitutional term limit deletion was approved by the legislature with only two dissenters among 2,964 votes[179] does not mean there was virtually no opposition to the change. The formal publicized legislative approval is meant to consolidate the legitimacy of the constitutional change, and this does not mean there is no opposition behind the constitutional negotiation table. For the second element, formal constitutional amendment in China is not straightforward at all. Formally, China's constitutional amendment is simple due to the ordinary nature of the amendment process and the absence of an eternity clause. However, as discussed above, the amendment culture, which emphasizes the concerns of opposition and stability, makes formal amendment difficult. Presidential term limit evasion through formal amendment in China might been achieved with some difficulty.

China's presidential term limit evasion has exceptional dimensions. From a global comparative perspective, although the Chinese experience resonated with the global trend of term limit evasion, it has distinctive institutional and personal concerns to do so rather than to follow "a script using tactics" it borrows from other countries.[180] Institutionally, the constitutional removal of presidential term limit aims to synchronize state's formal constitution with the party's constitution. The personal concern is to enable Xi to continue his anti-corruption campaign.[181] From an intra-socialist comparative perspective, China's move is opposite to those of Laos and Cuba where their respective new constitutions imposed a presidential term limit for the first time.

The second structural change through the 2018 amendment added a new independent institution to the centralized constitutional order: the supervisory institution. The new Section 7, consisting of four articles, stipulates the creation of Supervisory Commissions, including the State Supervisory Commission and local supervision commissions at various levels (Article 124). The rationales for this creation are to institutionalize and centralize the bodies dealing corruptions among party cadres and state officials, which is consistent with Xi's socialist ideology (party discipline) and his vehement anti-corruption campaign. State Supervisory

[178] Zhang and Ginsburg, "China's Turn Toward Law" (n 3) 355.

[179] Nectar Gan, "Xi Jinping cleared to stay on as China's president with just 2 dissenters among 2,964 votes" (*South China Morning Post*, March 11, 2018) <https://www.scmp.com/news/china/policies-politics/article/2136719/xi-jinping-cleared-stay-president-chinas-political> accessed November 28, 2019.

[180] Scheppele argues that legalistic autocrats "are often following a script using tactics that they borrow from each other." Kim Lane Scheppele, "Autocratic Legalism" (2018) 85 University of Chicago Law Review 545.

[181] Lin Feng, "The 2018 Constitutional Amendments " (n 1) 14.

Commission merges several party and state anti-corruption bodies.[182] The independence of these institutions is constitutionally protected: "The supervisory commissions exercise supervisory power independently in accordance with the provisions of law, not subject to interference by any administrative organ, social group, or individual" (Article 127). The Supervision Law enacted in the same legislative session as the 2018 amendments govern the operation of this new institution.[183]

To deal with corruption at a constitutional level is common in global constitutional design. For example, Tunisia's 2014 Constitution, Egypt's 2014 Constitution, and Mexico's 2015 constitutional amendments created specialized anti-corruption agencies.[184] But, China's supervisory institution stems from the country's own contemporary practice and tradition. The distinctive constitutional integration of party and state institutions reflects the anti-corruption efforts of the current socialist China. Moreover, the supervisory institution echoes the long tradition of institutionalized administrative supervision (e.g. the Censorate) in imperial China. The creation of supervisory institution, therefore, indicates Chinese exceptional constitutional change.

The anti-corruption institution in China now enjoys constitutional status. The Supervisory Commission is at the same constitutional level as the executive and judicial branches, which according to Lin Feng, "have changed the constitutional structure of China, the relationship between different state powers, and the party-state relationship."[185] Zhang and Ginsburg contend that "The creation of the Supervisory Commission not only promises to make anti-corruption investigations more frequent, predictable, and procedurally transparent, but also accomplishes this through formal constitutional authorization."[186] The constitutional provisions on the Supervisory Commission sent a signal to the public and state officials: the regime is committed to strenuously fighting against corruption. To the public, this constitutional message may appeal to the public's concern about corruption, which is useful in boosting the regime's legitimacy. To the state officials, this constitutional message may have a preventive effect: the mere existence of this anti-corruption at a constitutional level may deter state officials from engaging in corruption.

The third notable amendment requires all State officials to "take a public oath of allegiance to the Constitution when assuming office" (Article 27), which actually gives a constitutional status to the same requirement put forward by the

[182] Chen, *Introduction to the Legal System of the Peoples Republic of China* (n 14) 717.
[183] Lin Feng, "The 2018 Constitutional Amendments" (n 1) 15.
[184] Courtney Millian, "When Should We Put Anticorruption Agencies in the Constitution?" (*GAP*, July 18, 2016) <https://globalanticorruptionblog.com/2016/07/18/when-should-we-put-anticorruption-agencies-in-the-constitution/> accessed December 16, 2019.
[185] Lin Feng, "The 2018 Constitutional Amendments" (n 1) 16.
[186] Zhang and Ginsburg, "China's Turn Toward Law" (n 29) 362.

party in 2014.[187] The rationale of this change is "to promote the authority of the Constitution, and to derive legitimacy from it."[188] Given the constitutionalization of party vanguardism, taking the constitutional oath implies loyalty both to the party[189] and to its socialist ideologies.

The constitutionalization of term limit removal, anti-corruption institutions, and taking a public oath indicates that the party-state has increasingly adhered to the legal legitimacy of the constitutional distribution of power. The Constitution, therefore, operates as a legal blueprint for power distribution. However, the constitutional provisions that facilitate term limit evasion and the creation of anti-corruption institutions also function as an advertisement to highlight the party-state's resistant and exceptional messages: the party-state in China has no interest in Western institutions of limited government, and has its own ways to distribute and supervise the use of public power.

D. Universalizing Rights

China's 1982 Constitution includes rights provisions in the spirit of socialist statism. The Constitution establishes the principle of unity of rights and duties.[190] The practice of rights is limited by the state and collective interests.[191] Yet, China has adapted its understanding of rights, evident by the incorporation of the idea of "human rights" in the Constitution through the 2004 constitutional amendment. Before that, the idea of human rights was rejected in China as a "bourgeois sentiment."[192] The 204 amendment introduces the statement that "The State respects and preserves human rights" (Article 33). For some comparative constitutional law scholars, this amendment "was progress in the sense that the term "human rights" had never before appeared in the [China's] Constitution."[193] For some Chinese scholars, the constitutional incorporation of human rights "was one of the two most significant changes in China's constitutional reform at the beginning of the new century."[194]

The constitutional adoption of human rights can be explained by external and internal dynamics. Externally, this amendment is a response to international criticism of the human rights situation in China. One commentator states that the constitutional incorporation of the idea of human rights presents "China's pragmatism on foreign policy" because the amendments "to some extent, narrow the gap of

187 Annotated Translation: 2018 Amendment to the P.R.C. Constitution
188 Chen, *Introduction to the Legal System of the Peoples Republic of China* (n 14) 318.
189 Ibid.
190 China's Constitution, art. 33.
191 Ibid. art. 51.
192 Zhang, *The Constitution of China* (n 23) 57.
193 Wen-chen Chang and David Law, "Constitutional Dissonance in China" (n 157) 505.
194 Hua, *Chinese Legal Culture and Constitutional Order* (n 43) 111.

understanding of human rights between China and the West. This kind of pragmatism illustrates that an emerging China is a predictable power with rationality and responsibility, both domestically and internationally. This will also help in building a peaceful image of China in the international community."[195] In addition to international pressure, the incorporation of human rights in the 2004 amendment is a response to pressure exerted by the *weiquan* movement. The timing is relevant. It is not a coincidence that the amendment on human rights was introduced shortly after the Sun Zhigang incident. The amendment was introduced to signal the commitment to human rights to domestic (and international) audiences to appease the *Weiquan* movement actors.

With this amendment, commentators believe that China has adopted a universalist concept of fundamental rights. Qianfan Zhang suggests that "what are to be respected and protected are not only rights for workers, peasants and other 'good class' but rather 'human' rights in general—that is, rights of all human beings, which literally understood, include even such 'enemies' as those who used to be called 'counter-revolutionaries.'"[196] Jianfu Chen also comments that "this unqualified declaration perhaps means that China has now finally come to accept universal human rights, rather than insisting on an 'Asian' or 'Chinese' conception of human rights."[197] The constitutional adoption of the idea of human rights indicates that China *partially*, rather than fully, adopts the universalist conception of rights. The statist conception of rights remains hegemonic. Human rights are contextualized within the statist rights framework: human rights, as well as citizens' rights, are accompanied by duties (Article 33), and are not used to harm the interests of the State and society (Article 51). Rights statism remains the dominant feature of the Chinese constitutional polity although it is adapted by a more universalist understanding of human rights.

The constitutional provision on human rights raises concerns about its implementation. One argument is that "this provision has lacked any meaningful enforcement mechanism—judicial review or otherwise—and its impact has been questionable."[198] Judicial review is not a single mechanism to inforce constitutional rights. Comparative experience indicates that constitutional rights can be implemented through legislation.[199] China has had a similar experience. For example, the Property Law was enacted in 2007 to implement the property right provision introduced in the 2004 constitutional amendment.[200] But, statutes facilitated the protection and the restriction of rights at the same time. For example, Jyh-An Lee demonstrates that China's 2016 Cybersecurity Law "provides citizens with

[195] Li Li, "China's Constitutional Amendments and Their Implications" (n 15) 81.

[196] Zhang, *China Constitution* (n 23) 57.

[197] Chen Jianfu, "The Revision of the Constitution in the PRC" (2004) 53 China Perspectives 3.

[198] Chang and Law, "Constitutional Dissonance in China" (n 157) 505.

[199] G. Webber and others, *Legislated Rights: Securing Human Rights through Legislation* (Cambridge University Press 2018); Adam S. Chilton and Mila Versteeg, *How Constitutional Rights Matter* (Oxford University Press 2020, forthcoming).

[200] Wang, *The Constitutional Protection of Private Property in China* (n 16) 4.

unprecedented protection of their data privacy" but "it also creates numerous opportunities for the government or third parties to infringe upon citizens' privacy."[201] Consequently, "network operators are obliged to provide individuals with an impressive degree of privacy, yet individuals cannot claim any remedies for the infringements of their privacy carried out by the state government."[202] The explanation for this is that Chinese right statism was adapted by a partially universalist outlook. The partially universalist outlook expands on the protection of rights, while the dominant rights statism legitimizes the state's restrictions of rights, which cannot be claimed by individuals.

E. Marketizing the Economy

Economic statism remains at the core of the Chinese constitutional economy but has been adjusted by new market ideas and institutions. The "socialist public ownership of the means of production," "State-owned economy" as "the leading force in the national economy," state and collective ownership of land, are all constitutionally confirmed.[203] But, Dengism has adopted a pragmatic approach to the socialist economy, leading to the practice of the opening and reforming policy. The fundamental aspiration of the Chinese party-state is to build "socialism with Chinese characteristics" or "Chinese style socialism."[204] This has resulted in the adjustment to economic statism by adapting liberal economic principles. Consequently, the Constitution is committed to "socialist market economy," "diverse sectors of the economy developing side by side," the land use rights, and inviolable lawful private property.[205] These fundamental commitments have, in fact, informed the workings of the Chinese constitutional economy as economic dynamics in the country, as illustrated by the last three decades.[206] Thus, the Constitution confirmed the socialist economy but at the same time adopted capitalist economic elements, creating a disharmonic condition for the continuing development of the Chinese constitutional economy.

Several important amendments in 1999 introduced more market elements to the constitutional economy, which signaled the commitment to continuing reforms: "In the primary stage of socialism," multi-forms of ownership are allowed although the public ownership remains dominant; and private economic sectors are now constitutionally recognized as not "supplements" but "important components" of the socialist market economy.

201 Jyh-An Lee, "Hacking into China's Cybersecurity Law" (2018) 53 Wake Forest Law Review 100.
202 Ibid. 111.
203 China's Constitution, arts 6, 7, and 10.
204 Chen, *Chinese Law* (n 21) 117.
205 China's Constitution, preamble, arts 6, 10, and 13.
206 For China's transition to socialist market economy, see generally, John Wong, *Understanding China's Socialist Market Economy* (1993).

The 2004 amendment further fortified the private economy by the commitments that the state *protects* "non-public sectors of the economy such as the individual and private sectors of the economy" and that the state "encourages, supports and guides the development of the non-public sectors of the economy" (Article 11). Concomitantly, constitutional protection of private property was further strengthened. Citizens' lawful private property is now entrenched as "inviolable" (Article 13). The State may expropriate or requisition private property for the public interest but with compensation (Article 13). One scholar comments that "for the first time in the history of China since 1949, her Constitution says that private property rights will be protected to the same extent as that afforded to state- and collective-owned property rights."[207]

The 2004 constitutional protection of private economy is driven by a combination of both global and local dynamics. First, this is a response to the impact of economic globalization. China's accession to the WTO in 2001 opened the door for the flow of foreign investment into the domestic market, and concomitantly, foreign investors demanded stronger protection of their private property.[208] To attract more foreign investment, the constitutional commitment to private property sent a signal to foreign investors that their property would be protected at the highest legal level. In addition, the constitutional protection of private economy was animated by local dynamics. A decade of development of the "socialist market economy" led to the rapid emergence of private economic sectors in China: e.g. 1.5 million privately owned companies and 31 million households-based small businesses by 2000.[209] This development was accompanied by the domestic citizens' stronger demand for private property protection.[210] The constitutional protection of private property is a response to the dynamics of the local market and local need.

However, the emergence of capitalist entrepreneurs and private economy may challenge the socialist political and economic systems. Particularly, as one scholar indicates, "private enterprises had grown so large and the government was in danger of losing control if no measures were taken."[211] The party-state responded to this potential threat in two ways: the absorption of capitalist entrepreneurs into the existing socialist system, and the reservation of the hegemony of economic statism. In the first instance, Jiang's Three Represents, which is incorporated in the constitutional preamble in the 2004 amendment, facilitates the admission of private entrepreneurs into the communist party membership.[212] This was to

[207] An Zhiyong, "Private Property Rights and Capital Structure: Empirical Evidence from the 2004 Constitutional Amendment in China" (2017) 173 Journal of Institutional and Theoretical Economics 3, 454, 465.
[208] Wang, *The Constitutional Protection of Private Property in China* (n 16) 90.
[209] Hua, *Chinese Legal Culture and Constitutional Order* (n 43) 115.
[210] Wang, *The Constitutional Protection of Private Property in China* (n 16) 90.
[211] Hua, *Chinese Legal Culture and Constitutional Order* (n 43) 115.
[212] Ibid. 115.

ensure that the emerging capitalists would support the party's socialist policy. In the second measure, although market institutions were adapted, the Constitution entrenched the dominant role of the state in the national economy to avoid the turn of social and economic evolution in a capitalist direction. The state retains the power to exercise "supervision and control over the non-public sectors of the economy" (Article 11). Thus, the constitutional protection of private economy is within the hegemony of the statist economy to facilitate the progress of the society toward socialism.

IV. Conclusion

As China has emerged as a global power, the party-state has become sufficiently confident to move in its own socialist constitutional way in the opposite direction from, and as an explicit alternative to, Western democratic constitutional models. This exceptional constitutional move is a part of the broader project led by the party-state to move the Chinese society toward socialism within Chinese characteristics. Chinese constitutional exceptionalism informs the amendment culture, the choice of amendment rather replacement, the ordinary amendment process under party-supremacy, and the resistance to domestic constitutional mobilization and the aversive attitude toward institutions of Western constitutionalism.

Although China's constitutional change has been under centralized control, there is room for continuing constitutional dynamics. The first is the gap internal to China's Constitution. The Constitution together with its amendment include internal discordant provisions: a multi-party system under the communist party leadership; constitutional supremacy under the party's leadership; democratic centralism with distribution of power; human rights and statist rights and communitarian duties; capitalist institutions under the socialist market economy. The second is the gap between the constitution and society, particularly the socialist constitutional aspirations and the increasingly sharp inequality.[213] The third is the gap between the Chinese socialist constitutional ideals and general constitutional ideals (e.g. constitutionalism, separation of powers, human rights). These constitutional gaps create room (contradiction, complexity, ambiguity, and generality) for continued constitutional dynamics in various forms: social mobilization, discourse, legislative constitutional decisions, and even further formal constitutional change.

[213] Sonali Jain-Chandra and others, "Inequality in China—Trends, Drivers and Policy Remedies" (*IMF Working Papers*, June 5, 2018) <https://www.imf.org/en/Publications/WP/Issues/2018/06/05/Inequality-in-China-Trends-Drivers-and-Policy-Remedies-45878> accessed December 16, 2019.

8

The Personal Model

North Korea

Introduction

After the 1992 amendment in response to the fall of the Soviet Union, the Socialist Constitution of the Democratic People's Republic of Korea (DPRK or North Korea) was further amended two times under Kim Jong-il in 1998 and 2009, and five times under the Kim Jong-un era in 2012, 2013, 2016, and 2019. Particularly, in 2019, two separate rounds of amendments were introduced in April and August. This chapter focuses on these seven constitutional amendments.

The Constitution defines the Democratic People's Republic of Korea as "an independent socialist state."[1] The North Korea regime is socialist in the sense that it shares core features with other socialist countries: a constitution institutionalizing a political and social-economic program, a single communist party, a centralized political structure, rights and the national economy controlled by the state. The North Korea regime, however, is different from the four other socialist states in that it operates a unique "*Suryong*-Dominant Party-State System."[2] Created in 1967 and having experienced subsequent institutional reforms, this system is characterized by the supreme personal power of a *Suryong* or a "supreme leader" over the triple institutional powers of the communist party, the government, and the military.[3] The ideological base for this system is the so-called "theory of a socio-political organism" first introduced by Kim Jong-il in 1986 and subsequently modified with a more concrete definition of the role of different actors within that system.[4] Accordingly, *Suryong* is the great leader of the masses and unities the people; the party, an autonomous nucleus of the political system, implements *Suryong*'s ideas and guidance; the government administers the party's lines and policy; and the

[1] Socialist Constitution of the Democratic People's Republic of Korea (1972 amended through 2019), art. 1.

[2] Kap-sik Kim, "Suryong's Direct Rule and the Political Regime in North Korea under Kim Jong Il" (2008) 32(3) Asian Perspective 91.

[3] Ibid. 90–1.

[4] Ibid. 92.

Constitutional Change in the Contemporary Socialist World. Bui Ngoc Son, Oxford University Press (2020). © Bui Ngoc Son.
DOI: 10.1093/oso/9780198851349.001.0001.

military, the armed organization, supports the three entities of the system.[5] Under this system, the power is concentrated on a single leader, either Kim Il-sung, Kim Jong-il, or Kim Jong-un.[6]

The *Suryong* system informs and legitimizes the process and substance of constitutional change in North Korea, the experience characterized here as the personal model of socialist constitutional change. The subsequent *Suryong* chooses to amend rather than replace the 1972 Constitution due largely to the adherence to the founding *Suryong*. The change of *Suryong* normally induces constitutional change. The Constitution was, also, amended to incorporate *Suryong*'s new ideas and guidance. Procedurally, the constitutional amendments are formally approved by the legislature with a two-third majority vote, but the amendment approval is effectively controlled by a *Suryong*.

Substantively, constitutional change in North Korea improves the *Suryong*-Dominant Party-State System to facilitate the government's role in improving the material wellbeing of living conditions. Particularly, economic hardship due mainly to international sanctions renders improving the living conditions of the local residents the key concern of the Kim regime, which is reflected in constitutional change. Consequently, many amendments directly affect the constitutional economy by introducing more market elements. The other amendments related to ideology, political institutions, and rights are also animated by the imperative to improve the living conditions. The need to improve the material wellbeing generates new ideas about socio-economic development, the institutional adjustment to facilitate effective management of the economy and the society at large, and empowering the citizens to some extent. As a result, constitutional change in North Korea is progressive albeit less so compared with the other socialist countries.

This chapter relies on both English and Korean academic and popular materials on constitutions, law, society, and politics in North Korea. The Korean materials on North Korea's constitutions and their amendments (including the texts of the latest constitutional amendments, academic articles, and popular commentaries) are published in South Korea and are accessed via translation.

This chapter is organized as follows. Section I explains the factors and contents of constitutional amendments. Section II addresses procedural and legal questions pertaining ordinary amendments, choice, and rate. Section III turns to substantive progressive constitutional changes. Section IV concludes.

[5] Ibid.

[6] For more details on the personal rule model in North Korea, see Atsuhito Isozaki, *Understanding the North Korean Regime* (Woodrow Wilson International Center for Scholars 2017) 37–41.

I. Constitutional Amendments: Factors and Contents

A. Amendments under the Kim Jong-il Era: 1998 and 2009

Under Kim Jong-il, North Korea's Constitution was amended two times in 1998 and 2009. The 1998 constitutional amendment was adopted on September 5, 1998, at the First Session of the Tenth Supreme People's Assembly of the Democratic People's Republic of Korea. According to the succession plan, Kim Jong-il was designated to succeed his father Kim Il-sung who passed away in 1994. During the "transition" period (1994–1997), Kim Jong-il deployed "balancing" strategy (inclusive politics, honor-power sharing arrangements, and divide-and-rule tactics) to avert internal cleavages, which led to the conclusion of the succession plan.[7] He was officially selected to his father's former position as General Secretary of the Workers' Party of Korea on October 8, 1997.[8]

The 1998 constitutional amendment was driven by three major factors: leadership change; new policy (Kim's endorsed ideology of military-first politics (*Songun jeohgchi*), and the pressures to deal with economic hardship. First, although Kim's power was unquestionable, he inherited the power from his father, and this inherited power must be constitutionally legitimatized. Second, although the *Songun* ideology, "politics which solves all problems arising in the revolution and construction on the principle of giving priority to the military affair and advances the overall cause of socialism relying on the army as the pillar of the revolution,"[9] was traced back to his father, Kim Jong-il formalized and enforced it as his centrality since 1995. Kim Jong-il believed that the military is central to regime survival. He interpreted the failure of communist regimes in the Soviet Union and Eastern Europe as due to the lack of a strong army to build a socialist society. For him, the ultimate goal of constructing a powerful and prosperous nation (*gangseongdaeguk*) depends on the existence of a strong army.[10] The third factor has to do with gravity of economic difficulty. The isolation of the national economy from the outside world, the limits of reform due to the state's heavy control of the economy, along with natural floods culminated in the catastrophic famine from 1994 to 1998 threatened the regime's survival.[11] This requires constitutional change

[7] Jei Guk Jeon, "North Korean Leadership: Kim Jong Il's Balancing Act in the Ruling Circle" (2000) 21 Third World Quarterly 5, 761, 764.

[8] Jasper Becker, *Rogue Regime: Kim Jong Il and the Looming Threat of North Korea* (Oxford University Press 2005) 129; Adrian Buzo, *The Making of Modern Korea: Asia's Transformations* (Routledge 2002) 175; Michael Breen, *Kim Jong-Il—North Korea's Dear Leader: Who He Is, What He Wants, What to Do about Him* (John Wiley & Sons 2011) 77–88.

[9] "Songun Chongch'i [Army First]" (*Global Security.org.*, April 27, 2005) <https://www.globalsecurity.org/military/world/dprk/songun-chongchi.htm> accessed December 24, 2019.

[10] Jongseok Woo, "Kim Jong-il's Military-first Politics and Beyond: Military Control Mechanisms and the Problem of Power Succession" (2014) 47 Communist and Post-Communist Studies 2, 117, 118–19.

[11] Marcus Noland, "Famine and Reform in North Korea" (2004) 3 Asian Economic Papers 2, 1, 506.

to alleviate the economic situations and by which to fortify the sociological foundation of the regime's legitimacy.

Consequently, the substances of constitutional amendments dealt with three major issues. A preamble was introduced for the first time to glorify Kim Il-sung. Kim Il-sung was constitutionally credited as a "great leader," "the founder of the Democratic People's Republic of Korea and the father of socialist Korea," "the sun of nation," "a veteran statesman in the world," and "the eternal President of the Republic" (Preamble). On that base, the Preamble concluded that the socialist Constitution of North Korea "shall be called Kim Il Sung's Constitution, the codification of the great leader Comrade Kim Il Sung Juche-oriented ideas on and exploits in State building." (Preamble). Kim Jong-il devoted the constitutional preamble to laud his father, as the legitimacy of his power depended on his father's work.

Turning to the body of the Constitution, the centralized structure was changed along the line of the military-first politics. As Kim Il-sung was constitutionally venerated as "the eternal President," the presidency was abolished. A related change concerned the elevation of the National Defense Commission to "the highest military leadership body of State power and the organ of overall administration of national defence" (Article 100). That means this institution is not merely in charge with national defense. Most importantly, it is a political-military institution taking leadership in using the state power. Correspondingly, the Constitution provided that the Chairman of the National Defense Commission "commands and directs all the armed forces and guides national defence as a whole" (Article 102). Kim Jong-il was elected to this position in 1992 and reelected in 1998 with the amended Constitution.[12] Accompanying the abolition of the presidency was the transfer of presidential powers to the Presidium of the Supreme People's Assembly (e.g. the powers related to foreign and external affairs) or to the Cabinet (e.g. the power to manage the government as the head of the executive).[13]

In response to the imperative of economic elevation, the constitutional economy witnessed significant changes. While the statist nature basically remained, market elements were further introduced. Apart from the state and co-operative organizations, social organizations can now own the means of production (Article 20). The objects of private property include kitchen gardens, and the income from other legal economic activities (Article 24). That meant citizens can conduct commercial activities to make money. This is considered "the initial reception of a primitive market economy."[14] Particularly, intellectual property rights to copyright, inventions, and patents are constitutionally protected (Article 74). Another notable

[12] Woo, "Kim Jong-il's Military-first Politics and Beyond" (n 10) 121.

[13] Dae-Kyu Yoon, "Constitutional Change in North Korea" in *Constitutionalism in Asia in the Early Twenty-First Century* (Albert H.Y. Chen (ed.), Cambridge University Press 2014) 111.

[14] Ibid. 112.

change is the addition of the constitutional right to travel (Article 75), which is a response to the citizen's need to travel to seek food due to local famine.[15] The amendment also stipulated that the state shall "make proper use of such economic levers as cost, price and profit" in economic management (Article 33). Thus, some market concepts were introduced into the constitutional economy. Foreign trade is no long monopolized by the state, as social, co-operative organizations are also allowed to conduct these activities (Article 36). The amendment also created economic zones, which expanded the freedom of foreign investment through joint ventures and co-operation of enterprise (Article 37). With the introduction of market elements to constitutional economy (private property, foreign trade and investments, special economic zones), North Korea attempted to establish the so-called "North Korean socialist market economic system."[16] Although the statist constitutional economy essentially remained, some market elements were tolerated to facilitate economic development due to the pressures of economic hardship.

Another constitutional amendment was adopted in the First Session of the Twelfth Supreme People's Assembly on April 9, 2009. When Kim Jong-il suffered a stroke in August 2008, power succession became the pressing issue and his third son (Kim Jong-un) was officially designated as his heir.[17] In addition, in response to the increased pressures from the international community led by the United States, the North Korean regime considered the development of nuclear arms the most important means to protect it from the outside threats. Consequently, constitutional amendment became necessary to incorporate new military ideology and to provide an updated framework for new leadership.

The amendments added military-first politics (*Songun*) as official ideology, along with *Juche* ideology (Article 3). Meanwhile, all references to "communism" were deleted.[18] This is due to the regime's development of its own internal ideologies of socialism: *Juche* and *Songun*. In addition, the abolition of the term "communism" in the Constitution may be also because it bears a negative image as it is associated with collapsed and repressive regimes in international discourse. While Marxism-Leninism and communism were expunged from the Constitution, socialism was retained as this allowed the state to implement a centrally planned economy which is constitutionally entrenched.[19]

[15] Ibid.

[16] Chang Myung-Bong, "A Study of North Korea's Constitutional and Economic Changes in the Changing Internal-External Environment" (2004) 32(5) Public Law 43 (Korean).

[17] Yoon, "Constitutional Change in North Korea" (n 13) 112–13.

[18] The word "communism" appeared in Articles 29, 40, and 43 of the Constitution through the 1998 amendment.

[19] Darren C. Zook, "Reforming North Korea: Law, Politics, and the Market Economy" (2012) 48(1) Stanford Journal of International Law 131, 146; Christopher Green, "Wrapped in a Fog: On the North Korean Constitution and the Ten Principles" in *Change and Continuity in North Korean Politics* (Adam Cathcart, Robert Winstanley-Chesters, and Christopher Green (eds), Routledge 2017) 27; Jon Herskovitz and Christine Kim, "North Korea Drops Communism, Boosts Dear Leader" (*Reuters*, September 28, 2009) <https://www.reuters.com/article/idUSSEO253213> accessed December 24, 2019.

To prepare for power succession, the amendments created the position of Chairman of the National Defense Commission. A new section of six articles was added to the Constitution to deal with this position (section 2, chapter VI). Accordingly, the Chairman is the supreme leader of the state (Article 100) and the supreme commander of the overall armed forces (Article 102). The Chairman is vested with the power: to guide overall affairs of the state, to directly guide the work of the National Defense Commission, to appoint or dismiss important members of the national defense force, to ratify or to abrogate significant treaties concluded with other countries, and to declare a state of emergency, among others (Article 103). The 2009 amendments, therefore, established unique leadership centered on the Chairman of the National Defense Commission.[20]

One notable change is related to rights. While the statist features of individual rights essentially remain, the amendment included, for the first time in North Korea's constitutional history, the state's commitment to respecting and protecting "human rights" (Article 8). This change may be a response to the international criticism of North Korea's violation of human rights, especially under Kim Jong-il's rule.[21]

The constitutional economy was not affected by the 2009 amendment. Yet, the operational economy experienced significant changes, including the creation of special economic zones (e.g. the Gaeoseong Industrial Complex and the Mount Geumgang Tourist Zone) as stipulated by the 1998 amendment.[22] As possible changes to the constitutional economy had been addressed in the preceding amendments, the 2009 one focused on political issues.

B. Amendments under the Kim Jong-un Era: 2012, 2013, 2016, and 2019

Kim Jong-un was selected as the first Chairman of the National Defense Commission by the Supreme People's Assembly on April 13, 2012, four months after his father's death.[23] Two days before that, at the Party Congress, he was selected as the first secretary of the Workers' Party of Korea and the Chairman of the Central Committee of the party. Kim Jong-un, therefore, formally assumed the

[20] Chang Myung-bong, "65 Years of Division-Change and Continuation of North Korean Constitution" (2011) 13 North Korea Law Studies 318 (Korean).

[21] According to Human Rights Watch, the North Korean government under Kim Jong-il's rule was "among the world's most repressive governments ... Virtually every aspect of political, social, and economic life is controlled by the government." Human Rights Watch, "Human Rights Watch World Report 2005—North Korea" (*Human Rights Watch*, January 1, 2005) <https://www.refworld.org/docid/421da31725.html> accessed December 24, 2019.

[22] Yoon, "Constitutional Change in North Korea" (n 13) 114.

[23] "Kim Jong Un Elected First Chairman of National Defense Commission" (*Xinhua*, April 13, 2012) <http://www.china.org.cn/world/2012-04/13/content_25140405.htm> accessed December 24, 2019.

position of the supreme leader of the party, the state, and the military.[24] Under his leadership, constitutional amendments were introduced in 2012, 2013, 2016, and 2019.

The 2012 amendment did not affect the body of the constitution, but changed the preamble to glorify Kim Jong-un's father. Kim Jong-il was constitutionally credited as the defender of socialism in North Korea, who allegedly transformed North Korea into "an invincible politico-ideological power, a nuclear armed state and an unchallengeable military power," the author of the Songun idea, and the "eternal Chairman of the National Defense Commission" (Preamble) similar to the way Kim Il-sung's was memorized as the eternal President of the Republic by the 1998 amendment. Kim Jong-un then renamed the Constitution to bear his father's and grandfather's names: the charter is now called "Kim Il Sung and Kim Jong Il Constitution" (Preamble). One notable change to the preamble is that the regime formally declares itself as a "nuclear-armed state" which is attributed to Kim Il-sung's achievement. With this change, nuclear power in North Korea is an issue of constitutional significance, not merely a military policy. This change attracted great international attention as the denuclearization negotiations may be confronted with a constitutional bar.[25]

The 2013 constitutional amendment added this sentence in the preamble: "the Kumsusan Palace of the Sun where Comrade Kim Il Sung and Comrade Kim Jong Il are preserved in their lifetime appearance is a grand monument to their immortality and a symbol of the dignity and eternal sanctuary of the entire Korean nation" (preamble). This amendment further consolidates the legacy of the former leaders.

The 2016 constitutional amendment introduced an important structural change. The amendment was adopted in the fourth session of the Thirteenth Supreme People's Assembly (SPA), held in Pyongyang on June 29, 2016, which aimed to constitutionalize the policy introduced in the 7th Congress of the Workers' Party of Korea convened from May 6 to 9, 2016. The amendment created the State Affairs Commission (SAC) that replaced the National Defense Commission (NDC). Concomitantly, the amendment created the position of the Chairman of this institution. The SAC is defined as the supreme policy-oriented leadership body of State power (Article 106), and its Chairman is "the supreme leader" of the state (Article 100). The SAC has the broader powers to decide major national policies, not limited to issues of defense and security. After the constitutional amendment, Kim

[24] Yoon, "Constitutional Change in North Korea" (n 13) 115.

[25] Ibid. 116; Green, "Wrapped in a Fog: On the North Korean Constitution and the Ten Principles" (n 19) 28; KJ Kwon, "North Korea Proclaims Itself a Nuclear State in New Constitution" (*CNN*, May 31, 2012) <https://edition.cnn.com/2012/05/31/world/asia/north-korea-nuclear-constitution/index.html> accessed December 24, 2019; "The DPRK's Nuclear Constitution" (*NAPSNet Policy Forum*, June 13, 2012) <https://nautilus.org/napsnet/napsnet-policy-forum/the-dprks-nuclear-constitution/> accessed December 24, 2019; S Haggard and J Ryu, "The DPRK Constitution and Nuclear Weapons" (*Peterson Institute for International Economics*, June 5, 2012) <https://piie.com/blogs/north-korea-witness-transformation/dprk-constitution-and-nuclear-weapons> accessed December 24, 2019.

Jong-un was selected as the first Chairman of the SAC, effectively becoming the supreme leader of North Korea.[26]

The constitutional change "shows the coherence of Kim Jong-un's political line, aimed at differentiating his leadership from that of the father and projecting the image of a leader more interested in 'improving the people's living standards' through the economic development of North Korea."[27] The creation of the SAC is consistent with Kim Jong-un's *Byungjin* policy characterized by simultaneous economic and nuclear development. The introduction of this institution signals that the regime has achieved great achievements in its nuclear program and now turns the focus on economic development. The chief duty of the SAC is to implement the Five Year Strategy for State Economic Development.[28] Constitutional change to the structural political institution was, therefore, animated by the concern to improve the material wellbeing of living conditions.

North Korea's Constitution was amended twice in 2019, respectively, at the First and Second plenary sessions of the Fourteenth Supreme People's Assembly on April 11 and August 29. Choe Ryong Hae, the president of the Supreme People's Assembly Presidium, said in his legislative report that constitutional amendments aim "to provide a firm legal guarantee under Kim Jong-un's monolithic guidance."[29] The 2019 constitutional amendments aimed to further institutionalize Kim's power and the regime's new economic policy.[30] These internal needs may be also connected to external events: the 2019 North Korea–United States Hanoi Summit and the 2018 North Korea–United States Singapore Summit. Through his summit diplomacy, Kim Jong-un became more confident, and constitutional change was necessary to locate him in an equal constitutional position (head of state) with US President Donald Trump and Chinese President Xi Jinping.[31] In addition, the failure of the Hanoi Summit where no agreement was reached means that international sanctions have been continued, and the regime needs to find solutions to

[26] J.H. Ahn, "N. Korea Updates Constitution Expanding Kim Jong Un's Position" (*NK News*, June 30, 2016) <https://www.nknews.org/2016/06/n-korea-updates-constitution-expanding-kim-jong-uns-position/> accessed December 24, 2019.

[27] Maria Rosaria Coduti, "The State Affairs Commission and the Consolidation of Kim Jong Un's Power" (*NK News*, July 13, 2016) <https://www.nknews.org/2016/07/the-state-affairs-commission-and-the-consolidation-of-kim-jong-uns-power/> accessed December 24, 2019.

[28] Ibid; Scott A. Snyder, "The Motivations Behind North Korea's Pursuit of Simultaneous Economic and Nuclear Development" (*Council on Foreign Relations*, November 20, 2013) <https://blogs.cfr.org/blog/motivations-behind-north-koreas-pursuit-simultaneous-economic-and-nuclear-development> accessed December 24, 2019.

[29] Jong Kyo Jin, "North Korea's Latest Constitutional Revisions are a Retreat to the Past" (*Daily NK*, September 23, 2019) <https://www.dailynk.com/english/north-korea-latest-constitutional-revisions-retreat-past/> accessed December 24, 2019.

[30] "Changes in Economic Provisions in the 2019 Constitution of North Korea: Meaning and Evaluation" (2019) 7(2) IFES BRIEF 6 (Korean).

[31] Atsuhito Isozaki, "North Korea Revamps Its Constitution" (*The Diplomat*, August 26, 2019) <https://thediplomat.com/2019/08/north-korea-revamps-its-constitution/> accessed December 24, 2019.

boost the economy,[32] such as fortifying foreign investments, particularly from the socialist allies. Consequently, the 2019 amendments institutionalize Kim's power and introduced significant changes to the economic provisions of the Constitution.

Instrumentally, the amended Constitution modifies the regime's ideology. Article 3 replaced the *juche* (self-reliance) and *songun* (military first) ideas with "the Great Kimilsungism-Kimjongilism" "as the only guiding principle to state construction and activity."[33] As one commentator notes, the fact that the Constitution names the past leaders rather than the name of ideology "suggests that the regime of their successor, Kim Jong-un, is becoming a more personal rule."[34] The deletion of the references to the two specific ideas may aim to enable the flexible adaption of constitutional ideology in response to domestic and international change. Particularly, the deletion of the reference to *songun* indicates the trend to de-emphasize the military in constitutional amendments under Kim Jong-un era.[35] The removal of *juche* (self-reliance) may signal the regime's intention to further open up the country to the outside world, e.g. foreign investment.

On the centralized constitutional system, the amendments greatly consolidate the powers of the Chairman of the State Affairs Commission. Choe Ryong Hae said in his legislative report that the amended charter "constitutionally revises the status of the State Affairs Commission chairman as the Supreme Leader of the Party, state and armed forces of the DPRK."[36] One amendment defines "the Chairman of the State Affairs Commission assumed by Kim Jong-un" as "the supreme leader who represents the state."[37] This amendment institutionalizes Kim Jong-un as the head of state, not merely the leader of military force. Like China, North Korea wrote the name of the current leader in the Constitution for the first time. Yet, the difference is that North Korea's Constitution designates a particular personal leader to assume a particular state position. This illustrates a personal feature in constitutional change in North Korea.

One newly added provision stipulates that the State Affairs Commission Chairman shall not be elected as a deputy to the Supreme People's Assembly.[38] The Chairman is not subject to popular election as a candidate for membership of a legislature but is selected by the Supreme People's Assembly in its plenary sessions. In fact, before the constitutional amendments, in election of deputies to the

[32] H. Lee-hun, "N. Korea Revises Constitution to Include Kim Jong-Un's Reform-Oriented Approach to Economy" (*The Hankyoreh*, July 12, 2019) <http://english.hani.co.kr/arti/english_edition/e_northkorea/901610.html> accessed December 24, 2019.

[33] Socialist Constitution of the Democratic People's Republic of Korea (1972, amended through 2019), art. 3.

[34] Atsuhito Isozaki, "North Korea Revamps Its Constitution" (n 31).

[35] Lee Ho-Ryung, "Fourth Socialist Constitutional Amendment of the Kim Jong Un Era and North Korean Military Forces" Foreign Academic Activities Series 2019–39 (Korean) p. 7.

[36] Jong Kyo Jin, "North Korea's Latest Constitutional Revisions" (n 29).

[37] Socialist Constitution of the Democratic People's Republic of Korea (1972, amended through 2019), art. 100.

[38] Ibid. 101.

Fourteenth Supreme People's Assembly on March 10, 2019, Kim Jong-un was the first North Korean leader to not participate as a candidate.[39] The first session of the Fourteenth Supreme People's Assembly re-selected Kim Jong-un as Chairman of the State Affairs Commission,[40] and amended the Constitution to legitimize the existing practice.

Another amendment added two more powers to the Chairman of the State Affairs Commission: to promulgate the statutes of the Supreme People's Assembly and important statutes and decisions of the State Council; and to appoint or summon diplomatic representatives from other countries.[41] These are normally powers assumed by the head of state. This change, therefore, aimed to locate Kim Jong-un in the equal constitutional position with presidents in other countries to facilitate his future diplomatic activity.

Apart from political institutions, the 2019 amendments introduce significant market elements to the socialist economy. Five articles (26, 27, 32, 33, and 36) in Chapter II—Economy were amended for this purpose. One major change is the replacement of the Taean Work System, "the traditional party-centric method of managing the economy,"[42] by the Responsible Management System for Socialist Corporations,[43] "which increases the autonomy of managers at production sites and introduces market elements."[44] The amendment also added "decisively increasing the role of the Cabinet" in economic management.[45] This change underlines the shift of economic management from party to the administrative system. One commentator contrasts the two constitutionalized models of economic management as below:

> The Taean Work System was the result of an order given by former North Korean leader Kim Il-sung during an "on-the-spot guidance" at an electrical equipment factory in Taean in December 1961. This is a method of economic management in which the ultimate authority and responsibility for managing and operating a factory lies with the party committee at the factory. This is one of the pillars of North Korea's party-centric collectivist approach to economic management, along with the principle of uniform and detailed planning.

[39] "North Korea Election: Surprise as Leader Kim Jong-un 'Not on Ballot'" (*BBC News*, March 12, 2019) <https://www.bbc.com/news/world-asia-47535658> accessed December 24, 2019.

[40] 'North Korean Parliament Re-Elects Kim Jong Un to Key Panel' (*Al Jazeera*, April 12, 2019) <https://www.aljazeera.com/news/2019/04/north-korean-parliament-elects-kim-jong-key-panel-190412005145509.html> accessed December 24, 2019.

[41] Socialist Constitution of the Democratic People's Republic of Korea (1972, amended through 2019), 103.

[42] Lee-hun, "N. Korea Revises Constitution" (n 32).

[43] Socialist Constitution of the Democratic People's Republic of Korea (1972, amended through 2019), art. 33.

[44] Lee-hun, "N. Korea Revises Constitution" (n 32).

[45] Socialist Constitution of the Democratic People's Republic of Korea (1972, amended through 2019), art. 33.

> In contrast, Kim Jong-un has stressed the Responsible Management System for Socialist Corporations since coming to power in December 2011. The crux of this system, which was first formalized as a sub-category of the "economic management method with North Korean characteristics" during the 7th Congress of the Workers' Party of Korea in May 2016, is institutionalizing the market and harmonizing it with central planning. One way this works is by allowing businesses, once they've satisfied the production quota allotted by the state, to make money for themselves by manufacturing products and selling them on the market to meet demand.[46]

In addition to market elements internal to this new administrative form of economic management, the amendments fortify the state's commitments to protecting their "actual profits"[47] of economic agents; promoting "the leading role of science and technology in all economic activities"; and promoting foreign trade by protecting credit in foreign trade, improving trade structure, and expanding and developing foreign economic relations.[48] These changes add more market elements to the socialist economy to foster economic development. Particularly, the constitutional language reflects the market language, such as "profit," or "credit."

A former high-ranking official in the South Korean government said that "This revised constitution [of North Korea] is transitional in nature. When the negotiations with the US are finally concluded, the final version of the state envisioned by Kim Jong-un will be codified in the constitution."[49] The constitutional mandate of a particular individual, Kim Jong-un, as the head of the state also indicates the Constitution is not designed as stable.

II. Ordinary Amendment, Choice, and Rate

Constitutional amendments in North Korea belong to the kind of ordinary amendment. They are ordinary in the sense that the amendment power is formally exercised by an ordinary legislature, not separate from ordinary politics, and not demanding (e.g. public engagement). Formally, the amendments are adopted by the ordinary legislature (the Supreme People's Assembly) with two-thirds majority votes according to the rules created by the existing Constitution.[50] In reality,

[46] Lee-hun, "N. Korea Revises Constitution" (n 32).
[47] Socialist Constitution of the Democratic People's Republic of Korea (1972, amended through 2019), 32.
[48] Ibid. art. 36.
[49] Lee-hun, "N. Korea Revises Constitution" (n 32).
[50] Socialist Constitution of the Democratic People's Republic of Korea (1972, amended through 2019), arts 91 and 97.

however, the amendment power is controlled by a personal leader who is able to dominate the legislature and the party. This indicates a distinctive feature of the personal model of constitutional change in North Korea.

Substantively, ordinary constitutional amendments in North Korea do not merely introduce technical and policy changes, but substantively alter constitutional ideology (e.g. the deletion of *juche* and *songun* ideas), state structure (e.g. the creation of the State Affairs Commission, and its Chairman as the head of state), rights (e.g. the introduction of the concept of human rights), and the economy (e.g. the creation of the Responsible Management System for Socialist Corporations).

With substantive changes through nine amendments, the current version of North Korea's Constitution is significantly different from the original 1972 version. The document is substantively equal to a new Constitution. Despite that, amendment rather than replacement is chosen as a form of constitutional change. Unlike China, North Korea does not have the concern that constitutional replacement may create the platform for popular resistance mainly because the Kim regime can completely control the public constitutional discourse. So, what explains the choice of amendment over replacement? The amendment choice is stemmed from subsequent leaders' loyal adherence to and respect for their founding father Kim Il-sung. To appreciate this, it should be noted that the attachment to the founding farther is a crucial element for the legitimacy of personal rule of the subsequent leaders in North Korea. Particularly, the *Ten Principles for the Establishment of a Monolithic Ideological System* appearing in 1974 and attributed to Kim Jong-il, require absolute respect and loyalty to the founding father Kim Il-sung.[51] These principles are living super-constitutional norms as they penetrate and govern the entire society, including the activities of citizens and leaders.[52] The socialist Constitution of 1972 was made under Kim Il-sung leadership and embodied his ideology. The adherence to this document to show the loyalty and respect to the founding father is essential to the legitimacy of constitutional change. The subsequent leaders, therefore, changed the original Constitution incrementally through amendments rather than replacing the document associated with the founding framer.

The same Constitution with the same amendment procedure has different amendment rates under two different leaders. The Constitution was amended only two times within nearly a decade under Kim Jong-il, but five times within seven years under Kim Jong-un. The explanation of this variation has to do with factors beyond the length and substantive contents of the Constitution. Constitutional

[51] Ralph Hassig and Kong Dan Oh, *The Hidden People of North Korea: Everyday Life in the Hermit Kingdom* (Rowman & Littlefield Publishers 2009) 140.

[52] The Ten Principles are even "above the Constitution and the Party rules." See Han Myung Sub, "Main Contents and Problems of North Korean Human Rights Laws" in *Report on Human Rights in North Korea* (Korean Bar Association (ed.), 2017) 49.

endurance under Kim Jong-il can be attributed to the relative stability of the domestic society and its external isolation. But, Kim Jong-un amended the Constitution more often to respond to the more internal and external dynamics. First, the frequent amendments are due to the changing society animated by economic dynamics, including foreign investments. In addition, despite the consistent isolation, the North Korea regime under Kim Jong-un has been more open in international relations (e.g. Inter-Korean summits and the North Korea–United States summits), which requires frequent constitutional adjustment to empower the leader in diplomatic affairs.

III. Progressive Change

A. The Dynamic Constitution

Dae-Kyu Yoon notes that "All constitutional processes in North Korea are, by design, endorsed without opposition and manipulated by the country's top leadership—an undisputable reality of the totalitarianism housed within the country's borders."[53] Due to the isolation nature of the Kim regime and the lack of transparency in the constitutional amendment process,[54] it is nearly impossible for outside observers to understand the actual dynamics of the amendment process. Yoon contemplated that "predictably, constitutions have been adopted or amended by a unanimous vote of the SPA without public debate in advance."[55]

But, the observation of what has been publicized may lead to some insights on the dynamics of the Constitution in North Korea. Surveying constitution-making and constitutional amendments in North Korea through 2016, Immanuel Kim argues that: "The discursive alterations in the North Korean Constitution reflects the shifting political agenda since the inception of the nation."[56] Another commentator observes that: "Like its Chinese and Vietnamese counterparts, the DPRK Constitution is a dynamic, prescriptive document that outlines the institutional apparatus of the State and delineates the current policy objectives of the Party. It marks turning points in the overall progression of the country's development."[57] North Korea's Constitution is predominantly an instrument to institutionalize the

[53] Yoon, "Constitutional Change in North Korea" (n 13) 101–2.

[54] The details of constitutional amendments adopted April 11, 2019, were only disclosed three months later. Isozaki, "North Korea Revamps Its Constitution" (n 31).

[55] Yoon, "Constitutional Change in North Korea" (n 13) 102.

[56] Immanuel Kim, "Presentation on Reading the Discursive Changes in the DPRK Constitution" (2017) Cornell International Law Journal Symposium (only file with author). I thank Professor Kim for sharing the notes for this presentation.

[57] Patricia Goedde, "Law of Our Own Style: The Evolution and Challenges of the North Korean Legal System" (2004) 27 Fordham International Law Journal 1275–6.

discursive change of political agenda. The instrumental nature of the Constitution seems to become more important under the Kim Jong-un era. The frequent amendments under this era indicate that the Constitution in North Korea has been become a more significant instrument for the use of power and for socio-economic development.

The significance of the Constitution in North Korea may be due to the fact that the regime needs to use it more as an *operating manual, billboard, blueprint,* and *window dressing*, to borrow Ginsburg and Simpser's theory.[58] First, the Kim regime may need to rely more on the Constitution as a manual to co-ordinate the operation of various institutional players. This is connected to the increased institutionalization of power under the Kim Jong-un era. Kim Jong-un tends to rely on institutional instruments to consolidate his power, evident in his amending the party's constitution and the *Ten Principles for the Establishment of a Monolithic Ideological System*, and his holding of the Seventh Party's Congress in 2016.[59] In such a trend of institutionalization, it is understandable that the Constitution, which deals with major institutions, has become a more significant manual. Second, the Constitution seems to become a more important billboard for the Kim regime to signal their intentions (e.g. to create "a nuclear-weapons state" or the constitutional position of head of state similar to presidents in other countries) to both domestic and international audiences. Third, as the regime has planned to reform the economy, the Constitution has become a more significant blueprint to institutionalize the economic reform program and grand aspirations to pursue the "well-being of the people."[60] Finally, to respond to increasing international criticism and to consolidate domestic legitimacy, the Constitution tends to become a more important window dressing to pronounce the promises to constitutional ideals, such as human rights and "people-centered" governance, and judicial independence.[61]

The increasing instrumental importance of the Constitution is a sign of the improvement in the constitutional system in North Korea. This indicates that the Constitution is, to some extent, relevant to institutional design and socio-economic development in the country. In addition, constitutional juridification of personal power and a developmental plan is at least better than the lawless use of personal power at will and arbitrary policy. To be sure, this is by no means a sign of rule of law and constitutionalism.

[58] Tom Ginsburg and Alberto Simpser, "Introduction: Constitutions in Authoritarian Regimes" in *Constitutions in Authoritarian Regimes* (Tom Ginsburg and Alberto Simpser (eds), Cambridge University Press 2013) 6.

[59] Chang Hee Kim, "An Analysis on the Political Institutionalization Process of the Kim Jong-un Era" (2017) 84 Journal of Northeast Asian Studies 160 (Korean).

[60] Socialist Constitution of the Democratic People's Republic of Korea (1972 amended through 2019), art. 2.

[61] Ibid. arts 8 and 167.

B. Constitutionalizing the Party

Like other socialist countries, North Korea constitutionalizes the role of the communist party or the Workers' Party of Korea. Despite many amendments, the following Article remains intact: "The Democratic People's Republic of Korea conducts all activities under the leadership of the Workers' Party of Korea."[62] However, due to personal rule within the *Suryong* System, the role of the communist party in North Korea is weaker and less institutionalized than in other socialist countries. Commentators of North Korea's politics have different views about the party's role.[63]

Despite complicated historical trajectory, the communist party in North Korea has been institutionalized in recent years. The North Korean Communist Party was established in 1946 based on merging the Communist Party and the Nationalist Party, renamed as the Korean Workers' Party in 1949. Under Kim Il-sung in the 1970s, the *Suryong* ruled through the party, and therefore "the party apparatus was at the center of the North Korean political regime," as indicated in the phrase "Party Center" (*tang chungang*).[64] Kim Jong-il, however, reached outside the party to directly rule the government and the military, criticized the party for "not dealing properly with the food shortages in the country," and said that he "did not owe anything to the Party" in a speech to party members at Kim Il-sung University in December 1996.[65] But, the party returned as a player in the economic domain in 2005 when the regime began to implement market and economic reforms. Furthermore, through attempts to consolidate the party's role in the oversight of state institutions in 2007, Kim Jong-il "had brought the party back to the center of politics in the regime."[66] Notably, the third Party Conference in 2010 significantly institutionalized the party, through amending the party's constitution (the Charter of the Workers' Party of Korea), fulfilled the party's vacant positions, and increased members of key party institutions, including the Central Committee (from 151 to 229), Politburo (from 10 to 37), Secretariat (from 7 to 11), and the Central Military Committee (from 12 to 19).[67]

The party's role has been further consolidated and institutionalized under the Kim Jong-un era. One commentator contended that that Kim Jong-un wanted to fully restore the party's authority.[68] Particularly, he convened the Seventh Party Congress in 2016 for the first time in twenty-six years. The previous six party

[62] Ibid. art. 11.
[63] Gause Ken, "The Role and Influence of the Party Apparatus" in *North Korea in Transition: Politics, Economy, and Society* (Kyung-Ae Park and Scott A. Snyder (eds), Rowman & Littlefield Publishers 2012) 27.
[64] Ibid. 30.
[65] Ibid. 31–2.
[66] Ibid. 34.
[67] Ibid. 28.
[68] Kim, "An Analysis on the Political Institutionalization Process of the Kim Jong-un Era" (n 57) 151.

congresses were held in 1946, 1948, 1956, 1961, 1970, and 1980.[69] The Seventh Party Congress "symbolized the emergence of a new party-first policy in the Kim Jong-un era to replace the military-first policy of the Kim Jong-il era."[70] This Party Congress adopted amendments to the party constitution, elected Kim Jong-un to the leader of the party, and approved his proposed five-year economic plan.[71]

What explains the return of the party in North Korea's politics? One theory focuses on the external influence from China: Chinese communist party leadership might encourage North Korea to return to party-centric governance to push economic reform to stabilize the North Korea regime around the party.[72] In addition to this, internal demands to reform the economy may also induce the restoration of the party's role and its institutionalization. The Kim regime may rely more on the party as an institutional platform to deliberate and lead the reform projects. The dynamic change to the communist party in North Korea is conditioned by the gap between its formal constitutional position as the leading force of the regime and the functional *Suryong* system which places the power on a single leader. Efforts to restore the party's role and institutionalize its structures and functions have incrementally bridged the hole between the formal constitutionalization and the workings of the party.

C. Distributing Powers

Despite serial amendments, the Constitution retains the confirmation that "All State organs in the Democratic People's Republic of Korea are formed and function on the principle of democratic centralism."[73] In a formal sense, North Korea is not different from other socialist countries in adopting this constitutional principle. The Constitution's Chapter Six—State Organs provides in details the formal "democratic" centralized constitutional structure. The Supreme People's Assembly locates at the top of the constitutional pyramid, while other central state institutions are created by and accountable to the former.

Although there is no separation of powers and checks and balances, the Constitution formally distributes the legislative, executive, and judicial powers

[69] A. Zhebin, "The Seventh Congress of the DPRK Workers' Party: Preliminary Outcomes" (2016) 44 Far Eastern Affairs 3, 75.

[70] S.Y. Lee, "Political Transition in North Korea in the Kim Jong-un Era: Elites' Policy Choices" (2017) 41 Asian Perspective 3, 449.

[71] A. Fifield, "North Korea Announces Five-Year Economic Plan, its First Since the 1980s" (Washington Post, May 8, 2016) <https://www.washingtonpost.com/world/north-korea-announces-economic-plan-after-unprecedentedly-grim-struggle/2016/05/08/c84088e2-1214-11e6-a9b5-bf703a5a7191_story.html> accessed December 24, 2019.

[72] Jinwook Choi and Meredith Shaw, "The Rise of Kim Jong Eun and the Return of the Party" (2010) 19(2) International Journal of Korean Unification Studies 193.

[73] Socialist Constitution of the Democratic People's Republic of Korea (1972 amended through 2019), art. 5.

to different state institutions. Like other socialist legislatures, the Supreme People's Assembly in North Korea is defined as the "highest organ of State power," elected for a term of five years, and vested with the powers to legislate, amend the Constitution, adopt major policy, and select major state positions.[74] Its Presidium, like the standing committee of other socialist legislatures, enjoys the delegated legislative power, interprets the Constitution, and supervises other state bodies, among others.[75] The executive branch, however, is quite distinctive to North Korea, which reflects the *Suryong* system. It is comprised of the Chairman of the State Affairs Commission—the supreme leader presenting the state, the State Affairs Commission—"the supreme policy-oriented leadership body of State power," and the Cabinet—the body of overall state administration.[76] The Public Prosecutors Office, the soviet-style procuracy, is created at the central level and three local levels (province, district, or county), and is vested with the powers to supervise the strict observation of the law, investigate and prosecute offenders.[77] The court system includes the Central Court, and courts at three local levels (province, district, or county), and the Special Court.[78] Like in other socialist countries, the court system in North Korea is centralized on the Central Court, the highest judicial organ supervising the judicial activities of all the Courts.[79] Local government is created in three levels (province, district, and county), and is constituted by the Local People's Assembly, a deliberative body elected by local constituencies;[80] and the Local People's Committee, an administrative body accountable to the former.[81] Local government is empowered to formulate and implement local plans for development of the national economy.[82]

Under the Kim Jong-un era, the overall trend of constitutional amendments regarding the power distribution is to demilitarize the executive, as evident in the replacement of the National Defense Commission by the State Affairs Commission, its Chairman as the head of state, and the Cabinet's decisive role in in economic management. These reforms aim to turn the executive body from a military institution into the institution for policy-making and economic management to facilitate the active role of the executive in promoting the material wellbeing of living conditions through economic development. These structural changes are consistent with other constitutional adjustments which de-emphasize the military ideology and marketize the statist economy.

74 Ibid. arts 89, 90, and 91.
75 Ibid. art. 116.
76 Ibid. arts 100, 116, and 124.
77 Ibid. arts 154 and 157.
78 Ibid. art. 160.
79 Ibid. art. 168.
80 Ibid. arts 138, 139, and 141.
81 Ibid. arts 146 and 153.
82 Ibid. arts 141 and 148.

D. Universalizing Human Rights

North Korea's Constitution has a long list of rights in Chapter V—Fundamental Rights and Duties of Citizens, ranging from political to social and economic rights. These constitutional rights remain strongly statist. This is manifested in two overreaching principles governing constitutional rights. The first is the collective principle. Article 63 provides that "In the Democratic People's Republic of Korea the rights and duties of citizens are based on the collectivist principle: 'One for all and all for one.' "[83] That means rights are not separated from the citizens' duty to the state. Rights are granted by the state to the residents in exchange for "their revolutionary vigilance and devotedly fight for the security of the State."[84] The second principle establishes the socialist boundary of rights. Article 64 provides: "The State shall effectively guarantee the genuine democratic rights and freedoms as well as the material and cultural well-being of all its citizens. In the Democratic People's Republic of Korea the rights and freedoms of citizens shall be amplified with the consolidation and development of the socialist system."[85] Thus, rights are not entitlements but statements of developmental policy formulated and implemented by the state within the socialist system.

Under the hegemony of statism, however, the idea of "human rights" was formally introduced in the Constitution through the 2009 amendments. The provision that the State shall "respect and protect human rights"[86] was incorporated in Chapter I—Politics rather than Chapter V—Fundamental Rights and Duties of Citizens. The implication is that North Korea treats human rights as an issue of political regime, which stems from their accusation that foreign governments employed "the pretext of human rights protection" to overturn their socialist political regime.[87] In addition, North Korea considers human rights a serious political and legal matter of national sovereignty and resists the intervention of foreign countries and international organizations through human rights advocacy.[88]

North Korea's constitutional incorporation of human rights is addressed mainly to the outsiders rather than domestic audience. The idea of human rights has little to do with domestic legitimacy in North Korea. The source of domestic legitimacy in North Korea relies more on security particularly through consolidation of the nuclear power[89] rather than rights.[90] Human rights are not the daily language of

[83] Ibid. art. 63.
[84] Ibid. art. 85.
[85] Ibid. art. 64.
[86] Ibid. art. 8.
[87] Patricia Goedde, "Human Rights Diffusion in North Korea: The Impact of Transnational Legal Mobilization" (2018) 5 Asian Journal of Law and Society 181.
[88] Cho Jae Hyun, "Characteristics of Changes in the Basic Right Provisions of the North Korean Constitution, and the Development Direction" (2017) 19 North Korean Law Studies 43 (Korean).
[89] For the history of North Korea's nuclear weapons program, see Gregory S. Gordon, "'Fire and Fury' at the 38th Parallel: Exploring the Law of War's Twilight Zones in a Potential Future Conflict on the Korean Peninsula" in *Asia-Pacific Perspectives on International Humanitarian Law* (Suzannah Linton, Tim McCormack, and Sandesh Sivakumaran (eds), Cambridge University Press 2019) 747–51.
[90] Goedde, "Human Rights Diffusion in North Korea" (n 87) 190.

the North Korean residents.[91] Some North Koreans in South Korea said that they escaped the country not because of human rights violations but for the reasons of hungry, poverty, family support, among others.[92] Under such circumstances, the constitutional provision aim to send a signal to foreign governments and international agencies promoting for human rights in North Korea. The signal is aversive rather than convergent. Due to its consistent isolation, the country does not have incentive to signal its commitment to converge with universal human rights standard to gain international legitimacy. Rather, the constitutional inclusion of human rights tends to send a resistant signal to outsiders: the Kim regime resisted at the authoritative level of fundamental law the international criticisms of its human rights violations.

North Korea has formally engaged in the international human rights regime to some extent. It acceded to the International Covenant on Civil and Political Rights and the International Covenant on Economic, Social, and Cultural Rights in 1981, and the Convention on the Rights of the Child in 1990, and more recently, ratified the Optional Protocol to the Convention on the Rights of the Child on the sale of children, child prostitution, and child pornography in 2014, and the Convention on the Rights of the Persons with Disabilities (CRPD) in December 2016.[93] Foreign governments (particularly the US and South Korea), various NGOs, and UN agencies have actively promoted human rights in North Korea, despite the minimal impact.[94] Treaty signature and ratification and formal constitutional integration, of course, do not necessarily guarantee human rights protection. According to the North Korean human rights survey in 2014, 74.4 percent of the North Korean defectors who participated in the survey said their human rights were violated, 62.1 percent of the survey participants said they had never heard of human rights, and 85.5 percent said they had never been educated about human rights.[95] The constitutional status of human rights and its dissonance with statist citizen's rights may provide the base for the continued dynamics of transnational human rights discourse between North Korea and the international community.

E. Marketizing the Economy

North Korea's Constitution's Chapter II—Economy comprising of nineteen articles provides a foundational legal framework for a socialist economy. The constitutional

[91] Ibid. 194.
[92] Ibid. 194.
[93] Ibid. 180.
[94] Ibid. 177, 198; Danielle Chubb, "North Korean Human Rights and the International Community: Responding to the UN Commission of Inquiry" (2014) 15 Asia-Pacific Journal on Human Rights and the Law 51.
[95] Cho, "Characteristics of Changes in the Basic Right Provisions" (n 88) 49.

economy remains predominantly statist: a planned economy;[96] means of production are owned by the State and social, co-operative organizations;[97] "all natural resources, railways, air transport service, post and telecommunications establishments, as well as major factories and enterprises, ports and banks of the country are owned solely by the State," and "there is no limit to the property which the State can own";[98] "the steady improvement of the material and cultural standards of the people" as the goal of the economy.[99] Despite that, North Korea's Constitution, particularly through the 1998 and recent 2019 amendments, has introduced some market elements to the statist, socialist economy, including the constitutional commitments to the protection of private property and foreign investments.

Consider first the private property protected by the 1998 constitutional amendment. Article 24 of the Constitution provides that: "Private property is property owned and consumed by individual citizens. Private property is derived from socialist distribution according to work done and from supplementary benefits granted by the State and society. The products of individual sideline activities including those from kitchen gardens, as well as income from other legal economic activities shall also be private property. The State shall protect private property and guarantee by law the right to inherit it."[100] While this is not an explicit constitutional recognition of private enterprise, this allows the citizens to earn money by legal economic activities. After the constitutional amendments, in 2002, North Korea's government introduced measures for economic changes in a document called the July 1 Economic Management Improvement Measure, which "officially recognized markets as necessary but tried to keep them within the controlled economy."[101] Accordingly, farmers were able to sell goods at the markets under the ceiling prices, and sellers were required to pay fees and taxed for their incomes.[102] Although the government subsequently attacked markets via several measures (e.g. a 2008 measure's limitation of the operation of markets to three days per week), hundreds of legal markets have been operated, in addition to private market economy most of which is illegal. A publication estimated that in 2014 there were half a million private enterprises in North Korea.[103]

The dynamics of the economy in North Korea are conditioned by the disharmony surrounding the constitutional provision of private property. The constitutional protection of private property is a pragmatic and dissonant modification to the statist, socialist planned economy. The constitutional protection of private

[96] Socialist Constitution of the Democratic People's Republic of Korea (1972 amended through 2019), art. 34.
[97] Ibid. art. 20.
[98] Ibid. art. 21.
[99] Ibid. art. 25.
[100] Ibid. art. 24.
[101] Hassig and Oh, *The Hidden People of North Korea* (n 51) 44, 47.
[102] Ibid. 47.
[103] Ibid. 48, 67.

property is also ambiguous: this allows citizens to conduct legal economic activities based on their own property, but private enterprises and markets are not explicitly constitutionally recognized. This constitutional ambiguity provides space for the emergence of markets without rigid constitutional barriers. In addition, the gap between the implicit parsimonious constitutional toleration of market through the recognition of private property and the real demands of the citizens to improve their living conditions animates the functional dynamics of market sectors in the economy.

Another market element is the constitutional commitment to promote foreign trade and investment through joint ventures and enterprises in special economic zones.[104] To implement the commitment to promoting foreign investment in special economic zones promised by the 1998 constitutional amendment, North Korea passed the Gaeseong Industrial Zone Law 2002. In the next year, 2003, to implement that Law, several regulations were enacted, including the Development Regulations, Company Establishment and Management Regulations, Tax Regulations, Labor Regulations, Establishing and Operation Regulations for the Management Office, Entry, Visiting and Residency Regulations, and Customs Regulations.[105] From 2013 to 2018, more than twenty special economic zones were created in North Korea.[106] For political considerations, trade zones are located far from Pyongyang and business centers. Chinese businesses are by far North Korea's biggest investors and traders. Especially, to attract foreign investors, North Korea established the Sinŭiju Special Administrative Region in 2002, modeling after China's Special Administrative Regions (SARs). Like Hong Kong, Sinŭiju has a "Basic Law" (기본법; Kibonpŏp).[107] Sinŭiju's Basic Law promises that in the next fifty years the city would be governed by its own legislative, executive, and judicial systems staffed by foreigners and North Koreans.[108] Sinuiju is, however, described as "largely dysfunctional."[109]

The dynamics of foreign investment in North Korea is conditioned by competing constitutional commitments to self-reliance and promotion of foreign investment. In addition, the constitutional commitment to promotion of foreign investment is at odds with the real isolation of the country and the real need of foreign investment, which may explain the dysfunction of legal and constitutional measures like the Sinŭiju project. Looking forward, the competing aspirations to isolation and

[104] Ibid. arts 37 and 38.

[105] Joongi Kim, "The Challenges of Attracting Foreign Investment into North Korea: The Legal Regimes of Sinuiju and Gaeseong" (2004) 27 Fordham International Law Journal 1309.

[106] T Clément, "Failed Attempts at Cross-Border Economic Integration: The View from Sinuiju" (*38 North*, October 28, 2019) <https://www.38north.org/2019/10/tclement102819/> accessed December 24, 2019.

[107] For a comparison, see Patricia Goedde, "The Basic Law of the Sinuiju Special Administrative Region: A Happy Medium Between the DPRK Constitution and Hong Kong Basic Law?" (2003) 3(2) Journal of Korean Law 77.

[108] Hassig and Oh, *The Hidden People of North Korea* (n 51) 49, 51, 56.

[109] Théo Clément, "Failed Attempts at Cross-Border Economic Integration" (n 106).

foreign investment, and the gap between the constitutional commitment and the reality of foreign investment may put pressures on the government to undertake some measures to bridge the gap.

IV. Conclusion

Due largely to internal personal rule and external isolation, North Korea does not have substantive constitutional reforms like Vietnam, China, Laos, and Cuba. The Kim regime changes the Constitution mainly to modify ideology, the state structure, and the economy. This constitutional change, however, improves the socialist constitutional order and facilitates the role of the leader, party, and state in improving the material living conditions. After serial amendments, North Korea's Constitution has been no longer a monolithic charter. While Marxist and local socialist ideas and principles remain predominant, alternative universal or market ideas and institutions have been introduced into the Constitution: such as human rights, private property, foreign trade, profit, or credit. The coexistence of the dissonant ideas and institutions may create the space for continued constitutional dynamics. In addition, the external gap between the constitutional commitments to socialist ideals and the social reality of rising inequality[110] and economic hardship is the condition for further constitutional reform. Finally, the sharp gap between socialist constitutional principles internally promoted by the North Korea leaders and the constitutional norms (e.g. human rights) externally promoted by various actors of the international community may animate further constitutional dynamics in the Kim regime.

[110] Hassig and Oh, *The Hidden People of North Korea* (n 51) 90.

Conclusion

The End of the End of History?

After the collapse of the Soviet Union, American political scientist Francis Fukuyama published the influential book *The End of History and the Last Man*.[1] The idea of the end of history was first published in an earlier essay, in which he argues that, "What we may be witnessing is not just the end of the Cold War, or the passing of a particular period of postwar history, but the end of history as such: that is, the end point of mankind's ideological evolution and the universalization of Western liberal democracy as the final form of human government."[2] The recent tension of liberal constitutional democracy around the world[3] provides empirical points for critical debates on the end of history thesis. To illustrate, Kim Lane Scheppele discussed "the end of 'the end of history.'"[4] She argues that "Liberal, democratic constitutionalism is—to borrow the language of marketing—a damaged brand. If the end of history was supposed to represent the moment when liberal, democratic constitutionalism triumphed across the world and was so normatively powerful that no state that had achieved it would ever renege on its pledges, then the end of history is clearly over."[5]

In his recent book *Identity* published in 2018 as a response to current tension of liberal democracy, Fukuyama said that his critics have misunderstood his thesis.[6] He explains that he "was using the word *history* in the Hegelian-Marxian sense—that is, the long-term evolutionary story of human institutions" and the word *end* to refer to "target" or "objective" not "termination."[7] Fukuyama writes: "Karl Marx had suggested that the end of history would be a communist utopia, and

[1] F. Fukuyama, *The End of History and the Last Man* (Free Press 1992).

[2] F. Fukuyama, "The End of History?" (1989) 16 National Interest 4.

[3] Tom Ginsburg and Aziz Z. Huq, *How to Save a Constitutional Democracy* (University of Chicago Press 2018); Mark A Graber, Sanford Levinson and Mark Tushnet (eds), *Constitutional Democracy in Crisis?* (OUP 2018); Cass R. Sunstein (ed), *Can It Happen Here?: Authoritarianism in America* (Dey Street Books 2018)

[4] University of Delaware, "The End of 'The End of History' lecture by Kim Scheppele" (November 28, 2017) <www.youtube.com/watch?v=r9XfiHg8l5A>

[5] K.L. Scheppele, "Autocracy under Cover of the Transnational Legal Order" in *Constitution-Making and Transnational Legal Order* (Gregory Shaffer, Tom Ginsburg, and Terence C. Halliday (eds), Cambridge University Press 2019).

[6] F. Fukuyama, *Identity: The Demand for Dignity and the Politics of Resentment* (Farrar, Straus, and Giroux 2018) xii.

[7] Ibid.

Constitutional Change in the Contemporary Socialist World. Bui Ngoc Son, Oxford University Press (2020). © Bui Ngoc Son.
DOI: 10.1093/oso/9780198851349.001.0001.

I was suggesting that Hegel's version, where development resulted in a liberal state linked to a market economy, was the more plausible outcome."[8]

Fukuyama's account of human progress is a mix of both explanatory and normative enterprise. My purpose is not to provide a normative defense of socialist constitutions but to provide an exploratory explanation for their continuing progressive change that after the Cold War. Their history or progress indicates the trend to incremental adaption of core socialist constitutional institutions. In some case, socialist constitutional change leads to partial adoption of some institutions of liberal democracy and market economy (e.g. liberal rights, private ownership, private property rights, and private enterprises). But, the resistance to institutions of liberal constitutional democracy is also vehement in several cases, especially in China and Cuba. In addition, resistance to market economy is also evident, particularly in North Korea. In addition to adoption and resistance, the divergence between socialist and liberal political and economic institutions is increasingly sharp. This institutional divergence is mainly due to socialist and local constitutional innovation. The divergence is manifested in grand innovative projects such as the "socialist rule of law state" (constitutionally adopted in China, Vietnam, and Cuba) and the "socialist market economy" (constitutionally adopted in China, Vietnam, and Laos), which are resulted from the creative marriage of liberal institutions with socialist institutions and local experiential practices. The divergence is also evident in some specific institutions, such as China's supervisory institutions and legislative constitutional review body; Cuba's controlling institutions; North Korea's the Responsible Management System for Socialist Corporations. The partial adaption, resistance, and local innovation suggest that socialist constitutional change has not converged with "the end of history."

The "end" or objective of socialist constitutional evolution is informed by socialist ideals. The major concern shared among the five socialist countries is to facilitate the role of the state in improving the material wellbeing of living condition, not to limit the state power to protect liberal rights. This does not mean that the socialist countries do not have concerns about liberal rights and limited powers: consider the supervisory and controlling institutions. But, the prevailing "end" of socialist constitutional change is to improve the living condition of residents ensured by economic development and enabling institutions rather than to protect liberal rights by constitutional constraints. This progressive concern is informed by the constitutional commitment to achieve socialism and even communism (as the case of Cuba).

Table 1 below summarizes trends and major points in socialist constitutional change.

[8] Ibid.

Table 1 Constitutional Change in the Contemporary Socialist World

Country	Vietnam	Laos	Cuba	China	North Korea
Model	Universal: participation, international engagement; constitutionalizing some universal ideas	Integration: participation; intra-socialist engagement; constitutionalizing the "Lao multi-ethnic people"	Reservation: participation (referendum); regional and intra-socialist engagement; constitutionalizing communism	Exceptional: non-participation; external resistance; constitutionalizing national leaders' ideologies	Personal: non-participation; system; external isolation; constitutionalizing *Suryong's* ideologies
Constitution	1992 constitution; 2001 amendment; 2013 replacement	1991 constitution; 2003 replacement; 2015 replacement	1976 constitution; amendments in 1992, 2002; 2019 replacement	1982 constitution; amendments in 1988, 1993, 1999, 2004, 2018	1972 constitution; amendments in 1992, 1998, 2009, 2010, 2012, 2013, 2016, 2019
Party	public connection and oversight; constitutionality and legality required	constitutionality and legality required	public connection	three represents; constitutionality and legality required	return; institutionalization
State	distributed powers; controlled powers; constitutional oath; new independent institutions (audit and election); local decentralization	distributed powers; new executive term limits; new independent institutions (audit and election); local decentralization	distributed powers; new presidential and PM posts; new executive term limits; new independent institutions (supervision and election); local decentralization	distributed powers; constitutional oath; constitutional review; new supervisory institutions; local decentralization	distributed powers; demilitarizing the executive

(*Continued*)

Table 1 Continued

Country	Vietnam	Laos	Cuba	China	North Korea
Rights	human rights and proportionality included	human rights included	human rights included; rights increased from 19 to some 34	human rights and "harmonious society" included	human rights included
Economy	socialist market economy: multiple ownership and economic sectors; property rights; private enterprises; foreign investment; international and regional integration	socialist market economy: multiple ownership and economic sectors; property rights; private enterprises; foreign investment; international and regional integration	socialist economy: multiple forms of ownership; private ownership; foreign investment	socialist market economy: multiple ownership and economic sectors; property rights; private enterprises; foreign investment; international and regional integration	socialist economy; property rights; foreign investment

With these changes, the socialist constitutions are increasingly dissonant documents, which is the condition for continuing evolution of the socialist constitutional order. Internally, while socialist ideas and principles remain dominant, the socialist constitutions adopt competing ideas: liberal, universal, communitarian, and locally religious. This creates the dissonant and ambiguous space for the continued constitutional dynamics. Externally, the actual social and economic dynamics incrementally bridge but create new gaps (e.g. increasing inequality and corruption) between the formal constitutional commitments to socialist ideals and the social reality. This gap is the condition for the continued constitutional change in the socialist world as different actors of the polity may struggle to bridge the gap. Finally, the normative gap between the socialist constitutional ideals and ideals of constitutionalism provide the conditions for global diffusion which may animate the future constitutional change in the development world.

Socialist constitutional change is connected to the broader global constitutional landscape. Many current societies in the developing world are struggling for the improvement of the living condition by reforms, including constitutional reforms, to address problems, such as unemployment, crimes, public education, medicine, the backwardness in science and technology, caused by similar factors, such as urbanization, industrialization, and corruption in government.[9] Constitutional reform to improve the living condition is particularly dynamic in many countries in Asia, Africa and the Arab world.[10] For example, Kenya's new Constitution of 2010 includes many progressive provisions protecting the rights of oppressed, vulnerable, and marginalized group, such as children; minorities, women, and marginalized communities; senior citizens; and the disabled.[11] Constitutional change to improve the material wellbeing of living condition is a part of human's development.

[9] See generally, Human Development Report (The United Nations Development Programme 2016).

[10] See generally, Andrew Harding (ed.), *Constitutionalism and Legal Change in Myanmar* (Hart 2017); Charles Manga Fombad, "Constitutional Reforms and Constitutionalism in Africa: Reflections on Some Current Challenges and Future Prospects" (2011) 59 Buffalo Law Review 1007; Rainer Grote and Tilmann J. Röder (eds), *Constitutionalism, Human Rights, and Islam After the Arab Spring* (OUP 2016).

[11] David Okech et al, "Constitutionalism and Social Development in Kenya" (2014) 1 Social Development Issues 77, 81.

Index

Note on index: *For the benefit of digital users, indexed terms that span two pages (e.g., 52–53) may, on occasion, appear on only one of those pages.*
For subjects relating to each country, please see main entries on that particular country.
Tables are indicated by *t* following the page number